DATE DUE

NO 197			
JE 5'97			
NO 16 '92			
MR 26 '95			
NO 5'96			
MR 26 '92			
MY 24 02			
OC 19 07			

DEMCO 38-296

Whence the Goddesses
A Source Book

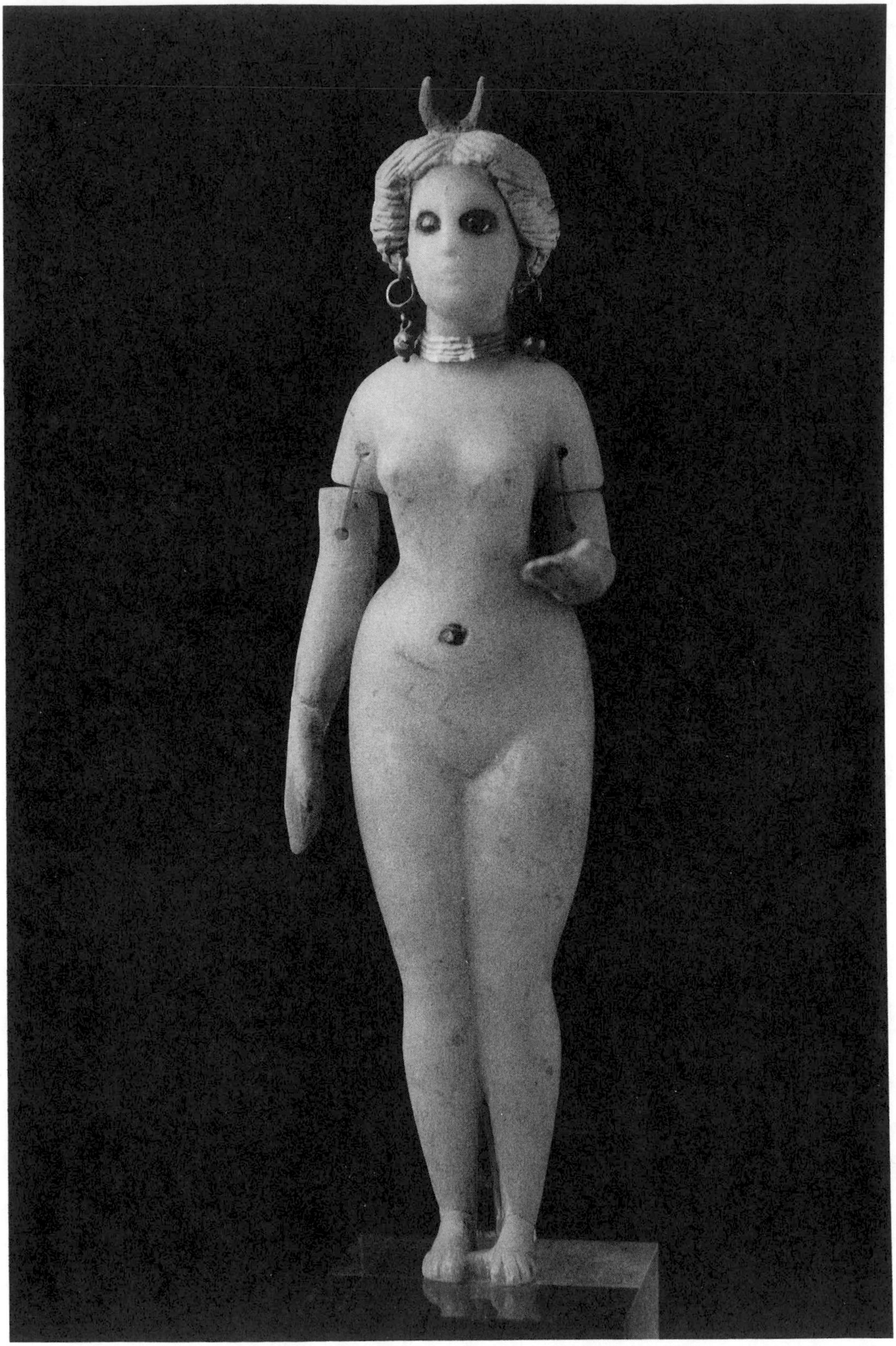

Whence the Goddesses
A Source Book

Miriam Robbins Dexter

PERGAMON PRESS
Member of Maxwell Macmillan Pergamon Publishing Corporation
New York Oxford Beijing Frankfurt São Paulo
Sydney Tokyo Toronto

Pergamon Press Offices:

U.S.A.	Pergamon Press, Inc., Maxwell House, Fairview Park, Elmsford, New York 10523, U.S.A.
U.K.	Pergamon Press plc, Headington Hill Hall, Oxford OX3 0BW, England
PEOPLE'S REPUBLIC OF CHINA	Pergamon Press, Room 4037, Qianmen Hotel, Beijing, People's Republic of China
FEDERAL REPUBLIC OF GERMANY	Pergamon Press GmbH, Hammerweg 6, D-6242 Kronberg, Federal Republic of Germany
BRAZIL	Pergamon Editora Ltda, Rua Eça de Queiros, 346, CEP 04011, Paraiso, São Paulo, Brazil
AUSTRALIA	Pergamon Press Australia Pty Ltd., P.O. Box 544, Potts Point, NSW 2011, Australia
JAPAN	Pergamon Press, 8th Floor, Matsuoka Central Building, 1-7-1 Nishishinjuku, Shinjuku-ku, Tokyo 160, Japan
CANADA	Pergamon Press Canada Ltd., Suite 271, 253 College Street, Toronto, Ontario M5T 1R5, Canada

---

First edition 1990

Library of Congress Cataloging in Publication Data

Dexter, Miriam Robbins, 1943-
Whence the goddesses : a source book / Miriam Robbins Dexter.--
1st ed.
p. cm. -- (The Athene series)
Bibliography: p.
Includes index.
ISBN 0-08-037279-1 : -- ISBN 0-08-037281-3 (pbk.) :
1. Goddesses. I. Title. II. Series.
BL473.5.D48 1990
291.2'114'089034--dc20 89-35838
CIP

Printed in the United States of America

The paper used in this publication meets the minimum requirements of American National Standard for Information Sciences—Permanence of Paper for Printed Library Materials, ANSI Z39.48-1984

Photographs by Gregory L. Dexter

To my Mother,

Frances Ruth Glick Elbaum,

who taught me that I,

just as every woman,

can accomplish all that I wish.

Her inspiration lives on in my heart.

CONTENTS

INTRODUCTION

Once there was a goddess born of the foam at the churning of the Ocean, in the Golden Age.[1] She was a goddess of love, fortune, and beauty, and she had a young son, "Love-God."[2] The story of her birth is similar to that of another goddess described by the Greek poet, Hesiod:

> Int.1. *"A white foam arose from the immortal flesh*
> [of the castrated genitals of Ouranos, the sky-god];
> *in it there grew a maiden.*
> *First she floated to holy Cythera,*
> *and from there, afterwards,*
> *she came to sea-girt Cyprus.*
> *There came forth an august and beautiful goddess . . .*
> *gods and men call her Aphrodite . . .* "[3]
> Hesiod, Theogony 190–197; *ca.* 750 BCE.

The beautiful foam-born Greek goddess of love, *Aphrodite*, gave birth to the young love-god Eros ("love" or "lust" in Greek), just as *Shrī Lakshmī*, the lovely Indic goddess of love and fortune, born at the churning of the ocean, bore the young Kamadeva ("lovegod" in Sanskrit).

Ancient myth and literature abound with parallels such as those between the Greek Aphrodite and her son Eros (and their Roman counterparts Venus/Cupid) and the Indic Shrī Lakshmī and her son Kamadeva. If we allow for several themes which are probably common world-wide, and which may derive from archetypal images or species-wide human perceptions, myths which share specific details may be traced to links between cultures. In this case, both the Greek and the Indic have probably borrowed from a common source, perhaps a Near-Eastern myth describing the castration of a sky-god and the birth of several deities, including the love-goddess, from his genitals or blood.[4]

The meanings of individual myths are often obscure, since their origins frequently lie in prehistory. However, when similar myths from related cultures are found, then the precursors of the myths may be discovered, and much evidence about the mythology and even the sociology of the cultures becomes manifest. This method of finding out about the myths by using the texts, themselves, in comparison with related mythic texts from other cultures, is known as the *comparative* method.[5] Thus, the myths speak for themselves.

This book is an exposition into the religious systems of ancient cultures, in particular religious cult and myth regarding female figures.The goddesses and heroines are multiple, and this book will identify them in their multiplicity. However, we should also remember that the goddess-*energy*, the divine feminine, is also a *unity*. Even a single goddess, such as the Indic Devī, is both singular and multiple, and she represents both life and death. This is the true state of the goddess, and of the divine principle in mortals as well.

This is a book for students of ancient myth, especially those students interested in female figures: goddesses and heroines. I will be presenting the primary sources,[6] the ancient myths and hymns, and I will cite authors and dates so that the work may more easily be used for reference. I have translated most of the source materials in this book. When I have used the translations of others, I have indicated this in endnotes. This sampling of sources represents, of course, only a minute portion of the material available to us; I hope that you will continue to read these texts, most of which are available in excellent translations.

Because I am focusing on primary sources, you will have the tools to draw your own conclusions about the goddesses and their myths. Although I draw some conclusions from the myths, I am minimizing theory in this book. I include little exegesis of the excellent research in the field that has been done by contemporary scholars, nor is there a great deal of my own theory, except that which relates to the interconnections between the goddesses. I hope that you will be able to enlarge upon the conclusions given, and that you will see the significance of how the earliest historic female figures were viewed.

In presenting the primary sources, I have used two sorts of indentations to indicate the different types of materials. General information is presented in the body of the text. Synopses of myths and folk-tales are set off by indentation and spacing. *Translations* of primary sources are further indented, set off by spacing, and put into italics for easier identification. Authors and dates are given with each quotation; question marks following dates indicate those dates for which there is no irrefutable evidence, but which represent the closest deductions of scholars.

The goddesses are often syncretized. There are different cult forms of the goddesses, for example Aphrodite *Ourania*, an Eastern form of Aphrodite; Aphrodite *Areia*, the warlike Spartan form of the goddess; and Aphrodite *Hetaira*, the Aphrodite who was protectress of courtesans. These cult forms are assimilated in this book, so that we discuss a generalized Aphrodite, or Athena, or Artemis. The *general* attributes of those goddesses are highlighted. Keep in mind, however, that powerful single goddesses often grew out of various local goddesses. Each local goddess would be worshipped as "Athena" or "Aphrodite," but her functions or origins might differ. These local goddesses were often syncretized into the more popular generalized goddesses. Mythopoets such as Homer, in his *Iliad* and *Odyssey*, depict broader, more popularized goddesses.

I give chronologically disparate information in this book: I do not distinguish, for example, the archaic Artemis from the later, larger perspective of the individual goddesses. Further, I give data for culturally related societies, even though the written evidence may vary widely. For example, Baltic folktales and folksongs were recorded quite late, but, nonetheless, both Baltic language and Baltic folklore preserve very archaic vestiges. The inflectional system of the language and the mythological tales show many parallels with those of the Indo-European culture for which we have the most ancient records: the Indic. Naturally, sources will vary from culture to culture. Where there are ancient sources for mythological material, I use them. Otherwise, I use folktales and other more modern materials.

There are two themes interwoven into this book: it is both a *motif* book and an *overview* of female figures who were celebrated in ancient Indo-European pantheons. Part One explains the motifs found in European Neolithic iconography and in ancient Near-Eastern iconography and myth. The most prevalent motifs were those of bird and snake goddesses, and "mistresses of animals." Many early historical goddesses reflect a goddess who gave life and death, and new life again. This "goddess of regeneration" may appear with or without bird or snake iconography. Some iconography in the ancient Hebrew culture coincides with European Neolithic and Near-Eastern iconography; that is also briefly discussed.

Part Two demonstrates the assimilation of these motifs by Indo-European goddesses; each chapter in Part Two gives an overview of the pertinent pantheon, discussing the important characteristics of the female figures who were worshipped in each of the cultures.

Finally, Part Three synthesizes the function given by the patriarchal Indo-Europeans to Indo-European goddesses, which function is, generally, to bestow energy of various sorts upon the male members of their societies. The goddesses bestow sovereign or ruling energy; martial strength; and nurturance, or generalized energy. We must remember that myth is political: it represents not only the world-view as it is, but the world-view as the mythopoets wish it to be viewed. Thus, when the goddesses of a culture have the function of conferring their energies upon the male members of their societies, we understand that the mythopoets wished the mortal females of the societies to be educated, "led forth," by those principles. The deities of a given mythology thus serve as the ideals, models upon which the society is to be based. Myths give divine sanction to the social patterns of a culture. Part Three describes the ways in which the idealized female, in each of her life phases, gave energy to people in her society, and it describes how society viewed her in terms of the gifts of energy which she did or did not give.

This book, then, tells of the accrual of characteristics, powers, and functions among goddesses throughout ancient Europe and other areas inhabited by Indo-European-speaking peoples. Through the stories of the goddesses, we may view the values and the idealized social structure of these societies.

Illustrations

Frontispiece:
Inanna; alabaster with garnets; gold necklace and earrings; ht. 25 cm (9-7/8″); Babylonian, Seleucid period, fifth century BCE; Louvre #AO20127.

Chapter 1:
Top right—Bird headed figure with stump arms; Tiryns; ht. 13.7 cm (5.4″); ca. 1200 BCE; Louvre #CA 589.
Bottom left—Athene; from the Gigantomachy, depicted on the pediment of the temple of the Peisistratidai; note snakes coiled around her cloak; ca. 520 BCE; Acropolis Museum, Greece #631

Chapter 2:
Top right—Hathor; bronze; fourth century BCE; Serapeion Memphis; Louvre #AF 303.
Center—Winged Anat with deer and lion; hematite cylinder seal; Ras Shamra, tomb IV; sixteenth to thirteenth centuries BCE; 1.9 cm X 1 cm (.75″ X .4″); impression = Louvre # AO17.242; cylinder = Louvre #R.S. 5.089.
Bottom left—Winged Inanna/Ishtar; Accadian cylinder seal; ca. 2550 BCE; British museum #89115; 1891.5-9.2553.

Chapter 3:
Cylinder seal engraved with a scene representing two figures seated facing a tree bearing fruits; behind one figure is a serpent; ca. 2550 BCE; British Museum #1846.5-23.347.

Chapter 4:
Crouching Aphrodite ("Lely's Venus"); note the snake coiled around her arm; first century CE; British Museum #1963.10-29.1

Chapter 5:
Ashtarte; bronze; first century CE; British Museum #1966.10-10.1

Chapter 6:
Maat; bronze; seventh to fourth centuries BCE; Louvre #E4436.

Chapter 7:
Bottom right—Manasa with cobra hood; Bronze; Eastern India; 750 CE; British Museum #1969.1-15.1.
Top left—Sarasvati; white marble; Malwa, Central India; early eleventh century CE; British Museum #1880-349.

Chapter 8:
Winged Eos carrying off Kephalos; terracotta relief; Melos; ca. 450 BCE; ht. 16 cm (6.25″); British Museum #1864.10-7.134.

Chapter 9:
Persephone carried off by Hades; ca. 450 BCE; Locri; terracotta relief; ht. 14 cm (5.5″); British Museum #1865.7-12.37.

Chapter 10:
Bottom left—Demeter; on a panther; a serpent around her neck; terracotta relief; ca. 350 BCE; Thebes; Louvre #CA 1447 (9830743-AGR).
Top right—Aphrodite and Eros on a goose; ca. 380 BCE; made at Tarentum; ht. 18.5 cm (7.25″); British Museum #GR1903.4-12.1

Chapter 11:
Bottom right—Diana; silver statuette; found in the Macon hoard; note the crescent moon over her forehead; first to third centuries CE; British Museum #1824.4-26.5
Top left—Fortuna holding a cornucopia; silver and gold statuette; found in the Macon hoard; 14 cm (5.5″); first to third centuries CE; British Museum #1824.4-24.1.

Chapter 12:
Top left—Durga dancing; Gurjara-Pratihara, Central India; tenth century CE; British Museum #1872.7-1.82.
Bottom right—Isis and Horus; bronze; seventh to fourth centuries BCE; Louvre: unnumbered.

Chapter 13:
Left—Winged Artemis with wild animals; ca. 550 BCE; Magna Graeca; ht. 17.8 cm (7″); Louvre #CA 1810.
Top right—Winged Medusa being slain by Perseus; terracotta relief; Melos; ca. 450 BCE; British Museum #1842.7-28.1134.
Bottom right—Siren; terracotta vase; Sicily; ca. 500 BCE; British Museum #1846.5-12.14.

Chapter 14:
Athena; owl perched on her hand; first century BCE to first century CE; bronze; Louvre #BR 4450.

ACKNOWLEDGMENTS

I would like to thank the following for their careful readings of parts of this manuscript, and their very helpful suggestions: Marija Gimbutas, whose exhortations to "produce!" and exceptional modeling in that realm greatly inspired my own work; Eve Michaelson, who facilitated the conversion of an ivory-tower esoteric feminist into a more pragmatic one; Carolyn De Wald, Niall Slater, Jeffrey Henderson, Micaela Janan, Don Maguire, Martha Malamud, and Richard Caldwell, Classical colleagues who made many helpful recommendations both Classical and otherwise; Bruce Zuckerman, who made his wonderful Ugaritic library accessible to me; Susan Gitlin-Emmer, whose careful reading produced suggestions both functional and succinct; Barbara Bradshaw, who read and reread much of the manuscript beyond the call even of friendship; Leslie Bockian, who helped me to give clarity to my feminist thoughts; Jean Des Marteau, who offered advice both textual and spiritual. I am also very grateful to Jaan Puhvel, who guided much of my doctoral work on both language and female figures.

The textual illustrations and documentation for figurines were greatly facilitated by the following: Dyfri Williams, Bill Cole, Lloyd Gallimore, Christine Bard, Christopher Gravett, Christopher Collins, T. Richard Blurton, and Tony Brandon, of the British Museum; Catherine Belanger, Marie Montembault, Beatrice Abbo, and Antoinette Decoudin, of the Louvre; Aris Lazaridis, of the Acropolis Museum in Athens; Antonis Vasilaikis, of the National Archaeological Museum in Crete; and D. Eric Pals, of the Los Angeles County Museum of Art.

I am also very grateful to my editors for their encouragement and their belief in my work; I thank Gloria Bowles for her numerous and timely notes of support, Renate Klein for her careful criticism of the manuscript, and Lisa Tantillo and Deborah Leary for bringing the book to completion. I also give heartfelt thanks to Susan Hawthorne, whose reading of the manuscript in the editing stage produced forthright comments which greatly clarified my thoughts regarding feminist politics.

Words cannot express my gratitude to my family: Greg, Jacob, Leah, and Joliene, for their support on every level, from listening to my theories to putting up with my constant attention to the word-processor. In particular, to my husband Greg, for his hours of devotion to perfecting the photographs for the illustrations, I tender my deep appreciation and my love.

Part One

Ancient Female-centered Theologies & Ancient Male-centered Theologies

CHAPTER 1

Bird and snake iconography

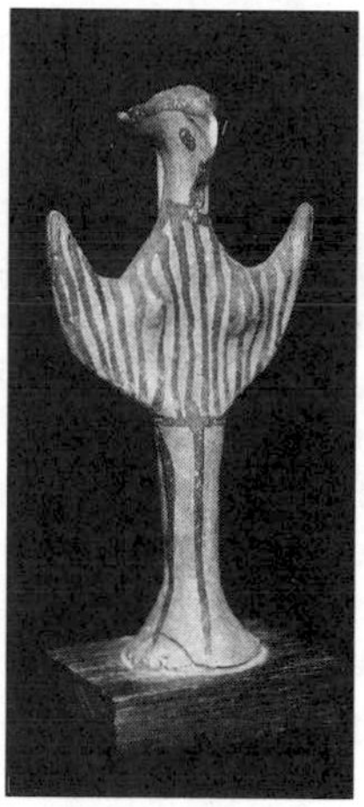

GODDESSES OF THE EUROPEAN NEOLITHIC

Throughout Southeastern and East Central Europe, during the Neolithic or "New Stone" age, from about 6500 BCE[1] to about 3500 BCE—and continuing in Greece, the Cyclades, and Crete to *circa* 1500 BCE—there lived sedentary agriculturalists who raised predominantly cattle and pigs. They built their dwellings in locations which offered good water and soil, rather than on high, steep hills; fortifications were minimal, indicating that they did not fear intruders. They produced gold and pure copper, but they had not yet learned to amalgamate it with strengthening substances, so their weaponry was relatively unsophisticated; indeed, they had no identifiable weapons at all until after 4500 BCE.[2]

Individuals were buried with grave goods, particularly tools and objects of ornamentation: both male and female graves show an equalitarian, if somewhat gender-specific, division of wealth.[3]

Although individuals in these societies were buried with some grave goods, the temples, or ritual dwellings, contained the objects of highest quality: gold, copper, marble, and highly decorated ceramics.[4] That is, the temples or sacred meeting places were more wealthy than individuals in Neolithic Europe. Therefore, it is a common hypothesis that religion occupied the focal point in these societies.

Further, goddesses rather than male deities occupied the focal point of Neolithic European religion, rendering these cultures *theacentric*,[5] or goddess-centered; *twenty times* more female figurines than male figurines have been excavated from Neolithic European sites thus far.[6] Often, the facial characteristics of these female cult figures are de-emphasized,[7] if facial characteristics are shown at all; gender (breasts, hips, pubic triangle), on the other hand, is indicated on most artifacts. This gender (or "sexual") characterization has given rise to the belief that the goddesses represent *fertility* figures.[8]

The term "fertility goddess" may be a narrow one; the goddesses so described may actually have been multi-functional, as were early historical goddesses such as *Inanna* and *Isis*.[9] However, the promotion of animal and vegetal fertility was indeed an important function of such goddesses, and the female principle may well have become primary as an object of worship. The biological role of the male in impregnation was not always given credence in ancient "history" and mythology; women thought to have been impregnated by immortal gods rather than mortal men were described in myths and literature even in historical eras:

> I.1.1. "*Mars sees* [Rhea Silvia],
> *and once having seen her,*
> *he desires her,*
> *and he possesses that which he desires . . .*
> *Silvia becomes a mother.*"[10]
> Ovid, Fasti III.21–45; 43 BCE to 17? CE.

In fact, goddesses and heroines were often described as having given birth parthenogenetically: that is, they became pregnant autonomously, without the fertilization of any man or god:

> I.1.2. "*Hera bore Hephaestos,*
> *apart from the marriage bed*
> [that is, without going to bed with Zeus]."[11]
> Apollodorus of Athens (b *ca.* 180 BCE)
> Atheniensis Bibliothecae I.iii.5.

Woman *per se* was probably believed to have potent, even "magical" powers of fertility, and her birth-giving powers on a personal scale mirrored the feminine principle of birth and regeneration on a cosmic scale. The goddess embodying the female principle had power over the earth and upon the human body, and it was most likely believed that when she was propitiated, the earth too would become fruitful.

That these deities were already worshipped in an organized fashion during the Neolithic is evidenced by ritual pottery, figurines, and graffiti, which were found in natural caves, and in ritual edifices, where the rites may have taken place.[12]

Neolithic European goddesses represented various physical phenomena. They were the "Earth Mothers" and the waters; they were responsible for both human beings and animals. Some goddesses, often designated as "Mistresses of Animals," were associated with pairs of lions or other animals. Their historic descendants include the Egyptian *Neith*, and the Greco-Roman *Artemis-Diana*.

Although the female principle was venerated for its fertile, life-giving properties, life occupied only one end of the spectrum. Neolithic peoples inhabiting parts of Europe, Asia, and the Near East may indeed have worshipped a goddess who embodied the entire life process: birth, life, and death. Those goddesses who were responsible for both the creation of life and for life's cessation were worshipped well into the historic eras. The Indic goddess *Devī*, who is represented as *Umā* and *Parvatī* in her beneficent aspects, and as *Durgā* and *Kalī* in her terrifying aspects, manifests the all-inclusiveness of the divinity. Devī appeared in many forms, and then withdrew them all into herself, saying

I.1.3. "*. . . truly,* [now] *I am a unity.*"[13]
Devī māhātmyam XI.24; *ca.* 550 CE.

This life-and-death-bringing goddess has been called by some the "Goddess of Regeneration."[14] In her life-giving aspect, the "Goddess of Regeneration" was creatrix, bestowing fertility upon the womb and fruitfulness upon the Earth. In her death-giving aspect, she became queen of the underworld, withdrawing the same life which she had created, and she held responsibility for the wintry barrenness of the Earth. Several goddesses, including the Sumerian queen of the underworld, *Ereshkigal*, the Greek *Hecate* and *Persephone*, and the Indic *Nirṛti*, all of whom we shall discuss below, represent the underworld aspect of the "Goddess of Regeneration."

Just as the goddess removed life, at the end of the spectrum of life through death, so she was capable of creating it *again*. Thus, the sequence is a dual one: life through death and *death through life*. The goddess became a deity of life and death *and life*, the magician-goddess who brought the miracle of rebirth, the "Goddess of Regeneration." The goddess was responsible for the processes of rebirth in all things, in the cyclical existences of trees, crops, people.

The forces underlying plant and animal regeneration were probably celebrated early on; we have mythological evidence in the early historic period that the goddess took a consort who was ritually sacrificed each year, or at the end of a given number of years. The death of the consort was short-lived, for with the advent of the new crops the consort-god too was reborn.[15]

Iconographically, the Neolithic European goddesses were represented in mortal female form, in animal form, and as an animal-human combination. Two prevalent hybrids in the European and Near Eastern Neolithic were those of *bird-woman* and *snake-woman*. Figurines of such goddesses have been found in Greece, Italy, Yugoslavia, Bulgaria, Rumania, and Central Europe,[16] and nearly forty percent of the figurines excavated in these areas are combinations of female figures with these avian or serpentine attributes.[17]

These figurines date from *circa* 7000 BCE to *circa* 3500 BCE, although they have Palaeolithic precursors.[18] They are quite numerous, and they are, moreover, remarkably similar to each other. Snake-goddesses are represented with stripes or spirals; they often have snake-like heads; some have mouths depicted as a long slash.[19] Bird-goddesses are represented with beaked, bird-like faces and prominent breasts, and, occasionally, wings or arm stumps.[20]

There is much evidence to demonstrate that these figurines represented the mythological and iconographic precursors of bird and snake goddesses depicted in art and myth in the early historical Near East and elsewhere. In the next sections of this chapter, I will discuss ancient iconographic remains of snake-figures, and then of bird-figures. Later, in Part Two, we will compare bird and snake symbolism in Indo-European historic cultures. The continuation of the symbolism in historic cultures demonstrates a continuity between the female religious symbolism of the European Neolithic and the earliest historic cultures, with regard to the later Indo-European cultures described in Part Two.

SNAKE GODDESSES OF NEOLITHIC EUROPE AND THE ANCIENT NEAR EAST

Snake-figures, both viperimorphic and anthropomorphic, dating to the Neolithic, have been found throughout Europe. The oldest Neolithic snake-figurines found so far were those excavated from shrines in Achilleion, a Greek site near Farsala, Thessaly. Female figures with snake-arms and with stripes or spirals, as well as snake-heads, were found at this site.[21]

The Vinča culture in Yugoslavia yielded snakes incised in vases, coiled snakes of pottery, and curling snakes carved out of bone. Ritual pottery with snake detail was found in Bulgaria, and an anthropomorphic terracotta figurine, with human female breasts and serpiform legs, was found in Kato Ierapetra, Southern Crete;[22] striped serpent-like female figurines, alone and as part of temple models, have been found as well.[23] These figurines date to the late Neolithic, *circa* 3500–2800 BCE. The snake was thus most likely worshipped in many areas of Neolithic Europe, and perhaps identified with the "Goddess of Regeneration:" the snake was able to slough off its old skin, and miraculously renew itself, and such properties may well have been identified with the divine.

Although proof of snake worship in the Neolithic must rest with the iconographic, in the periods succeeding the Neolithic, written and iconographic material gives evidence of snake goddesses. Among the earliest records of the divinity of the snake are those from dynastic Egypt, although iconographic evidence in Egypt too goes back to the prehistoric, predynastic period (that is, no later than the end of the fourth millennium BCE). The snake was so important that it became the symbol of Lower (that is, Northern) Egypt, in the form of the *uraeus,*[24] the serpent which bites its tail and thus, in circular form, represents the eternal cycle of birth, death, and rebirth. The uraeus served as a symbol of sovereignty throughout the dynastic period. The goddess represented by the uraeus was called *Uatchet*.[25] The worship of the uraeus was centered in the Nile Delta, at a place called by the dynastic Egyptians *Per-Uatchet,* "house of Uatchet," and by the Greeks and Romans Butos. Per-Uatchet was an oracular shrine.[26] Uatchet was the twin sister of the vulture goddess *Nekhebet,* whom we shall discuss shortly. Iconographically, Uatchet was represented both as a woman and as a large *winged serpent*.[27]

It seems particularly significant that the Egyptian hieroglyphic determinative for the classifications of both "goddess" and "priestess" was a serpent;[28] a common hieroglyph for the word "goddess," *Netrit,* was composed of the symbols for *god, t, ri,* and *serpent*."[29] That is, the serpent represented the goddess *par excellence*; the two were identified not only mythologically but also as an integral part of the Egyptian language.

Sumerian cylinder seals often depict snakes alongside deities, and the serpent-goddess figured in the earliest extant Sumerian mythology.[30] Syrian iconography dating to 2500 BCE likewise depicts the serpent in concert with the goddess. An interesting representation, for comparative purposes, is that of a female figure whose shoulders are encircled by a serpent;[31] as we shall discuss shortly, iconography in other cultures echoes this depiction.

Female figurines, whose bodies were encircled with snakes, were also found in ancient Crete, dating to the time of the Minoan civilization, from the third to the second millennia BCE. Minoan shrines bore equipment and votive offerings analogous to those in Neolithic "Old European" shrines.[32] Vessels entwined by snakes, perforated vessels covered with coiled snakes, and the serpent-enfolded female figurines have been found in Minoan shrines.[33] The latter figurines, which have been described *in sum* as the "Knossos goddess," were often made of ivory and decorated with gold.[34]

The Greek Mycenaean civilization, which flourished in the latter half of the second millennium BCE, was described by the Greek poet Homer in his epic poems, the *Iliad* and the *Odyssey*. The Mycenaeans borrowed much of the art of the Minoans, and a continuation of the Neolithic European snake worship is evidenced by figurines such as the seventeen terracotta sculptures of snakes excavated at Mycenae, and dating to *circa* 1250 BCE.[35] Snake worship *per se* is not described by Homer or subsequent Greeks, but we will see in Part Two that the iconography of snakes associated with goddesses continued among the Greeks for over a millennium after the Mycenaean era.

Descendants of the Serpent-Goddess

The serpent-goddess was represented not only in classical Greece but in Rome as well, since the Romans borrowed much iconography and mythology from the Greeks. The snake became associated with healing: the Greek serpent-god Amphiarios was a healer, and the Roman goddess of health, *Hygieia*, was portrayed with a serpent encircling her shoulders, a snake-entwined caduceus at her side;[36] the latter is evocative of the prehistoric Syrian goddess described above. Snakes were also thought to confer prophetic powers. The famous oracular shrine at Delphi, the "navel" of the Greek world, was said to have belonged, in prehistoric times, to the goddess Themis. The shrine was guarded by a female serpent, the Python. Later, the god Apollo slew the Python and took over the oracle.[37]

Sacred snakes were believed to be responsible for the mantic powers of the Trojan Cassandra, who, when a child, was left overnight at Apollo's shrine. When her mother, Hecuba, returned in the morning for her daughter, she found the girl surrounded by the sacred snakes which were kept in the shrine. The snakes were licking Cassandra's ears, and thereafter she possessed the gift of prophesy. However, to her misfortune, and that of the other Trojans, her prophesies were not believed, and the Trojans, never heeding her warnings, were overcome by the Greeks.[38]

A similar tale is told of the Greek prophet, Melampus. He saved a brood of young snakes, and when the latter were full-grown,

> I.1.4. *"standing at each of his shoulders,*
> *while he was sleeping,*
> *they licked his ears.*
> *Rising up, frightened, [Melampus]*
> *understood the voices*
> *of the birds flying overhead, and,*
> *from what he learned from them,*
> *he prophesied the future to men."*[39]
> Apollodorus of Athens [b *ca*. 180 BCE]
> Atheniensis Bibliothecae I.ix.11.

Note here the continuing interrelationship of birds and snakes in Classical mythology: while the snakes gave the gift of prophesy to Melampus, it was the conversations of the birds which formed the *material* for the prophesies.

Snakes played many roles in Greek and Roman mythology; their influence was at times quite apparent and at other times quite subtle. As we will discuss in Part Two, many Classical Greek and Roman goddesses were associated in some way with snakes.

The snake was believed to have positive powers in many geographical areas. However, as we stated earlier, although snake iconography has been found all over the world, we will concentrate on serpentine influences in Indo-European spheres.

In India, the snake was both feared and revered. It received and still receives mystical status among adherents of *Tantric* principles. In Tantric belief, there is an energy called the *Kuṇḍalinī shakti*.[40] An active energy, it is personified as a coiled serpent which is believed to reside in the first *chakra*, "district" or "hollow," that is, the first energy center.[41] When awakened, this energy passes along the spinal column, through all of the chakras, activating all of them as it goes, and thus advancing the spiritual abilities of the adherent.[42]

The Indic people also worshipped deified personifications of the serpent. The goddess *Manasā*, sometimes called *Manasā Devī*, was a gynomorphic epiphany of the snake-goddess. She was called *Nityā*, "eternal woman," and, as *Visha-harā* or *Visha-harī*, "she who takes away venom," she had the power to protect humanity from the venom of poisonous serpents.[43]

Kumarī or *Kaumarī* was wife of the warrior-god Skanda, also called Kumara. Although *Kumarī* means "the maiden," it is not her chastity that is in evidence, but her youth. Indeed, among her iconographical representations, a figurine dating to the sixth century CE shows her as a *pregnant* woman, with a *snake draped around her shoulders* . . . ,[44] again, similar to the Syrian goddess. The snake may represent the fertility inherent in her pregnancy.

In some regions, such as the Baltic, snakes were worshipped well into the modern era; indeed, the Balts retained linguistic forms, myths, and cult practices which have been largely unchanged since antiquity.[45] In Lithuania, for example, as late as the nineteenth century CE, snakes, which represented deities, were worshipped, and they were fed milk in rituals. According to Lithuanian folklore, they insured good fortune, as well as plant and animal fertility.[46]

> In one tale, the hero, a farmhand, came upon three men trying to kill a large snake. The farmhand took pity upon the snake, and, wishing to save it, offered the men money if they would set the snake free. The three men accepted, and the snake slithered away.
>
> The farm boy continued along, and, after some time, he came to a river. An old woman, beaten and ravaged, sat on the bridge. The youth was about to turn back when she said,

I.1.5. "*Do not be afraid, young man.*
You rescued me from death . . .
I was the snake whom you ransomed."[47]
from "Aukso Žiedas," Lithuanian Folktale
Second Millennium CE.

> The old woman then gave the boy a gold ring, as a reward for saving her, and the ring granted all of his wishes.

The Slavs too preserved many vestiges of ancient religious practice. In nineteenth-century Russia, although there were many folktales about evil snakes, in reality snakes were often regarded as bearers of good fortune. It was considered sinful to destroy house- or water-snakes, and, indeed, peasants showed respect for them by leaving out milk for them to drink,[48] as did the Balts.[49]

The Fall of the Sacred Serpent

The serpent was a power to be reckoned with, and consequently to be feared. Therefore, in the mythologies of many post-Neolithic societies, serpent-deities representing negative forces were pitted against young hero-deities. Often, one culture housed both positive and negative myths about the serpent.

People of the Near-East and the early historical Europeans shared similar myths of a battle between a warrior-deity and a snake. Ugaritic, Hebraic, Egyptian, and Sumerian mythology describe the clashes between the heroic god and the forces of evil, embodied in the snake.

Hebrew scriptures describe a battle between the heroic father-god, Yahweh, and the monster Leviathan. Yahweh

> I.1.6. *"dashed into pieces the heads of Leviathan"*.[50]
> Old Testament, "Psalms" 74.14. First Millennium BCE.

Yahweh also

> I.1.7. *"broke to pieces*
> *the heads of the sea-monsters* (taninim)
> in the waters . . . "[51]
> Ibid, 74.13.

According to another text,

> I.1.8. *" . . . the Lord,*
> *with his hard, great, strong sword,*
> *will strike Leviathan,*
> *the fleeing serpent,*
> *Leviathan indeed,*
> *the crooked serpent; and*
> *he will slay the sea-monster*
> *that* [is] *in the sea."*[52]
> Old Testament, "Isaiah" 27.1. *ca.* 800 BCE.

Yahweh was thus an enemy of the serpent-monster on both land and sea. It is interesting, therefore, that Yahweh was represented as a snake-footed deity on Jewish amulets dating to the second or first century BCE.[53] Perhaps one method of overcoming an enemy was that of assimilating it, thereby absorbing its power. We shall see below that this assimilation of the snake by the warrior-deity also appears in the Greek iconography and mythology.

Among the *Ugaritic* peoples, those who dwelled in Northern Syria in the second millennium BCE, the father-god was *El*, but the heroic deity who slew the serpent-monster was the younger god, the thunder and storm god, *Baal*, who was responsible for rain, and, consequently, for good harvests. Baal fought various demon-gods, including *Mot*, god of the underworld:[54] the battle was one between the light and the darkness. Mot killed Baal, but Baal's sister, the young warrior-goddess *Anat*, came to his rescue. She descended into the bowels of the earth, where she found the dead Baal.[55] After bewailing him and then burying him with fitting honors,[56] she went to Mot and asked him to restore Baal to life. Mot refused and Anat "cleft him" with her sword.[57] Baal, the year-god, was alive again.[58]

Baal's remission was always a temporary one, however. He had to fight Mot during periods of drought, which often lasted seven years,[59] just as mortal people of the Near-East fought seasonal periods of drought. Further, he also was made to fight the god of the waters, "Prince Yamm, Judge Nahar." Thus the gods of the heavens (Baal), the underworld (Mot), and the waters (Yamm) were not as comfortable about their distribution of powers as were the Greek Zeus, Hades, and Poseidon. It is interesting that, although Baal, in one text, slew Prince Yamm,[60] in another text, it is the goddess Anat who declares,

> I.1.9. *"Truly, I killed Yamm* (Sea),
> *beloved*[61] *of El;*
> *Indeed, I destroyed the great Nahar* (River) *of El."*[62]
> Ugaritic Text KTU 1.3.iii. *ca.* 1200 BCE.

Thus both the god who brings the rains and the powerful warrior goddess defeat the serpents who threaten both death and drought.

In Egypt the young god *Osiris*, husband of the goddess *Isis*,[63] was the god who succumbed to death. Although Isis did not *exactly* bring Osiris back to life, as Anat did with Baal, Osiris was indeed restored in another form. Osiris fought and was overcome by the god *Set*, his brother who brought death.[64] Death, however, was overcome, because Osiris continued to rule as god of the underworld[65] and, further, he was transmuted into his son, *Horus*.[66] His influence thus was extended doubly. The principle of regeneration was expressed both in a generational sequence of lives, wherein the child Horus received the life-spirit of Osiris, and in the afterlife of Osiris himself.

In the Mesopotamian Babylonian civilization, which flourished in the first millennium BCE, but contained mythological elements one to two millennia older, a dragon-goddess was described in the epic poem, the Enuma Elish.

> The primordial goddess of sea-water and mother of the gods was *Tiamat*. She was often described as a monstrous serpent, albeit one who possessed a neck and legs or "roots."[67] Tiamat and her husband Apsu, god of fresh water, represented the earliest creation. As the first couple, they were the male and female halves of the primeval chaos, out of which everything and everyone were created.
>
> After some time, the younger gods, the new powers, came together to dance, shaking the waters, and Apsu plotted to destroy them—against the will of his wife—so that peace might prevail again, and, further, so that the older gods might get some sleep. The young gods discovered the plot and were terrified. Finally, the wise and cunning god of running waters, *Ea*, put a spell on Apsu and killed him while he slept.
>
> This parricide upset some of the older gods, and they convinced the erstwhile reluctant Tiamat to avenge her husband. Although she had not wished to harm the young deities, who were after all descended from her, she became riled—or roiled—and she created a group of monsters which headed an avenging army.
>
> Now the younger gods became frightened, and they finally appealed to the young hero-god, *Marduk*,[68] Ea's son, to whom they gave the kingship and the mandate to kill Tiamat. After a terrible battle, Marduk aimed an arrow at the goddess. The arrow tore through her belly[69] and her "inner parts,"[70] and her life was "extinguished."[71]

This theme of the battle with the serpent-monster was borrowed by the Greeks in several different forms. The heroic father-god *Zeus* clashed with the monster *Typhon*, whom, according to one source, Zeus' wife *Hera* had borne parthenogenetically.[72]

> A similar monster, the female dragon Python,[73] whose oracular connections we discussed above, was sent by Hera against her rival, Leto, when the latter was giving birth to the god Apollo. Python was unable to find Leto, and so she went back to her lair in the forests on Mount Parnassus. Four days after he was born, Apollo, armed with arrows, travelled to Parnassus, where he found and killed the serpent. The place where the serpent lived was first called Pytho, and then Delphi.[74]
>
> Apollo then retreated to Thessaly, where he underwent a period of purification.[75] Afterwards, purified and perhaps "reborn," he returned to Delphi; henceforth, all of the prophecies given there were said to come from Apollo.

Just as the god took over the "lair" or sanctuary of the serpent-goddess, so he also took over her prophetic functions.

Another Greek mythological figure, the hero Herakles, slew the Hydra, the many-headed water serpent which lived in a swamp at Lerna;[76] and the Tyrian hero Cadmus, who settled the site of Thebes, killed the great dragon which stood guard over the Spring of Ares, later called the Castilian Spring.[77] Another Greek hero, Perseus, was renowned for his murder of *Medusa*, the snaky-haired Gorgon;[78] Medusa, by the way, had avian and serpentine attributes; she was depicted by some authors and artists as a *winged* deity.[79]

Just as the Hebraic deity Yahweh, whom we discussed above, was identified with the snake, so the Greek god Zeus, as "Zeus Meilichios," was at times depicted in snaky form.[80] This epiphany of Zeus was propitiated by those who sought expiation from sin.[81] As serpent, the god seems to have represented both the earth and the lower world;[82] thus the warrior god Zeus became the deity of the three realms of sky, earth, and underworld, absorbing the chthonic powers of the serpent-deity into his already considerable powers as god of the heavens.

The Near Eastern monster-myth, which told of the battles between the serpent and the young warrior-god, was also known to the earliest Indic peoples. Their most ancient writings, those of the *Rigveda*, describe the goddess *Danu*.[83] Danu, probably a primeval, and certainly an ancient, goddess, was described as the consort of two of the most powerful gods in the Indic pantheon: *Mitra* and *Varuṇa*.[84] She was also, however, viewed as a demon; she was the mother of the arch withholder of the cosmic waters, Vṛtra, and as such it was the duty of *Indra*, the Indic warrior-god, to kill her, along with her son:

> I.1.10. *''Indra bore the weapon down upon her.*
> *Danu was lying*
> *like a cow with [her] calf.''*[85]
> Rigveda I.32.9; *ca.* 1200 BCE.

This myth pervaded classical mythologies and remained popular in Medieval and Renaissance Europe. Both *Saint George*[86] and *Saint Michael*[87] were famous for their dragon-slaying, and the Persian hero *Rustem* likewise slew a dragon as the second of his seven trials.[88] The metaphor was—and continues to be—one of good or the higher self, upheld by the hero, overcoming evil or the lower self, symbolized by the dragon.

In the earliest myths of the hero and the dragon or serpent, the serpent was often a goddess: the Greek Python, the Sumerian Tiamat, and the Indic Danu may have been successors to the Neolithic European snake-goddess. The new, young, warrior-hero (Zeus, Marduk, Baal, Indra, Yahweh, Horus) slew the serpent of darkness, thus killing off the old order of deities, the ancient dragons and serpents, who were viewed as "chaotic."

There are several functional levels to these primordial serpent-myths. The first and the most evident function is a mythological and religious one, explaining the origins of creation. However, these myths of chaotic serpents may have also had sociological and psychological functions. The ancient serpents may have represented the earlier, indigenous peoples, clashing with the warlike newcomers; on the other hand, they may also have represented a primeval chaos on a cosmogonic level.

BIRD GODDESSES OF NEOLITHIC EUROPE AND THE ANCIENT NEAR EAST

Just as snake-iconography is evident world-wide, so the bird, too, has represented the divine in many areas throughout the world. Again, we will concentrate on iconography in the areas which influenced the Indo-Europeans.

As was mentioned earlier in this chapter, there is ample prehistoric evidence for bird-goddesses. Some figurines, such as those found at the Copper Age (fifth millennium BCE) Vinča site in Northern Yugoslavia, are incised with elaborate symbols.[89] Many figurines have very large eyes,[90] reminding one of the fourth and third millennia Sumerian figures of both deities and devotees.

The figures from Achilleion,[91] a Neolithic Greek site of the Sesklo, Proto-Sesklo, and the earliest ceramic periods, are among the earliest European Neolithic figures that have been found: the site dates from 6500–5700 BCE.[92] Bird and snake figures were found in shrines. Many of the bird-figures are beaked and have cylindrical necks.[93] Some have turbans or headdresses,[94] and some are marked with V's and triple lines,[95] markings similar to those found on Vinča figurines. Also, similar to the Vinča figurines are clay figures dating to the Greek Neolithic, which have heads resembling bird-masks.[96] A fragment of a bird-figurine and the head of a snake were found at Knossos, Crete,[97] and clay schematic figurines were also found at Knossos. The latter have stumpy arms which resemble wings.[98] These sites have yielded abundant evidence that Neolithic peoples across Europe celebrated female figures with the beaks or eyes or schematized shapes of birds.

The figures in all likelihood attest to the existence of a religious system encompassing avian goddesses, and not "dolls," as some have claimed, since the figures were found in shrines and in graves.

One may presume, then, that the figures did represent bird-goddesses, and that these Neolithic bird-goddesses were remembered, even if at times only in iconographic hints, in the later Near Eastern and European cultures which absorbed the socio-religious practices of the earlier Neolithic folk.

Several Mesopotamian cultures give evidence of a continuation of this avian iconography. The large eyes on figures of Sumerian devotees, as we observed, recall the eyes of Neolithic and Copper-Age bird-figures, figures such as those from the Vinča culture. Again, note that many of these features can be found elsewhere in the world,[99] but it is likely that the European and Near Eastern cultures assimilated traits from the earlier European and Near Eastern cultures from which they arose, and from geographically contiguous cultures.

The Syrians depicted both female and male winged figures, similar to the West Semitic "angels."[100] Sumerian and Accadian cylinder-seals also depict winged deities; the goddess *Inanna-Ishtar* was often both winged and associated with birds.[101] Inanna and other Near Eastern winged deities will be discussed in more detail in Chapter Two.

The Neolithic tradition was also continued in Minoan Crete, where bird-woman hybrids remained a popular iconographic image. A beaked female figure, dating to the proto-palatial period (2000–1700 BCE), was depicted on a stem of a round altar table from Phaistos.[102] The Cretans also practiced, and the later Greeks preserved, the "geranos" or "crane-dance," which was a type of circle-dance, one which perhaps imitated the circling passages in the Cretan Labyrinth.[103]

The Mycenaeans perpetuated the artistic culture of the Minoans, preserving the bird-goddesses as small terracotta figures with cylindrical bodies and wing-shaped arms.[104] Stripes that may have represented feathers were often found on these figures.

The bird-goddesses found their way into the iconographies and mythologies of many other early historical cultures. Upper (Southern) Egypt, as early as the Predynastic Period, was represented by a bird, a hawk. The vulture was the symbol of the goddess *Nekhebet*, and the swallow and the goose were associated with the goddess *Isis*. Isis, moreover, was sometimes represented as a *winged* goddess.[105]

The Celtic warrior-goddess *Badb* was identified as a "vulture" or "royston crow," similar to the Indic *Nirṛti*, described as a "black bird."[106]

Among the Greeks and Romans, wings were given to many goddesses, both positive and negative figures in the mythologies: as we discussed earlier in this chapter, the Gorgon Medusa was winged and snaky. Further, Sirens, Harpies, and most other negative Greco-Roman goddesses which were not snaky, were provided with wings or other avian paraphernalia. A detailed discussion of these Greek and Roman goddesses, as well as the Indic, Celtic, and other "bird-goddesses," will follow in Part Two.

Throughout the next chapters, we will be relating the goddesses of historic cultures to the prehistoric female figures which we have just discussed. The "Mistress of Animals" and the bird and snake goddesses found their way into historical European and Asian mythologies.

Some of the early historical cultures which will be discussed were of particular significance. They formed pantheons which included these assimilated prehistoric goddesses, and then, in turn, passed on elements from their pantheons to other cultures. The next chapter examines the mythologies of several early historic Near Eastern cultures, and notes their prehistoric elements.

CHAPTER 2

Goddesses of the ancient Near East

The worship and customs of ancient Neolithic European and Near Eastern goddesses were transmitted to early historical Near Eastern societies. In these societies, goddesses manifested attributes of their ancestresses, attributes such as the power over birth and death. The new goddesses also developed new attributes, to conform to the needs of their societies, and they thus represented an assimilation of old and new—an assimilation that would continue through the millennia, as new peoples came together.

Two cultures played an important role in the development of Classical European religions: the *Mesopotamian*, including the *Sumerian* and the *Babylonian*; and the *Egyptian*. Further, there are a few *Ugaritic* goddesses who seem to have affected both the related Semitic cultures, such as the Hebraic, and the historical European Mediterranean cultures. Examination of some goddesses from these societies will provide insight into the amalgam of attributes of which later goddesses were composed.

GODDESSES OF ANCIENT MESOPOTAMIA

The earliest historical culture which inhabited Mesopotamia was the Sumerian, which dated from about 3500 BCE. The Sumerians lived in the lower part of this once arid land bounded by the Tigris and Euphrates Rivers; an enterprising and cooperative folk, they used the overflow from the rivers to irrigate their lands, thus rendering them arable.[1]

This spirit of cooperation led to a synergy evident in many aspects of their culture: the Sumerians developed a writing system consisting of cuneiform, or wedge-shaped, symbols, a strong central government, and a complex religious ideology.

Goddesses played important roles in the Sumerian pantheon; we will discuss six of them, although special attention will be paid to the goddesses Ereshkigal and, particularly, Inanna. One of the earliest Sumerian goddesses was *Ninhursag*. She was apparently worshipped by a prehistoric Mesopotamian society, the *Ubaid*, since a small temple dedicated to her was found in Al-Ubaid, a low Ubaidian mound.[2] Ninhursag was a "Great-Mother" goddess, who brought both life and death to animals and plants, and she was a central figure in the Sumerian Paradise myth.[3] Early on, she was called *Ninlil*, "lady of the storm;"[4] she was queen of the universe, the eloquent goddess, the goddess who decreed the fates in the "place where the sun rises."[5] She was given a vast stone pile, called a *hursag*, which she provided with vegetation, wildlife, and minerals; and she became Nin-hursag, "lady of the mountain."[6]

Nidaba was goddess of the grasses, grain, and *reeds*. She became the patroness of the reed-stylus and writing, and she gave counsel regarding what was written.[7] She was a wise goddess.

Another wise goddess was *Geshtinanna*, sister of the divine consort *Dumuzi*; she chose to become her brother's substitute in the Underworld for half of each year.[8] She was a divine poetess, singer, and interpreter of dreams.[9]

The goddess *Nanshe* was also a divine interpreter of dreams.[10] Further, she played a role in moral and ethical conduct: she cared for the oppressed, and she judged humanity on New Year's Day.[11]

Ereshkigal was the Sumerian goddess of the Underworld. She had been abducted, and carried off to the Netherworld;[12] at first a goddess without consort, she later, in Accadian and Assyrian texts, takes the god Nergal as lover and husband:

> In the Accadian myth, Ereshkigal, angry with the god Nergal for not paying proper respect to her vizier, orders Nergal to come down to the Underworld to be killed by her. Nergal weeps, but descends; however, once there, it is he who overcomes Ereshkigal, and she takes him as consort.[13]
>
> In the later, Assyrian myth, Nergal prepares to go down to the realm of the goddess, to

make a visit of conciliation rather than to be killed by the goddess. He is warned by the god Ea not to eat or drink anything in the Underworld kingdom, if he wants to have the option of returning to the upper world. He is also warned not to have sexual intercourse with the goddess. When he arrives in the Underworld, he remembers not to eat or drink, nor to accept any other hospitality of the Underworld. The goddess goes to change into something more comfortable, however, and he forgets his other injunction. The two make love for six days and six nights.

On the seventh morning, Nergal was missing, and Ereshkigal wept for her lost lover, for she was not yet sated with his charms. She again sent her vizier to the gods, to announce that, if her lover did not return to her, she would send up the dead to devour the living. Nergal returned to her. He seized her by her hair, dragged her from her throne, and made passionate love to her for another six days and nights. And the two lived together happily ever after.[14]

It is easy to see the similarities between the myth of Ereshkigal and that of the Greek goddess, Persephone. Ereshkigal, at first the reigning deity of the Underworld, by more male-centered Assyrian times was sharing her throne with a powerful consort—one who announced his erotic presence with cave-man tactics. As we shall discuss in Part Two, Persephone, in the Greek pantheon, became the consort of the Underworld-god, Hades-Pluto, after he abducted her. We may recall that Persephone, just as Nergal, was not to eat anything in thc Underworld. Nonetheless, she ate some pomegranate seeds, and she was therefore to inhabit the dark kingdom for a part of every year.[15] Perhaps in an earlier form of the myth it was her intercourse with Hades which determined her mandatory sojourn in the Underworld.

There is a Sumerian myth which shows similarities to the myth of Persephone's partial inhabitation of the Underworld; in this case Persephone may be compared to the goddess *Inanna's* consort, the shepherd Dumuzi, and to Dumuzi's sister, Geshtinanna.

Inanna decided to visit her Underworld sister, Ereshkigal. As Inanna passed through each of the seven gates to the Underworld, she was compelled to divest herself of clothing, jewels, and prerogatives. By the time she reached the Underworld, she was stripped of all her external goods. Then Ereshkigal and the seven judges, the Anunnaki, fastened upon her their eyes of death; they expropriated her vital forces, killing her and hanging her corpse on a peg. The corpse of Inanna turned into a side of green, rotting meat.

As long as Inanna was without vitality, the mortal world followed suit. Nothing grew, and neither mortals nor animals copulated. The world was sterile.[16]

Inanna was a goddess, however, and she was therefore able to be resurrected.[17] After three days and three nights, *Enki*, the god of the waters and of wisdom, rescued her; he sent asexual lamenting spirits, the *kurgarru* and the *kalaturru*, down to the Nether World. They were to sprinkle the "food of life" and the "water of life" upon Inanna's corpse. They did so, and Inanna was revived.

However, the reprieve was a conditional one. Inanna must send a substitute, a scapegoat, to take her place in the Underworld.

Inanna departed for the Upper World, accompanied by infernal spirits, to find out how her people were faring without her.[18] She found everyone lamenting her death: everyone but Dumuzi. Inanna, angry with her consort, condemned Dumuzi to the Nether Regions.[19]

Even Dumuzi had a partial reprieve, though, because his sister Geshtinanna offered to sacrifice herself in his place. Inanna decreed that brother and sister would divide up the year. Each would inhabit the lower regions for half of the year, and spend the other half in the light, in an alternation of life and death:

I.2.1. *"Your . . . exactly half the year,*
your sister, exactly half the year"[20]
Sumerian Fragment; Recorded 2000–1500 BCE.

Thus sister and brother were, like Persephone, partial inhabitants of the infernal kingdom; the goddess of birth, death and rebirth, Inanna, is similar to Persephone's mother, Demeter. In their "barren" or "dead" state, both cause the flora and fauna of the earth to become barren as well.

Although this was a poem about the journey of Inanna, it was nonetheless a poem *in honor of* her elder sister, Ereshkigal. From this myth, we also learn that even the goddesses and gods feared the goddess Ereshkigal, for she could cause them to die. The poem ends,

> I.2.2. *''Shining Ereshkigal,*
> *Your praise is good, indeed!''*[21]
> Ibid.

Ereshkigal, the mighty goddess of death, had strangely human characteristics. In the "Descent of Inanna," when the *kurgarru* and the *kalaturru* came upon her, they found

> I.2.3. *''The mother giving birth to infancy,*
> *Ereshkigal . . .*
> *She has hair on her head*
> *like leeks.*
> *She says, 'Ouch, my insides!'''*[22]
> Ibid.

However, she has the characteristics of familiar goddesses as well as of mortals. Her leeky—or cucumbery[23]—hair evokes the Greek Gorgon Medusa with her "snaky hair."[24] Ereshkigal may, for several reasons, be related to the Neolithic European snake goddess. The snake, chthonic creature *par excellence*, certainly belongs with a chthonic-Underworld goddess such as Ereshkigal. Further, as a symbol of regeneration, the snake, which sheds and renews its skin, represents the goddess of life and death; her Sumerian epiphany, Ereshkigal, represents her death-aspect. The ancient undifferentiated goddess of life and death has thus been split by the Sumerians, just as she was by many other peoples. The Sumerian Underworld-goddess Ereshkigal bears similiarities with the Indic chthonic and death-goddess, Nirṛti,[25] and with the Greek witch-goddess, crossroads-goddess, and goddess of the Underworld, Hecate.[26]

Even though Inanna had to go through death and rebirth at the hands of her sister, she was one of the most powerful Sumerian deities. Her descent to the Underworld tells a story of birth, death, and rebirth. Inanna accrued many powers and functions, becoming a "Great"-goddess. In the poem, The Exaltation of Inanna, the poet-priestess, princess Enheduanna, described the goddess as the

> I.2.4. *'' . . . preeminent one,*
> *of heaven and earth,*
> *Inanna . . . ''*[27]
> Enheduanna, "Exaltation of Inanna" 12; *ca.* 2500 BCE.

Inanna was the

> I.2.5. *'' . . . great queen of the foundation of heaven*
> *and of the upper realm of heaven.''*[28]
> Enheduanna, "Exaltation of Inanna" 112; *ca.* 2500 BCE.

She was the evening star and the morning star,[29] and the mistress of the elements; she could wreak havoc upon the land:

> I.2.6. *''Like a dragon,*
> *you have thrown venom upon the land.*
> *When you roar upon the earth,*
> *like the Thunder,*
> *in that place the Grain does not exist.*
> [*You are*] *a flood,*
> *descending from the mountain.''*[30]
> Enheduanna, "Exaltation of Inanna" 9–11; *ca.* 2500 BCE.

Further,

> I.2.7. *''On the mountain,*
> [*when*] *homage is taken away from you,*

Grain is diseased.''[31]
Enheduanna, "Exaltation of Inanna" 43; *ca.* 2500 BCE.

She could also destroy people. She was a warrior goddess, whose strength was associated with the lion. A cylinder seal which dates to *ca.* 2300 BCE shows Inanna seated on a throne with two crossed lions. Weapons emerge from her shoulders.[32] Her association with the lion is a common one, shared by many European and Near Eastern goddesses. It also relates her to the Neolithic "Mistress of Animals." Mythology corroborates the iconography; Inanna is

I.2.8. '' . . . *the lady riding on a beast.*''[33]
Enheduanna, "Exaltation of Inanna" 14; *ca.* 2500 BCE.

and

I.2.9. '' . . . *the lion of battle* . . . ''[34]
Inscription of Utu-hegal, king of Erech. *ca.* 2500 BCE.

On another seal,[35] the goddess stands with a foot upon the back of a lion, and weapons again rise from her shoulders. In this figure she is *winged*; that is, she has accrued the attributes of the ancient bird-goddess. Again, the texts corroborate the iconography:

I.2.10. ''*In the vanguard of the battle,*
everything is beset by you.
My Lady, [flying about] on your own wings,
you feed on [the carnage].''[36]
Enheduanna, "Exaltation of Inanna" 26–27; *ca.* 2500 BCE.

The poet proclaims Inanna's destructive powers:

I.2.11. ''*That you destroy the rebellious land,*
let it be known! . . .
that you devour corpses like a beast,
let it be known!
that your eye is fierce,
let it be known!
that you lift up your fierce eye,
let it be known!
that your eye is flashing,
let it be known! . . .
that you achieve victory,
let it be known!''[37]
Enheduanna, "Exaltation of Inanna" 125; 127–130; 132; *ca.* 2500 BCE.

However, Inanna was a goddess of regeneration, and as such, she brought life as well as death:

I.2.12. ''*When Inanna*
looked at [Gudea]
with her eye of life . . . ''[38]
Gudea, Statue C; *ca.* 2600 BCE.

Even though Inanna was goddess of both life and death, the functions of a goddess of regeneration seem to have been divided, in a rather complex manner, between Inanna and her sister, Ereshkigal. Ereshkigal had charge over the kingdom of death, the Underworld, and was thus the actual Sumerian death goddess. But one cannot make a clear distinction between Ereshkigal as goddess of death and Inanna as goddess of life, for it was Ereshkigal who gave *birth* to "infancy," whereas, Inanna was *not* herself a giver of birth. Rather she was a *life*-goddess, goddess of the process of living and goddess who caused the procreation of others, but who did not herself procreate. Like many Classical virgin goddesses,[39] Inanna was addressed as "Mother:"

I.2.13. *"Oh, Mother Inanna, Inanna, goddess of Heaven,*
your dress, your dress!"[40]
Sumerian Fragment; Recorded 2000–1500 BCE.

She was not herself a mother, however. Her capacity, like that of virgin goddesses such as the Greek Artemis, was that of aiding motherhood. But Inanna, unlike Artemis, was not required to be a virgin, for she was a fertility-goddess as well as a "Mistress of Animals."

Inanna not only had charge over life and procreation; she could also cause devastation and death. Thus Ereshkigal was goddess of both birth and death, and Inanna was goddess of both life and death. Although their functions overlapped, their animal associations made their *primary* functions clear. Ereshkigal, the chthonic goddess, was associated with snakes, and Inanna was associated with birds. Thus Ereshkigal was the chthonic goddess, with the connections to death which that function brings; and Inanna was the Queen of Heaven, and the bird who flew to and from the heavens, with attendant connections to life. The two goddesses, with their interwoven functions, constituted a whole; the two were descendants of the ancient goddess of regeneration, depicted in Neolithic Europe as the goddess who was often both bird *and* snake.

As goddess of life, Inanna was also goddess of love, fertility, and sexuality. That is, she had charge over whether or not those qualities existed in a given society. In a city where the inhabitants failed to honor her,

I.2.14. *"A woman does not speak with favor*
to her spouse;
she does not reveal to him
her pure heart."[41]
Enheduanna, "Exaltation of Inanna" 55, 57; *ca.* 2500 BCE.

Nor does she reveal anything else.

Therefore, neither love nor procreation can take place where Inanna is not worshipped. Where she *was* worshipped, however, she brought fertility of all sorts to her people; the concepts of both mortal and vegetal fertility were conveyed through the metaphor of sexual love. The *Uruk Vase,* which dates to the fourth millennium BCE,[42] shows the god of the date palm, *Amaushumgalanna,* approaching the gate of Inanna, his bride, who may represent the storehouse.[43] The god leads a retinue, all of whom bring wedding gifts. Standing at the gate of her temple, Inanna receives him. This vase depicts the *hieros gamos,* the "sacred marriage" rite in which the goddess, represented by a priestess, had intercourse with the young vegetation god, represented in Sumeria by the reigning king.[44] This ritual ensured that the fertilization of the whole society, people and crops, would ensue; to the Sumerians and people of other ancient societies the ritual was vital to the well-being of the populace.

The iconography of Inanna and the vegetation-god is sometimes quite stylistic. Inanna is often shown with a date palm,[45] which represents the god; frequently, the goddess too is depicted symbolically: she is represented by *rosettes*[46] and by *gateposts.*[47]

The god had several names. Sometimes he was called *Dumuzi,* literally the "young son" or "male child;"[48] sometimes he was invoked by other names, such as Amaushumgalanna. He could be farmer or shepherd, representing the herds or the crops which were meant to be fecundated. This was the year-god, the god who had to die at the end of the year or of the season, in a cycle imitating that of the crops. In poems celebrating the sacred marriage, pastoral and agricultural metaphors abound. In eagerness for the ceremony, and in celebration of her body, Inanna exclaims,

I.2.15. " . . . *I am the queen of Heaven . . .*
My husband . . .
the wild ox, Dumuzi . . .
Inanna . . .

[sings] a song
about her vulva . . .
'[my] vulva . . .
like a horn . . .
the ship of Heaven . . .
like the new crescent moon . . .
I, the young woman,
who will plant it?
My vulva . . .
I, the queen,
who will place the bull?'
'Lady, let the king plant it for [you];
Let Dumuzi, the king,
plant [it] for [you].' ''[49]
Sumerian Fragment; Recorded 2000–1500 BCE.

Inanna addresses Dumuzi in loving metaphors of the crop; he is

I.2.16. '' *. . . the honey of my eye;*
he is the lettuce of my heart.''[50]
Ibid.

In sharp contrast to what was believed in later Western religions, the goddess' body and her sexuality were subjects for celebration, not for reticence and shame.

Both the sacred marriage and the subsequent death of the year-god were frequent subjects for Sumerian poems. In some poems, Inanna was held responsible for the death of the god, as she was in the poem, "The Descent of Inanna."[51] In other poems, she mourns the death of the god, citing causes outside her control.[52] In actuality, whether Dumuzi was depicted as innocent or as worthy of death, his death was necessary to the culture; the lament over his death was a ritual one.

The concept of the dying year-god carried over into later Mesopotamian religion. Thus the Babylonian *Ishtar*, with whom Inanna was assimilated, lamented over her beloved, the young year-god *Tammuz*. This concept also underlies the myth of Isis and Osiris, and the resurrection of the god into his son, Horus.[53] The Greek myth of Aphrodite and Adonis, although different in its particulars, also celebrates the union of the love-goddess and her young consort, and his subsequent death.[54]

Unlike Aphrodite, however, Inanna represented much more than fertility. She held charge of all of the heavenly prerogatives, the *me's*; she was the

I.2.17. *''Queen of all the me's . . .*
whose hand has gained the seven me's;
My lady: you safeguard the great me's.''[55]
Enheduanna, "Exaltation of Inanna" 1; 5–6; *ca.* 2500 BCE.

The *me's* included high priesthood, kingship, truth, the dagger and sword, the art of lovemaking, speech, power, and all of the crafts.[56] One of the *me's* was that of judgment, and she decreed the fates of both mortals[57] and gods.[58] Closely aligned to judgment is wisdom, and, even though wisdom was, strictly speaking, the prerogative of the Wisdom-god, *Enki*, Inanna too was praised:

I.2.18. *''You [are] extremely wise,*
Oh, queen of all the lands.''[59]
Enheduanna, "Exaltation of Inanna" 62; *ca.* 2500 BCE.

Inanna was wise and beautiful:

I.2.19. *''To my queen,*
wrapped in beauty,
praise to Inanna!''[60]
Enheduanna, "Exaltation of Inanna" 153; *ca.* 2500 BCE.

The two qualities, wisdom and beauty, were often given *in tandem* to a goddess or heroine.[61] In ancient societies, the dumb but beautiful image was not an ideal. A "Great"-goddess represented excellence in all things to her people.

The Sumerian "Great"-goddess, Inanna, was a goddess of great powers and status in her society, although those powers fluctuated, depending upon the mood of the people and, more particularly, upon the religious and political interests of the rulers. It is interesting that she was the most highly acclaimed in the poem of Enheduanna, daughter of Sargon, the first ruler of Akkad, or Accadia. *Circa* 2500 BCE, Sargon gained control of the most powerful Mesopotamian city-states, and hence established Accadian rule. His elevation of Inanna, and the assimilation of Inanna to Ishtar, were probably politically inspired; Inanna was given rank equal to that of the heaven-god, *An*, and Enheduanna was regarded as the earthly personification of Inanna.[62]

Although it was the Semitic Sargon who elevated the status of the goddess, mortal women apparently had higher status in early Sumeria than they did later, under the rule of the Semitic Babylonians and Assyrians. The status of women seems to have been particularly high before the twenty-fourth century BCE, although even after that time they could still own property.[63] Women could also engage in business transactions and qualify as witnesses.[64]

However, Babylonian temple records give evidence, in objective monetary terms, of the value of women in Accadian society, which both succeeded and existed contemporaneously with the Sumerian. One text lists

> I.2.20. "*Ninety-three female slaves at ten* [*qa*] *each;*
> *forty-two female workers at thirty* [*qa*] *each . . .*
> *six old female slaves at twenty* [*qa*] *each;*
> *thirty-eight boys at twenty* [*qa*] *each . . .* "[65]
> Babylonian Temple Record; *ca.* 2700–2580 BCE.

Another reads

> I.2.21. "*Seven strong workmen at fifty* [*qa*] *each . . .*
> *thirty-three strong workmen at sixty* [*qa*] *each.*"[66]
> Ibid.

Men, as we can see, earned more than women, and women—other than female servants—earned more than children. Male labor in Semitic Accadian society was obviously more highly valued than female labor. A detrition of the value of women commenced in Mesopotamia with the Accadians' rise to power.

EGYPTIAN GODDESSES

As did the Mesopotamians, the Egyptians too preserved the iconography of the old bird-snake goddess, sometimes as a composite, represented, for example, by the two-headed, winged serpent which guarded the land of Seker, in the Underworld.[67] At other times, the deity was divided into distinct bird or snake figures. As we discussed earlier, the uraeus, or the snake biting its own tail, was the symbol of Lower Egypt, while the vulture represented Upper Egypt.[68] Other birds were worshipped as well as the vulture; the hawk was an object of veneration very early on, probably in Predynastic Egypt (that is, at least before 3000 BCE[69]). The bird also became a common determinative of words and names indicating divinity.[70]

The vulture was personified as the goddess *Nekhebet*; her headdress was a vulture, and she sometimes held a sceptre encircled by a serpent.[71] Nekhebet was the mother of the sun-god, and the serpent-goddess *Uatchet* was his nurse.[72] Uatchet was represented as a large winged serpent[73] or as a woman holding a staff encircled by a serpent.[74]

The lions, which accompanied the ancient "Mistress of Animals," were also represented in Egypt. The goddess *Sekhet* was depicted with the body of a woman and the head of a lioness. Her headdress was composed of a solar disk, often encircled by a uraeus.[75] In the Pyramid Texts, Sekhet declares that she keeps evil foes away from Osiris.[76] Sekhet was thus a warrior goddess and a protectress, and may be compared to the Ugaritic *Anat* and the Greek *Athena*.[77] Anat too was represented in the Egyptian pantheon, and called *Ānthȧt*. A warrior-goddess as was her Syrian namesake, Ānthȧt was depicted with shield, spear, and club.[78] The Egyptians borrowed Ashtarte/Ashtoreth[79] as well, calling her *Āsthȧrthet*; she was represented with the head of a lioness, standing in a chariot, driving over a prostrate man.[80]

Tefnut was another leonine goddess, the personification of celestial moisture.[81] Similarly to Sekhet, she was depicted as a woman with the head of a lioness. Her headdress, like that of Sekhet, was often a solar disk encircled by a uraeus.[82]

The personification of justice, rectitude, law, and order was the goddess *Maāt*; her symbol was the ostrich feather, which was affixed to her headdress or held in her hand;[83] in some illustrations she was given wings.[84] In the *Book of the Dead* she was a dual goddess, the Maāti of the South and of the North, who heard the "confession" of the dead.[85]

One of the oldest Egyptian goddesses[86] was the goddess of the watery mass of the sky,[87] the primeval mother, *Nut*. She was generally represented in human form, and the disk of her headdress was sometimes horned and encircled by a uraeus.[88] At times, her headdress was simply the ideogram for her name, a vessel.[89] Nut was the female equivalent of her consort, *Nu*, who also represented the primeval watery mass; the two consorts played equal roles.[90] Nut may be compared to the Sumerian Tiamat, the primordial goddess of salt-water whom we discussed earlier.[91] Nut, however, did not succumb to a young patriarchal conqueror, as did Tiamat, and the Egyptian goddess enjoyed unbroken esteem in the Egyptian pantheon.

Nut was often represented stretched across the sky,[92] and she was sometimes depicted as the cow of heaven.[93] As such, her body represented the heavens, and her arms and legs represented the pillars on which the sky rested:[94]

> The god *Rā* became tired of the earth, and so he mounted upon the back of Nut, who had metamorphosed into a cow. Nut and her consort Seb, who was the earth, had been locked in an embrace. The cow began to tremble, and Rā ordered Shu, Nut's father, to hold up Nut's body in the sky. Nut and Seb were permanently separated, and thereafter the heavens and the earth came into being; Nut was the heavens and Seb the earth.[95]

If we compare the Egyptian myth to the Classical Greek concept of heaven and earth, we note a decided difference; the Greeks, as did most of their Indo-European relatives, believed in a female "mother" earth. Even though mythologists have claimed that earth is "naturally" feminine, that sky is "naturally" masculine, and that it is in the nature of things for the sky to cover and to inseminate the (passive) earth, the Egyptians conceived of the opposite gender personification. The masculine sky-god was *not* a universal one.

Although Nut was depicted in some mythology and iconography as a cow-goddess, the goddess *Hathor* was more often shown in bovine form. She was worshipped as a cow in the early part of the archaic period (*ca*. 3000 BCE),[96] and she was depicted in iconography as both cow[97] and woman with horned[98] or other headdress.[99] She was the consort of the bull-god *Apis*, who later became *Serapis*. The ancestress of the "cow-eyed Hera"[100] may have had qualities similar to those of Hathor. The golden Hathor was the patron goddess of lovers:

I.2.22. "*I adore the golden lady;*
I exalt her majesty.
I fashion praise for the Lady of Heaven,
my song of praise for Hathor,

the goddess.
I proclaimed [*my desire*] *to her.*
She gave heed to my prayers.
She directed [*my*] *mistress to me . . . ''*[101]
Papyrus Chester Beatty I verso C page 3; *ca.* 1550–1080 BCE.

Similar to the Greek "golden Aphrodite,"[102] Hathor was the goddess to call upon if one was in sexual need. She was also the goddess of singers, dancers, artists, and intoxicating drinks.[103] Her emblem was the sistrum.[104]

Hathor was associated with the "sacred tree," usually the sycamore:

I.2.23. *''I constructed . . .*
the house of Hathor,
goddess of the sycamore-tree
in the land of the South.''[105]
Inscription of Petosiris; Third Century BCE.

She was also associated with the date palm:

I.2.24. *'' . . . I eat* [*bread*]
under the foliage which is on [*the palm tree*]
of Hathor, my goddess . . . ''[106]
Book of the Dead lxxxii.7; *ca.* 1550–1080 BCE.

One is reminded of Inanna and her consort, the god of the date palm.[107] That such trees were sacred and potent is evident from the folkloristic element of the tree which remains to this day: the powerful *fairy* carries a *magic wand,* and with it she can cause wonderful things to occur.

Hathor was a goddess of fate:

> Once upon a time, there was a childless king. After waiting a long time for a son, he prayed to the gods, and in due time his wife gave birth to a son.
>
> Shortly thereafter, the *Hathors* came to determine a fate for the baby boy. They announced that he would die by means of a crocodile, a snake, or a dog.[108]

In another story,

> A wife was once fashioned for a young man, the younger of two brothers. She was the most beautiful woman in the world, for the essence of every god was within her.[109]
>
> Soon after she was created, the *seven Hathors*[110] came to her, in order to announce her fate. They unanimously declared that the lovely woman would die by the knife.[111]

Thus, the Hathors were prophetesses of fate, or of the future. The seven Hathors at Dendera were personified as young women who wore tunics and headdresses.[112] Perhaps in accordance with this function, the goddess also received the dead when they arrived in the Underworld.[113]

As well as receiving the dead, and determining the deaths of mortals, Hathor also caused the untimely ends of those deemed deserving of death. As a warrior goddess, Hathor rather enjoyed wreaking havoc upon humanity:

> The sun-god Rā was insulted, because men began to speak disparagingly of him: they said that he was becoming old. The god decided to devastate them, to teach them respect. He spoke to the other gods, who suggested that Hathor, the Eye of Rā, be sent to destroy the blasphemers. So,

I.2.25. *''Hathor . . .*
Now this goddess went out;
she slew humanity . . . ''[114]
"The Destruction of Humanity;" 14th to 12th Centuries BCE.

Hathor enjoyed her task. After the blasphemers had been slain, she said,

I.2.26. *"I prevailed over humanity;*
it was a delight to my heart!"[115]
Ibid.

The goddess did not really wish to cease the bloodshed, and the gods finally resorted to a ruse to stop her. They prepared a sleep-inducing beer-mash. The goddess enthusiastically partook of the mash, and she returned drunk. Her seige was over. However, gods and mortals decided that they needed insurance against another attack. In order that the goddess might be propitiated, from that time forth vases of sleep-inducing beer would be made at the festival of Hathor.[116]

The relationship between the father-god Rā and Hathor is similar to that between the Greek Zeus and his daughter, Athena.[117] Note, however, a difference between the powers of the two goddesses. The Egyptian father-god had to appease the powerful warrior-goddess Hathor; he could not have ordered her to terminate her carnage. Zeus, on the other hand, was given omnipotence by his Greek worshippers. His command was law. There was thus a greater *balance* of power among the Egyptian female and male deities than among the Greek.

Hathor had many different functions. She was goddess of love, supporter of the arts, goddess of fate, and warrior-goddess. She was both benevolent and malevolent, determining the course of life and the death of mortals. Many of the aspects of the "Goddess of Regeneration" are thus apparent in Hathor.

Hathor was not the only Egyptian warrior-goddess. The goddess *Neith*, the patron goddess of the city Saïs, was represented holding two arrows and a bow in her hands;[118] she seems to have been a hunting goddess or "Mistress of Animals" as well as a warrior. She may have been of Libyan origin.[119] Neith was worshipped as early as the First Dynasty, *circa* 3000 BCE,[120] and she was called "the great lady, the mother-goddess, the lady of heaven, and the queen of the gods."[121] She was her own parent, having created herself:

I.2.27. *"Oh, great mother!*
Her birth has not been revealed!"[122]
"Lady of the Sycamore House;" *ca.* 550 BCE.

That is, no one knows by what means, or through whom, she was born. Further, Neith was mother of the sun-god Rā, through parthenogenesis:

I.2.28. *"Neith,*
the great mother,
[who] bore Rā,
the Sun-God."[123]
Naophore Statue, Vatican, No. 1370, d.8; *ca.* 500 BCE.

The name *Neith* may possibly be derived from the root *+netet*, "to knit, to weave,"[124] which brings to mind the Greek goddess of weaving and other domestic arts, Athena. Neith also provided *clothing* for the dead.[125]

Neith was a virgin goddess,[126] and, as such, she was similar to both the Greek warrior-goddess Athena, and to the Greek "Mistress of Animals," Artemis. Artemis wielded bow and arrows, as did Neith. The Egyptian Neith, virgin warrior or huntress, and also possibly weaver goddess, thus bears similarities in both mythology and iconography to Greek female figures.

One of the most popular and powerful Egyptian goddesses, who accrued powers and functions with time, was *Isis*, goddess of regeneration, consort of *Osiris*, and mother of *Horus*. The goddess was

I.2.29. *"Isis the great,*
Mistress of the Gods."[127]
"The Legend of Isis and Rā;" *ca.* 1350–1200 BCE.

Isis is generally represented iconographically as a woman wearing a crown which consists of a pair of horns surrounding a solar disk,[128] and usually a uraeus peeks out from her headdress.[129] At times, a throne-shaped ideogram, the symbol of her name, appears on or over her head.[130] The goddess is often represented with wings, which she holds outspread to protect her charge.[131] In the Book of the Dead Isis says to the deceased,

> I.2.30. *"I come*
> *[so that] I might be*
> *as a protection for you."*[132]
> Book of the Dead CLI.I.1; *ca.* 1550–1080 BCE.

She had produced air by the beating of her *wings* when she restored Osiris to life:

> I.2.31. *"Isis . . .*
> *created wind with [her] wings;*
> *she made ritual wailings*
> *[for] the death [of] her brother."*[133]
> "Hymn to Osiris" 14–15; *ca.* 1500 BCE.

In later literature Isis also had avian attributes. In the Late Kingdom story of Horus' conflict with Set, dating to *ca.* 1100 BCE, she changed herself into a *kite*.[134] In a Demotic[135] tale from the seventh century BCE, Isis went to Egypt in the form of a *goose*.[136]

Perhaps the best-known story about Isis relates the birth of her son, Horus.

Osiris was both brother and consort of Isis, and his lot was typical of year-gods or consorts: he had to die. The prince of darkness, his evil brother Set, murdered him, dismembered him, and hid the pieces of his body. Isis traveled widely, searching for the members of her dead husband:

> I.2.32. *"Isis . . .*
> *went around this world*
> *in grief;*
> *nor did she alight without finding him."*[137]
> Ibid.

She finally located all of the pieces of Osiris but his penis. She fashioned a golden phallus and then performed a spell over him: he became alive again:

> I.2.33. *"She lifted up from inactivity*
> *[him whose] heart was motionless;*
> *she drew out his essence;*
> *she made the heir."*[138]
> Ibid, 16.

Thus Isis conceived the child, Horus, by means of the golden phallus.

Note that this birth was an all-but-parthenogenetic one: Isis received minimal help from her husband in conceiving the child. As we have discussed above, parthenogenetic, or "virgin," conceptions were known in many ancient mythologies.[139]

Isis and her sister *Nephthys* both cared for the child:

> I.2.34. *"His mother Isis gave birth to [Ani];*
> *Nephthys nursed him*
> *just as was done by them for Horus."*[140]
> Book of the Dead CXXXIV; *ca.* 1550–1080 BCE.

As they cared for the living, so Isis and Nephthys also became protectresses of the dead.[141]

Isis conceived her son "magically," reciting a spell over her husband and restoring him to potency. The goddess was well versed in verbal magic, and she often used her powers to aid herself as well as others. In the Book of the Dead her words of power are invoked:

I.2.35. ''[*May the*] *magic incantations of Isis . . .*
[*be*] *an amulet of protection*
[*for*] *this nobleman.*''[142]
Ibid, CLVI.I.

Isis decided to increase her powers by learning the secret name of the sun-god *Rā*.

I.2.36. ''*The divine one was an old man;*
he drooled in his mouth . . .[143]
his saliva fell upon the ground.
Isis, she ground [*it*] *in her hand*
along with soil which was on it;
she moulded it
into a holy serpent . . . ''[144]
"The Legend of Isis and Rā;" *ca.* 1350–1200 BCE.

The serpent bit the sun-god as he was taking his daily walk, and, as the "living fire"[145] began to ebb within him, Rā cried out in pain, asking for help.

Then Isis came to him with her

I.2.37. ''*speech,*[146]
with the breath of life,
and with her charms
[*which*] *drive out illness . . .* ''[147]
Ibid.

Isis was the only deity who had the power to cure the god; indeed, it is the belief in many societies that the one who pronounces a curse is the only one who can break the spell.[148] Isis promised to help the god, if he would only tell her his secret name:

I.2.38. ''*Oh, pronounce to me your name,*
father god;
that man will live
upon pronouncing his name.''[149]
Ibid.

The sun-god tried to enumerate his deeds and qualities, without giving up his secret name, but Isis refused to cooperate. She said to Rā,

I.2.39. ''*Your divine name is not numbered*
among these [*things*]
you have told me.
Oh, tell it to me;
[*then*] *this venom will come out.*''[150]
Ibid.

The god could bear the burning of the poison no longer, and he gave up his secret name, his name of power, to Isis. Isis caused the poison to leave the body of the sun-god; he lived, and the power of Isis waxed. Henceforth, she had eternal power over him.

By the first century BCE, Isis had became popular in Greece and in Rome as well as in Egypt. Plutarch identified her with the Greek goddess, Athena.[151] Her rites in Greece and Rome were never assimilated to the Olympian religion; Roman temples to the goddess were built and torn down several times in the first century BCE.[152] Those following traditional religion viewed her with suspicion, and her adherents were considered effeminate and somewhat perverted.[153] Through the Romans, however, Isis found her way into many different geographical areas, where her cult became assimilated to those of indigenous goddesses. Many believe that figurines of a Black Virgin Mary, which have been found throughout Europe, were chiefly representations of Isis.[154]

Although Isis was a powerful and popular goddess throughout Egyptian history, her powers appear to have waxed with time as she acquired the functions of several other goddesses. She became a goddess of vegetal fertility as well as a mother goddess *par excellence*.[155]

The increasing potency of female deities such as Isis did not necessarily mirror the status of mortal women in Egyptian society. Women occupied a rather ambiguous place among the Egyptians. In the early second millennium BCE, a woman could hold property equally with a man.[156] Further, a man could own land acquired for him by his mother rather than by his father.[157] However, at the same time, women often lived in restricted quarters[158] similar to those occupied by Classical Athenian women of the upper class.[159] Moreover, preference was given to male offspring at this time, and we are told that one man gave charge of his tribe to his eldest son.[160]

In the middle of the second millennium BCE, Queen Hatshepsut reigned, and, to strengthen her position, she gave herself both masculine and feminine designations, calling herself son and daughter of the god Rā.[161] Alternating gender designation was used through at least the first millennium BCE; one used a matronymic as well as a patronymic. For example, in his autobiography, Ahmose refers to himself as the son of the woman Abana,[162] and another man describes himself as the son of a nobleman and of the priestess Tawosre.[163]

Thus we see that women in Egypt retained relative freedom to own land and some measure of visibility within their families. In other respects, their status waxed and waned. Egyptian goddesses, on the other hand, remained consistently potent as both nurturers, such as Isis as mother and Hathor in her aspect as goddess of love, and destroyers, such as Hathor in her aspect as bloodthirsty avenger of Rā.

GODDESSES OF ANCIENT UGARIT

In the middle of the second millennium BCE, there flourished an ancient Canaanite city, *Ugarit*, on the Mediterranean coast of Northern Syria. The civilization was a Semitic one, and thus related to that of the Accadians and the Hebrews. Excavations of the mound now called *Ras Shamra*, in the first quarter of this century, revealed a multitude of tablets in the Ugaritic language. Many of the tablets contain mythological texts.

The pantheon of deities mentioned in Ugaritic myths is similar to those in the ancient Egyptian and Mesopotamian cultures. The love-and-warrior-goddess *Ashtarte* was the West Semitic equivalent of the Babylonian Ishtar, both in name and in function. The people of Ugarit thought her most beautiful:

> I.2.40. ''*Give to me the Lady Hriya,*
> *the well-bred, your first-born,*
> *whose loveliness is like the loveliness of Anat;*
> [*whose*] *beauty is* [*like*] *the beauty of Ashtarte.*''[164]
> "Legend of King Keret;" KTU 1.14.iii.39–42; *ca*. 1350 BCE.

Ashtarte was associated with the snake. This is illustrated iconographically by a gold pendant from Ras Shamra, dating to *ca*. 1500 BCE. Ashtarte is standing on a lion, and she is flanked by serpents.[165] Another Ugaritic female figurine of the same date represents a goddess with a snake winding around her neck and arms.[166] The snake-entwined goddess appears in later iconographies, such as the Indic and Roman.[167]

Ashtarte was also borrowed as a warrior-goddess into Egyptian mythology and iconography.[168]

We have already discussed the young storm god *Baal*, his conflict with his brother *Mot*, god of the Underworld, and the rescue of Baal by his sister, *Anat*.[169] The strife between the two brothers parallels that between the Egyptian Osiris and Set, and the part played by Anat resembles that of the less aggressive Isis. The Ugaritic myth may display Egyptian influence, since the two cultures had close relations throughout the second millennium BCE.[170]

There are connections between Ugaritic and Hebraic texts as well. The mother-goddess *Asherah*, described in Ugaritic myths, was also popular in Israel, where she remained prominent long after the official Hebrew religion became monotheistic.[171] The Ugaritic father-god, *El*, was paralleled in Israel by the monotheistic deity known to the Hebrews by several names, including *El*.[172]

In the Ugaritic texts, Asherah was generally known as the wife of the father-god, El.[173] She was given as epithet the feminine form of El, *Elat*:

> I.2.41. " . . . *to Asherah and her children;*
> *to Elat and her group [of offspring].*"[174]
> KTU 1.4.iv.49; *ca.* 1300 BCE.

She was the "Great-Mother:"

> I.2.42. "*Propitiation to the great lady Asherah of the Sea;*
> *honor to the Creatrix of the Gods . . .* "[175]
> KTU 1.4.i.21–22; *ca.* 1300 BCE.

The gods were collectively her children:

> I.2.43. "*The seventy*[176] *children of Asherah shout:*
> *let the . . . gods drink . . .* "[177]
> KTU 1.4.vi.45–47; *ca.* 1300 BCE.

In keeping with Asherah's role as nurturer, her name may mean "sanctuary," as *Asherat* did in Phoenician, and as *Ashirtu* did in Accadian.[178]

It is possible that Asherah, although wife of El, transferred her affections to the storm-god when the popularity of the latter grew. According to a Hittite text, dating from the fifteenth to the twelfth centuries BCE, *Ashertu*, the Hittite equivalent of Asherah, was the consort of the father-god *Elkunirsha*, the Hittite El. Ashertu grew tired of her husband and tried to seduce the storm-god.[179]

If Asherah was the Ugaritic mother *par excellence*, then *Anat* was the prototypical daughter-goddess, the beautiful[180] young maiden. To be sure, she was not a maiden in the sense of "untouched virgin," for she, just as Asherah, was viewed as a wet nurse:

> I.2.44. " . . . [*who*] *sucks the milk of Asherah*
> *sucks the breast of the young girl, Anat,*
> *the wet nurses . . .* "[181]
> KTU 1.15.ii.26–28; *ca.* 1300 BCE.

Further, the texts indicate that Anat was the lover of her "brother," Baal, and she may have changed herself into a cow and subsequently borne to him an ox.[182] She was not primarily a goddess of love, however, and her significant relationship with Baal was as his defender. She was the Ugaritic warrior goddess, combining the functions of love and war in a manner similar to the Mesopotamian Inanna-Ishtar, or to the Egyptian Hathor, who also was depicted in bovine form.

Anat defended the young storm-god, Baal, when the latter was attacked by his brother Mot, and she thus preserved for her people the life-giving waters of Baal's rain.[183] When Baal disappeared, Anat searched throughout the universe for him,[184] much as Isis searched for Osiris. But Isis, a mother goddess, regenerated her husband, and conceived her son, Osiris; Anat was not mother goddess but warrior goddess, and she rescued the dead Baal in a fitting manner, by taking vengeance upon the monster Mot. She killed Mot, and Baal was then restored to life.[185]

The maiden Anat was much like the Greek virgin *Athena*; Anat

I.2.45. "... *killed the crooked serpent,*
the powerful [*serpent*] *which* [*had*] *seven heads.*"[186]
KTU 1.3.iii.41–42; *ca.* 1300 BCE.

and Athena slew the serpent-footed giant, Enceladus.[187] Athena, however, was best known for the *inspiration* of male warriors. Anat, like the Egyptian Sekhet, or Hathor in her warrior-aspect, delighted in carnage:

I.2.46. "*Anat ... violently slays the sons of two cities;*
she hews the people of the sea-shore;
she destroys the people of the rising sun;
under her, heads [*fly*] *like vultures;*
over her, hands [*fly*] *like locusts ...*
she attaches heads to her back;
she attaches hands onto her girdle;
she wades knee-deep in blood ...
Anat exults.
Her liver is filled with laughter,
her heart with rejoicing."[188]
"Hymn to Anat"; KTU 1.3.ii.5–14; 24–26; *ca.* 1300 BCE.

Anat manifested her power within the Ugaritic pantheon, and on the battlefield. The storm-god Baal turned to Anat when he was in need, and, indeed, Anat was not fearful of any of the male deities. Once, when she wished to procure a favor for Baal, she decided to take the offensive with her father El:

I.2.47. "*The maiden Anat answered* [*El*] ...
Do not rejoice,
Do not rejoice,
Do not exult! ...
I shall cause your gray head
to flow with blood,
your gray beard with gore!"[189]
Ibid, v.19–25.

One might have expected El to strike down his daughter in wrath. Instead, he replied:

I.2.48. "*I know you, daughter,*
as an implacable [*goddess*] ...
What do you request,
Oh maiden Anat?"[190]
Ibid, v.27–29.

Anat tended to achieve her desires, even if she had to threaten violence, or even resort to it.

Anat once asked the young hero, Aqhat, for his bow, a wonderful bow given his father by the craftsman god, Kothar wa-Khasis, himself. Anat offered Aqhat many things: silver and gold, life and deathlessness. But he taunted her, questioning how a mere mortal could possibly achieve immortality, and thus impugning her veracity. Furthermore, he asked what a *woman* might have to do with a bow, a warrior's weapon.

Anat was not pleased by the young man's arrogance, and she was determined to obtain his bow whether or not he was willing to give it to her. She threatened her old father, El, with assault, unless the god lent her his support in her quest for the bow, and El agreed to help her.

With the support of the father-god guaranteed, Anat then ordered her assistant, whom she turned into a *falcon,* to kill the hero. And then, after Aqhat was dead, she wept for him, for his death caused the earth to become barren.[191]

The weeping of Anat was similar to that of Inanna, who also wept for *her* hero. Although the circumstances of Aqhat's death were far different from those of Dumuzi—

Aqhat did not even have the honor of serving as the goddess' consort—yet the memory of the dying year-god survived among the people of Ugarit.

Anat could metamorphose others, such as her assistant, into birds, and she could also change *herself* into a bird; like Inanna-Ishtar, Anat was winged:

> I.2.49. ''*The maiden Anat lifts up her wing,*
> *lifts up her wing and soars in flight . . .* ''[192]
> KTU 1.10.ii.10–11; *ca.* 1300 BCE.

Thus Anat and the other Ugaritic goddesses bore many similarities to other Near Eastern goddesses: Anat was a warrior-goddess, whose father El both respected and feared her; their relationship was similar to that between the Egyptian Rā and Hathor. Anat, a beautiful young woman, appeared in the form of a bird, while other goddesses in her pantheon are represented with snakes. We will discover that many later goddesses of Europe and neighboring areas shared these characteristics, although none quite had the power of an Anat. The attributes of other Near-Eastern goddesses seem to be echoed in Classical-Age mythology. The cow-headed goddesses such as Hathor and Nut may be reflected in the common epithet for the Greek Hera, the "cow-eyed," and the Greek "golden" Aphrodite is evocative of Hathor in her aspect as love-goddess.

There is a significant number of martial goddesses in these societies. In particular, the Accadian Ishtar, Egyptian Hathor, and Ugaritic Anat show qualities of rage and destructiveness as well as love and creativity. Their plurality of characteristics reflects their origins as goddesses of the "life continuum." Most of the Classical-Age Indo-European goddesses, while retaining this spectrum of functions, become strategic warriors rather than raging ones.

Thus, some of the attributes of Classical-age goddesses were inherited from their European forebears, and some were borrowed from their Near Eastern neighbors. The patterns of influence will emerge in Part Two. For the moment, we will turn to two ancient patriarchal societies which also influenced both the ancient Europeans and much of the modern western world.

CHAPTER 3

Male-God-centered societies

THE PROTO-INDO-EUROPEANS

Proto-Indo-European is a linguistic term; it designates the language or dialects spoken by those people who now speak Indo-European languages. The *Indo-Europeans* were and are all those peoples who speak the historical descendant languages.

Although the term Proto-Indo-European does not relate to a specific physical stock, in addition to a linguistic entity, it is also used to indicate a group of related Neolithic peoples whose homeland probably lay in the south Russian forested and grassy steppes and river valleys, the Pontic-Caspian region.[1] The question of the original Indo-European homeland is a much-debated one, but this region offers, in my opinion, the best correlation for both archeological and linguistic evidence. Upon studying the archeological remains of the presumed Proto-Indo-Europeans, along with linguistically related words or *cognates*, one may determine many of their economic and social characteristics.

If the Proto-Indo-Europeans were indeed those groups which inhabited the Pontic-Caspian region, they raised horses,[2] which were also used in ritual; sheep, cattle, dogs, and, in some areas, pigs. At least in the later stages of the Eneolithic, about 3600 to 2200 BCE, they were probably nomadic or semi-nomadic pastoralists; there is evidence of wheeled vehicles,[3] which would have been used to transport household goods and families seeking new pasture ground in their nomadic migrations. The mobility offered by wheeled vehicles and domesticated horses provided both economic and martial advantages.

Although there is evidence for small settlements, most of the evidence for these cultures comes from burials. Most groups buried their dead—at least men and children—in pit graves, and many erected a tumulus or *kurgan* over these graves. In some areas, the deceased was ritually strewn with ochre. Many of the graves contained wealthy grave goods, which included ornaments, arrowheads, daggers, stone battle axes, and maces.

There is evidence for fishing, hunting and agriculture: they knew the plough, yoked animals, and grinding of grain. Climatic change may have led to decreased agricultural productivity, on the one hand, and, on the other hand, conditions which favored stock-breeding: that is, pastoral nomadism.

Not only is there testimony to animal, particularly horse, ritual, but there are also remains of stone stelae engraved with anthropomorphic figures; there are male figures, accompanied by battle-axes, and female figures as well.[4]

It may be possible to trace the migration patterns of this folk in conjunction with their sociological characteristics, since their artifacts and burial patterns contrasted sharply with those of the people whom they displaced or with whom they assimilated, as they migrated. They may have migrated in several waves, from the fifth millennium through the third millennium BCE,[5] moving from the steppes southeast to India and Iran; west to Europe: Greece, Italy, Germany, Britain, Ireland, Wales; west to Anatolia; north to Latvia and Lithuania; and east to Chinese Turkestan. Some, too, remained on the Russian plains.

Both the Anatolian Hittites and the Tokharians of Chinese Turkestan became extinct, but the present-day Greeks, Italians, East Indians, Persians, Germans, Russians, Latvians, Lithuanians, Armenians, Albanians, and Welsh, and British, and their descendants in various parts of the world, such as the Americas, speak Indo-European languages.

Although "Indo-European" refers primarily to a language family, and is thus a linguistic designation, there is, as we noted, both linguistic *and* archaeological evidence for Proto-Indo-European sociological structure and for their migrational patterns.

The Proto-Indo-Europeans lived in small *patrilineal* units, socially stratified according to the functions performed by the males in the societies. Burial rites give evidence of the social stratification: some wealthy graves, probably those of chieftains, show an abundance not only of weapons[6] but of ornaments, sacrificed animals, and human sacrifice.

One particular type of human sacrifice found in Proto-Indo-European graves indicates that these peoples were *patriarchal* and patrilineal in social structure: *suttee* burials—that is, burials named after a classical Indian practice in which a widow is immolated and interred with her dead mate—have been found in prehistoric sites in the Danube delta, in Tuscany,[7] and the environs of the lower Dnieper river, in the southwestern Soviet Union.[8] Females in such burials showed signs of injury, while the males were usually accompanied by an abundance of grave goods; the latter might, therefore, have been tribal chieftains. The immolated women may have been intended to follow their masters to the next world, so that the males could continue to enjoy their usual comforts. These burials indicate, of course, the relative expendability of human female lives, and indeed, among the later historical Indo-European cultures, the father or master of the house had unrestricted right of property, and often of life, over his wife and children.[9]

The patriarchal structure of the Proto-Indo-Europeans may have been due in part to the status of their warriors; migratory existence leads to an elevation of the warrior, since his role is important to a group which is encroaching upon the lands of others. If the warriors in a particular society are mostly male, as was the case among the Indo-Europeans, then the males in the society are its most important members.

There is ample archaeological evidence of the importance of warrior-tools to the early Indo-Europeans. Their graves yielded bows and arrows, spears, antler axes, and proto-daggers.[10] These tools were often engraved and inlaid, and they thus seem to have been signs of wealth and power among the ancient Indo-Europeans.

It therefore appears that warriors were of high status among the Proto-Indo-Europeans.[11] The warrior-caste was the second caste in their "tripartite" social system of priests-lawgivers, warriors, and nurturers.

The "tripartite" theory was evolved by the French comparative mythologist Georges Dumézil and his followers.[12] According to Dumézil, Proto-Indo-European society was divided into three functional levels, and this division was reflected in their mythology. The priest-class or caste, which included priests and judges or lawgivers, occupied the first functional level; the warrior class was termed the "second function;" and the nurturing class, composed of farmers, herdsmen, artisans, and women, was collectively described as the "third function" class. These three classes formed a "tripartite society."

The priest-lawgiver caste was one of high esteem, as was that of the warrior. Not surprisingly in a patriarchal social system such as that embraced by the Proto-Indo-Europeans, the most prestigious two castes were male-dominated. The third caste was of lesser status. The members of this caste nurtured the others; that is, they were the caretakers, or the servants, of the warriors and priests.

The "tripartite" Proto-Indo-European society of priests-lawgivers, warriors, and nurturers was echoed in the Indo-European religious pantheons. These mostly male-dominated pantheons reflected complex ideology, but Indo-European *goddesses* appear to have been few and relatively powerless. We will find, indeed, that when a goddess fulfilled several different functions instead of the nurturing one alone, she was most likely of *non*-Indo-European origin. There were, as we shall discuss in Part Two, many trifunctional, or *transfunctional* goddesses in the later Indo-European cultures, goddesses who fulfilled the "priestess"-function, gave energy to warriors, and were also nurturing figures. This plurality of functions is an indicator of great power, power that appears to have been lacking in the Proto-Indo-European goddesses.

Proto-Indo-European goddesses seem to have represented natural phenomena, and several are weakly personified. Some of them, however, gained prominence in their later pantheons, and they have acquired rich mythologies. Few goddesses can be definitely distinguished as Proto-Indo-European; positive identification relies, first of all, on linguistic correlation: that is, on *cognate* names. Words are said to be cognate when they are found in related, or "sister"-languages, and can be traced back to a "parent" or "proto"-language by means of consistent sound equivalences. Thus cognate names such as those for the Indo-European dawn-goddesses: Greek *Eos*, Indic *Ushas*, Roman *Aurora*, and others can, through sound laws, be traced back to a common Proto-Indo-European root-word.

The other criterion used for identification of related goddesses is similarity in their mythologies. Comparison of Indo-European mythologies carries risk, because historical attestations for goddesses range over a very broad time-frame. Thus, while Indic, Greek, and Roman myth has a relatively long history, with texts dating to the first millennium BCE and earlier, Germanic, Baltic, and Slavic myth was *recorded* at least a thousand to fifteen hundred years later. This historical disparity is somewhat mitigated by the fact that the oral tradition preceding the texts could have existed for millennia; however, one can not be certain whether similar myths shared by the Romans and the Balts, for example, were part of a common Indo-European tradition or were borrowed much later. With this caveat in mind we will explore the similarities between a few groups of goddesses which share cognate names and similar mythologies.

A goddess of the dawn, an earth-goddess, a stream-goddess, and a sun-maiden meet these two criteria; other goddesses found in later Indo-European cultures do not. That is, although other Proto-Indo-European goddesses may have been worshipped, there is not enough corroborative evidence to name them. We will need, then, to decide whether the criteria of comparable myths and of comparable naming are sufficient for identifying Proto-Indo-European goddesses, and we must determine the significance of this identification. This knowledge will become important when, in the next section, we discuss the multitude of goddesses who appear in Indo-European pantheons, and who may *not* have originated with the patriarchal Proto-Indo-Europeans. Possible sources of these other goddesses will then be explored.

THE DAWN-GODDESS

A goddess of the dawn was present in many of the Indo-European cultures.[13] Among the Greeks she was personified rather late, in the Hellenistic period, but both her name and her mythology are cognate with that of other Indo-European dawn-goddesses. She was called *Eos*, and she was often invoked as a goddess who separated lovers, by bringing the morning light:

> I.3.1. "*. . . you are growing old, Tithonus,*
> *or why have you thus chased*
> *your bedfellow Eos from your bed?*"[14]
> Antipater of Thessalonica, <u>Palatine Anthology</u> V.3;
> 1st Century BCE to 1st Century CE.

Eos had fallen in love with the mortal, Tithonus, and she had begged Zeus, king of the gods, to grant immortality to her lover. The request was granted, but Eos had forgotten to ask that her lover be rendered eternally youthful as well. So Tithonus, never dying, continued to age through the eons. Eos, faithful, spent her nights with her immortal, but aged, lover. In fact, she left his bed but reluctantly, and

> I.3.2. "*unwillingly fulfilled her duty for the world.*"[15]
> Propertius II.18.A.7; born *ca.* 50 BCE

The Roman elegist responsible for the previous line was describing *Aurora*, the Roman equivalent of Eos. Eos-Aurora was

I.3.3. *" . . . the golden one*
who has an old consort . . . "[16]
Ovid, Amores I.13; 43 BCE to 17? CE.

and she bore to Tithonus a son, Memnon.[17]

Much of Aurora's mythology was given to *Mater Matuta*, "morning mother," another Roman goddess of the dawn. In the Roman rites of the *Matralia*, "the mothers," Mater Matuta took care of her sibling's offspring:

I.3.4. *"Now, Phrygian Tithonus,*
you are complaining
that you have been abandoned
by your wife (dawn),
and the watchful morning star
goes forth from the eastern waters.
Go, good mothers
(the Matralia is your festival)
and offer yellow cakes
to the Theban goddess . . .
the scepter-bearing hands of Servius
consecrated a sacred temple
to Mother (parenti) *Matuta.*
She excludes female slaves
from the threshold of her temple
and calls for toasted cakes . . .
let not a devoted mother
pray to her
on behalf of her own offspring:
she herself was seen to have been
a rather unfortunate parent.
You should rather entrust to her
the progeny of another."[18]
Ovid, Fasti VI.473–568; 43 BCE to 17? CE.

Several rites of the dawn-goddess are described in this passage. Of interest are the rites which exclude female slaves from her temple, and those in which she takes care of her sister's offspring. The Greek philosopher and biographer Plutarch expanded upon these themes:

I.3.5. *"The women,*
leading a handmaid into the shrine,
strike her with sticks,
then drive her forth again;
they take in their arms
the children of their brothers
in preference to their own children."[19]
Plutarch, Parallel Lives, "Life of Camillus" V.2; born *ca.* 46 CE.

These rites seem, at first glance, to be rather arbitrary, and thus perhaps insignificant. Indic mythology, however, gives evidence of similar mythology surrounding their dawn-goddess, *Ushas*, and further, explains the two themes.

Ushas, just as Eos and Aurora, was the "lingering dawn," and since she shortened the productive day's work of men because of her reluctance to leave her bed, the authors of the Rigvedic hymns thought it necessary that she be brought to task; the patriarchal warrior-god Indra therefore punished her for attempting to forestall the day:

I.3.6. *"And indeed you have achieved*
this manly heroic deed,
Indra,
that you destroyed the woman,
daughter of heaven,

meditating ill . . .
Ushas fell down,
truly frightened,
from her crushed chariot,
when the mighty god had crushed it.''[20]
Rigveda IV.30, 8, 10. *ca.* 1200 BCE.

The Indic peoples apparently had no compunctions about the punishment of a goddess. The more circumspect Romans, on the other hand, called in what they probably considered to be the lowest order of mortals: the lowest caste of females, to act as scapegoat for the goddess. There was no memory evident among the Romans that the punishment bore relationship to the reluctance of the goddess, the "lingering dawn," to leave her bed. In Roman mythology the dawn-goddess committed no punishable offense. Instead, female slaves were castigated, "struck with sticks," although the Romans could provide no conscious reason for the punishment of those slaves.

The theme of interparental nurturing, and that of castigation, is likewise shared by Indic and Roman mythology. In the first book of the Indic Rigveda, the two goddesses of the Dawn and of the Night, Ushas and her sister Rātrī, cared for the same child:

I.3.7. ''*Night and Dawn,*
changing color,
united,
nurse the same infant;
glowing he shines between heaven and earth.
May the gods preserve Agni,
giver of goods.''[21]
Rigveda I.96.5. *ca.* 1200 BCE.

Perhaps the origin of this second theme is to be found in the relationship between Night and Dawn, and their shared child, Agni. Agni's principal realm was fire, but in some hymns he was invoked as a moon-god. He most likely represented the moon when, as Rātrī's child, he dwelt in the realm of Night.[22]

The Greek and Roman dawn-goddesses, Eos and Aurora, were but little personified; in Rome, dawn-ritual was largely taken over by Mater Matuta. In India, however, the cognate dawn-goddess, Ushas, increased in importance to such an extent that more hymns were addressed to her than to any other goddess in Rigvedic literature. (Nonetheless, the majority of the Rigvedic hymns were addressed to male deities.) Ushas was regarded as a "Great"-goddess: she was described as such in Rigvedic hymns,[23] and, moreover, she was transfunctional, embodying all possible powers. She was "*endowed with knowledge*,"[24] "*strong with strength*,"[25] and "*bestowing all treasures*."[26] Her nurturing aspect was made clear not only by her nursing of the child, Agni, but also by her designation as "*mother of the gods*."[27] In spite of her many epithets, however, Ushas' real power was slight, as evidenced by the facile punishment given for her "reluctance."

Among the Baltic Lithuanians, the cognate dawn-goddess was *Aushrinė*. This goddess lit a fire for the sun, to start the day:

I.3.8. '' . . . *I went to the Dawn.*
The Dawn answered,
'I have to kindle the (dear little) fire
for the (dear little) sun
early in the morning.' ''[28]
Lithuanian Folksong; Second Millennium CE.

Similarly, I.3.9. '' '*Dear sun-maid, daughter of heaven,*
who kindles the fire in the mornings,
in the evenings,
[*who*] *spreads out a bed for you?*'

—*The Dawn, The Evening Star:*

'Dawn kindles the fire,
the Evening Star spreads out the bed.' '[29]
Ibid.

The Latvian equivalent of Aushrinė was *Auseklis*:

I.3.10. *''The sun-maiden went to rest*
with the morning Dawn.''[30]
Latvian Folksong; Second Millennium CE.

Auseklis did not always rise in the morning:

I.3.11. *''For three mornings I have not seen*
Auseklis rise:
The sun-maiden has locked her up
in an oaken chamber.''[31]
Ibid.

The Latvians had various explanations for the whereabouts of the Dawn, when she failed to rise:

I.3.12. *''For three mornings I have not seen*
Auseklis rise:
Auseklis [is] in Germany;
She is sewing velvet skirts.''[32]
Ibid.

Finally,[33] the Old Prussians, who were Baltic cousins of the Latvians and Lithuanians, had a closely-related dawn goddess, whose name was *Ausca*.[34]

THE SUN-MAIDEN

Another cult which was based upon a naturalistic phenomenon was that of the sun-maiden, who, like the dawn, also seems to have had linguistically and functionally related avatars throughout the Indo-European realms.[35]

The Indic sun-maiden, *Sūryā*, was daughter of the stimulating power of the sun, *Savitṛ*. She was sometimes described as the bride of the twin gods, the *Ashvins*:

I.3.13. *'' . . . you were the lords*
of Sūryā's daughter.''[36]
Rigveda IV.43.6; *ca.* 1200 BCE.

Elsewhere, the twins served as groomsmen, when they arranged a marriage between Sūryā and Soma. Soma was the patron god of the soma-plant, and he was also commonly worshipped as the moon-god:

I.3.14. *''Soma was the bridegroom;*
the groomsmen were both Ashvins,
when Savitṛ bestowed
his promised Sūryā
on her willing husband.''[37]
Rigveda X.85.9; *ca.* 1200 BCE.

Similarly, in Baltic mythology, the sun was always a goddess, and the moon a god, as the following Lithuanian folktale illustrates:

Once upon a time, the moon and the sun fell in love and were married. The sun-goddess, *Saulė*, gave birth to a daughter, the earth.

Meness, the moon, and Saulė lived happily together for many years, but, after some time, they began to quarrel. Since they were such opposites, the sun so hot and the moon so cold, they could not live together comfortably. They decided, therefore, to separate.

Separation was the only thing the two could agree upon. They could *not* agree upon custody of their daughter, the earth, and so it was determined that the thunder-god, Perkūnas,[38] would serve as arbiter. Perkūnas,

I.3.15. *"with thundering voice, said:*
'Let it be thus:

Saulė will take care of her daughter,
the earth,
during the day,
and Meness will care for her at night.' "[39]
Lithuanian Folktale; Second Millennium CE.

And so it is.

The ancient Prussians too sang to the sun as goddess:

I.3.16. *"O mother sun,*
to us here, to us here!
O father cloud,
to Prussia, to Prussia!"[40]
Old Lithuanian Folksong; Second Millennium CE.

The earth was just one of the daughters of the Baltic sun-goddess. She gave birth to a "sun-maiden," just as did the Indic sun-deity. The myth of the Baltic sun-maiden and the twin sons of the sky-god is also preserved among the Balts, in folk-songs:

I.3.17. *"Where did the horses of God stay?*
The Dieva Dēli [sons of God] *rode them.*

To where did the Dieva Dēli ride?
To search for Saules Meita [the sun-maiden].*"*[41]
Latvian Folksong; Second Millennium CE.

The twin sons of the sky-god, the Dieva Dēli, jointly courted the sun-maiden:

I.3.18. *"The silver cocks are crowing*
beside the golden stream.
They were rousing the Dieva Dēli,
suitors for Saules Meita."[42]
Ibid.

But there is also a myth regarding a wedding of the sun-maid to the moon, wherein the Dieva Dēli were but a part of the bridal party:

I.3.19. *" . . . Meness* [the Moon]
was wedding Saulė's daughter.
He asks me to join
in the bridal train . . .
now I can gallop hard
in company with God's sons!"[43]
Ibid.

This Baltic song recalls the double myth of the Indic Sūryā, who was betrothed to both Soma as moon god, and to the twin Ashvins.

Among the Greeks, there was a heroine who shared some of the mythology of the sun-maiden, and whose name evoked a sense of the sun's function. *Helen*, the heroine for whom the Trojan war was fought, was said to "burn homes"[44] through her overwhelming beauty, and her name may well be derived from a Proto-Indo-European root-word which means "to burn."[45]

Helen was related to the divine twins,[46] the Dioskouroi, Kastor and Poludeukes, one of whom at least was a horseman.[47] They were the Greek equivalents of the Indic Ashvins and the Baltic Dieva Dēli. Although Helen was not betrothed to them, she was their sister, and they were her protectors:

> I.3.20. *"Come, you two,*
> *in your horse [-drawn] wagon,*
> *crossing the clear sky,*
> *protectors of Helen . . .*
> *cast away from your sister*
> *the shame of foreign beds."*[48]
> Euripides, Helen 1495–1507; 485? to 406? BCE.

The two brothers attempted to choose a husband for her, but the suitor whom they chose was unsuccessful:

> I.3.21. *" . . . and indeed Kastor and mighty Polydeukes*
> *would have worked hard*
> *to make [Philoktetes] their brother-in-law,*
> *but Agamemnon,*
> *being son-in-law [to Helen's father Tyndareus],*
> *wooed her for his brother Menelaus."*[49]
> Hesiod, Catalogues of Women, 68: 13–15; *ca.* 750? BCE.

At any rate, the twin Dioskouroi, the Sons of God, had *attempted* to be groomsmen.

Helen's groom was, of course, Menelaus, and her Trojan "husband," Paris, is a later addition to Helen's myth. Menelaus, however, may play a more integral role in the myth. Although the name *Menelaus,* is not related to the Indo-European word for moon, *mēn,* yet this may be a *double entendre*—a subtle play on words.[50] The two terms, *mēn* and *mĕn,* are almost comparable phonologically. Further, there did exist a non-Greek Indo-European moon god, *Men,* who had centers of worship in what is now Turkey. *Men* appears on steles dating to the early centuries CE.[51] Therefore, there are parts of Helen's myth that correspond to those of the Indic and Baltic sun-maidens.

Thus, the Indic and Baltic mythologies give evidence that there was a Proto-Indo-European myth whose central characters were a sun-maiden and two sets of suitors, a moon-god *and* the twin sons of the sky-god. The Greeks may have preserved some vestiges of this myth.

THE EARTH-GODDESS

Several Indo-European cultures also appear to have worshipped an earth-goddess. In Greek mythology she was *Semele*[52] mother of the vine-god Dionysos. The mythology of Semele became quite changed from that of the ancient Indo-European "earth-goddess."

Zeus, the king of the Olympian gods and goddesses, had an affair with *Semele,*[53] and Zeus' wife, Hera, manifested her jealousy in her usual manner:

> I.3.22. . . . *now (Hera) was letting loose her tongue,*
> *(readying herself) for a quarrel (with Zeus)*
> *(but)*
> *"What, in fact, have I accomplished*
> *so many times,*
> *through reproach?"*
> *she asked.*
> *"(Semele) herself must be attacked by me . . . "*[54]
> Ovid, Metamorphoses III.261–263; 43 BCE to 17? CE.

So Hera decided to effect an indirect attack upon her omnipotent husband's mistress, knowing from long experience that it was useless to rail against Zeus.

Hera disguised herself and went to Semele, advising her to test her lover's divinity by asking him to reveal himself to her in her true form.[55] Zeus, who had promised to grant to Semele any request she might make, metamorphosed into a thunderbolt, and Semele was consumed by its fire (or by fright).

Semele had been pregnant, and Zeus, taking up the unborn child, sewed it into his thigh. In due time the child Dionysos was born from the thigh of his father Zeus.[56]

> I.3.23. *''And now*
> *both (Semele and Dionysos)*
> are gods.''[57]
> Hesiod, Theogony 942; *ca.* 750? BCE.

Semele received a rather elaborate mythology, although the Greeks never actually described her as an earth-goddess. In contrast, the Balto-Slavic earth-goddesses were concerned chiefly with the earth, and they were given but slight personification.

In Latvia the earth-goddess was *Zemes Māte*, "earth mother."[58] Similarly, Lithuanian *Žemyna*[59] was *"pure and just."*[60] In an old poem, she was invoked thus:

> I.3.24. *''Žemyna, blooming one,*
> *bloom with rye,*
> *with barley corn*
> *and with all cereals.''*[61]
> Lithuanian Poem; Second Millennium CE.

Finally, in East Slavic her name was *Mat' Syra Zemlya*, "mother[62] moist[63] earth."[64] She was a powerful goddess among Slavic peasants, playing the roles of both earth-mother and prophet.[65]

> Among some Slavic peasants, in the month of August, there was a custom which prescribed that they go down to the fields at dawn carrying jars filled with hemp-oil. They would turn to the east and invoke the goddess, asking her to subdue every evil and unclean being, so that they might not cast a spell upon them or otherwise harm them. Then they would pour oil upon the ground: in religious terms, they were pouring a libation to the earth.
>
> Turning westward, they would ask Mother Moist Earth to engulf evil beings in her burning fires, that is, in the fires of Hell. Turning to the south, they would further invoke the goddess, begging her to calm the south winds, moving sands, whirlwinds, and all bad weather.
>
> At length, they would turn to the north and ask the goddess to calm the north winds, the clouds, the snowstorms, and the cold.[66]

Not only was the Earth in control of the elements; she was also omniscient, and she could prophesy to mortals. All her people need do was dig into her and apply an ear to the hole. She made a special sound if a crop was to be good, and another sound if the crop was to be poor.[67]

Peasants settled property disputes by calling upon the earth-goddess as witness. Oaths were taken by swallowing a lump of earth.[68]

To the Slavic farmers, the earth was of great, perhaps primary, importance. Zemlya was thus transmuted from simple personification of the earth, such as were her Baltic cousins, to goddess in charge of many elements, rendering them benign for the farmer's crops.

*DANU

The last Proto-Indo-European goddess whom we shall discuss was, in all likelihood, the personification of a watery place, a river or stream; we shall arbitrarily name her **Danu*. In many mythologies she was magical, often monstrous, and associated in some way with water. She became personified in Indic mythology as the monstrous serpent-goddess *Dānu*. Dānu was the mother of Vṛtra, the arch-withholder of the heavenly waters.[69]

I.3.25. *"Now I tell the heroic deeds of Indra,*
which he performed first with his thunderbolt.
He smote the serpent and released the waters;
the bellies of the cloud-mountains split open.

He smote the serpent
lying upon the cloud-mountain . . .

Indra slew Vṛtra,
the arch-withholder . . .
As tree-tops cut asunder with an ax,
the serpent will lie close to the earth . . .

Vṛtra lay scattered in many places . . .

She whose son is Vṛtra
became one whose strength is low;
Indra bore the weapon down upon her.
The mother was above,
the son below.
Dānu was lying
like a cow with [her] calf."[70]
Rigveda I.32.1–9; *ca.* 1200 BCE.

In some hymns Vṛtra was called *Dānava,* "son of Dānu,"[71] while elsewhere the *Dānus* were a class of demons:

I.3.26. *"[Indra] overcame the seven Dānus*
with his strength."[72]
Rigveda X.120.6; *ca.* 1200 BCE.

Likewise, in the ancient Iranian book of sacred hymns, the Avesta, mention is made of the *Danava* tribe, along with other enemies of the Iranians:

I.3.27. *"Then they entreated her:*
give us good fortune,
O good, most strong
Arədvī Sūra Anāhita,
so that we may be defeaters
of the Turian Dānava . . . "[73]
Avesta, Yasht V.73; Composed 5th to 1st Centuries BCE.

In Celtic mythology *Danu became the Irish *Danu,* eponymous ancestress of the mythical magical folk, the *Túatha Dé Danann,* "the people of the goddess Danu."[74]

The Túatha Dé were very learned in the healing arts and in magic. For example, when their king, Nuada, lost an arm in battle, the youth Miach, son of the great doctor, Diancecht,

I.3.28. *"put . . . joint to joint,*
and vein to vein,
of his hand
and he heals [it]
in three times nine days."[75]
Lebor Gabála Érenn VII.310R[1]; *ca.* 1100 CE.

Further, when the sons of Mil came to Ireland to attack the people of Danu, the latter protected themselves at first by means of Druid magic:

I.3.29. *"Their Druids and their poets*
recited poems against them,
so that [the Sons of Mil]
saw that they were [only] sods of the bog
and of the mountain."[76]
Ibid. VIII.414.

Moreover,

> I.3.30. "*. . . the Druids threw magic winds*
> *after them,*
> *so that the lower part of the sea-gravel*
> *was put upon the upper part of the sea.*"[77]
> Ibid. VIII.415.

These Druids had the power both to transform themselves and to affect the elements as well. Because of their magic, they were feared as demons, and so the battle of Sliab Mis was one wherein the Sons of Mil fought

> I.3.31. "*against demons and sea-demons,*
> *that is,*
> *against the Túatha Dé Danann.*"[78]
> Ibid. VIII.435.

Among the Celtic Welsh *Danu appeared as Dôn. One poem describes a leader in war

> I.3.32. "*. . . of duty and promise,*
> *wise as Dôn.*"[79]
> Book of Taliesin XXXVI.10;
> Recorded *ca.* 1300 CE.

Elsewhere in the poem, the poet claims that he was

> I.3.33. "*called a cunning man*
> *in the court of Dôn.*"[80]
> Book of Taliesin XVI.26;
> Recorded *ca.* 1300 CE.

The goddess also gave her name to a tribe of women whose story is told in Greek mythology, although the eponymous parent in this case was a male.

King Belus[81] fathered two sons, the twins Aegyptus and *Danaus*. Aegyptus became king of Egypt, and to him were born fifty sons. Danaus became king of the land of Libya, and he fathered fifty daughters upon various wives. The fifty daughters were called the *Danaïds*.

Upon Belus' death, the twins quarreled over their inheritance, and Aegyptus proposed, in conciliation, that the fifty princes marry the fifty princesses. Danaus, suspecting a plot, fled from Libya to Argos.

When Danaus and his daughters reached Argos, they found the town suffering from a drought. Danaus told his daughter Amymone to "appease" the water-god Poseidon, and she appeased the god so well that

> I.3.34. "*Poseidon revealed to her the springs*
> *at [the river] Lerna.*"[82]
> Apollodorus of Athens, Atheniensis Bibliothecae II.i.4;
> born *ca.* 180 BCE

The Danaïds were associated with water in other ways. They invented the art of sinking wells,[83] and they were also associated with water-jars in punishment for a rather macabre series of events:

Aegyptus sent his sons to Argos, begging that they be allowed to marry the Danaïds; Danaus refused, and the sons of Aegyptus laid seige to Argos. Danaus capitulated, promising a group wedding. However, on their collective wedding night, Danaus gave daggers to his daughters, and they

> I.3.35. "*killed their bridegrooms as they slept,*"[84]
> Ibid, II.1.5.

fearing that the latter would murder them if given the chance. Because of their misdeeds, the Judges of the Dead condemned the Danaïds to the endless task of carrying water in jars perforated like sieves.[85] No such punishment has been recorded for Danaus; only his daughters were connected with the watery motifs. Hence the young women, the Danaïds, although not watery monsters,[86] were nonetheless connected with the aqueous element of the goddess.

The great-great granddaughter of Danaus, *Danaë,*[87] played an active role in the other facet of the myth.

Her father Acrisius, king of Argos, was warned by an oracle that Danaë's son would kill him. Acrisius therefore decided to incarcerate Danaë in an inaccessible bronze chamber.[88] Although mortal men were thus unable to reach the princess, the undauntable king of the gods, Zeus, having metamorphosed into a shower of gold, descended upon the chamber, and upon the princess, and impregnated her.

Acrisius, when he learned that Danaë had borne a son, was quite dismayed but still unwilling to capitulate to the fates:

I.3.36. ''*Putting his daughter*
along with her child [Perseus]
into a chest,
he hurled it forth
into the sea.''[89]
Ibid, II.iv.1.

However, both mother and child survived. After Perseus was grown, he became a great hero, and he returned to Argos to see his grandfather. While taking part in some funeral games, he threw the discus, which accidently struck and killed Acrisius. The oracle was thus fulfilled. Perseus accomplished many heroic feats, including that of slaying the *female sea-monster* which Poseidon had sent to devastate the land of Philistia. Perseus

I.3.37. '' . . . *three times, four times*
thrust his sword
through [*the monster's*] *groin,*
again and again.''[90]
Ovid, Metamorphoses IV. 734; 43 BCE to 17? CE.

Perseus thus saved the monster's prey, the princess Andromeda.[91] The characters in the myth have been somewhat skewed, since Danaë, descendant of *Danu, was the mother of Perseus, instead of the female sea monster whom he heroically slew. (Of course, this deed was only considered heroic by those who disliked female sea-monsters.)[92]

There is little other myth relating to *Danu; but she has given her name to several bodies of water. The rivers Don, Dnieper, Dniester, and Danube bear her name, and the Balts borrowed river water names from the Slavic lexicon. In Lithuanian, *Dunõjus* is the term for the Danube,[93] or for any large stream, in some texts.[94] In Latvian, *Duņavas* indicates a small river or stream.[95] One may deduce, from this evidence, that there was a prehistoric tribe which inhabited an area near a watery place, perhaps a river. This water became deified, and the deity gave her name to the *Danuva-tribe.

Although I have described the group of *Danu-goddesses as Proto-Indo-European, the *Danuvas may simply have been a tribe which was contiguous to the Proto-Indo-Europeans at one point in the Indo-European migrations. The Irish Túatha Dé Danann were believed to have been a very ancient folk, with more than mortal powers, who settled Ireland. In the Indic Rigveda, the goddess Dānu was designated the "consort of Mitra and Varuna,"[96] that is, the consort of two of the most important gods in the Rigvedic Indic pantheon. This marriage may have been symbolic of a union between the two cultural groups in ancient India: the indigenous peoples and the Indo-Europeans. The union may be similar in function to the marriage between the pre-Indo-European Hera and the Indo-European Zeus.

Thus, in legends and myths of many cultures, the ancient goddess, *Danu, eponymous ancestress of the *Danuva-tribe, regularly takes the shape of a monster, one usually connected in some way with water; she is slain, in rather morbid fashion, by the young patriarchal hero-god. The mythology may reflect a historical occurrence in which the *Danuva tribe and its deity were subdued by the encroaching warrior-folk.

As we have discussed, only four or perhaps even three goddesses compose our rather short catalogue of Proto-Indo-European goddesses, at least if we employ the criteria of linguistic and mythological equivalences. For the moment, we will assume that the pantheon of Indo-European goddesses was indeed a small one, and we will explore different avenues of origin for the other goddesses which we will discuss.

A common feature is to be noted among the Proto-Indo-European goddesses: each of these goddesses personified a phenomenon of nature: sun, dawn, earth, perhaps river. To no one of these goddesses was any appreciable power given. Most were rather weak personifications of the phenomena which they represented. Only the Indic *Ushas*, the goddess of the dawn, held a position of any real importance in her pantheon, and her powers were few indeed. She may have been "great" and even "strong with strength," but she was nonetheless castigated by Indra much as if she had been a recalcitrant child. Thus even Ushas was viewed as little more than a relatively powerless, but beautiful, decoration to the Indic pantheon.

If the Proto-Indo-Europeans included no powerful goddesses in their original pantheon, then how do we categorize the important goddesses which we find among many of the later cultures? What is the origin of an *Athena*, an *Anahita*, an *Aphrodite*? In Part Two we will examine these goddesses in depth.

It is of use for our study to observe the means by which patriarchal warrior-societies assimilated the mythology, and particularly the goddesses, of the peoples whom they invaded. Therefore, before we turn to the goddesses assimilated by the Indo-Europeans, we will first note how another patriarchal warrior-society, the Semitic Hebrews, dealt with and assimilated the Near Eastern mythology of its neighbors.

THE HEBREWS

The Woman and the Man and the Tree and the Serpent: Near-Eastern Tree and Serpent Iconography

The social patterns of the early Hebrews were most likely similar to those of the Proto-Indo-Europeans. The early Semites were also migratory,[97] and they too developed martial prowess. It would appear that the migratory existence, and resulting need for grazing land that might have belonged to others, led to emphasis upon warrior ability, and subsequent elevation of the male warrior. (Semitic women were rarely noted for Amazonian abilities.) From there it is a small step to elevation of males *per se*.

The Hebrews became both patrilinear and patriarchal. Since, therefore, children inherited goods from their fathers, those fathers wanted to be sure that their reputed offspring really were of their own seed. It thus served their economic, as well as personal, interests to have control over the sexuality of their women.

This need was emphasized among the Hebrews perhaps because they were surrounded by neighbors who, although Semitic cousins, had evolved different social and religious practices. Among the Canaanites and Phoenicians, as we have discussed, goddesses such as Asherah and Ashtarte were enthusiastically worshipped, and these goddesses may indeed have counted some followers among the Hebrews;[98] the Hebrews gave to the neighboring goddess Ashtarte the substitute-name, Ashtoreth.[99] The goddesses posed a threat to the monotheistic Hebrew people, for both the goddesses, and the other Semitic societies which worshipped them, were considered dangerous to the very structure of Hebraic society. Goddesses worshipped by other Near Eastern cultures were celebrated with sexual rituals in which the priestess, who represented the goddess, had ritual intercourse with a priest, who represented a god of fertility. This union of priest and priestess, or god and goddess, was called the *hieros gamos*, or 'sacred marriage.' Through this intercourse, the fertility of humans, animals, and the land, was ensured. The female devotees or priestesses thus had some autonomy over their sexual lives; that is, they *belonged* to no husband or master but, nonetheless, they were not required to be celibate. The Hebrew patrilineal social structure was threatened by this female autonomy: if Hebrew women should become pregnant by men not their husband, how would they determine the paternity of their children, for purposes of name and inheritance? Their concerns, then, were economic.

Therefore, perhaps because the Hebrews wished to differentiate themselves from these neighbors who posed such a threat to them, they emphasized an omnipotent, omniscient male deity; to worship any other deity was forbidden. Monotheistic religion and stringent patriarchy may thus have been the result of a Hebrew attempt at both unification and differentiation from their neighbors, and a concern for rights of inheritance.

Thus, goddesses *per se* were absent from "accepted" Hebrew religion. Those goddesses who found their way into the Old Testament were altered to conform to the state religion; their powers were reduced, and generally their immortal status was taken away. One goddess in particular degenerated into a mortal scapegoat, in rather an interesting manner. She was addressed thus by the Hebrew deity:

> I.3.38. *"I will greatly multiply your sorrow*
> *and your conception;*
> *in sorrow you will bring forth children*
> *and your desire [will be] to your husband,*
> *and he will rule over you."*[100]
> Old Testament, "Genesis" 3; *ca.* 1000 to *ca.* 700 BCE.

These words, accepted by much of the Western world for over two millennia as the *earliest word* on woman's state, have had tremendous influence both upon society's treatment of women and upon its belief in woman's "culpability."[101]

> According to the Biblical story, the downfall of humanity was caused by the weakness or "sinfulness" of the woman, Eve. The first mortal, Adam, and his wife, Eve (she who was constructed from one of Adam's *ribs*), were for some time blissfully happy, while they lived in the Garden of Eden. But then, a serpent induced Eve to taste the forbidden fruit of the Tree of Knowledge, and the couple was subsequently banished from Eden.

The main elements in this story, the tree, the serpent, the woman, and the man, are elements found in other Near Eastern cultures, both in their myths and literatures, and in their iconographies. To better understand the interrelationship of the elements in the Hebrew story, we shall first examine a Sumerian paradise myth, which dates to approximately 3000 BCE.[102]

> The Sumerian story is a myth: that is, it treats of gods rather than mortals. In this myth, there is a paradisiacal land called Dilmun. Although the land is an almost perfect one, one element is lacking: fresh water. Therefore, the Sumerian water-god, *Enki*, causes the land to be filled with fresh water, and it becomes a lush garden.
>
> After many years of hard work, the "Great-Mother" goddess, *Ninhursag*, causes eight plants to sprout in this garden. She is justifiably angry when Enki makes a quick meal of them. She pronounces the curse of death upon him, and several of his bodily organs become diseased.
>
> Fortunately for the god, his friends in high places are able to talk Ninhursag into curing him: only she who pronounced the curse of death has the ability to remove it.[103] So she seats him by her vulva, and creates eight healing deities, one for each of his ill organs. The

goddess created for the healing of Enki's *rib* was *Nin-ti*, "the lady of the rib." In Sumerian *ti* has several meanings, including "rib" and "to make live."[104] Eve, Hebrew *Chava*, means, "she who makes live."[105]

It is interesting, I believe, to compare the power of Ninhursag, and the plant-plucking and ensuing illness of Enki, with the Hebraic scenario, wherein foolish Eve, who is so subordinated to Adam that she is born from one of his *ribs*, plucks an apple from the tree of knowledge (and, we must remember, wisdom and knowledge were particular realms of the goddesses), bringing ruin upon herself, Adam, and the rest of humanity, particularly female humanity. In contrast to the Hebraic Eve, the Sumerian goddess Ninhursag was considered to be neither foolish nor sinful. On the contrary, it was Ninhursag who punished Enki for plucking her plants, just as Yahweh punished Eve for plucking the apple. Thus, although the lexical similarities may have been simple coincidence, the precursor to the first mortal woman, Eve, may indeed have been a powerful goddess. In fact, Eve's tradition may have been borrowed, at least in part, from Sumerian mythology.

We have now to explain the significance of the man, the tree, and the serpent. In Near Eastern mythology, "Great"-goddesses are often represented with consorts.[106] Their union was the 'sacred marriage' which we discussed above. The Sumerian *Inanna* loved the shepherd *Dumuzi*, and their union, their "sacred marriage," was echoed in Babylonia by *Ishtar* and *Tammuz*, and in Greece by *Aphrodite* and *Adonis*. Each of these goddesses lost her lover yearly or cyclically, and, whether or not she had caused his death, she grieved over him when he died. The consort was often, then, a "year-god," a god who had to die annually, or after a given number of years, so that he could be reborn, just as the crops "died" and were harvested annually, and were annually "reborn" after replanting when they sprang up again.

Whether or not Adam would have undergone an annual death-ritual in an earlier myth, he *was* the husband and, thus, consort of Eve, the once-goddess.

The serpent and the tree may best be understood through Near Eastern iconography. We have already discussed the association of goddesses with serpents:[107] the serpent was very likely another manifestation of the goddess, and therefore a sacred entity. Likewise, iconography throughout Europe, Asia, and the Near East depicts the veneration of trees. In the pre-Indo-European Indus Valley, in Egypt, in Crete, in Greece, and in Syria men and women were represented in attitudes of worship, facing trees.[108] The tree, too, is rich in fertile power when it blooms and becomes heavy with fruit; it may also have been an epiphany of the goddess.[109]

Thus the focal points of the Hebrew Paradise story, the woman, the man, the serpent, and the tree, were most likely re-interpretations of earlier Near Eastern iconography and mythology. An original myth and icon, which consisted of goddess, sacred snake, sacred tree, and male consort, perhaps one who aroused the wrath of the goddess by eating her sacred fruit, became re-interpreted, among the Hebrews, into a story involving a foolish woman; a tree bearing fruit which must not be plucked but *was* plucked nonetheless by the foolish woman; a seductive snake; and a man who gave birth to a female. The Hebrew story not only changes the roles of the main characters in the story; it even shifts the birth process.

The Hebrew myth, then, was *not* the earliest word on the status of women. The antecedants of the Hebrew myth show quite clearly that at least the idealized woman, the goddess, held high status in early Near Eastern societies. This early status was considerably altered later in time by the Hebrews. The Near Eastern goddess, among the Hebrews, degenerated into a mortal scapegoat, one responsible for the "greatly multiplied sorrow," and the subservience of women in the ensuing centuries.

Part Two

Assimilation of Neolithic European & Near Eastern Goddesses

The Proto-Indo-Europeans, as we have discussed, were a martial, semi-nomadic folk, and many of the indigenous people whom they came upon in the course of their travels had considerably less warrior prowess than they. These indigenous peoples, whom we call the *Neolithic Europeans*, although they were not necessarily a homogeneous group, were no match for the martial skills and weapons of the encroachers. Further, the Proto-Indo-Europeans had domesticated the horse, and they might well have used it in war. In areas occupied by the Indo-Europeans, the lower Danube and parts of Eastern Europe, excavated domesticated animal bones include those of horses.[1] One can imagine a Proto-Indo-European cavalry of sorts, consistently victorious against the indigenous peoples defending their lands on foot. In some areas the conquered Neolithic Europeans fled, and they developed new settlements.[2] In other areas, the Proto-Indo-Europeans *assimilated* with the Neolithic Europeans, creating new cultural groups.[3] The Proto-Indo-Europeans adopted and absorbed some aspects of the indigenous cultures, but, on the whole, fine art began to decline in Europe. Frequently, painted pottery and figurines gave way to crude pottery: in the Danubian basin, in the western Ukraine, and in Moldavia, painted pottery, shrines, sculptures, symbols, cult vases, and script disappeared; pottery decorated with cord or stabbing impressions replaced painted pottery.[4]

Although religious iconographic *representation* on pottery and sculpture declined, Neolithic European religion did not entirely give way to Proto-Indo-European sky-god worship. Instead, Neolithic European and Near Eastern goddesses and gods were *assimilated* into the Indo-European pantheons, creating new pantheons which reflected the diverse beliefs of the merging cultures. In the following chapters, we will examine several goddesses, worshipped by historical-era Indo-European cultures, who have multiple attributes and powers. We will demonstrate that most of these goddesses owe their origins to Neolithic Europe and to the Near East, and not to the Proto-Indo-Europeans.[5] The multiple powers of the goddesses are a reflection of their importance in the earlier cultures.

To discover and define the early historic European cultures, we shall examine the mythological traditions of many historical Indo-European cultures, and in doing so, we once again meet the difficulty of broad differences in the time frames for attested literary materials. To be sure, we must question whether the Latvian and Lithuanian folklore, which was not written down until the last few centuries, can be compared with the earlier Celtic and Germanic myths, and with the much earlier Greek, Roman, Indic, and Iranian folktales, myths, and cult attestations. We can not be certain whether, in the later folktales, we are dealing with late borrowings from other, earlier cultures, or with inherited Indo-European myth. Nonetheless, these cultures *are* related to one another, and for that reason a comparison of their goddesses, heroines, and anti-heroines is useful. We will see the similarities of functions among goddesses in related cultures, in an effort to better understand the ideals of those cultures. Further, we will observe a consistent pattern of iconography which will relate many of these goddesses to their Neolithic and Near Eastern forebears.

In this section, we shall discuss goddesses in each of eight Indo-European societies, demonstrating their functions and the frequent modification of functions for the purpose of assimilating them to the new amalgamated religion. There will be an overview of each pantheon, wherein major gods as well as goddesses will be briefly discussed. Thereafter, the major goddesses of each pantheon will be discussed in detail. "Major," in this instance, indicates both those goddesses who have the most power in their pantheons *and* those goddesses for whom large amounts of source materials may be found. The sorts of goddesses who hold power will vary from pantheon to pantheon. I also include several goddesses which bore lesser import in their pantheons but which nonetheless illustrate the bird or snake motifs discussed in Chapter One, or which seem to echo traits of the Near Eastern goddesses discussed in Chapter Two.

The Indo-European pantheons are diverse in character, from the carefully delineated pantheons of the Greeks and Romans, which the ancient mythopoets structured as "families," to the less structured and less personified "pantheons" of the Balts and Slavs. It is to the folklore and myth of the latter group that we shall turn first. Although their pantheons were quite different from those of other Indo-European groups, their goddesses share many traits in common with the goddesses of the other cultures. Baltic folktales and folksongs, indeed, comprise an important cornerstone of Indo-European myth.

CHAPTER 4

Latvian and Lithuanian goddesses

In their migrations from the Proto-Indo-European homeland, the Balts probably first settled along the south-east shores of the Baltic Sea, about 1300 BCE. From there, they diffused somewhat, until, by about the sixth century CE, they had become three distinct cultures: the Prussians, the Latvians, and the Lithuanians. The Prussian language gradually died out, and it no longer existed as a living language after the seventeenth century CE. The Latvian and Lithuanian languages have continued to be used through the present; their literatures, which are similar to one another in many respects, are composed of both Christian and pre-Christian beliefs, and, for that reason, they probably reflect at least some ancient views of the deities.

The Lithuanian pantheon included a number of naturalistic deities. Many folk-songs celebrate the sun, the moon, the heavens. Some Lithuanian gods and goddesses show affinities with other Indo-European deities: the thunder-god and patron of martial expeditions, *Perkunas*; the sky-god *Dievas*; the sun-goddess, *Saulė* (and her daughter, the sun-maiden); the earth-goddess, *Žemyna*, and *Aushrinė*, goddess of the dawn. As we discussed earlier,[1] these goddesses were quite possibly of Proto-Indo-European origin. Two other important Baltic goddesses were the goddess or fairy of fate and destiny associated with the day and the sky, *Laimė*; and the fairy-witch who was allied with the earth and the night, *Laumė*.

These deities of the Lithuanian pantheon were celebrated in myth and song. Other deities were worshipped in a domestic setting: families worshipped spirits connected with the hearth. These spirits were personified as *serpents*; they received offerings, and, as we noted,[2] they were fed milk. Although there were sites for sacred fires,[3] temples did not exist as such in medieval Lithuania. Instead, rites were celebrated in the open air and in forests, paralleling a tradition prevailing throughout the ancient Near East, Europe, and Asia.

The Latvian pantheon included unnamed deities of the sky and of the earth and several goddesses equivalent to those of the Lithuanians: *Zemes Māte*, the goddess of the earth; the dawn-goddess *Auseklis*; *Saule*, *Laima*, and *Lauma*; and several other goddesses or spirits responsible for the forests, for the fields, for milk, for the sea, for cattle, whose names were prefixed or suffixed with the word for "mother," *māte*.

We shall not discuss at any greater length those goddesses which may have been inherited from the Proto-Indo-Europeans: the earth-goddess, the dawn-goddess, the sun-goddess, and her daughter, the sun-maiden, since they were described in detail above. These goddesses were the subjects of many folk-tales and folk-songs, and they were obviously very important throughout the history of the Balts.

The most powerful female deity among the Balts was called *Laima* in Latvian and *Laimė* in Lithuanian. Laima was a goddess of fortune, and she also aided women in childbirth. When she had thus cared for a woman, the birth was blessed:

> II.4.1. *"Every person is blessed upon birth."*[4]
> Basanavičius (1902) describing Laima.

One's fortune, however, is fickle, and subject to change, often because one is not always able to find her:

> II.4.2. *"The Laimas change daily:*
> *one day* [one is] *wealthy,*
> *another day* [one is] *of moderate means,*
> *another day one has nothing . . .*
> *therefore now we also say:*
> *'Laima thus destines' or*
> *'everyone is given a Laima by God,*

but not everyone can discover [*her*].' "[5]
Ibid.

In the Lithuanian folk-tale, "God's Share," the deity is tangible, rather than removed.

In this tale, an unlucky boy went to seek his fortune, and came to stay with a hermit. During his stay, he discovered three birds who took off their feathers and bathed themselves. The hermit, who happened to be God, explained to the boy that the youngest bird was his share of good fortune, and that he must watch for it again; when he had the opportunity, he must seize its feathers[6] and compel the bird to return to the old hermit with him. The youth caught the youngest bird and followed the hermit's instructions, and the hermit, transforming the bird into a beautiful maiden, said to her:

II.4.3. "*This young man has had no share of good fortune.*
Marry him and be his share."[7]
Lithuanian Folk-Tale (This Lithuanian folk-tale, as well as subsequent folk-tales and songs cited in this chapter, was recorded in the nineteenth to twentieth centuries CE).

The young man and the beautiful young woman married, became very rich, and lived happily ever after.

The Lithuanian Laima in this tale seems to have had little of the power that might be accorded to a goddess; on the contrary, in this context she appeared to be the pawn of the hermit-deity. Since Lithuania and Latvia became Christianized when these folk-tales were being transmitted, the new religion most likely deprived the old goddesses of their powers. What is particularly significant in this folk-tale is that Fortune appears as a bird, albeit without the power of the Neolithic bird-goddess.

Sometimes the goddess, not necessarily designated as Laima, but nonetheless a conveyer of nurturance and prosperity to a man, becomes another sort of bird, a *swan*. If her feathers are destroyed, she is changed into a mortal maiden.

In one folk-tale, Laima's feathers are burnt, and she is transformed into a beautiful mortal woman. She marries a prince, but later decides to become a swan again. Her lover throws feathers to her, and she flies away. From time to time she returns, to see her children, but she retains her bird-form thereafter.[8]

Laima had many forms, not always avian, but she was always the personification of prosperity. Folk-songs in Latvia likewise describe Laima as bestower of good fortune:

II.4.4. "*Oh, dear god, Good Fortune,*
on the farm
the little plowman grows up;
I will not lead my little calf
over the field, when I marry."[9]
Latvian Folk-Song.

Laima was more than just a goddess of fortune, however. The difference between a Fortune and a Fate is a slight one, and Laima as goddess of fortune in childbirth became a goddess of destiny as well:

II.4.5. "*Where did you sit, dear Laima* (Laimiņa)
When I was born from the mother?
Did you sit on the seat of good luck
or in a little pool of tears?"[10]
Latvian Folk-Song.

Laima determined the course of one's life:

II.4.6. "*Dear Laima determined my course of life,*
sitting on three seats.
Sit, dear Laima, on one seat;

Wish for me one good course of life . . . ''[11]
Latvian Folk-Song.

This function as goddess of destiny rendered Laima a powerful goddess, because she, equally with the god Dievas, the heavenly Father, determined who was to live and to die:

II.4.7. ''*God passes the day*
in conversation with dear Laima,
[*determining*] *who must die,*
who will live under the bright sun.''[12]
Latvian Folk-Song.

Thus, Fortune, among the Balts, could be a plural deity; the "Fortunes" could live with and bring prosperity to men, often men whom they married. The Baltic Fortune was not decried for her fickleness, as was her perhaps more famous Roman equivalent. Further, she attained greater powers than did the Roman Fortuna, becoming a goddess of fate or destiny, as well as a goddess of good fortune. She became one of the most potent of Baltic goddesses.

Another Baltic goddess, who possessed a name similar to that of Laima, but who fulfilled quite different functions, was the chthonic goddess *Lauma*. Laumas were nocturnal beings, more terrestrial, more of the earthly plane, than were other deities.[13] The Latvian Lauma was a "witch" or "fairy,"[14] although other, post-Christian Latvian goddesses took on the function of death-goddess. Lauma's Lithuanian equivalent, Laumė, was often invoked as "earthly mother."[15] She was a "fairy" or "fay,"[16] although this version of the goddess as well was often presented in fairy-tales as vaguely or not-so-vaguely malevolent. She possessed, in fact, many characteristics of the witch.[17] She was sometimes—although not always—sexually attractive, large-breasted, with long, blond hair.[18]

Lauma was often depicted as a plural deity, as was Laima; if the Laumas became angry with anyone, they had the power to change her or him into anything they wished, animate or inanimate.[19] In ancient times, Laumas frequently appeared to mortals.

II.4.8. ''*In thickets and on foot-bridges . . .*
whoever, passing them,
spoke to them or greeted them, then
[*the Laumas*] *would thank them quite merrily.*''[20]
Basanavičius (1902) on the Laumas.

In a Lithuanian fairy-tale perhaps borrowed from the Slavs, "The Sun Princess and Her Deliverer,"[21] this witch-goddess[22] repeatedly tried to foil the attempts of a young prince to rescue the beautiful Sun Princess. Laumė was a "toothless old witch" who owned a rather disloyal cat. The witch promised the prince that he could have anything of hers he wished, if he were able to herd her mares for three days and bring them home safely every evening. If he were unsuccessful, however, he must pay with his life.

Of course, there was a trick to this horse-herding: the mares were in reality the witch's daughters and granddaughters, and she commanded them to turn into different animals, to hide from the prince, so that he would be unable to find them and bring them home, and would thus forfeit his life. Laumė commanded her daughters to turn into tiny fishes the first day, but the prince was enabled to outsmart them and to force them to return to their original shapes. At the end of the day, he returned them, rather bedraggled, to the witch. The next day she commanded them to turn into woodpeckers, but she was foiled yet again. The third day they metamorphosed into grubs, but they were again discovered. The prince returned, successful, to Laumė.

Thus the prince had the right to ask whatever he wished of the witch. He asked for her youngest filly, who happened to be her favorite granddaughter and as strong as twelve ordinary mares. The filly also had supernatural powers: she could talk with a human voice and fly.[23] She was able to help the prince complete the tasks necessary to rescue the Sun

Princess, who was held prisoner by a wicked giant, and the prince and Sun Princess lived happily ever after.

The Laumas could, on occasion, be beneficent. From time to time, they would do a woman's spinning for her[24] and they would give gifts—often of linen.[25] However, if annoyed, they were ready to persecute their victims.[26] For example, they helped the infants of industrious mothers, and ate the children of the lazy.[27] Thus, Laumas were neither "good" nor "bad" fairies, but, rather, powerful creatures who used those powers in many different ways.

Lauma presents many characteristics of the goddess-turned-fairy/witch. She was a shape-changer, turning herself into various animals and birds. Sometimes she appeared with human breasts, but with a hen's feet,[28] thus embodying characteristics of the ancient *bird-goddess*. She was also the mother of daughters who could change their forms upon her command, a "Mistress of Animals" as well as witch, similar to Homer's *Circe*, who transformed Odysseus' men into animals.[29] The companion of the Baltic witch, Lauma, was a cat, similar to the cats found in the fairy-tales of witches in many cultures. The witch's cat, one suspects, is the descendant of the ancient lions which flanked the "Great"-goddess, just as the "wicked" witch is a descendant of the goddess herself.[30]

Thus, Lauma-Laumė was sometimes benevolent, sometimes malevolent, often feared. She embodied characteristics of both the ancient bird-goddess and the "Mistress of Animals," and she was an earth-goddess who was transfigured into a fairy or witch in Christianized fairy-tales. Although she could perform magic, and had the power of shape-changing, under the influence of Christianity, Lauma lost some of her potency. The very strong and good, the heroic, were able to prevail over her, and even to outsmart her. Laima, on the other hand, a goddess of hope and fortune, light and life, was able to retain a greater part of her pre-Christian powers.

We have noted that the Neolithic European bird-goddess was echoed in the Baltic pantheons. The snake-deity, too, may be found among the Balts, not only as the personification of the deity who lived in the hearth, but as a goddess in folk-tales. Earlier in this book, we discussed the female serpent who brought luck to a kind farm-boy.[31] Another tale describes a young woman who found herself wed to a serpent.

The Lithuanian folk-tale, "Eglė, the Queen of Serpents,"[32] tells of a young woman, Eglė, who was the youngest of three daughters. One day she, along with her two sisters, went swimming in a lake; leaving their clothing in piles on the shore, the girls went to bathe. After bathing, when Eglė returned to her clothes, she found a serpent (it was actually an adder) coiled upon her clothes:

> II.4.9. *"Give your word that you will marry me,"*
> *the serpent said to Eglė,*
> *"and I'll peacefully creep away."*[33]
> Lithuanian Folk-Tale.

The girl was compelled to give her promise to the serpent, and the serpent, satisfied, glided back into the water from whence he had come. Eglė and her sisters returned home and told their parents what had happened. The girls' parents were not pleased.

A few days later, several snakes slithered into the yard of the young girl and her family, and let it be known that they were matchmakers for the serpent to whom Eglė had promised herself. Her parents tried mightily to dissuade the serpent-matchmakers, but the snakes would only repeat that Eglė had given her promise.

Finally, Eglė's parents agreed to give up their daughter, so the serpents departed for their home, meandering back into the waters with the girl in tow, leaving the maiden's family in tears.

The home of the serpent, the young bridegroom, was a sumptuous palace under the sea, and the serpent, who was a serpent-king, was in reality a handsome prince.[34] The wedding took place with great festivity, and Eglė was very happy.

Life continued quite pleasantly for Eglė; in fact, she forgot all about her parents, and she spent several years devoted to the prince and to the children she bore for him. But one day, her eldest son asked her about his grandparents, and she suddenly realized that she missed her family. She became quite homesick, and she begged her husband to let her take the children and go to visit her family.

The reluctant prince attempted for a long time to dissuade his wife from visiting her relatives, because he did not quite trust them:

> II.4.10. *''Sure, I'll let you visit* [*them*],''
> *he said,*
> *''but first finish spinning this little bit*
> *of silk flax.''*[35]
> Ibid.

She spun day and night, but, no matter how much she spun, the bit of flax never diminished. Losing patience, Eglė went to an old woman, who knew magical lore and enchantments, to ask for help. The wise old woman told her to throw the flax in the fire. The girl returned home, threw the flax in the fire, and, as the flax burned, she saw a beetle writhing in the flames. The dead beetle could no longer make new silk for her to spin, and so Eglė was able to finish spinning the flax.

That task accomplished, she returned to the serpent-king, and again asked that she be allowed to visit her parents. Her husband readily agreed, but again forestalled her with seemingly impossible tasks which she was only able to accomplish with the advice of the wise old woman. Finally, the serpent-king was not able to think of any new tasks for Eglė to complete, and he was compelled to allow her to visit her family. He taught her a song, which contained the secret name by which she might call him when she was ready to return to the palace under the sea:

> II.4.11. *''Žilvine, dear Žilvine,*
> *if you are alive,*
> *let milk foam up.*
> *If you are not alive,*
> *let blood foam up!''*[36]
> Ibid.

and he warned his children not to divulge his secret name to anyone.[37]

So Eglė returned home; once her family had her back with them, they did not want her to return to the underwater palace. So they frightened the youngest child into divulging her father's secret name; then Eglė's brothers went to the lake and called the serpent, reciting his secret song. When the serpent-prince appeared, they savagely cut him down with scythes, well-substantiating his fears regarding their trustworthiness.

That same day, Eglė readied herself to return home to her husband. She took her children and went to the banks of the lake. When she sang her husband's secret song, his incorporeal voice came to her from the depths of the lake, telling his wife how he was slain. Eglė ordained that she and her children be changed into trees, and they became birch, oak, ash, poplar, and fir.

The snake, the serpent-king, was in this case a male, and not a snake-goddess. However, it is quite possible that his story has bearing upon our inquiry. The male serpent in the earlier versions of Near Eastern and European myths is often the son of a female serpent which is slain by the warrior-hero of the new order. Thus Indra slays Danu and her son Vṛtra, and Beowulf slays Grendel's mother as well as Grendel. The serpent was the symbol of the old order, since it was one of the epiphanies of the ancient bird and snake goddess. This serpent, which was slain by the representative of the conquering folk, could be female, as it was in Mesopotamia and later Western Europe, or male, as it was in some Ugaritic and Egyptian myths, or it could be both female and male, mother and son.[38]

The serpent in Near Eastern and European myth is often represented as the "arch-enemy" of the young, heroic warrior; in Northeastern Europe, however, the vestiges of this ophidian negativity are far fewer. The snake might be somewhat feared by the Balts, but it is also respected and venerated. Thus it is significant that the serpent in the Lithuanian story about Eglė has few of the sly or slippery qualities found in the serpents celebrated in Judeo-Christian and Western European folklore. On the contrary, the human brothers and parents of this "queen of serpents" were much craftier than the serpent, and they were dishonorable and murderous as well.

In an earlier chapter,[39] we discussed Baltic goddesses who had inherited Proto-Indo-European characteristics, goddesses such as the sun-maiden. The following Lithuanian mythological song pictures the pantheon of sun, moon, and stars:

> II.4.12. *''Dear mother sun*
> *dear mother sun*
> *accumulated a dowry;*
>
> *dear father moon*
> *dear father moon*
> *apportioned the share.*
>
> *Dear sister star*
> *dear sister star*
> *sat on a stool;*
>
> *dear brother Pleiades*
> *dear brother Pleiades*
> *accompanied [me] outside.''*[40]
> Lithuanian Folk-Song.

The most important Baltic goddesses thus shared many characteristics in common with goddesses from varied sources: both the major Baltic goddess, Laima, who brought fortune to mortals and determined their destinies, and the chthonic goddess-turned-witch, Lauma, were associated with the bird. Some manifested snake-characteristics or were personified as sun, dawn, and earth.

CHAPTER 5

Ancient Slavic goddesses

The Slavs originally lived between the Oder and Middle Dnieper rivers. Through several migrations they were extended to the Balkans and to the upper Dnieper. Written attestation for Slavic folklore and myth was sparse until the Middle Ages. By that time, there had been connection with many other cultures, including those of the Romans and the Celts, so there was great opportunity for borrowing of folkloristic and mythological elements. Further, the introduction of Christianity to the Slavs—early on to the Southern Slavs—added to and changed their religio-mythological viewpoints. The earliest written texts among the Slavs are translations of the Christian New Testament, dated to the ninth century CE, although general Christianization of the Slavs did not take place until almost 1000 CE, when Prince Vladimir was baptized and had pagan idols destroyed.

There is some earlier written *description of* the Slavs, but it is not produced *by* the Slavs. In the fifth century BCE the Greek historian, Herodotus, described a Slavic tribe called the Neuri; according to the Scythians and Greeks living in Scythia, Herodotus says, the Neuri performed a yearly ritual:

> II.5.1. ''*Once every year, each of the Neuri becomes a wolf,*
> *for several days,*
> *and then turns back into his former [shape].*
> *But, as for me, I don't believe these stories . . .* ''[1]
> Herodotus, Histories IV.105; fifth century BCE.

Tales of werewolves are still found in Russian and Polish folklore, survivals of wolf-cults that had parallels in many parts of Europe. Other cults of demons, witches, seers, sorcerers, and spirits coexisted with Christianity for several centuries. Among the Southern Slavs, it was believed that spirits, whom they called *Vila* or plural *vilas*, appeared in many forms to charm young men: a vila appeared as a beautiful young girl, whose long hair fell over her back and breasts.[2] She would punish a man who happened upon her revels, by dancing him to death.[3] She could appear as a horse, a swan, or a falcon,[4] as well as a young woman. She could cause hail-storms or stop the heavenly waters.[5] There were vilas of the water, vilas associated with the mountains, and others who dwelled among the clouds. One cloud-vila turned into a "swan maiden" in the following tale:

> A youth met a Vila who was about to "drink out his dark eyes" in return for a drink of water from the fountain which she was guarding. Before she could do so, the hero seized her, threw her across his horse, and took her to his earthly home. He tore off her right wing, placed it in a chest, and made her his wife.[6]

Apparently, the power of the vila was such that she must be "grounded" before she could be rendered innocuous to man. That is, she could no longer be the "bird-goddess." Swan-maidens appear in the folklore of many cultures; in these stories, if their wings or swan-plumage are removed, they become vulnerable. Those who possess the avian attributes of these swan-maidens could literally become their masters, so wings and plumage were in great demand.[7]

There are many tales of bird-maidens.

> In one folk-tale a young hero, whose name is Prince Ivan, is hiding among some bushes on the shore of a lake, waiting until twelve pigeons arrive. When the pigeons land on the ground, they metamorphose into beautiful young women.
>
> The maidens run into the water and frolic about. Then a thirteenth pigeon arrives, and she too becomes a maiden: *Vassilissa the Wise*.
>
> Prince Ivan steals Vassilissa's shift, and she searches for it in vain, until she promises herself to the robber. Eventually, the two are married.[8]

The clothing of the maiden, Vassilissa the Wise, was the human counterpart of her pigeon-plumage.

The Slavic goddess *Lada* was also connected with birds. Lada was the goddess of the spring and of lovers, and she was the patroness of marriage and happiness.[9] She had a male counterpart, *Lado*, a fertility deity. At the beginning of spring, Slavic peasants would make clay images of *larks*, smear them with honey, and tip their heads with tinsel. They would carry these images about, while offering songs to Lada.[10]

Thus, the bird-goddess found her way into Slavic folklore and mythology. The Neolithic worship of the snake likewise seems not to have been neglected by the Slavs. As did the Balts, the Slavs personified the spirits of the hearth as serpents. Further, the Slavs knew a folk-tale similar to the Lithuanian story, "Eglė Queen of Serpents," which was told earlier.[11]

> In this tale, "The Water Snake," a girl went to bathe and a snake curled up on her shift, refusing to let her have her clothes until she promised to marry him. She married him, under compulsion similar to that of her Lithuanian counterpart, Eglė, and she bore him two children. She lived happily with her husband, the serpent, for some time; finally, again as in the Lithuanian tale, the girl begged her husband to let her go to see her mother.
>
> Just before she set out for her parental home, the girl asked her husband how she might address him when she returned to him. He told her to call out his name, "Osip" (Joseph), and he would appear.
>
> When the girl was again with her family, and chatting about various things, she foolishly revealed to her mother the words which she would use to call her husband. Her mother went to the dike and called the snake. When he showed his head, she cut it off.
>
> When the girl found out that her mother had killed her serpent-husband, she changed her children into *birds*—a wren and a nightingale—and she changed herself into a cuckoo.[12]

We might note that the bird and snake elements come together in this variant, rather than the snake and tree elements of the Lithuanian tale. It is interesting, moreover, that similar elements are found both in the tale of the *bird*-maiden, Vassilissa, and in this tale of the *water-snake*.

Many spirit-deities were propitiated by the Slavs: deities which presided over births were called *Rod* or *Rozenitsa* by the Russians, and *Rodienitsa* by the Croatians.[13] Russian *Dolya* and Serbian *Sreča* represented one's portion in life, or good fortune, as did Russian *Schastie*. Their antitheses, the goddesses *Nesreča*, *Nedolya*, and *Neschastie*, brought misfortune.[14] Both Sreča and Dolya were depicted as lovely young girls who spun golden thread,[15] but fortune could also be a gray-haired old woman.[16] Misfortune, too, spins thread;[17] the two are obviously two aspects of the same goddess, a goddess who is at once young and old, and who can bring fortune or misfortune.

Fortune could remain near her protégée, as a protectress, or she could just as easily abandon the person. Everyone had a personal Fortune, and one's life was directed by the goddess. One Serbian peasant would greet another thus:

> II.5.2. *"Your Sreča [is] kind!"*[18]
> Reported in Afanes'ev (1865–1869).

That is, *may your Fortune be kind.* To an unfortunate person, one would say,

> II.5.3. *"Your Sreča [is] angry."*[19]
> Ibid.

To this concept of the individual Fortune, we may compare the similar Baltic concept of *Laima*, and the Romans concept of the more removed *Fortuna*.[20]

The Slavic goddesses of fortune and misfortune represent the two poles of possibility for the individual in Slavic societies. The two poles are represented in related societies, such as the Indic, where fortune and misfortune are depicted as *Lakṣmi* and *Alakṣmi*.[21]

Keep in mind, however, that these poles always represent two aspects of the same goddess, the goddess of happiness and unhappiness, fortune and misfortune, life and death.

Fate in her deathly aspect was also known as *Mora, Mara,* or *Smert. Mor* in Russian indicates "pestilance, plague,"[22] and *Mar* or *Maruchi* (Serbian *Mora,* Polish *Mora* or *Mara*)[23] was a

> II.5.4. " . . . *little, old female creature*
> *who sits on the stove*
> *and spins thread at night* . . . "[24]
> Ibid.

Mora could be troublesome if not properly propitiated. Sometimes she smothered sleeping people at night,[25] and she could sabotage the spinning of the careless. One old woman, documented by the nineteenth century Russian mythographer, Afanas'ev, would not leave her spinning without praying to Mara, just in case the goddess might appear at night, and tear up and entangle her thread.[26]

The goddess was wont to gallop furiously about on horses, and she liked to braid their manes and tails. In Serbian legends, she transmuted *herself* into a horse.[27]

Mora was a spinner and entangler of thread, and she thus literally and metaphorically spun and entangled people's lives. Her additional involvement with and characterization as a horse demonstrates the animal's continued importance to Slavic peoples from the Neolithic through the nineteenth century of this era.

A goddess similar to Mora was *Smert*. This term indicates "death, decease" in Russian.[28] The goddess Smert was sometimes depicted as

> II.5.5. "*a scrawny skeleton* . . . "[29]
> Ibid.

Songs of exorcism were still sung to her in the nineteenth century:

> II.5.6 "*On the steep, high mountain,*
> *boiling cauldrons boil;*
> *in these boiling cauldrons there burns,*
> *with inextinguished fire,*
> *every life under the heavens.*
> *Around the boiling cauldrons*
> *stand old men;*
> *the old men sing*
> *about life, about death,*
> *about all sorts of people;*
> *the old men promise*
> *long lives for the whole world.*
> *How annoyed is Smert at that;*
> *the old men heap up great curses*
> *[upon her]!*" [30]
> Ibid.

The Slavic spirits were worshipped—whether with songs of exorcism or with songs of celebration—in the open air or under trees, just as were the deities of the Balts.

Although there is abundant evidence of spirit-cults, traces of an ancient pantheon of gods and goddesses, common throughout the Slavic regions, are more difficult to find. Many of the major Slavic deities were similar to Baltic goddesses and gods; several share cognate names and functions. The Slavic warrior-god and god of the thunderbolt was *Perun*. He was celebrated by the Russians in Kiev and by the Serbs in the Balkans; his worship may have been brought to Kiev by the Germanic warriors who founded the principality. The Lithuanian equivalent of Perun was *Perkunas*.[31]

The Slavic personification of the sky was the god *Svarog*.[32] Svarog had two sons, *Dazbog*, the god of the sun,[33] and *Svaroghits* [Svarozhich], who personified the fire.[34] *Veles/*

Volos was the god of cattle and protector of the flocks.[35] There was a custom, among the Slavs, in which patches of unreaped corn were left in the fields, while bread and salt were placed on the ground nearby. These ears were eventually knotted together, in a ceremony called "the plaiting of the beard of Volos." It was believed that after this ritual had been performed, no evil person would be able to harm the produce in the fields.[36]

Many Slavic deities were female personifications of natural phenomena. The earth, *Mat' Syra Zemlya,* has already been mentioned above.[37] There were also several goddesses of the "dawn." The goddess of the morning-dawn, *Zarya Utrennyaya,*[38] opened the gates of the heavens when the sun rose, while *Zarya Veckernyaya,* "Evening Twilight,"[39] closed the gates of the heavens in the evening: she was the afterglow of sunset.[40] Among the Serbs, the two "dawns" stood beside the sun. Depicted as a single goddess, Zarya was said to work along with the thunder-god;[41] in this connection, she was represented as an *armed virgin warrior:*

> II.5.7. "*I exhort you, Oh maiden,*
> *bearing the treasure*
> *of your father's sword,*
> *having inherited the ancient coat of mail,*
> *oh helmeted heroine,*
> *riding at full gallop*
> *on a black horse . . .*
> *may you give [to me]*
> *a fine field*
> *worth a mighty fight . . .*
> *may you divert my fate,*
> *oh maiden,*
> *from my enemy's might . . .* "[42]
> Ibid.

Thus, similar to the Greek Athena, she was a virgin patroness and protectress of warriors.

In some myths, one of the "dawns," the "morning star," replaced the sun-goddess as the bride of the moon:

> II.5.8. "*The morning star is quite delighted:*
> *She is marrying her brother,*
> *the shining moon.*"[43]
> Recorded in Lebesgue (1920).

The mythology of the Slavic dawn-goddess is similar to that of other Indo-European dawn-goddesses. Zarya herself does not always linger, but she is regularly aligned with lovers who may not tarry beyond Dawn's light. In one song, a woman invites her lover to spend the night with her:

> II.5.9. "'*Spend the night, my sweetheart,*
> *spend the night with me!*'
> '*I'd love to stay, my darling,*
> *[but] my will is not my own . . .*
> *still more,*
> *I fear that I will sleep*
> *until the light.*'
> '*Do not fear*
> *do not fear, my sweetheart:*
> *I shall not sleep*
> *for the whole night.*
> *I shall awaken you before dawn,*
> *before the morning dawn,*
> *I shall see you off and far away!*'"[44]
> Folk-Song recorded in Sobolevskii (1895–1902).

Similarly, in another song, a Hussar comes to visit his mistress, enjoining her to

> II.5.10. *"Awaken me early in the morning,*
> *my sweet one,*
> *before the white dawn,*
> *lest the daylight come."*[45]
> Ibid.

The moon, too, was invoked by lovers:

> II.5.11. *"Oh Moon, dear Moon,*
> *go behind the shed*
> *so that I may speak a little*
> *with my darling.*
> *Oh Moon, dear Moon,*
> *shine out; do not hide—*
> *and even though you depart, my love,*
> *come back to the farm."*[46]
> Ukranian Folk-Song, Nineteenth Century CE;
> Recorded in Hatto (1965).

In some myths, the Slavic moon-deity, *Myesyats*,[47] was personified as a young woman, despite her masculine name; she was married to the sun. In other myths, the sun was personified as a goddess, *Solntse*,[48] and the moon was her husband. In one song, the two live together with their children, the bright Stars:

> II.5.12. " . . . *in the midst of the Court*
> *there are three rooms:*
> *In the first room*
> *is the bright Moon;*
> *in the second room,*
> *the red Sun;*
> *and in the third room,*
> *the many Stars."*[49]
> Recorded in Ralston (1872).

The song goes on to explain that the Moon is the master of the house, the Sun is the mistress, and the stars are their children.[50] This myth corresponds to that of the Baltic moon and sun deities.

All of the natural forces, including the sun, the moon, the stars, and the dawn, were celebrated by the Slavs in song, particularly in love-song. In one song, a young woman was waiting in her bed-chamber for her lover, trembling with anticipation, when she experienced a miraculous phenomenon: she saw

> II.5.13. " . . . *a miracle.*
> *In the heavens [is the] sun—*
> *in [her] chamber the sun.*
> *In the heavens the moon—*
> *In [her] chamber the moon.*
> *In the heavens the stars—*
> *in [her] chamber the stars*
> *In the heavens the dawn—*
> *in [her] chamber the dawn,*
> *and all the beauty beneath the skies."*[51]
> Russian Folk-Song, Fifteenth Century CE;
> Recorded in its present form in the Nineteenth Century CE.
> (Hatto, 1965).

Thus, the great marvels of the universe are its heavenly phenomena, its sun, moon, stars, dawn; and the great power of love can reflect these heavenly forces into one's terrestrial domain.

Not all Slavic goddesses represented natural phenomena. A "Mistress of Animals" was also worshipped by the Slavs of Bohemia, Poland, and Lusatia, those Slavs who were in contact with Germanic peoples. This "Mistress of Animals" was a young, beautiful goddess of the hunt, *Dziwica*,[52] who

> II.5.14. *''loves to hunt in the light*
> *of the moonlit night;*
> *she rushes along, with weapons in her hands,*
> *with a fleet horse, through the woods,*
> *accompanied by hunting dogs,*
> *and she chases animals when they have run away.''*[53]
> Reported in Afanas'ev (1865–1869).

This goddess was called *Devana* among the Czechs and *Dzievona* among the Poles.[54] The name may have been a Slavic translation of the Roman "Diana,"[55] which was perhaps brought from the Romans to the Slavs by the German soldiers.

Although the spirits and fairies of the various Slavic folk were quite different from the well-organized pantheons of other Indo-European peoples, there are several similarities. The Slavic goddesses of the sun, dawn, and earth were similar to those found in sister-cultures, and elements in folk-tales show a continuing lineage from the Neolithic bird and snake goddess, or "Goddess of Regeneration."

CHAPTER 6

Iranian goddesses and Zoroastrianism

Those Indo-Europeans who became the historical Iranians settled in Southwestern Asia, in the area which became modern Persia or Iran, around the beginning of the second millennium BCE. Their first writings, royal inscriptions, appeared almost fifteen hundred years later, after the Persian king Cyrus seized Babylon in 538 BCE. Inscriptions offer the earliest evidence for Persian deities; the earliest *literary* work, the Zend-Avesta, was not actually written until the first centuries CE, during the Sassanian dynasty (224–729 CE). The Zend-Avesta does, however, record oral tradition from at least a millennium earlier. The Zend-Avesta was the earliest Iranian "bible" or collection of sacred writings; it contained hymns to both *pre-Zoroastrian* and *Zoroastrian* deities.

Among the pre-Zoroastrian deities, two were preeminent: *Mithra* (Miϑra), a god of contracts, judge of the dead, and sun-god who later became a solar-warrior-god in the Mithraic religion; and *Anāhitā*, the personification of the waters who also granted wisdom and strength.

Arēdvī (Arədvī) *Sūrā Anāhitā*, "the moist one, the strong one, the pure one," was the most powerful Iranian pre-Zoroastrian goddess; she was the only *goddess* to whom a hymn was addressed in that part of the Zend-Avesta which celebrated the pre-Zoroastrian deities. Anāhitā was mentioned in other writings of the ancient Persians: King Artaxerxes II was one of the earliest known to invoke her, in an inscription dating to the fourth century BCE:

> II.6.1. " . . . *by the will of Ahura Mazda,*
> *Anāhitā,*
> *and Mithra . . .*
> *may Ahura Mazda, Anāhitā,*
> *and Mithra protect me.*"[1]
> Artaxerxes II (Mnemon), Susa A; 405–359 BCE.

Anāhitā was a multifunctional goddess. She was well-incorporated into the tripartite religious structure of the Indo-European Iranians, since her powers were divided among the three functional levels which a deity could fulfill. She bestowed wisdom to the *priests*, valor to *warriors*, and fecundity to everyone else:

> II.6.2. "*strong warriors ask of you* (Anāhitā)
> *possession of a rapid horse*
> *and the superiority of glory . . .*
> *the priests . . . ask of you*
> *wisdom and prosperity . . .*
> *maidens pray to you*
> *for a well-working field [to be sown]*
> *and a brave husband . . .*
> *young women who [are] giving birth*
> *pray to you for an easy delivery . . .* "[2]
> Avesta, Yasht V.86-87;
> 5th to 1st Centuries BCE;

She was also a great river-goddess, mother of the waters:

> II.6.3. "*Hither flowed Arēdvī Sūrā Anāhitā . . .*
> *she causes some waters to stand still,*
> *she lets others flow, suitably,*
> *she makes free a dry passage*
> *through the Vanghuī* (Vaŋhuī)
> *and the Vitanghvaitī* (Vītaŋhvaitī)
> *rivers.*"[3]
> Ibid, Yasht V.78.

Anāhitā possessed that special Iranian attribute, *Khvarēnah (xᵛarənah)*, a fiery spirit of *creative energy* which had a mythology of its own; it indicated "light," "majesty," "energy," and "brilliance;" it sometimes appeared as a halo or aura around the head of a deity:[4]

> II.6.4 " . . . *through the splendor*
> *of my* (Anāhitā's)
> *Khvarēnah* . . . "[5]
> Ibid, Yasht V.89.

Anāhitā was, therefore, a personification of *creative energy*. As embodiment of the three socio-religious functions, of the fructifying waters, and of the divine energy or Khvarēnah, Anāhitā was indeed a potent goddess in a pantheon composed primarily of male deities.

Just as Anāhitā was an important goddess in the ancient Iranian *polytheistic* religion embodied in the Avesta, so the goddess *Spēnta* (Spənta) *Ārmaiti*, "holy devotion," held an important place in the ancient *henotheistic*—almost monotheistic—Zoroastrian religion.

Henotheistic religions are characterized by the predominant worship of one deity without denying the existence of other deities. Although other entities were included in the Zoroastrian religion, it was Ahura Mazdāh, the "Wise Lord" (in Medieval Persian he was known as *Ormazd*), the god of the Achaemenian kings (558–330 BCE), who was the essential deity. Although the priest Zoroaster[6] retained the old Iranian gods in his religion—a religion which reconciled the religion of the Median Magi with that of the Achaemenian kings—the hymns which he composed, probably between 660 and 583 BCE, were addressed primarily to Ahura Mazdāh and to the Mazdean spirits.

These spirits, the other deities which made up the Zoroastrian "pantheon," were not viewed as autonomous deities, and that is why Zoroastrianism can be considered a monotheistic or henotheistic religion. The spirits were thought to be archangels or "augmentative spirits." They were not only subordinated to Ahura Mazdāh; they were *aspects* of the "one god,"[7] even though they were personified and characterized to some extent. They were called *Amesha Spēntas* (Ameša Spəntas), "holy immortals."

There were six "holy immortals," and several *daevas* or evil spirits whom the good spirits opposed. The chief daeva was *Angra (Aŋra) Mainyu*, who became the demon *Ahriman* in Medieval texts. As Ahura Mazdāh represented life and truth, so the demon Angra Mainyu represented death and "The Lie."

The six "holy immortals" were *Vohu Manah*, "Good Spirit," who was responsible for useful animals, such as the cow; *Asha* (Aša) *Vahista*, "Best Law, Righteousness," who presided over fire; *Khshathra* (Xšaϑra) *Vairya*, "Precious Dominion," who was the patron deity of the warrior-class; *Haurvatat*, "Welfare," who ruled the waters; *Ameretat*, "Immortality," who governed plants and represented divine deathlessness; and, finally, *Spēnta Ārmaiti*, "Holy Devotion," who personified the earth and its bounty, and had other functions as well.

Since Ārmaiti was personified as an aspect of *Ahura Mazdāh*, she was said to have been born androgenically of this god:

> II.6.5. "*O Ahura,*
> *who created dear Ārmaiti . . .*
> *by these [questions]*
> *I am trying to get to know you,*
> *O Mazdāh,*
> *[as] the creator of all . . .* "[8]
> Avesta, Yasna 44.7; composed *ca.* 660–583 BCE.

The virgin Ārmaiti represented a "purity" of thought. Further, just as did Anāhitā, the Zoroastrian goddess served several functions. She represented wisdom, giving advice about the role of the spirit:

> II.6.6. *"Going from one to the other,*
> *Ārmaiti confers with spirit*
> *where there is vacillation."*[9]
> Ibid, Yasna 31.12.

and she taught the path of truth:

> II.6.7. *"Oh, holy Ārmaiti,*
> *instruct the inner nature [of people]*
> *in the Truth* (Asha)."[10]
> Ibid, Yasna 33.13.

Further, she was similar to the Roman and Baltic goddesses of fortune, Fortuna and Laima, for she too controlled the destiny of mortals:

> II.6.8. *"Through Ārmaiti,*
> *destiny [is to be invoked]."*[11]
> Ibid.

And, just as was the Roman Fortuna, she was the cornucopia of the fruits of the land:

> II.6.9. *"May you give to me,*
> *Oh Ārmaiti,*
> *that portion of riches."*[12]
> Ibid, Yasna 43.1.

In fact, Ārmaiti *was* the personification of the land itself, and the earth was, thus, her proper realm:

> II.6.10. *"Then, [Ahura Mazdāh created]*
> *Ārmaiti,*
> *granting peace*
> *for her pasturage."*[13]
> Ibid, Yasna 47.3

As goddess of the earth, the goddess, by extension, sustained the earth of the *khshathra*, the "realm" or "dominion," and she was responsible for its growth:

> II.6.11. *"Ārmaiti causes*
> *the undiminishing realm to increase."*[14]
> Ibid, Yasna 28.3

Although her personification as goddess was slight, Ārmaiti, just as Anāhitā, was well-integrated into the tripartite religious system. She fulfilled the priestly function by giving advice about the role of the spirit; she also fulfilled the second function, by bestowing strength, much as a warrior-goddess of the spirit:

> II.6.12. *"Through Ārmaiti,*
> *Oh Ahura,*
> *grant strength."*[15]
> Ibid, Yasna 33.12.

Finally, although a virgin, she even fulfilled the mothering or nurturing function: as the medieval Iranian goddess *Spendarmat*, she caused the first human couple to be born.[16]

In sum, Ārmaiti was an aspect of the all-spirit Ahura Mazdāh, somewhat limited in personification to suit the Zoroastrian religion. Her powers were broad, however, and she appears to have been a sublimation of a more personified goddess such as Anāhitā. While Anāhitā was a creatrix of *life*, one who granted both female and male fertility,

Ārmaiti echoed the duality of the "Goddess of Regeneration:" she controlled the destiny of mortals, both good destiny and bad, and, like the Roman *Fortuna*, she bestowed wealth. Ārmaiti was similar to the Greek *Athena* as well: thoroughly assimilated to the patriarchal Iranians, she was born androgenically of Ahura Mazdāh, just as Athena was born of Zeus. Further, she conferred both wisdom and martial ability, as did Athena. Thus, while Ārmaiti was somewhat subsumed under her more potent father, and while her sexuality was repressed—as was common of most Indo-European goddesses—her functions and powers were numerous indeed.

CHAPTER 7

Indic goddesses

The Iranian and the Indic cultures were closely related, since the Indo-Iranians had lived in close proximity before they settled into their final geographical domains.[1] Both were Indo-European societies, and both assimilated cultural aspects of the indigenous peoples whom they came upon when they reached their final destinations, around the beginning of the second millennium BCE.

Before the arrival of the Indo-Europeans in India, the pre-Indo-European, indigenous *Indus* civilization worshipped a "Great-Mother" goddess. Archaeological excavations from the civilizations of *Mohenjo-daro* and *Harappa* revealed a preponderance of female figurines—as was the case in Neolithic Europe—some of which were manifestly connected with religious rites. For example, cups were found in the headdresses of some female figurines, and smoke stains could be seen on the insides of the cups.[2] Oil or incense may have been burned in the cups, and the figurines may, therefore, have been cult objects. Some of the figurines were *horned,* and associated with a *sacred tree*. They can be compared with similar figurines found in Indo-European Greece and Anatolia.[3]

With the arrival of the Indo-Europeans, who predominantly worshipped male deities, the indigenous goddesses lost their prestige for some time. In the earliest Indic texts, the hymns of the *Rigveda,*[4] the Indic socio-religious culture was manifestly male-centered. Most of the Rigvedic hymns were addressed to male deities, particularly to *Mitra,* the ruler of the day who beheld all creatures with an unwinking eye; *Varuna,* the personification of the sky and king of the universe; *Indra,* the warrior-king; and *Agni,* god of the fire and of the sacrifice. A number of hymns were addressed to the goddess of the dawn, *Ushas* (Uṣas), whom we discussed earlier, but the most important function of the dawn-goddess seems to have been that of "beautiful woman." That is, Ushas "decorated" the old Indic pantheon, and, in addition, either brought the morning or caused the morning to tarry. Ushas thus may be considered a "token female" among the Rigvedic deities.

Other goddesses were mentioned in the Rigveda, and it seems as though some of them had been quite powerful in an earlier era. They may have lost some of their powers with the advent of the Indo-Europeans. The goddess *Aditi,* for example, was described in the *Rigveda* as the mother of the *Adityas*. Literally "sons of the Aditi," the Adityas counted among their number several of the most powerful Rigvedic gods, including Mitra, Varuṇa, the sun-god *Surya,* and others.[5] Further, Aditi represented procreation, as both mother and daughter of the creative god *Daksha* (Dakṣa):

> II.7.1. *"Daksha was born of Aditi,*
> *and Aditi was born from Daksha."*[6]
> Rigveda X.72.4; *ca.* 1200 BCE.

And she was the manifestation of all of nature:

> II.7.2. *"Aditi is the heaven, Aditi is mid-air,*
> *Aditi is the mother and the father*
> *and the son.*
> *Aditi is all gods, Aditi is five-classed men,*
> *Aditi is all that has been born*
> *and shall be born."*[7]
> Ibid, I.89.10.

The "lap" of Aditi, the "boundless goddess,"[8] represented nature in its positive aspect:

> II.7.3. *"Aditi's lap contains*
> *the desired dwelling-places."*[9]
> Ibid, X.70.7.

and she personified the "bounty" of nature:

> II.7.4. *"I request the abundance of Aditi,*
> *sure, boundless, splendid,*
> *which does not injure,*
> *which is worthy of reverence."*[10]
> Ibid, I.185.3.

She was a protectress of the pious:

> II.7.5. *"May Aditi allot to us*
> *freedom from sin."*[11]
> Ibid, I.162.22.

She was ritually invoked by the poet, along with other major deities, in several prayers:

> II.7.6. *"May Varuna, Mitra, Aditi, and Sindhu,*
> *Earth and Heaven,*
> *bestow this [boon] upon us."*[12]
> Ibid, I.94.16; I.95.11; I.96.9 *et alia*.

Thus, although Aditi, in the Rigveda, was not a truly active or heroic goddess, she was a goddess of stature in the Rigveda. She may have been an indigenous goddess assimilated by the Indo-European Indic peoples as the mother of their greatest gods. Aditi was the creative goddess, mother of all mortals and immortals; she may have been an ancient "Great-Mother" goddess: the positive aspect of the "Goddess of Regeneration."

The negative aspect of Aditi was represented by *Nirṛti*, a goddess who may have been the death-aspect of the ancient "Goddess of Regeneration." Just as the "lap" of Aditi represented beneficence and munificence: the "desired dwelling-place," so the "lap" of the goddess Nirṛti was to be avoided, for it betokened death: she received the corpse back into her womb, the "lap of Nirṛti:"

> II.7.7. *"Those who wound, as is their custom,*
> *the one who speaks artlessly,*
> *or those who, by custom,*
> *violate the shining one,*
> *may Soma either deliver them*
> *to the serpent*
> *or place them*
> *into the lap of Nirṛti."*[13]
> Ibid, VII.104.9.

Note, in this example, that she was the manifestation of righteous anger against those who violated the laws of nature.

Nirṛti was a binder-goddess; such deities are feared, for if the binding is not loosened, it will bring death:

> II.7.8. *"That cord around your neck(s),*
> *not to be undone,*
> *which Nirṛti the goddess bound . . . "*[14]
> Atharvaveda VI.63.1; *ca*. 900 BCE.

We have already discussed the binder-god Vṛtra,[15] who withheld the waters of the heavens. On a cosmic level, Vṛtra, along with his mother *Danu*, threatened the death of all humanity.

Nirṛti was also associated with a *black bird of omen*, which was her "mouth:"

> II.7.9. *"What this black bird*
> *has wiped off with your mouth,*
> *O Nirṛti . . .*

may Agnī Gārhapatya . . .
release me from this sin.''[16]
Ibid, VII.64.

This association relates Nirṛti to the Neolithic European bird-goddesses, and to her later European avatars.[17]

Thus, Nirṛti was a chthonic and underworld goddess, one who functioned much like the Mesopotamian *Ereshkigal* and the Baltic *Lauma*. Her personification as a black bird links her to the Neolithic goddesses of life and death; Nirṛti, just as other post-Neolithic goddesses, represented but one part of the spectrum of life and death. Just as Aditi protected those in concert with nature—the pious—with life, so Nirṛti punished those who violated nature with death. It thus appears that the two goddesses, Aditi and Nirṛti, were descended from the one Neolithic goddess of regeneration and creation, life and death.

This positive-negative split between Aditi and Nirṛti was echoed later in Indic history, when the "Great"-goddess *Devī* was viewed as both one and many.[18] The Indic peoples seem early on to have set fluid boundaries for the "wholeness" of their deities, or at least for the Neolithic "Goddess of Regeneration," treating her at times as one deity, and at other times as two or more deities. One wonders at the psychological implications of this character-fragmentation, although it is difficult to determine why it actually took place. The irrevocable fragmentation of the deity of life and death, Aditi-Nirṛti, may have represented an unwillingness on the part of the earliest Indo-European Indians to visualize both birth and death, both beneficence and maleficence, in one deity. The later unification and fragmentation of the *Puranic* goddess[19] Devī was perhaps visualized by a different stock, since she most likely represented a re-emergence of the "Great"-goddess of the pre-Indo-European indigenous peoples of India.

The river-goddess *Sarasvatī*, the "great flood,"[20] was another goddess who was addressed several times in the Rigveda. Similar to the Iranian river-goddess, *Anāhitā*, Sarasvatī represented boundless energy: waters flow for all eternity, and water is, indeed, a *literal* source of energy. Sarasvatī gave sustenance to the deserving:

II.7.10. ''*For him,*
Sarasvatī causes milk,
melted butter,
[and] sweet water
to pour forth.''[21]
Rigveda IX.67.32; *ca.* 1200 BCE.

and suppliants did not hesitate to ask this of her:

II.7.11. ''*May Sarasvatī*
give nourishment
to the singer.''[22]
Ibid, X.30.12.

She was called "best mother,"[23] and she was invoked by those who wished to bear children:

II.7.12. ''*O Sarasvatī,*
O goddess,
give us progeny.''[24]
Ibid, II.41.17.

In fact, it was Sarasvatī who set the seed in the womb:

II.7.13. ''*O Viṣṇu, prepare the womb . . .*
Place the fetus [in the womb],

O Sarasvatī . . . ''[25]
Ibid, X.184.1–2.

Just as she bestowed wealth in terms of descendants, she also granted material wealth:

II.7.14. ''*O Sarasvatī . . .*
who [is] treasure-giving,
wealth-procuring,
who [is] bestowing beautiful gifts . . . ''[26]
Ibid, I.164.49.

She was, moreover, precursor to *Shrī Lakshmī* (Śrī Lakṣmī), as personification of good fortune:

II.7.15. ''*So may*
fortune-bearing Sarasvatī
effect good luck.''[27]
Ibid, VII.96.3.

She thus amply fulfilled the nurturing functions.

Further, although Sarasvatī was never described in the *process* of physically destroying her enemies, she was described as a "defeater of enemies,"[28] and enjoined:

II.7.16. ''*O Sarasvatī,*
dash to the ground
those who hate the gods.''[29]
Ibid, VI.61.3.

She was, moreover, the "hero's consort."[30] The warrior-function, therefore, was also fulfilled by the river-goddess, even though in this case the function may have been a metaphorical one.

Finally, Sarasvatī protected the prayers of the pious:

II.7.17. ''*May the goddess,*
Sarasvatī,
rich in gifts,
with her might,
be a protectress
of our prayers.''[31]
Ibid, VI.61.4.

She guided "all works of devotion"[32] and she caused "all prayers to succeed."[33]

Sarasvatī later became a goddess of speech,[34] music, and *wisdom*. Indeed, to this day she is worshipped in the Hindu religion as a goddess of wisdom and knowledge. *Mantras*, Hindu religious formulae, such as:

II.7.18. ''*Om, hail to Sarasvatī*''[35]
Hindu Mantra, Twentieth Century CE.

still address her, to increase the devotee's strength of mind and ability to focus intellectual concentration.[36]

As nurturer, slayer of foes, and both protectress of the pious and repository of wisdom, Sarasvatī manifested all of the three possible functions within an Indo-European religio-social structure. This multiplicity of functions rendered Sarasvatī, just as her Iranian counterpart Anāhitā, a powerful goddess, even though the powers, reduced to epithets, may have represented but a shadow of the earlier functions.

The final Rigvedic goddess whom we shall discuss was the Indic equivalent of the Iranian Ārmaiti. The Rigvedic *Aramati* was a goddess of devotion, as was her Iranian counterpart; the Indic Aramati was, however, mentioned rarely in the Rigveda. She was "worthy of worship:"[37]

> II.7.19. *"The great Aramati,*[38]
> *The lady, the goddess,*
> *to whom drink-offering has been brought*
> *with homage,*
> *the sublime one,*
> *who knows holy law."*[39]
> Ibid, V.43.6.

She may have fulfilled another of Ārmaiti's functions:

> II.7.20. *"Forth . . . go the rivers;*
> *through great Aramati have they run."*[40]
> Ibid, X.92.5.

In this context, Aramati may personify the earth, as did Ārmaiti. The two goddesses of devotion may be a personification of devotion, or proper thought, itself,[41] but it is quite possible that further personification and extension of their realms to the earth took place early on, before their migrations out of south Russia.

Although there has not been a profusion of Rigvedic goddesses for us to discuss, there was one more important Indic goddess who at least had her roots in the Rigveda. The term *lakshmī* (lakṣmī) originally indicated a "sign" or "token."[42] In the Atharvaveda it came to mean good or bad "luck,"[43] while in the Mahābhārata it indicated "beauty," "loveliness," "splendor."[44] Further, in heroic tales *Shrī Lakshmī* was personified as a goddess of fortune, beauty, and love,[45] the most beautiful women in the stories were compared to her.[46]

Shrī Lakshmī was composed of all good things. The Hindu gods, therefore, desired her, or at least her attributes. Hence, Agni took her food; the personification of the sacred drink, *Soma*, took her royal power; Varuṇa took her universal sovereignty; Mitra availed herself of her noble rank; Indra took her strength; the priest-god *Bṛhaspati*, who intercedes with gods on behalf of mortals, took her holy lustre; the stimulating sun-god *Savitṛ*, took her dominion; the surveyor of all and purveyor of prosperity, *Pūṣan*, took her wealth; the river-goddess Sarasvatī took her prosperity; and the heavenly builder, *Tvaṣṭṛ*, took her beautiful forms.[47] She thus was equal to a combination of two Greco-Roman goddesses, *Fortuna* with her cornucopia,[48] and her distribution of luck; and *Pandora*, the "gift of everything," or the "all-endowed."[49]

Just as the Greek goddess of love and beauty, *Aphrodite*, was born of the sea-foam,[50] so Lakshmī was born of the foam at the churning of the ocean.[51]

> The primeval Ocean, the "Ocean of Milk," was an undifferentiated mass of potential energy. The god *Vishnu* (Viṣṇu), who had metamorphosed into a tortoise, stood in the depths of this ocean; upon his back arose the axis of the world, Mount Mandara, and around Mount Mandara coiled the serpent *Ananta*, the "boundless one," the "infinite one."[52]
>
> The creator-god, Brahma, ordered the Hindu gods, or *devas*, to pull the serpent's head, while the *Asuras*, or demons, alternately pulled his tail. This was a cooperative venture between the two groups of beings, rather than a contest.
>
> Pulling in turn upon Ananta's head and tail, the devas and asuras caused Mount Mandara to rotate rapidly. In this way they churned the Ocean of Milk. The elements of creation, including Lakshmī and other divinities, came forth out of this Ocean.[53]
>
> Lakshmī is called *Padmā*, "goddess of the lotus,"[54] because she was holding a lotus in her hand when she came up from the ocean; the lotus is one of the attributes which she holds in her many hands.[55]

The mythology of Lakshmī was similar to that of Aphrodite in another respect as well: Aphrodite gave birth to *Eros*: literally love-god,[56] and similarly the Indic goddess Lakshmī had a young son, *Kāmadeva*: likewise "god of love."[57]

Lakshmī was named as consort to various Hindu gods in different texts. In the hymn to the Indic "Great"-goddess *Devī*, the Devī māhātmyam—a tale in seven-hundred verses from the Mārkāṇḍeya Purāṇa—she was said to be the consort of the god *Shiva* (Śiva):

> II.7.21. *"You are indeed Gaurī* (Pārvatī)
> *who has been made the support*
> *of the moon-crested god* (Shiva)*."*[58]
> Devī māhātmyam IV.11; *ca.* 550 CE.

She was also said to be the wife of Vishnu:

> II.7.22. *"You are Shrī [Lakshmī],*
> *who has, alone, made her home*
> *in the heart*
> *of the Enemy of Kaiṭabha* (Vishnu)*."*[59]
> Ibid.

She was thus Vishnu's *shakti* (śakti), his energizing consort, who awakened him:

> II.7.23. *"O goddess . . .*
> *let the Lord of the World*
> (Vishnu)
> *be awakened from sleep . . . "*[60]
> Ibid, I.85–87.

Another of her epiphanies was the goddess-heroine *Rukmiṇī*.[61] She was the principal wife of *Krishna* (Kṛṣṇa), the great teacher and avatar of the god Vishnu in the Classical Indian epic, the Mahābhārata.[62]

The powers of Shrī Lakshmī were broader than those of Rigvedic goddesses, just as the powers of other post-Rigvedic goddesses were broader than those of their Vedic predecessors. This great scope of power, however, need not have been a new phenomenon. More likely, later goddesses *retrieved* a more ancient prestige which they had lost when the Indo-Europeans entered India. In the post-Rigvedic era, the newness of the male-centered socio-religious system relaxed, allowing the tenets of the earlier, perhaps female- *and* male-centered religious systems of the indigenous peoples to resurface.

Lakshmī was but one epiphany of a very powerful goddess who had many names, but who was often known simply as *Devī*: "goddess." Devī was popular among the adherents of the *Tantric* religion throughout India, but she was particularly popular, in her various aspects, in Bengal. She was a "Great"-goddess who accrued many powers and functions.

Tantra means "rule" or "doctrine" in Sanskrit. The Tantric texts are magical and religious works which are devoted to Devī in large part; the Tantric religion celebrates Devī as activating female energy, or *shakti*. This shakti is the *activating* energy which awakens the *dormant* energy lying within the male. The female personification of this energy is the goddess *Shaktī* (Śaktī). She is manifested as the consort of the god Shiva, who in turn represents static energy:

> II.7.24. *"If Shiva becomes joined with Shaktī,*
> *he is able to be powerful.*
> *If not, then*
> *the god is not even able*
> *to move."*[63]
> Saundaryalaharī I; *ca.* 1000 CE.

The male and female principles were therefore complementary in Tantric theology. Tantric worship was and is devoted to the celebration of these deified principles of energy: Shiva and Shaktī. Shaktī, the personification of activating energy, is but one aspect of the great Tantric goddess, Devī, and conversely, each male deity had his female activating consort, or Shaktī.[64]

One of the most famous shaktis, at least in the Buddhist religion, was *Tara*, "she who carries across," "the savioress,"[65] who was sometimes worshipped as the plural *Taras*. She was the compassionate goddess, the powerful savioress and protectress of humanity.

> Tara was, according to some,[66] the wife of Bṛhaspati, the divine priest or sacrificer, the teacher of the gods, who interceded with gods on behalf of humans. Disregarding marital law, the moon-god, Soma, carried off the beautiful Tara, and this act led to a great war between the gods and the demons, or Asuras. The powerful god, Brahmā, finally put an end to the war and restored Tara to her husband.

The goddess who assimilated all of the shaktis, Devī, was known in several aspects, both beneficent and maleficent—or perhaps more correctly, both life-bringing and death-bringing. The death-bringing aspects of Devī were not necessarily regarded as maleficent, since she represented the *continuum* of life, death, and rebirth. Since death leads to rebirth, the goddess who brings death is just part of the continuum. This concept is different from that of the "grim reaper" espoused in Western culture, since death in Eastern philosophy is not viewed as an absolute end but rather as a middle ground between birth and rebirth. In fact, when true death, or the absence of further lives, finally comes to the person who has accrued sufficient virtue, that "death"—emergence into the all-deity and the only real bliss—is hailed as the great reward.

The three-eyed goddess[67] Devī was born from the united light which emanated from the bodies of Vishnu, Brahmā, Shiva, Indra, and the other gods.[68] The concentration of light was like

> II.7.25. *"a mountain glowing intensely,*
> *penetrating the quarters of the world*
> *with its flames."*[69]
> Devī māhātmyam II.10–11; *ca.* 550 CE.

Then this light

> II.7.26. *"pervading the three worlds*
> *with its splendor,*
> *cojoined and became a woman."*[70]
> Ibid, II.12.

We noted earlier that each of the principal Hindu deities *took* one of the goddess *Lakshmī*'s attributes, rendering her a "giver of all things." On the contrary, in the hymn to Devī, each of the principal deities *gave* her one attribute: weapons, jewels, the lion, lotuses, and armor.[71] Thus having *received* the energies and attributes of the gods, Devī was created to save the worlds from the gods' enemies.

Since Devī was the goddess *par excellence*, she accrued many different epiphanies. Each form of Devī had a somewhat different aspect or function. She was sometimes distinguished from these forms, while at other times they were assimilated to her. Whether described as distinct goddesses in their own right, or as aspects of Devī, in the hymn to Devī it was accepted that all of the goddesses were but a part of the "Great"-goddess, who asks:

> II.7.27. *"What other feminine force is there*
> *besides me?"*[72]
> Ibid, X.5.

and declares that all of the goddesses

> II.7.28. *''are but my own manifestations*
> *entering into my own self!''*[73]
> Ibid.

Thus all of the goddesses, or aspects of Devī

> II.7.29. *''passed into the body of Devī.''*[74]
> Ibid, X.6.

With regard to this assimilation, we recall that the term *devī* means, simply, "goddess." Devī, in her "positive" or more benevolent aspects, was worshipped as *Umā*, the goddess of "light, splendor;"[75] and as the daughter of the mountain-god, the *Himalaya, Pārvatī*, "mountain-goddess."[76] She also assimilated the river-goddess and goddess of wisdom, *Sarasvatī*.[77] The "negative" or death-bringing aspects of Devī were personified as *Kālī*, "the emaciated black goddess,"[78] who bore a skull-topped staff and a garland of skulls;[79] *Durgā*, "the inaccessible, unattainable goddess;"[80] and *Caṇḍikā*, "the fierce, passionate goddess."[81] Even in her death-avatars, Devī was beneficent to humanity. As bearer of fortune or happiness, *Bhagavatī*, Durga saved both gods and mortals by overcoming the demon-god of many shapes, the destructive *Asura* who was besetting the world, *Mahiṣāsura*.[82]

Devī, the many-aspected goddess, was known by other epithets as well; after she slew the asura Aruṇa, who, in collective bee-form, caused great havoc upon heaven and earth, she became known as *Bhrāmarī*, "the bee:"

> II.7.30. *''And then people*
> *will praise me everywhere*
> *as Bhrāmarī.''*[83]
> Ibid, XI.54.

She was *Ambikā*, "mother,"[84] and *Ishvarī* (Īśvarī), "mistress,"[85] and she embodied the dual goddess: *Lakshmī*, the personification of prosperity whom we discussed, and her opposite, *Alakshmī*, the goddess of misfortune:

> II.7.31. *''In time of prosperity*
> *she is indeed Lakshmī,*
> *bestowing good fortune on the home(s) of men.*
> *In the same manner,*
> *she thus becomes Alaksmī,*
> *[and] she comes forth to [cause] destruction.''*[86]
> Ibid, XII.40.

Further,

> II.7.32. *''You,* (Lakshmī) *go,*
> *with hair dispersed,*
> *and as death you love moist flesh.*
> *You are Lakshmī and Alakshmī.''*[87]
> Harivaṁśa, Appendix 1.8.19–20; *ca.* 1050 CE.

This "Great"-goddess, in all of her manifestations, was a goddess of every plane. She held sway over both life and death; she was

> II.7.33. *''The eternal one,*
> *the embodiment of the universe''*[88]
> Devī māhātmyam I.64; *ca.* 550 CE.

who

II.7.34. *"scratched the sky with her tiara."*[89]
Ibid, II.38.

She was, therefore, a celestial and a worldly goddess.

Devī was multifunctional; she was the "supreme knowledge"[90] and

II.7.35. *"Wisdom . . . [through whom] the*
quintessence of all precepts
is comprehended."[91]
Ibid, IV.11.

She was also a warrior-maid, an active fighting force in her own right, and not just one who gave strength to male warriors:

II.7.36. *"The great Asura*
(the demon-god Mahiṣāsura)

was overthrown by the Devī,
who cut off his head
with her great sword."[92]
Ibid, III.42.

She slew other monsters as well, coming to the rescue of gods and mortals when they were confronted with forces which they could not overcome.[93]

Devī, in her various epiphanies, had up to eighteen arms and hands, in which she held a number of weapons, including: sword, shield, mace, discus, arrows, bow, club, spear, missile, and rod. She also held a noose, a thunderbolt, and a trident.[94] She was not, therefore, a passive warrior.

As one would expect of almost any goddess, whether warrior-maid or goddess of love, Devī also fulfilled the nurturing function. It has already been mentioned that she was addressed as Ambikā, "mother." She was, in fact, the Tantric generative force and mother *par excellence*:

II.7.37. *"By you* (Devī) *this universe is brought forth . . .*
by you this world is obtained."[95]
Ibid, I.75.

And she conferred riches and children upon those whom she deemed worthy.[96]

By taking on the aspects and functions of the other Indic goddesses, Devī also was associated with the epiphanies of the Neolithic bird and snake goddesses. She rode

II.7.38. *"in a chariot yoked with swans."*[97]
Ibid, XI.13.

and she carried

II.7.39. *"the trident, the moon, and the snake."*[98]
Ibid, XI.14.

In fact, as Shaktī, the goddess represented the particular energy, the Kuṇḍalinī, which is depicted as a snake.[99] Moreover, as the goddess Durga, she has been represented iconographically holding snakes in her arms.[100]

Devī, therefore, accrued a wealth of epithets and functions. Her powers were great, and her popularity was widespread. We must not, however, assume that the society which worshipped her was feminist, just because they honored a female deity. Her hymn tells of the rewards gained from worshipping her:

II.7.40. *"[Devī], when celebrated and greatly honored*
with flowers and incense rich in fragrance,
thus grants wealth,
sons,
a mind inclined toward virtue,

and prosperity.''[101]
Ibid, XII.41.

Were the society a feminist one, the goddess would have granted daughters as well as sons.

Also note, in this regard, a precept widespread through ancient India and recorded in a Hindu Law Code, the Manu Smṛti, which dates to the fifth century BCE:

II.7.41. *''Her father protects* [*her*] *in childhood,*
her husband protects [*her*] *in youth,*
and her sons protect [*her*] *in old age;*
a woman is never fit for independence.''[102]
Manu Smṛtiḥ IX.3; 5th Century BCE.

The pre-Indo-European Indic society may have been a feminist culture, or at least an equalitarian one, but assimilation with the Indo-European invaders rendered Indic culture in general more male-centered than its worship of a female personification of activating energy and omnipotence might indicate. With this caveat in mind, one may assert that this society was, nonetheless, *less* male-centered than those which worshipped (and worship) an omnipotent male deity, exclusively.

Many Indic goddesses have been discussed in this section. The primeval mother Aditi, giver of life to many of the Rigvedic gods, is balanced by Nirṛti, the goddess who represented death. Aditi and Nirṛti represent the "Goddess of Regeneration," goddess of birth, life, and death, as two ends of the same pole. The many manifestations of Devī, on the other hand, give a more assimilated depiction of a single "Goddess of Regeneration." The chthonic Nirṛti may be compared to the Baltic Lauma, or to Sumerian Ereshkigal, or even to Greek Persephone.

The watery Rigvedic goddess Sarasvatī who brought fortune and treasure may be compared to the Avestan Anāhitā. The goddesses Lakshmi and Alakshmi represented the poles of fortune and misfortune; Lakshmi echoes the Baltic Laima, Roman Fortuna, and Greek Tyche.

The syncretized Devī embodies most of the attributes of the prehistoric goddesses. Devī rides "in a chariot yoked with swans" and carries the snake in her arms. She is a goddess who grants life and takes it away again, and then grants it once again. Devī thus re-echoes the iconography of the Neolithic bird and snake goddesses, and she re-echoes the functions of the ancient "Goddess of Regeneration."

In sum, the "Great"-goddess Devī has been a powerful force in Indic society. She was and is[103] a goddess of multiple functions and manifold nature: not two-fold, representing dark and light, positive and negative, life and death; but manifold, representing the continuum of the life force, and all aspects of the feminine deity which contribute to that life force. Although several other goddesses were mentioned in more ancient Indic texts, the earlier goddesses were not imbued with the powers and the broad appeal of the Tantric goddess, Devī.

CHAPTER 8

Irish and Welsh goddesses

Because Celtic literature dates to a relatively late period, the beginning of the second millennium CE, our early records of Celtic religion—the religion of the ancient Irish, Welsh, and early inhabitants of "Gaul," among others—are gleaned from inscriptions, figurines, and from Roman descriptions of the Celtic gods. The Romans gave their own names to deities worshipped by the Celts; they thus describe a Celtic Jupiter, Mars, Minerva, and Vulcan. Figurines of the antlered *Cernunnos*, a god of prosperity,[1] have been found. Triads of goddesses, one of whom often holds a child, are described as *Matrones*.[2] The goddesses *Macha* and *Brigid* (the latter may be correlated with the Dea Brigantia found in Roman Britain) were also depicted in tripartite form. Macha will be discussed below, while Brigid will be discussed in Part Three.

Although we have early iconography, the greatest source of knowledge regarding Celtic goddesses comes from later texts. From them we learn of deities such as the goddess *Danu*, the mother of the *Túatha Dé Dānann*, who was called *Dôn* by the people of Wales.[3] The Irish *Lugh*, Welsh *Lleu*, the god of "the skilled hand," possessed such a radiant face that mortals could not keep their eyes upon him for any length of time; he was probably a sun-deity. He was a "jack of all trades:" a sorcerer, a carpenter, a smith. The chief of the Irish gods was *Eochaid Ollathair*, called *The Dagda*, the "good god." He was a divine magician, a warrior-god, and a patron of artisans: one of the rare Indo-European male deities who fulfilled all three of the Indo-European functions.[4]

ANCIENT IRISH GODDESSES AND HEROINES

Among the Celts, both goddesses and mortal women retained a great portion of their earlier powers and their autonomous character. They reflected pre-Indo-European roots and superimposed Indo-European characteristics. Thus, their "earlier" powers refers to those powers which they held before the advent of the Indo-Europeans.

Celtic goddesses were often believed to be imbued with magic powers: the goddesses *Badb, Macha*, and *Morrigan*[5] were *sorceresses*, and they often figured prominently in male rites of passage.

Other goddesses also figured in male rites of passage: the goddess *Scathach* introduced the young hero *Cú Chulainn* into the realm of the *warrior*, and the goddess *Flaith*, "sovereignty," introduced men into the kingship.

Goddesses were often associated with caves, which were believed to be entrances to the nether-world: Morrigan—often called "The Morrigan"—came

> II.8.1. " . . . *out of the cave*
> *of Crunchu,*
> [*her*] *suitable home* . . . "[6]
> Metrical Dindshenchas "Odras" 56;
> Recorded *ca*. 800–1100 CE.

Morrigan was often found on the battlefield, and she availed herself of shape-changing as she fought the Irish heroes. The Táin Bó Cuailnge, or "The Battle of the Bull of Cooley," is an epic which describes a war between two Irish tribes, the people of Ulster and those of Connacht, over a bull which belonged to the Ulster folk. In this epic, Morrigan contested with *Cú Chulainn*, an Ulster hero. First

> II.8.2. "*The Morrigan* [*appeared*] *there*
> *in the form of a white heifer*
> *with red ears.*"[7]
> Táin Bó Cuailnge 1992–1993;
> *ca*. 400 BCE to 100 CE; Recorded 1st to 7th Centuries CE.

Cú Chulainn attacked Morrigan, shattering one of her eyes. Then, quickly changing shape,

> II.8.3. *"The Morrigan [appeared] there*
> *in the form of a slippery eel . . . "*[8]
> Ibid, 1997–1998.

She coiled herself around the hero's legs, rendering them vulnerable to the blow of the Connacht hero Lóch, with whom she worked in concert to attempt to defeat Cú Chulainn; she then metamorphosed one more time:

> II.8.4. *"The Morrigan [appeared]*
> *in the form of a mangy,*
> *greyish-red she-wolf."*[9]
> Ibid, 2001.

In another tale, the Táin Bó Regamna, which supposedly preceded and predicted the more famous Táin Bó Cuailnge,[10] Cú Chulainn has words with an old woman whom he encounters on the road. The woman is a goddess who turns into

> II.8.5. *" . . . a bird . . . upon the branch nearby . . . "*[11]
> Táin Bó Regamna 5;
> *ca.* 400 BCE to *ca.* 100 CE; Recorded 1st to 7th Centuries CE.

The bird-woman then predicts the shape changes she will undergo when contesting the hero in the Táin Bó Cuailnge: heifer, eel, and she-wolf. The old woman metamorphosed into bird goddess, of course, was Morrigan. Morrigan was not successful in her encounter against the Ulster hero: it was not his time to die. Nonetheless, she was a goddess who was feared and respected for her powers.

Another Irish battlefield goddess seems at times to be synonymous with Morrigan. The goddess *Badb* was often called "the Badb;" like "the Morrigan" she was an awesome and ominous deity. After he battled against Lóch and the Morrigan, Cú Chulainn complained that he was attacked by

> II.8.6. *" . . . Lóch*
> *together with Badb,"*[12]
> Táin Bó Cuailnge 1094;
> *ca.* 400 BCE to *ca.* 100 CE; Recorded 1st to 7th Centuries CE.

perhaps using Badb as an epithet indicating "the battlefield goddess."

The name "Badb" indicates "a royston crow or vulture;"[13] Badb was a warrior-goddess who generally assumed the shape of a bird, as did Morrigan. To her bird-attributes one may compare those of several goddesses from other cultures, including the Greek *Pallas Athena,* and the Indic *Nirṛti.*

Badb haunted battlefields and prophesied death thereon. In the battles of the Táin,

> II.8.7. *"The Badb will shriek [at] the ford."*[14]
> Ibid, 2808.

Her shrieking is a grim warning of the carnage of war, and, indeed, she is called the "blood-red-mouthed,"[15] a reminder of the blood spilled in war. Compare her to the Indic goddess Devī, whose teeth became red after she devoured her enemies.[16]

Not only goddesses prophesied the difficulties of war. Human women were prophetesses as well.

> Before the battles of the Táin, Queen Medb,[17] the queen who was responsible for the battles over the Bull of Cooley, was driving along in her chariot. She came upon a beautiful young woman who was graced with teeth white as pearls, lustrous skin, and long blond hair. This woman was the prophetess *Feidelm,* and Medb asked her to prophesy the effect upon her Connacht army of the conflict against the Ulstermen.

> II.8.8. *"Oh, Prophetess Feidelm,*
> *how do you see our army?"*[18]
> Ibid, 205 ff.

Despite the fact that Medb assured her of the superior forces of the Connacht warriors, Feidelm replied, several times,

> II.8.9. *"I see brilliant red upon them,*
> *I see red."*[19]
> Ibid, 207 ff.

So Feidelm prophesied, despite Queen Medb's protests, that Connacht blood would be spilled, and that the queen's warriors would suffer greatly in the war—as they did.

Thus women, mortal as well as idealized, warned of the ruin that would be caused by war, then as now.

Badb and Morrigan, both endowed with the avian attributes characteristic of the Neolithic bird-goddesses, were banished by the Irish to the nether-realms, and were associated with caves and with death.

Bird-personification was a common phenomenon among Irish female figures. The mother of the hero Cú Chulainn, *Dechtire,* appears at the beginning of one of the versions of Cú Chulainn's birth story. She first comes to the plain before Emain, accompanied by fifty young women, all

> II.8.10. *"in the form of a bird."*[20]
> Compert Cú Chulainn 4; *ca.* 800 CE.

Badb, Morrigan, and Dechtire were female figures who assimilated somewhat intact features from the pre-Indo-European culture which inhabited Neolithic "Ireland;" their "bird-goddess" affiliations are still quite evident. This was, however, not the only sort of assimilation practiced by the Indo-Europeans. They were often wont to impose their own attitudes or structure upon indigenous goddesses, rendering them a mixture of pre-Indo-European and Indo-European characteristics. Such was the case with the Irish *Macha,* who not only received Indo-European equine personification—that is, she was made to undergo the functions of a horse—but who also was given Indo-European tripartite functions.

One will recall that the Indo-European society was a tripartite one; that is, it recognized three functions, those of *priest, warrior,* and *nurturer of the population*. Macha, as a tripartite goddess—or rather, as a transfunctional one—was divided into three distinct mythological personages. She is designated a "transfunctional" goddess because she spans *all* of the possible functions, unlike a deity who would participate in only *one* of three possible functions. Although Macha spanned all three of the Indo-European functions, the Irish viewed her as three separate goddesses, each of whom fulfilled one or more functions, and each of whom had her own particular history.

The first Macha was a prophetess. Her husband, *Nemed,* was "the sacred one."[21] Macha both foretold and caused much of the distress suffered by the Ulstermen in the Táin.[22] She, therefore, served the first function of wisdom, knowledge, and prophecy, all qualities which belonged to the intermediaries of the deities: the priests.

The second Macha was called *Macha Mongruad,* "red-maned Macha." She was the daughter of Aed Ruad, one of three co-sovereign[23] kings of Ireland, according to a pact. Each of these kings was to rule for seven years, and each did indeed rule three times. Aed Ruad was the first of the kings to die. Upon her father's death, Macha Mongruad demanded that she be allowed to fulfill his term of office. A battle ensued, for neither of the kings would willingly give up the sovereignty to a woman. Macha was victorious;[24] she ruled for seven years. Then one of the two surviving kings, King Dithorba, died. Upon his death, his five sons wished to reclaim the throne from Macha. Unwilling to relinquish her rule, she made battle with them. Again victorious, she exiled the sons of Dithorba.

Macha than married a man called Cimbaeth, and she made him her general. However, it was *she* who retained the rule and the power. Afterwards, taking the shape of a leper, she pursued the sons of Dithorba. In spite of her leprosy, the youths were physically attracted to her. Each went alone with her to the woods, and she overcame each in turn and bound him. She then led all of the brothers to Ulster, and forced them to build a *rath*, a "fortress," for her in the city of Emain. She shaped the boundaries of Emain with her brooch,[25] and that city became the capital of Ulster.

Macha Mongruad later *fell in battle*, slain by a warrior whose name was *Rechtaid red-wrist*.[26] Thus war and warriors predominated in the second Macha's life; the martial blood-*red* color of her "mane" and of her slayer's wrist were integral parts of her characterization. She was a martial goddess, and one who held the sovereignty of Ireland.

The third Macha married a farmer, Cruin, who thereupon increased his material prosperity. Macha was a model wife, and she bore to Cruin two children in a rather curious manner.

> Cruin one day went to a fair, and, against his wife's wishes, revealed—indeed, bragged—to King Conchobor that his wife was more fleet of foot than the King's horses. The king, fascinated, ordered Cruin to bring his wife to a race. If she did not do so, added Conchobor, Cruin would lose his life.
>
> Although Macha arrived promptly at the fairgrounds, lest she incur the king's wrath, she begged him for a respite, because she was in her ninth month of pregnancy. The king remained fascinated but not troubled by compassion. The contest proceeded as ordered, and Macha raced the horses to the end of the green. She proved swifter than they, and she won the race. Just as she reached the finish-line she delivered "twins, a boy and a girl"[27] (some say that she delivered a mare and a boy).[28] As she died,[29] the infants screamed, and the sound cast the men of Ulster into a strange sickness: each man, and his descendants through several generations, at his time of greatest need, would suffer "pangs," becoming no stronger than a woman in childbed.[30] That is, when the Ulstermen needed their military strength the most, that was the time when they would be deprived of their martial prowess. Conchobor's victory was a "pyrrhic" one.

Thus, when the Ulster warriors battled those of Connacht over the Brown Bull of Cooley, the Ulstermen lost much fighting time, incapacitated by their "pangs." They were saved by Cú Chulainn, who was not originally of the Ulster line.

The three Machas cannot be divided into truly distinct functional levels, as some scholars have attempted to do.[31] The three often overlapped in the ancient Irish texts, and, further, the third Macha, wife of Cruin the farmer, was more than just third-function "fertility"-symbol. Although she did bring both prosperity and children to her husband, she had another, quite important, attribute: she fulfilled the function of a *horse*,[32] as manifested in her race with the horses of King Conchobor. Horses were generally representative of the warrior-function, since it was on horseback that the martial Indo-Europeans conquered their enemies in combat.

We briefly discussed *Queen Medb*, and her attempted seizure of the Brown Bull. Similarly to Macha, Medb was a transfunctional goddess-turned-heroine.[33] She too was portrayed in Irish literature as a multiple character. Separate histories were given for *Medb of Leinster* and *Medb of Connacht*, but Medb has the same character traits in both of her personifications.

Medb, queen of the Irish province of Connacht, was wife of King Ailill. In this king-queen relationship, the rules were quite different from those of other royal couples. Not only did Queen Medb *not* live in the shadow of her husband's sovereignty: he was quite overshadowed by *her*. Medb lived outside the boundaries of Indo-European male-centered mores, and she had the power to establish rules of behavior for her husband. Says Medb,

II.8.11. *"I asked for a wonderful bridal gift*
which no woman ever before
had asked
of a man of the men of Ireland,
that is,
a husband without stinginess,
without jealousy,
without fear.''[34]
Táin Bó Cuailnge 27–28;
ca. 400 BCE to 100 CE; recorded 1st to 7th Centuries CE.

How many Indo-European women, divine or mortal, could order their husbands to be without jealousy? In fact, she continued,

II.8.12. *"If the man with whom I should be*
were jealous,
it would not be proper,
for I was never before
without a man
[waiting] close by
in the shadow of another.''[35]
Ibid, 36–37.

Medb was anomalous in Indo-European literature, because the Indo-European men were quite possessive of their womenfolk.[36] Her powers, which we shall enlarge upon shortly, and her *autonomy*, must be explained in terms of economics.[37] In Ireland, inheritance was both matrilineal and patrilineal, and, further, women as well as men could inherit goods.[38] Thus economically independent women existed in ancient Ireland. This social independence was mirrored in Irish literature and mythology, where goddesses and heroines could be autonomous in a way impossible for female figures in strictly patrilineal cultures. Thus, the Greek *Hera*,[39] wife of the king of the gods, *Zeus*, was quite dependent upon her husband. In fact Hera, when confronted with Zeus' philandering, could respond only with anger, never with activity similar to his. Women in Greece, just as women in Rome, India, Iran, and throughout the rest of the Indo-European world, were expected to be chaste and faithful.

Irish women of means were well-regarded and given a place of substance in the society. In Ireland, if a woman had the same background and fortune as her husband, her rights tended to be equal to his. She was called *"a woman of equal lordship."*[40] The consent of such a woman was required for almost all of her husband's contracts. In fact, if a woman had a greater fortune than her husband, the man was called a *man of service* and the marriage was called *a man with a woman of property with service*.[41]

On an epic level, in the "pillow talk" between Medb and Ailill, where Medb made those remarkable statements about male jealousy, each of them tried to prove greater wealth. Medb knew that whoever possessed the greater wealth would "wear the pants" in the family. The whole epic of the Táin centers around Queen Medb's attempted robbery of a neighboring bull, "the Brown Bull of Cooley," and the ensuing war over the bull. Medb's wealth was just equal to that of Ailill—save one bull.

Economics, however, does not entirely explain Medb's power. As we mentioned above, she was a *transfunctional* goddess. Not only was she a *sovereign queen* in her own right, rather than just consort or "vice-president," a queen

II.8.13. *"of fiery power . . . "*[42]
Metrical Dindshenchas "Ath Luain" 17.
Recorded *ca.* 800 to *ca.* 1100 CE.

She was also a *warrior* in her own right, leading the campaign against the province of Ulster, in hope of capturing the Brown Bull; she was

II.8.14. " . . . *best . . .*
in battle and encounter and contention. . . "[43]
Táin Bó Cuailnge 16;
ca. 400 BCE to *ca.* 100 CE; recorded 1st to 7th Centuries CE.

rather than just a source of energy or encouragement for fighting *men*. She was, finally, a nurturing figure,

II.8.15. " . . . *the most generous* (lit. "the best")
[of all of her sisters]
in pledges and bestowal [of gifts] "[44]
Ibid, 15–16.

and she was a fount of sexuality as well, enjoying several husbands and numerous lovers. Medb's sexuality, and particularly, her numerous husbands and her *power over them*, can be explained by the fact that she *was* sovereignty; the kingship could come to a man only through marriage to her. Thus, a man who wanted to be king would do his best to retain her good will.[45]

Thus, Irish female figures in general, and Queen Medb in particular, enjoyed multiple functions and considerable power. The patri-matrilineal inheritance pattern, and potential economic viability of the Irish women, most likely explain their autonomy and sociological viability. *Whatever* factor is responsible for the autonomy of Irish female figures, it is significant that they resisted the dominance-subordination pattern imposed over the other Indo-European cultures by the Indo-European patriarchs.

WELSH GODDESSES AND HEROINES

Ancient Welsh female figures were not as autonomous as some of their Irish sisters, but their powers and myths were often similar.

One Welsh goddess in particular echoes many of the qualities of other goddesses in Indo-European cultures. Although *Rhiannon* has her own story, many of the characteristics of her myth and her *persona* may be recognized in other mythologies or epicized myth.

Rhiannon appeared in the first "*branch*," or chapter, of the Mabinogi[46] as a mysterious lady riding a white horse. No matter what the speed of the horsemen who pursued her, she could not be overtaken until *Pwyll*, prince of Dyfed, requested of her that she speak with him. The two had been fated to meet, and they soon married. Rhiannon subsequently gave birth to a son, which was spirited away on the night of its birth. The serving-women, who should have been watching over the mother and baby, fell asleep, and, terrified when they awoke to the loss of the child, they decided to cover their tracks. They killed some pups, and pretended that the bones and blood of the animals were those of the baby boy; they swore that Rhiannon herself had destroyed her son.

Pwyll could not divorce Rhiannon for the supposed murder of their son, since only barrenness rendered such a severe decree. Rhiannon was instead made to perform a substitute penance for her wrongdoing. The penance was a curious one: she was condemned to sit near a horse-block outside the city gate, and to carry passersby on her back to the king's fortress. She became, in essence, a *horse-substitute*.

The equine element in Rhiannon's story does not end here. At the very time that Rhiannon bore her son, the mare of Teyrnon Twrf Liant was about to foal. Just as the mare bore a large handsome colt, a great claw reached through the window of the house, attempting to seize it. Teyrnon drew his sword and lopped off the arm, and then heard a great noise outside. He rushed out, but could see nothing. However, when he returned to his house, he found an infant boy, of obviously noble birth, lying by the door.

Teyrnon and his wife raised the boy who grew quite large and strong for his age, and the colt was given to the boy when he was in his fourth year. At this time, Teyrnon heard of Rhiannon's misfortune, discovered a likeness between his foster-son and Pwyll, brought the boy to the castle, and related the whole adventure of the mare and the boy. Rhiannon cried out in joy,

> II.8.16. *''Between me and God . . .*
> *if that should be true,*
> *I [may] cast off*
> *my anxiety (pryder)!''*[47]
> Mabinogi "Pwyll Pendeuic Dyuet" 614–615; *ca.* 1300 CE.

and the boy was named Pryderi.

Rhiannon, however, was not yet delivered of her equine punishments. In the third *branch* of the Mabinogi, following the death of Pwyll, Rhiannon married Pryderi's friend, Manawydan. After a number of adventures, Rhiannon and Pryderi disappeared into the magic fortress of Llwyd son of Cil Coed. As punishment, Rhiannon was made to wear around her neck the collars of donkeys, after they had been carrying hay.

Rhiannon, the goddess-turned-magical queen, was similar to other Celtic goddesses, such as Macha, in that she was treated as a horse and underwent equine-related punishment. The Celtic horse-goddess seems to be relatively unique. Many Indo-European goddesses from other areas had hippomorphic characteristics. The Greek goddesses *Athena, Hera,* and the Mycenaean *Potnia Hippia* all were given the epithet *Hippia,* "horse-goddess." *Demeter Melaina of Phigalia* and *Demeter of Thelpousa* were given equine form. The Indic *Saraṇyū* metamorphosed into a mare. None of these other goddesses, however, were solely horse-goddesses. Only among the Celts was there a goddess specifically called "horse:" the Gaulish goddess *Epona*[48] was the only Indo-European goddess who was horse-goddess and nothing more.

Rhiannon may have been a more deeply personified version of the Celtic horse-goddess, or she may have been one of the Celtic versions of the sacrificed mare. Although she did not lose her life, as did her Irish sister, Macha, her horse-related punishments may indeed have been substitutes for the more extreme sacrifice.

Rhiannon was also connected with birds. In the second *branch* of the Mabinogi, the bodiless head of Bendigeidfran, son of *Llyr,* talked to his seven friends for seven years, while the *birds of Rhiannon* sang. The birds seem, in this case, to further underline both the magic of Rhiannon and that of the talking head, and they serve further to relate Rhiannon to the goddess associated with birds. As did "Queen" Medb, Rhiannon became an epic heroine, but her birds too invoke her original divinity. Rhiannon is thus not simply "magical woman" but a continuation of the Neolithic European goddesses.

Irish and Welsh folk-tales and myths bear similarities, but there are also differences in their characterizations of female-figures. The equine element is strong in the personification of both Irish and Welsh goddesses, but other features of their personification differ. Most importantly, there is a difference in the allocation of powers and functions. Whereas Medb and at least the second Macha were strong female figures with several functions and a good deal of autonomy, Rhiannon was to a great extent carried by the fates. Although she was a magical woman, she was not able to use that magic to relieve herself of her anxiety. Only the fates, and Teyrnon Twrf Liant, could release her misfortune.

One more tale, which we shall refer to again later,[49] illustrates the differences between Irish goddesses and their Welsh counterparts.

In the story of the Welsh *King Math,* which is found at the beginning of the fourth *branch* of the Mabinogi, Math was required to keep his feet *in a virgin's lap* during the intervals between wars. One maiden who thus served him was Goewin, daughter of Pebin. Her beauty caught the eye of one of Math's nephews, Gilfaethwy, son of Dôn, and he fell in "love" with her. He raped her, and she immediately became "defused," as it were; it became necessary for Math to seek another virgin to be his source of energy.

Throughout Indo-European societies both virginity and chastity are highly important commodities. A Medb, with her lovers closely succeeding one another, could only perhaps be duplicated by an Aphrodite, who was, however, *only* allowed the functions of love and sex.[50] All other female figures, divine and mortal, were closely overseen by their male husbands or guardians. In Wales, as in most other Indo-European societies, virginity had an almost concrete usefulness. In Ireland, neither virginity nor chastity were all-important, perhaps again because of the combined female-male patterns of inheritance.

Several Celtic goddesses manifest bird and snake iconography. The shape-changer, Morrigan, could metamorphose into many animals, including a bird and an eel. Badb was a warrior-goddess who assumed bird-form. Badb prophesied *death* on battlefields, and, as such, she may be compared to the Germanic Valkyries: the battlefield goddesses who also took on the plumage of birds. The magical Rhiannon is further associated with birds, and she and the three-fold Macha were associated with the *horse*. Other important Celtic female figures were the three-fold Brigid, and the queenly "wife," Medb.

Although Celtic female-figures share many features with other Indo-European goddesses and heroines, personifications such as Medb remind us that the *Irish* female-figure occupies a unique place in Indo-European society.

CHAPTER 9

Germanic goddesses

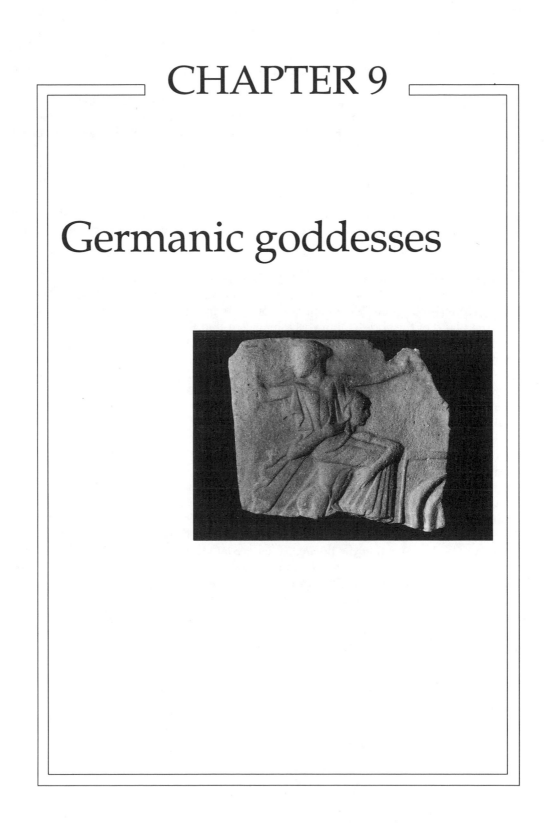

The ancient Germanic tribes lived south of the Scandinavian peninsula, in the islands of the Baltic Sea, and on the North Germanic plain between the Rhine and Vistula Rivers.

The Germanic peoples were actually three distinct tribes; they spoke dialects of one language but they fought with one another. Those who lived in the east, the Goths, migrated toward the Black Sea *circa* 200 CE. The Northern Germanic peoples, often called the Old Norse or Old Icelandic peoples, occupied the Scandinavian countries. The Germans who lived in the west were the ancestors of the modern Germans and of the Anglo-Saxons. The latter group were the progenitors of the modern English peoples.

We know nothing of the pagan religion of the east Germanic peoples, the Goths; their first writings date to after the fourth century CE, and they are a translation of the Christian Bible. The legends which were told by the West Germanic peoples were, for the most part, not handed down. The literati were monks, and they were not very interested in pagan religion.

Most of the legends and mythology of the Germanic peoples are preserved, then, in Scandinavian works, especially the Eddas. The Eddas describe several male deities, including *Oðin (Wodan)*, the chief of one tribe of Germanic gods, the *Aesir*, who inhabited *Asgard*, the "land of the gods." Oðin was a magician-god and a warrior-god. He received half of the dead from the battlefield, and he was a type of general, directing battles. The true Germanic warrior-god, however, was *Þor (Donar)*; he, like the Greek Zeus, wielded the thunder-bolt, and he was physically the most powerful of the gods. *Tyr (Tiwaz)* was a god who was courageous in battle, and was an upholder of contracts. The trickster god, *Loki*, was harsh-tongued, and he seemed to enjoy shocking his peers. He earned the gods' wrath by contributing to the death of *Baldr*, the most handsome and most innocent of the gods. Baldr represented the "dying" god whose sacrifice is described in mythologies worldwide.

Gods of the other tribe of deities, the *Vanir*, include *Njǫrðr*, who was invoked for seafaring and fishing, and who bestowed prosperity upon mortals, and his two children, *Freyr*, who controlled the sun, the rain, and the fruitfulness of the earth, and *Freyja*. We shall discuss Freyja and the other Germanic goddesses below.

The Eddas reflect early oral tradition, but the manuscripts date to the early second millennium CE. It seems that the poetic Eddas predate the prose Eddas, which are dateable to *circa* 1200 CE. The latter were composed by *Snorri Sturleson*, a man who included many of the poems from the earlier writings into his work.

We, therefore, have very little truly ancient literature written by the Germans; our earliest knowledge of their culture comes from a group which invaded their lands in the first century BCE: the Romans. The Roman historian *Tacitus* wrote a book called the Germania; in it he describes the culture and customs of the Germanic peoples with whom the Romans came into contact:

> II.9.1. ". . . *(girls and boys)*
> *who are of the same size,*
> *of similar height,*
> *and equal in strength,*
> *are mated . . .*
> *the children of sisters*
> *have the same status with an uncle*
> *as with a father.*
> *Some think that this blood-tie*
> *is even more sacred and closer*
> *than that between father and son . . .* "[1]
> Tacitus, Germania 20; born *ca.* 55 CE.

Many have assumed that this avuncular relationship indicates matrilineality, although the opposite has been argued.[2] Whether the society was matrilineal or patrilineal, we note that *uncles* are mentioned with regard to these children, but *aunts* are not mentioned. The society was not a *matriarchal* one. Tacitus gives further evidence of patriarchy:

> II.9.2. ''. . . *adulteries are very few . . .*
> *among such a populous folk,*
> *and punishment is immediate*
> *and is entrusted to the husband . . .* ''[3]
> Ibid, 19.

Thus, the double-standard was alive and well among the ancient Germans. In fact, Indo-European Germanic mythology was quite male-centered. The cults which have extant descriptions were predominantly masculine, involving male farmers and warriors. Pre-Indo-European evidence from the same area, on the other hand, reflects quite a different state of affairs. Many late Bronze Age female figures were found; they wore short skirts, neck torques, were bare-breasted, and had plaited hair.[4] It is interesting that bronze rings and neck-torques, and apparently sacrificed humans who wore blindfolds or nooses around their necks, were found in Danish peat-bogs.[5] The nooses closely resembled the neck-torques, since the latter were twisted and coiled. Some archaeologists believe that the neck torques, rings, and humans were offerings to an ancient goddess,[6] and Tacitus seems to support this view. He tells us that the goddess *Nerthus*[7] was led in ritual procession through a village, and then returned to her temple.

> II.9.3. ''*Then, the wagon and the robes, and,*
> *if you are willing to believe it,*
> *the deity in person,*
> *are washed in a sequestered lake;*
> *slaves ministrate to her,*
> *and then immediately the lake swallows them.*''[8]
> Ibid, 40.

This act of lustration was probably a symbolic re-actualization of renewal, a regeneration of the vital forces, of the creative energies, of the goddess. When slaves were sacrificed to her, this added more "fuel" to her energies, and, further, contributed to the fertility of the earth.

The Bronze Age female figures represented with neck-torque remind one of female figurines with similar torques found throughout Mesopotamia, dating from *ca*. 3500 BCE on.[9] The torques may reflect a European tradition which began no later than the Bronze Age, and continued in some areas until the Iron Age.

The torqued goddess appears on other artifacts, in addition to figurines: the famous silver *Gundestrup Cauldron*,[10] which was probably of Celtic workmanship but which shows Germanic religious scenes, depicts several female figures. One figure is a woman wearing a torque, surrounded by wheels and by fabulous animals, including *birds*. Once again, birds are connected with the goddess.

The torqued goddess, whether "Nerthus" or her precursor, was not a beneficent mother-goddess, but was a purveyor of death as well as of life, one who demanded human sacrifice. She may have been the "life force" personified.[11]

The Germanic pantheon contained several significant goddesses, some of which are quite similar to other European and Near Eastern goddesses. One, the goddess *Hel*, guarded the Germanic underworld. According to Snorri, Hel was a daughter of Loki. She had

> II.9.4. ''. . . *power over nine regions,*
> *[with the condition] that*
> *she share all [her] food and lodging*

with those who were sent to her,
that is, men who were dead of sickness,
and dead of old age.''[12]
Snorri, "Gylfaginning" 34; *ca*. 1200 CE.

She was a rather frightening-looking woman:

II.9.5. *She is half black,*
and half flesh-colored;
because of this she is easily recognizable;
moreover, she is rather stern-looking
and fierce-looking.[13]
Ibid.

Hel may be compared to *Persephone*, the queen of the Greek underworld; but she may be more particularly compared to the Sumerian goddess *Ereshkigal*, who was the true ruler of the lower realms, unlike the Greek queen-consort.

One triad of major Germanic deities, the virgin *Norns*, had functions and powers similar to those of goddesses in many other cultures. The Norns were the Germanic *fates*, and they determined the flow of one's existence, the length of one's life, and, ultimately, the moment of death. Their decisions were inescapable. The Norns were represented in varied numbers, but they were most commonly depicted as *three* in number. They were, therefore, comparable to the Baltic *Laima*, who sometimes appeared as a plural deity, and more particularly to the Greek *Moirai*, and the Roman *Parcae*, who often appeared as three entities. The Germanic Norns represented past, present, and future.

In their beneficent aspect, the Norns gave gifts and blessings to an infant at her or his birth. However, when malevolent, they could take away the baby's life. In this function the Norns were again comparable to Laima and the other goddesses of fate.

The Danish historian *Saxo Grammaticus*, who lived in the twelfth to thirteenth centuries of this era, wrote a history of the Danes in sixteen volumes, in Latin. He described a Danish king, Fridleif, who went to consult the oracles of the Fates (*Parcarum oracula*) about the destiny of his child Olaf. In the house of the gods (*deorum aedes*) he saw three maidens (*nymphis*) seated, who in answer to his request determined the character of his son. The first two granted boons to the child; the third gave him stinginess.[14]

This sort of tale, of course, gave rise to the fairy tale, "Sleeping Beauty," wherein three good fairies gave gifts to a princess, but a bad fairy conferred a cursed fate upon her.

In the Germanic poem, the Vǫluspá, a seeress tells of the beginning of the world: how the heavens and the earth were created out of nothingness. Then the gods built shrines and temples, and made implements for work, and they played games and had much gold. This "Golden Age" came to an abrupt halt when "three maidens" from the race of giants came along and spoiled things. They introduced the necessity of *fate*.

II.9.6. *''Thence come maidens*
three,
having knowledge of many things . . .
Urth[15] *one is called;*
the second Verthandi . . . [16]
Skuld[17] *the third.*
They laid down laws,
they chose life
for the children of people;
they tell fates.''[18]
Poetic Edda, "Vǫluspá" 20; *ca*. 1000 CE.

The poem goes on to tell of how the world will end.

The Fates or Norns were wise women, for they could prophesy, and even create, the future. There were mortal women among the Germanic peoples who were also believed to be possessed of prophetic powers. Several Romans, observing and writing about the Germanic tribes, described *priestesses* with prophetic powers:

> II.9.7. *The Germans "believe that [in women]*
> *there is a certain divine and prophetic sense:*
> *they neither spurn their counsels*
> *nor slight their answers."*[19]
> Tacitus, Germania 8; born *ca*. 55 CE.

Their counsels could even extend to the realm of war, usually a masculine sphere in Indo-European cultures:

> II.9.8. *"There was a custom among the Germans*
> *that their matrons should declare*
> *by lots and divinations*
> *whether it was expedient or not*
> *to engage in battle."*[20]
> Caesar, de Bello Gallico I.50; *ca*. 100 BCE.

Further, priestesses among one Germanic tribe, the Cimbri, were

> II.9.9. *". . . grey-haired seeresses, dressed in white . . .*
> *armed with swords*
> *[these priestesses] would meet*
> *with the prisoners of war*
> *throughout the camp . . .*
> *[and] would cut the throat*
> *of each [prisoner] . . .*
> *and from the blood which poured forth*
> *into the vessel*
> *some [of the priestesses]*
> *would make a prophecy . . . "*[21]
> Strabo, Geography VII.2.3; *ca*. 64 BCE to 21 CE.

And so, among the Germanic tribes, there was a belief that certain female entities were both powerful and wise. Wise women, mortal and immortal, were responsible for much of the process of birth, life, and death among those peoples.

Many female deities were described in both the Poetic Eddas and the Prose Eddas. The deities included giants and giantesses, and the deities more characteristic of the other pantheons we have discussed.

Skaði was a giantess. The gods had killed her father, the giant Þyassi, and she was quite angry with them.

> II.9.10. *"Further, Skaði,*
> *daughter of the giant Þjassi,*
> *took helmet and coat of mail*
> *and all [her] weapons,*
> *and she went to Asgarð,*
> *in order to avenge her father.*
> *Now, the Aesir offered to her*
> *a settlement and compensation;*
> *and first,*
> *that she should choose for herself*
> *a husband from among the gods,*
> *and [she had] to choose from his feet,*
> *and [she could] see nothing more of him.*
> *Then she saw one man's feet,*
> *exceedingly beautiful,*
> *and she said:*
> *"I choose him!*

There can be little [that is] ugly
in Baldr!''
(continued).

Since Baldr was the most handsome of all the gods, Skaði thought that those beautiful feet must surely belong to him. However, she had chosen the wrong feet:

II.9.11. ''. . . *that was Njǫrðr of Nóatún.''*[22]
Snorri, Prose Edda, "Bragarœður" 2; *ca.* 1200 CE.

Thus Skaði was given her choice of all the gods,[23] but, because of her handicap, she ended up with Njǫrðr,[24] a Germanic god associated with fertility and the sea. Skaði married Njǫrðr, but, having little in common, they lived apart. Skaði lived in the mountains, and her husband lived by the sea. According to Snorri, Skaði

II.9.12. ''. . . *often goes about*
on skis,
and with her bow
she shoots wild animals.''[25]
Snorri, "Gylfaginning" 23.

It would appear that Skaði, similar to the Greek *Artemis*, preferred autonomy to married togetherness. Like Artemis, Skaði was a "Mistress of Animals," content to roam the mountainside; and although Skaði was married, she lived as though she were a virgin, similar to the virgin Artemis.

Freyja, "the lady," was twin sister of Freyr and was the Germanic goddess of love. From her name was later derived the Germanic polite term "*frau*."[26] She was connected with war and with love. We are told that whenever she rides into battle, to her lot falls half of the slain warriors.[27] Her chariot is drawn by two cats,[28] animals which may represent the earlier Neolithic European lions which accompanied some of the goddesses.[29]

Her most important function, however, seems to be that of love-goddess. Love-poetry is pleasing to her; she is invoked for help in love-affairs.[30] In keeping with this function of fertility and nurturing, Freyja is sometimes called *Gefn*, "giver," and *Sýr*, "sow."[31] She was thus the mother *par excellence*, as was the sow.

Because she was goddess of love, the satirical poem, the "Lokasenna," accuses her of promiscuity:

II.9.13. ''*Freyja . . .*
all Aesir and alfs
who are here within
each one have you embraced,
you adulteress!''[32]
Poetic Edda, "Lokasenna" 30; *ca.* 1000 CE.

Further, the same poem states:

II.9.14. ''*Freyja . . .*
you're a whore,
and [you were] really mixed up in mischief
when the happy gods
caught you in your brother's [embrace] . . . ''[33]
Ibid, 32.

There is no myth of a love affair between Freyja and her brother, Freyr, and we may assume that Loki was casting vain aspersion upon the goddess. However, Freyja did represent desirable femininity to gods and mortals alike.

Once, we are told, a builder offered to make an excellent stronghold for the gods. He stipulated this, however, as his reward: he was to have Freyja as his wife and possession of the sun and moon besides. (Perhaps all three of the boons were considered to be equally wonderful, or equally impossible.) He built the stronghold, but Loki tricked him out of his reward.[34]

So, Freyja did not have to sleep with the master builder. However, to obtain her famous golden necklace from the four dwarves who crafted it, she was required to pass one night with each of them. She did so.[35]

Freyja had a falcon coat, and she often lent her "feather form" to others.[36] Thus, as goddess who could take on bird-shape, she was linked to the Neolithic bird-goddess. She was a love-goddess with avian attributes, the sort of goddess whom we will come across again, in the Greco-Roman personifications of Aphrodite and Venus.

As we discussed, one of the epithets for Freyja was *Gefn*, "giver." This epithet may be connected with the name of another Germanic goddess, *Gefjon*. Gefjon had a personality quite distinct from the usual personality of Freyja, however. She was one of the main pantheon of Germanic deities, the *Aesir*, and in the tales of King Gylfi, she was given the persona of a beggar-woman:

There was a beggar-woman who once entertained King Gylfi of Sweden so well that he promised to the woman an area of land as great as four oxen could plough in a day and a night. Since she was a goddess, she took four oxen from Giantland. These oxen happened to be her sons by a giant. The plough

II.9.15. *''went in so sharply and deeply*
that it loosened up the land
and the oxen dragged the land
out towards the sea,
and to the west,
and they stopped in a certain strait.
In that place Gefjon placed the land
and gave it a name,
and called it Sealand [Zealand].''[37]
Snorri, "Gylfaginning" 1; *ca*. 1200 CE.

It is interesting that it was her *sons* who ploughed the land for her, because Snorri says, later on in the Edda, that

II.9.16. *''. . . Gefjon,*
she is a virgin,
and [that woman] serves her
who dies when still a maiden.''[38]
Ibid, 35.

The term "virgin," in Old Norse and in most ancient European and Near Eastern cultures, indicated either a sexually untouched woman *or* a young woman who had never been married. Thus both the physical state of the goddess Gefjon, and her relationship to other goddesses such as Freyja, remain somewhat ambivalent.

A tale was told of Freyja's brother, *Freyr*, "the lord," and his "seduction" of the giantess, *Gerð* (Gerth).

One day, Freyr climbed up into the seat of the great god, Oðin. From there, he was able to see into all of the worlds. To the north, in the Underworld, he saw a beautiful maiden, a giantess, daughter of two cliff-giants. He exclaimed,

II.9.17. *''In the court of [the giant] Gymir,*
I saw walking along

a maiden for me to desire;
her arms shone;
and from them
[shone] all the air and sea.''[39]
Poetic Edda, "For Skírnis" 6; *ca.* 1000 CE.

The giantess was infused with light and bringer of the light:

II.9.18. *''When she reached up her hands*
and opened the door before her,
then her hands shone out
both in the heavens
and upon the sea,
and all the world
was illumined
from her.''[40]
Snorri, "Gylfaginning" 37; *ca.* 1200 CE.

Freyr's servant, Skirnir, was sent to woo the maiden. He first offered her the apples of eternal youth, and the ring, Draupnir.[41] Gerð refused all of the gifts. Then the messenger offered to cut off her head with his sword if she kept refusing to meet his master. He continued cajoling: he threatened to make her ugly with his magic wand, so that she would never be married, and that caused her to change her mind. She decided to meet Freyr after nine nights, and to grant him her "love."

The poem ends with Skirnir, the messenger, reporting back to Freyr, and with Freyr wondering how he can manage to wait until she arrives:

II.9.19. *''One night is long,*
two are longer,
how will I survive three?''[42]
Poetic Edda, "For Skírnis" 42; *ca.* 1000 CE.

However, one suspects that the story ends happily—for Freyr, at least.

Gerð, the giantess whose arms illuminated the world, was most likely a sun-maiden, although she was not related to the Indo-European sun-maidens whom we discussed above.[43] Gerð, as were many Germanic female figures, was a combination of goddess and vulnerable mortal. Her fear of ugliness connotes either a particular feminine vulnerability *or* what the male mythopoets *thought* would be a terrible thing for a woman.

Freyja may be considered the first *Valkyrie*[44] or battlefield-goddess, since she chooses half of those who were slain on the battlefield.[45] Unlike Freyja, however, the later Valkyries were required to be virgins.

The Valkyries were maidens who chose warriors destined to die in battle and to be awarded victory.[46] They also served as cup-bearers in Valhalla.[47] The Valkyries were helmeted goddesses who could turn themselves into *swan-maidens*. If a man succeeded in stealing their plumage, they could not escape from him, and they had to do his will.[48]

One particularly famous Valkyrie was the epic heroine, *Brynhild*. This warrior-maiden incurred the wrath of the great god, Oðin, because of events which occurred after she had allowed herself to be surprised by a man.

One day Brynhild and eight of her sisters descended from their swan flight[49] and removed their plumage. A hero-king saw their clothing and decided to steal it, thereby putting the maidens in his power. Brynhild, thus under thrall, was compelled to kill the king's adversary: a man who happened to be a protégé of Oðin.

Oðin was angry with Brynhild, and he pricked her with a magic thorn, throwing her into a profound slumber. He then enclosed her in a dwelling encircled by a wall of flame. The only man who could save her would be the brave hero who could ride his horse through the flames. The hero was meant to marry Brynhild, and this meant that she could no longer be a Valkyrie, since she would have lost her virgin status.

After some time, one such hero, Sigurð, was out on his travels, when he saw before him a great light, and flames reaching to the skies. He drew nearer to the light, and then he beheld a shield-hung castle before him. He entered the castle, and he saw a creature sleeping there, armed for battle. Curious as to what manner of man might be lying there asleep, Sigurð removed the helmet from the warrior's head, and

II.9.20. *''He saw that it was a woman.*
She was in a coat of mail,
and it was as tight
as if it were grown to her flesh.''[50]
Vølsunga Saga 21; *ca.* 1400 CE.

Nonetheless, he cut off her armor as easily as if it were cloth, and she awakened. Sigurð told her that he had heard of both her beauty and her wisdom.[51] Brynhild told him how she had come to be sleeping in a burning castle, fully armed, and she told him many runes besides. Then answered Sigurð,

II.9.21. *''In all the world*
there is found
[no] wiser woman than you,
and, as a matter of fact,
give me more wise counsel!''[52]
Ibid, 22.

Brynhild gave to Sigurð more advice. Then the hero once again told her that no one was wiser than she, and he further declared,

II.9.22. *''This I swear,*
that I shall marry you,
and you are equal in my mind.''[53]
Ibid.

So Brynhild was both beautiful and intelligent, so wise that Sigurð considered her his equal. Brynhild was a paragon among Germanic heroines: she was both a repository of wisdom and a warrior. Further, Brynhild was a heroine endowed with bird-plumage. All of the Valkyries, then, were connected to the ancient bird-goddess, beginning with the love-and-war-goddess, Freyja.

The ancient Scandinavian goddess *Frigg*, the "loved one,"[54] was the god *Oðin's* wife, and the protectress of marriage. Loki, in the satirical *Lokasenna*, tried to impugn her:

II.9.23. *''Frigg . . .*
you have always been wild for men,
for you, the wife of Vithris,
you let both Ve and Vili
into your bosom.''[55]
Poetic Edda, "Lokasenna" 26; *ca.* 1000 CE.

Vili, however, was "will,"[56] and *Ve* was a "priest" or "sacred one,"[57] so the insult did not hold for anyone who understood Old Norse. Frigg, then, still represented the typical Indo-European consort-goddess: she upheld the value of marital chastity.

Frigg had one other attribute: the ability to *prophesy*. In one lay, she is called *Sága*, "the one who tells."[58] However, Freyja said of her:

II.9.24. *''To my mind,*
Frigg knows the whole of fate,
even if she herself says nothing.''[59]
Ibid, 29.

Frigg "says nothing." That is, she does not use her knowledge to prophesy. So she "sees" only, but does not use her knowledge to benefit others. One wonders why she was not prophetess as well. Perhaps that function was not in keeping with her role as Oðin's wife.[60]

In Germanic society, goddesses *per se* were predominantly consorts and fertility figures. We know little of Nerthus, except that slaves were sacrificed to her by drowning, probably to add "fuel" to her fertile energies. *Giantesses,* such as Gerð, figure prominently in the Eddas, and they were relatively autonomous for female deities. Gerð was probably a sun goddess. Skaði was a "Mistress of Animals" who carried a bow, as did the Greek Artemis.

The goddess Hel may be compared to the Sumerian Ereshkigal, the Greek Persephone, the Baltic Lauma, and the Indic Nirṛti. The Norns, who represented fate and thus fortune, may be compared to the Baltic Laima, the Greek Moirai, and the Roman Parcae. Their gifts were both positive and negative, and thus they were similar to the Indic duality of Lakshmi and Alakshmi.

Freyja, the Germanic goddess of love, may be compared to goddesses such as the Sumerian Inanna and the Greek Aphrodite. As the first Valkyrie, to whose portion fell half the slain warriors in battle, she shares characteristics with the Sumerian Ereshkigal, the goddess who received all of the Sumerian dead; the Celtic Badb, and the other chthonic and underworld goddesses. Therefore, Freyja was responsible for life and love, but to her came death as well. She was the "Goddess of Regeneration." As did many of the other "Goddesses of Regeneration," Freyja had avian imagery: she possessed a falcon coat, a "feather-form."

A descendant of Freyja, the Valkyrie Brynhild, manifested not only ability on the battlefield, but great wisdom. She resembles, in both of those functions, the Greek warrior-goddess and goddess of wisdom, Athena.

Frigg was a "wife"-goddess; she was not very autonomous, but she had a significant function within the Germanic pantheon, which was apparently mirrored by women in Germanic societies. She was a *seeress* and *wise woman*. As seeresses and wise women, goddesses, heroines, and mortal women were powerful, and they were respected by the men both in their mythologies and in their societies.

CHAPTER 10

Greek goddesses

Perhaps the most widely-known of the ancient pantheons of deities is the Greco-Roman *Olympian* pantheon. Many deities, including *Zeus* and *Hera,* are mentioned as early as the twelfth century BCE, in the Mycenaean Greek *Linear B* texts. These texts, the oldest extant Greek writings, were translated in the last few decades. They include records of goods, including goods dedicated to various deities:

> II.10.1. "*For Zeus: one gold bowl*
> *and one male [attendant].*
> *For Hera: one gold bowl*
> *and one female [attendant].*"[1]
> Mycenaean Tablet PY 172; *ca.* 1200 BCE.

It is difficult to determine the precise roles of the Greek deities in the Mycenaean texts, since mythological stories as such have not been found in Linear B script. However, by the time of *Homer,*[2] who was believed to have written two epic poems, the Iliad and the Odyssey, in the eighth to seventh centuries BCE, the catalogue of Greek gods and goddesses was well-established. We shall make brief mention of the male deities, to put the pantheon into perspective, and then we will focus upon the female deities.

Zeus was the thunder-god and "king of the gods," and the goddess *Hera* was his consort, the "matron-goddess." Other significant gods included *Poseidon*, the "earth shaker" and god of the sea; *Ares*, the god of war and carnage; *Apollo*, the god of the sun, patron of music, and god of prophecy;[3] *Hades*, god of the underworld who was sometimes called the "underworld Zeus," and husband of the maiden-goddess *Persephone*, whom he abducted; *Dionysos*, god of the vine and of vegetation who was sometimes reckoned among the Olympians; and *Hephaestos*, the divine blacksmith, personification of terrestrial fires, such as volcanoes, and husband of the love-goddess, *Aphrodite*.

Although we will be discussing the Greek goddesses in detail, a short list of these deities, as well as the gods, may put the pantheon into perspective. We have already mentioned Hera, the "divine consort," and patroness of marriage, and Aphrodite, the "divine lover," goddess of love both within and outside of marriage. One of the most important Greek deities was the virgin goddess *Athena*, protectress of the city of Athens, goddess of wisdom, goddess of handicraft, and goddess of victory in war. Another virgin goddess, *Artemis*, was "Mistress of Animals," goddess of the chase, and one of the goddesses of the moon. The three-fold goddess *Hecate*'s functions overlapped those of Artemis, and it was not until late that she was associated with the moon. She was goddess of the crossroads and of ghosts and spirits, and she came to be associated with magic. Hecate has also been associated with *Demeter*, goddess of the fruits of the earth, and with the young *Persephone*, daughter of Demeter and wife of Hades, as a representation of the three phases of a woman's life: youth, middle age, and old age.[4] Most of these deities were included in the pantheon at Mount Olympus. They were considered to be the major Greek deities even though several more ancient deities, such as the earth-goddess *Gaia* and her daughter *Rhea*, mother of Zeus and Hera, were not part of the Olympian pantheon. Although there were several other Greek goddesses, this catalogue is sufficient for a representative picture of the Greek deities.[5]

To fully understand the Greek goddesses and heroines, it is necessary to understand the nature of the society. Homeric society differed from the heroic Mycenaean society, and the Classical Greek society of the fifth century BCE differed from Homer's society. The Mycenaeans were Indo-European, but they tempered their society with borrowings from the earlier peoples. They borrowed the pre-Greek *Minoan* writing system, and they may have borrowed Minoan social customs. We have artistic remnants of the Minoan society, but we have not deciphered their script, *Linear A*, so there are many questions about the society which are, as yet, unanswered. From Minoan frescoes depicting women hunting and participating in other aspects of the society, one can infer that women played a more active role in the society than did their later Attic Greek sisters, who were prohibited from participating in many functions of Greek life.[6]

Hints of early Greek society are given by Homer. We recall that Homer describes a time long past, the "heroic" age of the twelfth century BCE, even though he lived several centuries later. He tries to *interpret* the earlier society, and he sometimes combines values and character-types of his society with those of the later society. This leads to strangely composite characters among his heroes and heroines. One heroine in the Odyssey, *Nausikaa*, represents just such a combination of Homeric Greek and early Greek or pre-Greek characteristics.

The sixth and seventh chapters of the Odyssey describe the hero *Odysseus'* adventures in the land of the sea-faring Phaeacians. This land borders Greece, sociologically and geographically: that is, the culture of the Phaeacians was not a barbaric one to the Greek Odysseus.

As the adventure begins, Odysseus has just washed up on the shore of the island of Phaeacia, following a shipwreck. Meanwhile, the goddess Athena, in disguise, has made a telling suggestion to Nausikaa, daughter of the king and queen of the island, Alcinous and Arete. She has hinted that Nausikaa might be married soon, so perhaps she should get her wardrobe in order.

Nausikaa thus awakens at dawn and goes to find her parents, who are also up and about. Her mother is spinning, as women of that time and place were wont to do, and her father is going forth to join the other nobles in Council. Nausikaa asks her father to *allow* her to do the laundry, not telling him that her reason for doing so has more to do with excitement over a possible marriage than altruism. Alcinous suspects the truth; perhaps even Phaeacian teen-agers rarely begged to do the family's laundry. But he gladly grants to his daughter the necessary equipment, while his wife packs picnic delicacies. Nausikaa, accompanied by her handmaidens, eagerly sets off for the river to wash clothes and to have a picnic lunch.

The maidens washed the clothes, Nausikaa "treading on them in the trenches"[7] with all of the others. Then, waiting for the clothes to dry, the girls ate lunch and played ball, Nausikaa outshining her friends in loveliness. As they were frolicking about, an apparition came out of the woods: Odysseus, holding a leafy branch around his body to cover his nakedness, and otherwise covered with nothing but crusty sea-brine.

Most of the maidens, as protected maidens will, cringed with fear at this strange sight, but Nausikaa alone was undaunted:

> II.10.2. " . . . *only the daughter of Alcinous remained;*
> *for Athena placed courage into her heart,*
> *and she removed fear from her limbs.*
> *[Nausikaa] stood staunchly and faced him.*"[8]
> Homer, Odyssey VI.139–141; *ca.* 800? BCE.

Although Homer had to add the convention that Athena gave courage to Nausikaa, the maiden was *brave*. She showed no traces of the timidity which characterized a Classical, or even Homeric, Greek woman. Although Odysseus was naked, she faced him boldly, as a friend.

Odysseus and Nausikaa spoke, and the princess ordered her handmaidens to tend to the strange traveler, teasing them for being so frightened:

> II.10.3. "*Where are you running away to*
> *at the sight of a man?*"[9]
> Ibid, VI.199.

Odysseus bathed and anointed himself with oil, and then, to render him truly handsome, his patroness Athena

> II.10.4. " . . . *poured down grace*
> *upon his head and shoulders.*"[10]
> Ibid, VI.235.

At that, struck by Odysseus's beauty,

> II.10.5. *"the young woman gazed at him . . . "*[11]
> Ibid, VI.237.

Afterwards, Nausikaa advised Odysseus of the best approach to her father's court. He should let her return first, and then make his way to the palace alone. It would not do for him to be seen with the unmarried girl. This suggestion is in keeping with Homer's personification of the Greek female, but the next suggestion is not very Greek:

> II.10.6. *"But when the rooms and the courtyard contain you,*
> *swiftly pass quite through the hall,*
> *until you reach my mother.*
> *She sits at the hearth*
> *in the brilliance of the fire,*
> *spinning wool of sea-purple on the distaff . . .*
> *the throne of my father is there [as well] . . .*
> *passing him by,*
> *throw your hands around my mother's knees . . .*
> *if she should be disposed toward you in her heart,*
> *then there is hope that you may see your dear ones,*
> *and reach your well-built house*
> *and your fatherland."*[12]
> Ibid, VI.303–315.

So ends Chapter Six. Chapter Seven describes Odysseus' arrival at the court. Athena—disguised as usual—gives Odysseus the same advice, that he must make his request to Nausikaa's mother, Arete, rather than to her father, Alcinous. She tells the hero that, when he goes to the court of Alcinous, he will find the *kings* feasting at the banquet.[13] Homer assumes that the custom was the same in ancient Phaeacia as it was in Classical Attic Greece: women were not allowed to feast with their husbands. Nausikaa, in spite of her maturity and bravery, eats alone in her room, as would any Greek girl; her nurse had kindled her fire for her,

> II.10.7. *"and arranged her supper within [her chamber]."*[14]
> Ibid, VII.13.

Continuing his quest, Odysseus goes first to Arete, as he is instructed, and then he sits down in the ashes of the hearth as a suppliant.

The rest of the adventure follows the more typical Greek customs. It was Alcinous who took Odysseus' hand and raised him from the ashes, and ordered food and drink to be brought to him. It was Alcinous who then called for a council of Phaeacian leaders, to determine how to help Odysseus, and eventually Odysseus was enabled to leave the island and set out on his way again.

Thus Alcinous held authority among *men*. The rule in Phaeacia was not a matriarchal one. The culture in this land was typical of early Greece: it was more egalitarian than patriarchal, and, although it was the males who ruled, rule was *established through* a female.[15] The female could inherit the land, through the matri- patrilineal line of descent.[16] Arete may have owned the land which her uncle-husband Alcinous ruled, and he may well have married her to gain sovereignty over the island. Arete's material power, ownership of the land, would have given to her power over her subjects, and, by extension, power over any person who entered the kingdom seeking aid. For this reason suppliants were required to approach the queen before asking a favor of her husband. Homer, aware only of the inheritance patterns of his own day, tries to explain Arete's power:

> II.10.8. *"For she is not in any way lacking*
> *in noble understanding."*[17]
> Ibid, VII.73.

That is, because Arete is very wise, Alcinous has given her a very important position. He has shown her great honor:

> II.10.9. *"Alcinous made her his wife,*
> *and he has honored her*
> *as no other woman on earth is honored,*
> *of those women*
> *who now manage their homes*
> *in* subjection *to their husbands . . . "*[18]
> Ibid, VII.66–68.

Only in this way was Homer able to explain how a woman could be so powerful. We find, then, that Homer has effected a juxtaposition of the customs of two differing times, the Mycenaean age of *circa* 1200 BCE and the Homeric pre-Classical age of *circa* 800 BCE. He tries to explain the apparent anomalies by stating that Athena gave courage to Nausikaa, and that Arete was honored because of her great wisdom. However, as we know, customs can change considerably in four hundred years.

At times the customs of mortals may be explained by actions of the gods, and the advent of the male-centered Greek society and patrilinear inheritance pattern may perhaps be explained in this way. The Greek tragic poet *Aeschylus* described the "triumph of patriarchy" in the third play of his trilogy, the Oresteia. The background to the story of the Greek youth, Orestes, is useful for an understanding of the events of the third play.

In the first play of the trilogy, the "Agamemnon," Orestes' mother, *Clytemnestra,* killed her husband, King Agamemnon, the king who led the Greeks to Troy to avenge the seduction and kidnapping of his sister-in-law, Helen. Clytemnestra had fallen in love with another man during the ten years that her husband was away warring with the Trojans. Her "defection" was caused more by the fact that her husband sacrificed their daughter, *Iphigeneia,* so that propitious winds might blow for the Greek ships, than that he had spent so many years away from home.

In the next play in Aeschylus' trilogy, the "Libation Bearers," Orestes, by command of the god Apollo, killed his mother and her lover, Aegisthus. Orestes was then haunted by the *Erinyes* or *Furies,* goddesses who avenged wrongs done to kindred, especially the wrong of murder within the family, and particularly matrilineal murder. That is, the Erinyes supported the earlier descent pattern.

In the third play of the trilogy, the "Eumenides," the Erinyes continue to haunt Orestes. Finally, there is a tribunal, so that the gods may vote upon his guilt or innocence. The Furies state that his murder of his mother was the worst possible shedding of blood, for he killed his mother, his closest blood relative, while

> II.10.10. *"the man whom [Clytemnestra] killed*
> *was not related by blood."*[19]
> Aeschylus, "Eumenides" 605; 525/4 BCE to 456 BCE.

Apollo, in defense of Orestes, counters:

> II.10.11. *"The mother of that which is called her child,*
> *is not the parent,*
> *but only the nurse*
> *of the newly sown embryo."*[20]
> Ibid, 658–659.

Apollo gives as proof the fact that a man could give birth to a child without any help from a woman, just as Zeus gave birth to his daughter, Athena.[21]

Finally, Athena herself speaks, tipping the balance of the judgment in Orestes' favor:

> II.10.12. *"It is my duty to render final judgment here.*
> *This is a ballot for Orestes*
> *I shall cast.*

There is no mother anywhere who gave me birth,
and, except for [being a patroness of] marriage,
I am always on the male's side with all my heart,
and strongly on my father's side.
So, in a case where the wife has killed her husband,
lord of the house,
her death shall not mean most to me.
And, if the other votes are even,
then Orestes wins . . . ''[22]
Ibid, 734–741.

And Orestes won, while the Greek women became disenfranchized. The female, along with her birth-giving function, became devalued, and the Erinyes were mollified, and metamorphosed into *Eumenides*, kindlier powers who bestow fertility upon their society but who realize their place within a male-dominated pantheon.

Although the Greek pantheon was male-dominated, the goddesses nonetheless played a significant role in Greek religion and ritual. Many goddesses were worshipped in Greece, but we shall discuss only a few of them. As we consider the goddesses, keep in mind the process of *syncretism*, which played an important role in the development of Greek deities. As we discussed in the Introduction, local goddesses with varying functions were often given the names of goddesses whose worship was more widespread. Thus, a Near-Eastern mother-goddess might be assimilated with the Greek virgin goddess, *Artemis*, or a local Laconian warrior-goddess might be syncretized to the pan-Hellenic *Aphrodite*.

Aphrodite was one of the most important goddesses of the Olympian pantheon, the goddess of love and beauty. Homer linked her with the line of Zeus, calling her "daughter of Zeus,"[23] but Hesiod's description of her "theagony" was a more accepted version of her origins: the god *Kronos*, father of Zeus, has castrated his own father, *Ouranos*. He cast the severed genitals into the sea, and then,

II.10.13. ''*A white foam arose from the immortal flesh;*
in it there grew a maiden.
First she floated to holy Cythera,
and from there, afterwards,
she came to sea-girt Cyprus.[24]
There came forth an august and beautiful goddess . . .
gods and men call her Aphrodite . . . ''[25]
Hesiod, Theogony 190–197; *ca.* 750? BCE.

Hesiod's story correlates well with the "theagonies" of other Greek writers. The traveler, Pausanias, states that

II.10.14. '' . . . *there is a temple of Aphrodite Ourania . . .*
the cult of Ourania
was first established by the Assyrians,
and after the Assyrians
by the Paphians of Cyprus,
and the Phoenicians
who inhabit Ascalon in Palestine;
from the Phoenicians
the people of Cythera
learned her worship.''[26]
Pausanias, Description of Greece I.14.7; *ca.* 150 CE.

Herodotus tells us that

II.10.15. ''*The temple of Aphrodite Urania . . .*
[in the Syrian city of Ascalon]

is the oldest of all temples erected
for this goddess.''[27]
Herodotus, The History I.105; *ca.* 450 BCE.

Thus, although there is some disagreement regarding the order of the cities which first knew the worship of Aphrodite, there is still concordance in the fact that Aphrodite was not of Greek origin. The ancient Greeks seem to have believed that the goddess—that is, her cult—originated in the Near East. It is possible that the worship of a goddess such as the Eastern Mediterranean Ashtoreth or Ashtarte spread westward, and that the Greek name was given to the goddess after she became accepted by the Greek people.[28] She was then accreted to the Greek pantheon and Indo-European Greek characteristics were added to her Near-Eastern ones. At any rate, in designating Aphrodite as "daughter of Zeus," Homer was most likely attempting to integrate an Eastern goddess into the Zeus-dominated Olympian pantheon.

Aphrodite's iconography also sheds light upon her origins. She was shown on a clay drinking cup riding a *goose*,[29] and she was depicted with her son Eros, riding a *swan*.[30] The "crouching Aphrodite" by the Greek sculptor Diodalses has a *snake* coiled around the arm of the goddess.[31] Aphrodite was thus given the accoutrement of the Neolithic and Near Eastern bird and snake goddess, the "Goddess of Regeneration."

Aphrodite's Near Eastern origin may explain the presence of hierodules, or "sacred prostitutes," in her temple at Corinth:

II.10.16. *''Oh, girls visited by many guests,*
handmaids of the goddess Persuasion
in wealthy Corinth,
with your thoughts often darting up
to the mother of love,
Aphrodite Ourania . . . ''[32]
Pindar, Fragment 122; 518–438 BCE.

Aphrodite had connections with the sea, in Corinth and in other places. At Corinth, there was a temple of Aphrodite surnamed both *Pontia*, "of the sea," and *Limenia*, "of the harbor."[33] And, in Attica, there was a sanctuary to Aphrodite *Euploia*, "fair voyage."[34]

Aphrodite was *golden*, as was the Egyptian Hathor:

II.10.17. *'' . . . Hermione,*
who had the appearance
of golden Aphrodite.''[35]
Homer, Odyssey IV.14; *ca.* 800? BCE.

Although Aphrodite was primarily a love-goddess, she was, by extension, a mother-goddess. In Homeric Hymn V, Aphrodite represented the "Great-Mother," Cybele. On her journey to her liaison with the mortal, Anchises, she was accompanied by

II.10.18. *''gray wolves, wagging their tails,*
and bright-eyed lions, and bears,
and swift panthers, greedy for roe-deer;
and she, seeing them,
delighted in her soul,
and she put desire into their hearts,
so that they all lay down, two by two,
in shady dens.''[36]
Homeric Hymn V, to Aphrodite: 70–74; 8th to 6th Centuries BCE.

In the Iliad, Aphrodite was mother of the Trojan, *Aeneas*, through her union with Anchises:

II.10.19. *''And now the king of men,*
Aeneas,

would have perished,
had not the daughter of Zeus,
Aphrodite, his mother,
who conceived him to Anchises
as he tended his cattle,
quickly observed [him].''[37]
Homer, Iliad V.311–313; *ca.* 800? BCE.

Aphrodite had characteristics, not only of a mother-goddess, but also of a more powerful deity, whose abilities transcended the "fertility"-function. She was given the epithet *Areia* in her capacity as a Spartan goddess of love and war. Pausanias describes one of her shrines:

II.10.20. *''Behind the Lady of the Bronze House*
is a shrine of Warlike Aphrodite.
The wooden figurines are as old
as anything else in Greece.''[38]
Pausanias, Description of Greece III.17.5–6; *ca.* 150 CE.

Although Aphrodite was indeed invoked as a "warlike" goddess, we must remember that she was invoked in this capacity by the martial Spartans. Her "warrior"-powers were most likely derived from her nurturing function. The function of a political, protective city-goddess became that of defending the city in time of war and that of guarding it in peacetime.[39]

The epithet *Areia* was built upon the Greek name for the warrior-god, *Ares*, and the two deities are thus linked in terms of cult-epithet. However, although they were connected in this way as god of war and "warlike" goddess, it was their union as mythological lovers, as warrior-god and love-goddess, that was popular in tales told by the Romans and Greeks, who were fond of uniting the energies of love and war.

The love-goddess Aphrodite was married to the lame divine blacksmith, *Hephaestos*, and, although she accepted her married state, she was nonetheless not quite the ideal Greek housewife. In fact, she was caught in a rather embarrassing position—literally—when she fell in love with the physically superb warrior-god, Ares.

Ares and Aphrodite saw each other whenever possible, and, when Hephaestos found that his wife was making a common practice of deceiving him, he decided to catch her in the act. A talented craftsman, he forged a bronze hunting-net, invisible but unbreakable, and he attached it to his and Aphrodite's bed. Then he pretended to go away on a business trip. The watchful Ares saw Hephaestos leaving, and he immediately went to visit Aphrodite:

II.10.21. *''Come here, darling,*
let's go to bed . . . !''[40]
Homer, Odyssey VIII.292; *ca.* 800? BCE.

Aphrodite concurred, and the two went happily to bed, posthaste. Imagine their consternation when they found themselves entangled, nude, in Hephaestos' net! Caught *flagrante delicto*, the lovers were even more chagrined when Hephaestos summoned all of the gods (but not the goddesses: the scene was too shameful for women to look upon) to witness his wife's evil doings. Then,

II.10.22. *''unextinguishable laughter arose*
among the happy gods,''[41]
Ibid, VIII.326.

and many of them decided that they would rather be in Ares' position, embarrassing as it was, than Hephaestos'.

Not one of the gods reprimanded Aphrodite for failing to be a devoted wife. Even Hephaestos decided that he would rather be married to her, as she was, than not married to her at all.[42]

Aphrodite could be goddess of both the married and the unmarried, but it is clear that her primary function within the Greek pantheon was that of love-goddess. Although female chastity and fidelity figure prominently throughout Greco-Roman society and religion, the Greeks and Romans did *not* require a chaste love-goddess. Aphrodite could spark the lust of all men and gods, and remain exempt from the concept of female monogamy that was dear to the hearts of Greek and Roman men. The *autonomy* of Aphrodite, the fact that she was not bound by the rules of chastity which were imposed upon other goddesses and mortal women, also bespeaks her *power*.

Chastity *did* play an important role in the personification of the Greek goddess, *Artemis*. There is little clue to her personification in the earliest texts in which she is believed to appear: Mycenaean Greek inscriptions, dating to *circa* 1200 BCE, such as

> II.10.23. *"To Aigios, a servant of Artemis."*[43]
> Mycenaean Tablet PY ES 650; *ca*. 1200 BCE.

However, by the first millennium BCE, there were two rather distinct characterizations of the goddess. In Asia Minor, in the city of Ephesos, she was depicted as a polymastic, or "many-breasted," mother-goddess.[44] She was the "Great-Mother" of plants, animals, and men.

A more classical Greek representation of the goddess was to be found in her worship in the Dorian states, particularly in Laconia,[45] where she was a virginal huntress and "Mistress of Animals."[46] This Laconian goddess was also a protectress of the city in wartime, similar to the Spartan Aphrodite Areia:

> II.10.24. *"When they were no more than*
> *a stadium away,*
> *the Lacedaemonians sacrificed a she-goat*
> *to [Artemis] Agrotera,*
> *as they are accustomed,*
> *and they led the charge upon their enemy . . . "*[47]
> Xenophon, Hellenica IV.2.20; *ca*. 430 BCE to *ca*. 354 BCE.

Because the Lacedaemonians were relatively warlike, it is not surprising that many deities would be preempted from their more usual spheres, to do service as patrons of war. And again, we must recall that syncretism plays a large role in the accumulation of powers of a popular goddess.

The virginal Artemis was characterized as a member of the Olympic pantheon in the Iliad, as "chaste Artemis,"[48] and as

> II.10.25. *"the queen of the wild beasts,*
> *Artemis who loves wild places."*[49]
> Homer, Iliad XXI.470–471; *ca*. 800? BCE.

She had particular associations with the bear. In the chorus of the "Lysistrata," a play by the Greek comic playwright Aristophanes, a woman stated that she once played the "Brauron Bear" at the festival of Brauronian Artemis:

> II.10.26. *" . . . and then, wearing the saffron-colored robe,*
> *I was the Brauron bear."*[50]
> Aristophanes, "Lysistrata" 645; *ca*. 450 BCE to *ca*. 385 BCE.

The girl thus wore a yellow robe, in place of a bearskin. Further, mythological evidence[51] of Artemis' connection with bears is supplied by the story of Callisto and Zeus:

Callisto was a nymph who served Artemis. She

> II.10.27. *"chose to lead her life*
> *with wild animals,*
> *in the mountains*

together with Artemis.''[52]
"Hesiod," Astronomia 3; *ca.* 750? BCE.

and with other nymphs, all of whom chose to emulate Artemis' virgin state.

Unfortunately, Callisto received the glance of father Zeus' roving eye and he seduced her. She became pregnant, but for a while her pregnant state went unnoticed by the goddess. Finally, however, Artemis saw Callisto undressed, at her bath, and she could not help but note that the girl was pregnant.

Enraged that the girl was so obviously no longer celibate, Artemis changed her into a bear.[53] In this state, Callisto gave birth to a son, *Arcas*.

Callisto later wandered into Zeus' sacred precinct, and she was about to be killed by hunters. Zeus, however, took pity on her, and set her among the stars. She was called the "Big Bear," *Ursa Major*.[54] Some say that Arcas too was put into the heavens. He was called the "Little Bear," *Ursa Minor*.[55]

"Callisto," which means, "the most beautiful one," may have been an epithet of Artemis. Pausanias believed that the two were to be identified:

II.10.28. '' . . . *there is an enclosure of Artemis,*
and wooden statues of Ariste and Calliste . . .
I believe that . . . these are surnames of Artemis . . . ''[56]
Pausanias, Description of Greece I.29.2; *ca.* 150 CE.

Artemis was also associated with other animals. She was:

II.10.29. ''*deer-shooter, shooting arrows . . .*
ravaging the tribe of wild animals . . . ''[57]
Homeric Hymn XXVII, to Artemis: 1–2; 10;
8th to 6th Centuries BCE.

She was also goddess of more peaceful pleasures,

II.10.30. ''*arranging the charming dance*
of the Muses and the Graces.
There, hanging up her elastic bows and arrows,
she leads and heads the circle dance,
her body elegantly poised.''[58]
Ibid, 15.

The circle dance led by Artemis reminds one of the Minoan circle dance, which we know of from Minoan dancing figurines.[59] The dance was not always the dignified one of the Muses and the Graces. Cymbals—the accoutrement of those who danced as though they were possessed, the Maenads or Bacchantes—were found in the temple of Artemis *Limnatis*,[60] "Artemis of the Lake," in the borderland between Laconia and Messenia.[61] That Artemis was indeed associated with the Bacchantic tradition is further illustrated by a dedication to Artemis by the Milesian poet, Timotheus:

II.10.31. ''*To Artemis,*
Maenad, Thuiad, Phoibad, Lussad.''[62]
Timotheus, Fragment 1; *ca.* 450 BCE to *ca.* 360 BCE.

These epithets were all used of women who were possessed by gods such as Bacchus, gods celebrated with orgiastic rites.

Thus the "chaste huntress" was but one aspect of Artemis; her rites were quite varied. In Arcadia, the huntress-goddess was associated with snakes:

II.10.32. '' . . . *Artemis stands,*
clothed in the skin of a deer,
and carrying a quiver on her shoulders;
in one of her hands she holds a torch,
in the other two serpents.''[63]
Pausanias, Description of Greece VIII.37.4; *ca.* 150 CE.

We are reminded of the famous chryselephantine Knossos figurine: the gold and ivory woman, priestess or goddess, holds two snakes in her outstretched arms.[64] Serpents are depicted with most of the important Greek goddesses; in this way, many Greek goddesses bear attributes of the Neolithic European goddesses, and later Near Eastern and Minoan goddesses, many of which were also represented with snakes or as snakes themselves.[65]

Artemis was also identified with the moon, albeit not in the earliest Greek sources. In later myth, both Artemis and the chthonic goddess *Hecate*[66] became lunar goddesses.

Even in her Classical aspect as virgin huntress, Artemis reflected a memory of an ancient ritual held in common with other goddesses: that of human sacrifice. We are told, in a play of the Greek tragedian, Euripides, that King Agamemnon sacrificed his daughter Iphigeneia, to appease the gods, so that the winds, which were long still, might begin to blow, and might carry the Greek ships to their Trojan battleground. In this play, Iphigeneia was saved at the moment of her sacrifice, and a hind was substituted for her:

> II.10.33. ''*Then Calchas shouted,*
> *you can imagine how delightedly:*
> *'Oh, rulers of this allied Achaean army,*
> *do you see this victim*
> *which thc goddess set before her altar,*
> *a mountain-deer?*
> *This she prefers to the maiden,*
> *so that she not stain her altar*
> *with the murder of a noblewoman.'*''[67]
> Euripides, "Iphigeneia at Aulis" 1590–1595; 485? to 406? BCE.

So, at the last minute, the maiden was saved. She was saved in another of Euripides' plays, the "Iphigeneia in Tauris", but, if *she* was not killed on behalf of the goddess, other humans were. Iphigeneia was made a priestess in a temple of Artemis, and she did not enjoy all of her duties:

> II.10.34. '' . . . *and in her temple she made me her priestess;*
> *therefore in the rites of that festival*
> *in which the goddess Artemis takes pleasure . . .*
> *lovely is its name alone.*
> *But, for the rest, I keep silent,*
> *out of fear of the goddess—*
> *for I sacrifice,*
> *as was formerly the custom of this city,*
> *whatever Greek man comes to this land.*
> *I consecrate the victims;*
> *others take care of unspeakable slaughter*
> *within the temple of the goddess.*''[68]
> Euripides, "Iphigeneia in Tauris" 34–41; 485? to 406? BCE.

The depiction of Artemis as recipient of human sacrifice was a dramatic device, to be sure; yet it may have spoken to a memory of an earlier form of the goddess. Artemis was indeed a goddess who could bring death, to humans and to animals. One woman's cry again illustrates this function of the goddess.

The Greek hero Odysseus was absent from his home for many years. He finally returned to his home, Ithaca, under disguise. Although his wife, Penelope, did not recognize him, he somehow reminded her of the husband she had missed for so long. Penelope, out of longing for her husband, and grief at his long absence, cried out to the goddess:

> II.10.35. ''*Artemis, august goddess,*
> *daughter of Zeus,*
> *if only now you would cast your arrow in my breast*

and take away my life at once!"[69]
Homer, Odyssey XX.61–63; *ca.* 800? BCE.

Whether Artemis was originally a powerful mother-goddess, or primarily a nature goddess who then acquired the characteristics of "mother-goddess" in the Near East and those of "maiden" in Greece, has been disputed. As we have seen, she extinguished the lives of humans and animals. To be a true mother-goddess, she would have to fulfill the other end of the spectrum: she would also have to be responsible for birth. Because she was a "virgin" goddess, one might think that this possibility was precluded. But let us examine the significant meaning of her virgin status. Artemis was a member of the Olympian pantheon, and daughter of Zeus. As a member of this patriarchal body, she had to conform to the rules (those rules which applied to every goddess but Aphrodite, who held responsibility for human and animal fertility): she must be married or celibate. If she were married, she would become a consort-goddess, and her powers would be subordinated to those of her husband. If celibate, she could remain autonomous,[70] retaining her great powers for herself.

Although she was a virgin, she was also a goddess of fertility: she was often given the epithet "Eileithyia." Since Eileithyia was the goddess of childbirth, Artemis too was identified with childbearing. The philosopher Plato tells us that:

II.10.36. "*. . . Artemis . . . [although] unwedded,*
[lit. "unbedded"]
has been allotted [the sphere of] childbirth.'"[71]
Plato, Theaetetus 149B; *ca.* 429 BCE to *ca.* 347 BCE.

Artemis therefore retained the characteristics of a mother-goddess even when she was assimilated into the Classical Greek pantheon. Thus, it is most likely that Artemis was originally a "Mistress of Animals" *and* mother goddess. When she entered the Olympic pantheon, her most important role may have been that of "Mistress of Animals" and patroness of the hunt: hence, her designation as "bear"-goddess. Although she later received the designation of "virgin," she was also a goddess of fertility, of life for man and beast, and of death. She fulfilled the full spectrum of functions required of a mother goddess and a goddess of death and regeneration. Artemis thus inherited the mantle of the Neolithic "Goddess of Regeneration" and the "Mistress of Animals."

In Classical Greek mythology another virgin goddess, *Athena,* was a goddess of wisdom, and, as we have discussed, a patriarchal deity *par excellence*. She was born from the head of her father, Zeus, who had swallowed her mother, *Metis*:

II.10.37. "*Now [Zeus] himself*
[bore] sparkling-eyed [Athena] Tritogeneia
out of his own head.'"[72]
Hesiod, Theogony 924; *ca.* 750? BCE.

Athena was born out of the head of her father Zeus, without the participation of the woman whom Athena declined to identify as her mother. Zeus impregnated the goddess Metis, whose name means "counsel" or "wisdom" in Greek, and then, hearing from earth and heaven that she was destined to bear a warrior-god who would dethrone him, he swallowed her. Several months later, Athena popped out of his head, fully armed. Henceforth, Athena told everyone that she had no mother, only a father. But, interestingly enough, she was not only a warrior goddess. She personified many other functions, including that of *wisdom*. Therefore, she must have received at least *one* attribute from her mother. She may have received her martial inclinations from the thunderbolt-wielder, but she did not get her wisdom from her dad.

Zeus had swallowed Metis, so her participation in the birth was merely obscured, not nonexistent. Further, this "birthing" by the god is merely evidence of how well a strong pre-Greek goddess could be assimilated into the patriarchal Indo-European pantheon, for Athena shared attributes of the Minoan domestic goddess, and the snake and the bird, with Aphrodite and Artemis:

> II.10.38. " . . . *bright-eyed Athena departed,*
> *having the appearance of a sea-eagle.*"[73]
> Homer, Odyssey III.371–372; *ca.* 800? BCE.

Again,

> II.10.39. " . . . *bright-eyed Athena departed,*
> *and she flew away,*
> *up into the air,*
> *as a bird.*"[74]
> Ibid, I.319–320.

Athena was frequently represented on coins with her special bird, the *owl*. Athena occupied the obverse of the coins, and the owl occupied the reverse.[75] The owl, which is active at night, the time of darkness, may represent the "dark" or death-aspect of the regenerative goddess.

Athena was often depicted iconographically with the other dark aspect of the regenerative goddess, the snake. The "Varvakeion Athena" represents the goddess standing, fully armed, wearing an Attic gown girded with a serpent. Her chest is covered by an *aegis*, a breastplate or shield bordered with coiled serpents, in the middle of which resides the head of the snaky-haired Gorgon, *Medusa*.[76] Athena was frequently depicted with the Gorgon's head, which she inserted into the middle of her shield after Medusa was slain by Perseus.[77] The Athena represented on the pediment of the temple of the Peisistratidai, in the grouping from the Gigantomachy, wears a cloak bordered by a snake.[78] The goddess, as an assimilated member of the Greek patriarchy, was famous for battling against serpents. In this way, she plays a function similar to that of Zeus, just as, in Syria, both Anat and Baal, in different texts, fought the serpent of darkness. Athena killed the snake-footed giant Enceladus,[79] just as Anat killed the seven-headed crooked serpent.[80] Athena was not always the foe of the serpent; inside the shield of the Varvakeion Athena coils the sacred serpent Erichthonius, the guardian of the Acropolis. Athena therefore battles the serpent who threatens the (patriarchal) society, but the serpent who guards that society is her companion, just as the snake may have been the companion of the Neolithic "Goddess of Regeneration."

Athena was never merely a nature-goddess, but she was assimilated to some extent with the earth-goddess at Athens, and she acquired certain functions as a deity of vegetation. In particular, she gave the olive tree to the Athenians, and the Athenians apparently considered this gift to be of considerable importance:

> The water-god Poseidon wanted to own earthly kingdoms, and he once tried to take possession of Attica by thrusting his trident into the acropolis at Athens, where a well of sea-water immediately gushed out.[81] Later, Athena planted the first olive-tree beside the well, thus taking possession in a somewhat more gentle manner. Poseidon, angry because Athena had encroached upon his supposed territory, challenged Athena to single combat, but Zeus ordered the two to submit their dispute to arbitration.
>
> Somewhat late texts tell us that the *men* of Athens supported Poseidon while the *women* gave their support to Athena; Athena won the contest by one vote.[82] She became the patron deity of Athens and she

> II.10.40. " . . . *accordingly named the city, Athens,*
> *after herself.*
> *Poseidon,*
> *on the other hand,*
> *became filled with wrath,*

and he flooded the Thriasian plain,
and caused Attica to be
under the sea.''[83]
Apollodorus of Athens, Atheniensis Bibliothecae III.xiv.1;
born *ca.* 180 BCE.

To appease Poseidon's wrath, the Athenian men decided to subject the women to a triple punishment:

II.10.41. ''*that no woman should henceforth*
have the right to vote;
that none of their offspring
should bear his mother's name;
and that no one should call them
Athenian women.''[84]
St. Augustine, De Civitate Dei 18.9; 354 CE to 430 CE.

Thus, again mythology provided the Athenian citizens with a justification for women's loss of *personhood* in Athenian society.

Athena gave many gifts to the Greeks. She invented the flute and she was a patroness of feminine handicrafts, such as spinning and weaving. But her talents were not confined to the domestic, for, as the patron goddess of Athens, she was in charge of her city's protection. Thus, as we mentioned before, she became a martial goddess as well.[85]

Athena had a triple aspect, as did other goddesses in historic Indo-European spheres. That is, she was tri- or trans-functional. The essence of Athena's transfunctionality was that she, as one goddess, fulfilled three socio-religious functions.[86] She was worshipped as *Hygieia*, "health," *Polias*, "guardian of the city," and *Nike*, "victory."[87] As Polias, Athena represented sovereignty, an important function of goddesses which we shall discuss in Part Three. As Hygieia, she was a nurturing goddess. Further, she was invoked by women desirous of conception, as "Mother:"

II.10.42. ''*The women of Elis,*
because their land had been deprived of men
in their prime of life,
are said to have prayed to Athena
that they might conceive
at their first union with their husbands.
Their prayer was answered,
and they founded a temple of Athena
surnamed Mother.''[88]
Pausanias, Description of Greece V.3.2; *ca.* 150 CE.

Just as did Artemis, Athena became a goddess important to the personal cult of women. Both were invoked with regard to childbirth, even though both adamantly maintained their virginity. As we shall discuss later on, their virginity directly contributed to their power and to their autonomy.[89]

It is interesting to note that, as *Nike*, Athena was specialized in her martial capacity, for she was goddess of those battles which led to victory, and thus to peace and prosperity. She was rarely viewed as a savage warrior, as was the Greek male warrior-god, Ares.

Thus, Athena fulfilled many functions. Like Artemis, she represented several aspects of earlier Neolithic and Near Eastern goddesses. Her relationship to birds and snakes, and her function as one of the goddesses of motherhood, connects her to the Neolithic "Goddess of Regeneration," while her function as warrior-goddess and her patronage of the olive-tree relate her to aspects of divinity in the Near East. Athena was a goddess with a rich heritage, indeed.

The consort-goddess Hera embodied characteristics similar to those of Athena and other Greek goddesses. She had bird-attributes:

II.10.43. *"Then the two,*
[Hera and Athena]
went forth
with steps resembling [those]
of shy doves . . . "[90]
Homer, Iliad V.778; *ca*. 800? BCE.

In her iconography Hera was also associated with the serpent, for in her sanctuaries have been found votive offerings which include terracotta snakes.[91] Thus, Hera, just as most of the other Greek female deities, may be linked with the ancient Neolithic European "Goddess of Regeneration."

Hera was also closely connected with cattle, reminding one of the Egyptian goddess *Hathor* or the later depictions of *Isis*. Hera was called "cow-eyed:"

II.10.44. *"Then the mistress,*
the cow-[or ox-]*eyed Hera*
answered . . . "[92]
Ibid, I.551.

Hera's bovine associations may link her to the deity symbolized by horns of consecration in Minoan Greece.[93]

As we saw earlier, Hera's roots in Greek culture go back at least as far as Mycenaean Greece, where she—as well as other goddesses—was linked with Zeus. She became his consort early on:

II.10.45. *"In the sanctuary of Hera*
there is a statue of Zeus,
and the statue of Hera is seated on a throne;
[Zeus[stands beside her.
He has a beard and a helmet upon his head;
they are simple works."[94]
Pausanias, Description of Greece V.17.1; *ca*. 150 CE.

But Hera was not always merely the consort-goddess:

II.10.46. *"You, [Hera],*
the glorious Aeolian goddess,
origin of all."[95]
Alcaeus of Mytilene GI.6–7; born *ca*. 620 BCE.

Thus Hera was not merely the wife of the divine father-god; she was the progenitress herself.

The Zeus-Hera marriage was one between brother and a sister, the only such marriage "allowed" in the Greek sphere,[96] although it would have been common enough in the Near East. According to one myth, the marriage originated in the trickery of the father-god:

At first, Zeus was unsuccessful in his courting of Hera. He therefore decided to resort to trickery. He

II.10.47. *"plotted that he would sleep with Hera*
when he should see her go away
from the other gods.
Wishing to be incognito,
and not to be seen by her,
he changed his appearance
into that of a cuckoo,
and he perched on a mountain."
(continued).

It was a very cold day, and

II.10.48. *"Hera, traveling alone,*
arrived at the mountain,

and she sat down upon that [place]
where now there is a temple
of Hera the Complete One.
The cuckoo, seeing [her],
flew down and perched,
shivering and shuddering from the cold,
on her knee.
Hera, seeing it,
had pity for it,
and she put it into her blouse.
Zeus at once remetamorphosed
and seized Hera.
She averted his raping her
by begging him,
invoking the Mother,
and he promised to make her his wife.
Now, among the Argive people,
who honor the goddess more than any other Greeks,
a statue of Hera sits in a sanctuary
on a throne;
in her hand she holds a sceptre,
and on this sceptre is a cuckoo.''[97]
Scholia on Theocritus XV.64.
First Millennium CE.

One suspects that the myth was formulated around this figure of Hera and the cuckoo, and that the bird was originally an avian avatar of the goddess, rather than a tricky metamorphosis of her consort.

It is further said that the two spent their wedding night on the Isle of Samos. It lasted for three hundred years.[98]

So Zeus made Hera an "honest" woman. But, given his subsequent infidelities, and her subsequent subordination, one wonders who was the "victor" in this marriage. The marriage was a stormy one. Zeus was forever having affairs, and Hera was forever raging—impotently, to be sure—over his indiscretions. As we shall see in Part Three, this led Hera to bear some children in a unique manner.

One vestige of what may have been Hera's more ancient power remained: she was able to bestow the gift of *prophecy* upon anyone—human or animal—whom she wished to favor:

II.10.49. *''And the goddess,*
white-armed Hera,
caused [the horse, Xanthus]
to be gifted with speech.''[99]
Scholia on Homer, Iliad XIX.407.
First Millennium CE.

Xanthus then predicted to the hero Achilles his fate and his death. Further, Hera

II.10.50. *''used to give wise advice to* [Zeus],
as she sat on an intricately crafted chair.''[100]
Homeric Hymn III, to Pythian Apollo: 345–346
8th to 6th Centuries BCE.

So she was a wise woman as well. In this way, Hera resembled other consort-goddesses, such as the Germanic Frigg, who knew all things, even though she did not tell them to others. Hera was a first-function sovereign goddess,[101] albeit the weakened consort of the true sovereign god. It would seem that the concomitant function among such goddesses was that of priestess, represented as the ability to prophecy and to have foreknowledge of all things.[102]

Thus, the Classical Hera was a typical consort-goddess, but her roots and her powers ran deep: she was related not only to the Neolithic European "Goddesses of Regeneration," the bird and snake goddesses, but she also preserved a vestige of the Bronze-Age cow goddess.

The *Moirai*, the Greek *Fates*, were three female deities, similar to the Germanic *Norns* and to the Roman *Parcae*. We might recall that the Baltic *Laima* was also often conceived as a plural deity. Ancient goddesses were often multiplied into trinities, perhaps signifying the three stages of life: beginning, middle, and end; birth, life, and death. The Moirai determined the span of a person's life, and the content of that life. According to Hesiod, Fate, in the singular, was a terrible creature:

> II.10.51. *"And Night gave birth to horrible Fate."*[103]
> Hesiod, Theogony 211; *ca*. 750? BCE.

So Fate was born in darkness. And, as morning leads to night, so light and life lead to death and darkness. Thus, Fate could be miserable and frightening. But, we must remember, night and darkness also lead to the morning light, and death, in the same manner, leads to rebirth. Fate, therefore, represents a continuum similar to that depicted by the "Goddesses of Regeneration." And so, although Hesiod describes Fate as "gloomy," he also tells us that

> II.10.52. *"Zeus . . . bestowed the greatest honor*
> *upon [the Fates]."*[104]
> Ibid, 904.

Frightening as Fate or the Fates were, they were well-honored by the Olympian deities.

Just as the Moirai had power over the lives of mortals on a cosmic level, so similar powers, on a terrestrial level, were assigned to Greek seeresses, such as the *Pythia*. This prophetess and medium translated the intentions of the god Apollo, and she was inspired by, and related to, the moon:

> II.10.53. *"And after death*
> *she shall not lose her art of divination,*
> *but she shall travel around in the moon,*
> *becoming the so-called face*
> *that appears in the moon . . . "*[105]
> Plutarch, Moralia 398 C–D; born *ca*. 46 CE.

So the Pythia was the "woman in the moon."

The Classical Greeks did not believe that the Pythia had any oracular influence *in herself*:

> II.10.54. *"Now, just as we do not think*
> *that the oracular responses*
> *are those of the Pythia,*
> *but that the oracles are from the one*
> *who sent them to her mouth . . . "*[106]
> Libanius XII.60; Fourth Century CE.

She was merely the mouthpiece of the god Apollo, according to the Greeks. However, even before the advent of the Indo-Europeans, the site at Delphi where the Pythia gave her responses had been a sacred one, commemorated by the rock called the *omphalos*, the "navel," which was supposed to mark the center of the world. The deity responsible for the more ancient oracles was most likely the Python, the serpent-goddess whom Apollo slew upon taking over the site.[107] As we discussed, serpents were believed to have the power to confer the gift of prophecy,[108] so the serpent-goddess may well have been the goddess of prophecy. As we shall discuss in Part Three, the gift of prophecy was one given most often to female figures, rather than to male figures—whether or not the words of the prophetess were believed.

The Greek goddess of *fortune*, *Tyche*, was one of the eldest daughters of Ocean and Tethys;[109] both were, in turn, offspring of Earth and Heaven.[110]

Tyche was a companion of Persephone, daughter of Demeter; she was frolicking with her in the meadow, along with other young goddesses, just before Hades came up through the earth and changed Persephone's status from virgin daughter of Demeter to queen of the Underworld.[111] According to some, the goddess of fortune was the

> II.10.55. "*sister of Good Laws*
> *and Persuasion,*
> *and the daughter of Forethought.*"[112]
> Alcman, Fragment 62; *ca.* 650 BCE.

Although there are myths of her genealogy, there are no pre-Classical or even Classical Greek myths which embroider the story of Tyche. She began to become a major cult figure in the fourth century BCE.[113] By 335/4 BCE there was an Attic state cult of *Agatha Tyche*, "good fortune," gaining importance in Hellenistic Greece and in the Roman era. In the latter era she was identified with *Fortuna*.

Tyche, although not a goddess of the scope of a Roman Fortuna, is nonetheless important for our purposes because she is the Greek link in a tradition of Fortune-goddesses. The Indic Lakshmī, the Baltic Laima, the Germanic Norns, and the Roman Fortuna are each important to their cultures. In Greece, there was no deity personified as "bad fortune,"[114] so there was no exact Greek equivalence to the Indic Alakshmī. The slot of chthonic goddess was filled by Hecate, who did not, however, embody misfortune.

Often Fate and Fortune are synchretized in a mythology, as were Laima, the Norns, and Lakshmī. At other times, the two are distinct, as they were in Greece and Rome:

> II.10.56. "*Fortune and Fate*
> *give all things to man,*
> *Pericles.*"[115]
> Archilochus, Fragment 16; *ca.* 750? BCE.

In such societies, more power may be given to one than to the other. In Greece, Fate was the more celebrated personification, whereas in Rome, Fortune held greater prominence. The important indication of this female personification is that the lives of mortals are ruled by fortune and by fate: embodiments of the universal powers which give shape to our lives, powers within which our *karma* takes place. And those powers, among the Indo-Europeans, were feminine.

Hecate was a Titaness, one of the ancient group of Greek deities which preceded the Olympian gods. Most of the Titans were punished for rising against the Olympians, but Hecate—at least, according to Hesiod—retained much of her old honor, granted her by Zeus:

> II.10.57. "*The son of Kronos*
> *did not use violence against [Hecate],*
> *nor did he rob her of anything*
> *which was her portion among the former Titan gods . . .*
> *but she has honor*
> *on earth, and in the sky, and in the sea.*"[116]
> Hesiod, Theogony 423–427; *ca.* 750? BCE.

The potency of Hecate was reflected in her transformation into a *transfunctional*[117] goddess. Hesiod pictured her sitting

II.10.58. *"by august kings in judgement."*[118]
Ibid, 434.

and

II.10.59. *"in the assembly whom she wishes*
is distinguished among the people . . . "[119]
Ibid, 430.

Hecate was, then, a goddess who was a powerful force in the judgement-hall and in the Assembly. Her ancient wisdom was respected, even though other Titans were cast down into the Underworld.

The goddess fulfilled the martial function as well, in the typical manner of a female figure, for she was the power behind the warriors:

II.10.60. *" . . . and when men arm themselves*
for the battle that destroys men,
then the goddess stands by
to bestow victory and gladly grant glory
to whom she will . . . "[120]
Ibid, 431–433.

In this role she was similar, then, to the goddess Athena, who also brought inspiration and victory to the Greek soldiers. She also resembled the Celtic Morrigan, who took an active role in the outcome of battles, and the Germanic Freyja, the love- and battlefield-goddess.[121]

Of course, Hecate, just as the other Greek goddesses, also nurtured the populace. She was

II.10.61. *"a nurse of the young."*[122]
Ibid, 450.

She also

II.10.62. *"increases the herd . . .*
. . . if she wishes . . .
from a few she increases them
and from many she decreases them."[123]
Ibid, 444–447.

Hecate gave life and took it away again, as she willed, as did the other ancient "Goddesses of Regeneration." Later, her strong multi-functional aspects became subordinated to her characterization as a goddess of the underworld and death, of night, of ghosts and of *witches*.[124] She became, in particular, a goddess of crossroads:

II.10.63. *"Hecate, bewailed in nocturnal crossroads,*
through the cities . . . "[125]
Vergil, Aeneid IV.609; 70 to 19 BCE.

and she was depicted with triple aspect:

II.10.64. *"You see the faces of Hecate*
turning in three directions,
so that she may guard the crossroads,
divided into three paths."[126]
Ovid, Fasti I.141–142; 43 BCE to 17? CE.

The goddess of the *nocturnal* crossroads was also a goddess of death, since those who feared the obscurity of night also dreaded the "darkness" of the Underworld. Hecate had witnessed the rape of Persephone, hearing, from within her cave,[127] the cries of the young girl. Hecate became a favored companion of Persephone, the queen of the lower spheres:

> II.10.65. *"Hecate . . .*
> *greatly befriended*
> *the holy daughter of Demeter.*
> *From that time on*
> *the mistress was attendant and companion*
> *to [Persephone]."*[128]
> Homeric Hymn II, to Demeter: 438–440; 8th to 6th Centuries BCE.

Hecate, as chthonic goddess, was depicted with the chthonic creature, the serpent:

> II.10.66. *"Hecate Brimo . . .*
> *all around her*
> *awful serpents coiled*
> *among the oak branches."*[129]
> Apollonius Rhodius, Argonautica III.1211–1215;
> born *ca.* 295 BCE.

Hecate was banished, as it were, to the nether-regions. As we shall discuss in Part Three, the transformation of a goddess who reigned over heaven, earth, and sea, into a witch of the Netherworld, was not uncommon. In particular, the "Goddess of Regeneration," who could deprive a person or an animal of life, was often relegated by the Indo-European to the place of death, the Underworld.

Demeter too was a chthonic goddess, but earth was primarily her realm, although she did have some connection to the Netherworld. She was the Greek goddess of vegetation. She was responsible for plant growth, and for the lack thereof. At one time, the earth was perpetually abundant with growing things, but that abruptly changed when *Persephone* or *Kore*,[130] the daughter of Demeter, was abducted by *Hades*, the ruler of the Underworld.

Persephone was playing in the meadow one day, accompanied by friends. She stopped to pick a lovely flower, a narcissus, when, all of a sudden, the earth yawned open, and out came Hades. The Underworld king abducted the young girl and took her down with him into the depths of the earth, to his underground kingdom. Persephone cried out, and several deities heard her: the goddess Hecate, the sun-god Helios, and her own mother, Demeter.

Demeter, who heard the cry but could not see its source, began to search for her daughter. She searched the world, asking those whom she met if they had seen Persephone. She found Hecate, who told her that she had heard all, but had seen nothing. Then she went to Helios, who had both heard the cry and seen the rape, and he told the grieving mother everything. "However," he added,

> II.10.67. *"Stop your loud wailing . . .*
> *Hades, the Ruler of Many,*
> *is not an improper son-in-law for you,*
> *from among the immortal gods . . . "*[131]
> Homeric Hymn II, to Demeter: 83–84;
> 8th to 6th Centuries BCE.

This did *not*, indeed, assuage Demeter's grief. She wanted her virgin daughter back with her again; she did not want a "proper son-in-law."

And so she continued to wander through the cities of earth, much as did the Egyptian Isis in her search for Osiris.[132] Demeter avoided the Olympian assemblies, and her vigor and anger were redoubled. Her peregrination took her to Eleusis, where she disguised herself as an old woman. The king of Eleusis, Celeus, and his wife Metaneira hired her as a nurse for their infant son, Demophoon, and Demeter decided to render the boy immortal. Each day she anointed him with ambrosia, and each night she held him in the fire, to purge away his mortality. The boy grew rapidly, and he resembled an immortal.

One night, the boy's mother saw the old woman holding the boy in the fire. She screamed and wailed, and Demeter snatched the boy out of the fire. She angrily berated Metaneira for thus depriving the child of immortality, and then she mandated a temple to be built for her own worship. Since the Eleusinians had been kind to her, she promised to teach her rites to them. Eleusis would be the site of the Eleusinian Mysteries.[133]

Having spoken, the goddess revealed herself in all her lovely godliness.

Now, the goddess of vegetation was still overcome with sorrow, and she withdrew her gift to the world; she forbade the earth to yield its fruits, and it became barren. Zeus, fearing that the human race would be destroyed by famine, tried to get Demeter to change her mind, but she remained firm. The king of gods finally ordered Hades to give up his wife. Persephone was very happy, for she had greatly missed her mother. Before she departed for the upper world, however, Hades secretly gave her a pomegranate seed to eat: she had tasted the food of the Underworld (and also the food of fertility; she was definitely not a virgin any longer), and she thus belonged, at least in part, to the nether-regions.

Persephone, not understanding the significance of the food, returned to the upper world, and she joyfully embraced her mother. Then Demeter, as she held her daughter, suddenly feared a trick. She knew that the gods could be wily.

> II.10.68. *''Oh, child,*
> *you did not eat any food*
> *while you were in the netherworld,*
> *did you?''*[134]
> Ibid, 393–394.

Of course she had. In fact, she had acted similarly to the Sumerian god, *Nergal*.[135] Persephone had cohabited with the ruler of the Underworld, and that fact alone might have caused her to become subject to the Underworld realm. Persephone told her mother all that had transpired, and the two comforted each other. Hecate came and joined them, embracing the young goddess. And henceforth Hecate was companion to Persephone. Persephone could no longer live year-long in the Upper World. Because she had eaten while in the Underworld, she must spend a third of the year with her husband; the other two thirds of the year she would spend in the Upper World, with her mother and the other immortals.[136]

Demeter was asked to accept this compromise, and she did so. She caused the lands to be fruitful again, and further, she taught to the kings of Eleusis, including wise Triptolemus,[137] both her rites and her mysteries. However, the earth would be barren each winter, while Persephone lived with her husband in the Underworld. And each spring, when she returned to her mother, the earth would bloom again.

Thus we are taught not only about the seasons, and the reason for their existence; we are taught about the nature of the Underworld as well. Its ruler was a tricky god who "got his woman," at least on a part-time basis. If Persephone was an underground goddess, so was her mother—and so, indeed, was her older companion, Hecate. Hecate, as we know, was a chthonic and nocturnal goddess, and her connection with the nether-regions was an early one. Demeter's connection with the lower world is underscored by her epithets; she was *Demeter Erinys*, of Thelpusa,[138] "Demeter the Fury," named for the goddesses who mete out retribution for the spilling of kindred blood.[139] According to one theory, an Erinys was an infernal spirit representing the anger of the soul of the person who was murdered;[140] thus the Erinys would have originated in the lower regions, where the dead were thought to reside.

Demeter, while still searching for her daughter, was pursued by Poseidon, who had fallen in "lust" with her. Demeter metamorphosed into a mare, to outwit her pursuer, but the wily Poseidon changed himself into a stallion, and he thus raped the goddess.

> II.10.69. *''First off,*
> *Demeter was furious with this state of affairs;*
> *but later she checked her wrath . . . ''*[141]
> Pausanias, Description of Greece VIII.25.6; *ca.* 150 CE.

Demeter subsequently gave birth to a daughter and to a horse, Arion.

Demeter was also called the *Black Demeter* of Phigalia.[142] Her chthonian character is further underscored both by the serpent who draws Triptolemus' chariot, and by the snakes which are depicted along with her other attributes: sheaves of corn and poppies.[143] The serpents, of course, also serve to link her to the European Neolithic snake goddess.

Persephone remained queen of the Underworld, although not as potent a queen as was her earlier counterpart, the Sumerian goddess *Ereshkigal*.[144] She did have some Underworld functions, however, even though her husband was the true deity of death. She determined where souls should go after purgatory[145] and, further, she restored the spirits to the upper light.[146]

Persephone's sacrifices consisted of black sheep, and the person offering them had to turn away her or his face:

> II.10.70. *"Then sacrifice a ram*
> *and a black ewe,*
> *turning them towards Erebus,*
> *but you yourself turn away,*
> *going far away from the streams of the river."*[147]
> Homer, Odyssey X.527–529; *ca*. 800? BCE.

Following that,

> II.10.71. *". . . pray to the gods,*
> *to strong Hades and to awesome Persephone."*[148]
> Ibid, X.533–534.

The black sheep, probably a representative of death, indicates that the Underworld was Persephone's true, and perhaps original, realm. As her mother ruled over plant *life* in the upper world, on earth, so Persephone ruled over the sterile underground realms. Moreover, her role was a liminal one; she was both virgin daughter and wife, but wife in a setting of barrenness and death.

Demeter was thus the mother who gives fertility of vegetation and takes it away again, much as the goddesses of mortal life both gave it and removed it. Persephone, the *Kore* or "maiden" *par excellence*, was neither virgin nor mother, neither of the upper world nor of the Underworld—or, conversely, she was the goddess of both realms, and the matron whose maidenhood is eternally renewed.[149]

Connections between the Greek goddesses and the goddesses of the Near East, and their earlier Neolithic forebears, are numerous. Many Greek goddesses manifested the bird and snake iconography of the Neolithic "Goddess of Regeneration:" both Athena and Hera were represented mythologically as birds and iconographically with serpents. Aphrodite was represented with birds, such as swans and geese, and with snakes. Hecate and Demeter were represented with snakes, and Artemis, the "Mistress of Animals," was represented iconographically holding two serpents.

Bird and snake associations are not the only features which give us clues to the heritage of the Greek goddesses. The royal power of Nausikaa's mother, Arete, recalls the bestowal of *sovereignty* represented by the Egyptian Isis and by many Indo-European female figures. (See Part Three.) Hera was a repository of wisdom and a prophetess. The Greek fortune: Tyche, and the Moirai: the fates, had control over mortal lives, as did the Baltic Laima and her other Indo-European counterparts. The stories of Demeter and Persephone have elements which evoke the Egyptian myth of Isis and Osiris, and the Sumerian myths of Ereshkigal and Nergal, and of Inanna, Dumuzi, and Geshtinanna. Finally, Athena's warrior aspect may shadow, in rather mitigated form, the martial function of the Ugaritic Anat and the Egyptian Hathor and Sekhet. The Greek goddesses were rich indeed in their heritage of the myths and iconographies of earlier goddesses.

CHAPTER 11

Roman goddesses

Most of the deities in the Roman pantheon were borrowed wholesale from the Greek, but, nonetheless, there are many differences between Roman deities and their Greek counterparts. The Classical Roman era occupied a place in time later than the Greek: it flourished in the first century BCE, although various writings exist from two centuries or so earlier.

The Roman *Jupiter* was king of the pantheon, as was his Greek counterpart, Zeus, and *Juno* was his consort. The Roman *Mars* was a warrior-god similar to the Greek Ares. *Neptune* ruled the seas, as did the Greek Poseidon. The Greek Dionysos was worshipped as *Bacchus* in Rome, and the Greek Hephaestos was known as *Vulcan*. *Apollo*, the god of the sun, was known by the same name in Greece and Rome.

Although many of the female deities worshipped by the Romans were similar to those worshipped by the Greeks, we shall include Roman writings about the goddesses, to point out the Roman perspective of the deities, which differs from that of the Greeks.

Foreign "Great"-goddesses were imported into Rome; they were not assimilated into the pantheon, but rather they were borrowed wholesale from their neighbors. Rites were "foreign" ones. They enjoyed an enthusiastic following, so enthusiastic that at times the Roman State deemed it necessary to root out foreign religious rites. The Anatolian goddess *Cybele* was brought to Rome in 204 BCE.[1]

The festival of Cybele was called the *Megalensia* or *Megalesia*, from the Greek word *megas*, "great." Her rites—and the goddess herself, in the form of a sacred stone—were brought to Rome from mount Ida, in Phrygia.[2] When the boat which transported the "goddess" reached Rome, at the place

II.11.1. "*where the smooth Almo flows into the Tiber . . .*
a white-haired priest in a purple robe
washed the mistress and her sacred things
in the waters of Almo . . .
[Cybele] herself, seated in a cart,
rode in through the Capene gate . . . "[3]
Ovid, Fasti IV.337–345; 43 BCE to 17? CE.

The "bath" of the goddess is common in many cultures; earlier we discussed a similar ceremony in which the Germanic goddess *Nerthus* was bathed;[4] the ceremony is one of renewal and revitalization. After "Cybele" was washed in the Almo, she was "new again" for the Romans. The ceremony is similar to that in which a goddess or mortal woman bathes herself, and thus renews her virginity.[5]

Cybele thus arrived in Rome; then

II.11.2. ". . . *to the temple of Victory,*
which is on the Palatine,
they carried the goddess
on the day before the Ides of April . . .
the people, in great numbers,
bore gifts to the Palatine for the goddess,
and there was a feast offered to the gods,
and games called the Megalesia."[6]
Livy, ab Urbe Condita XXIX.xiv.14; 59 BCE to 17 CE.

By the time Vergil wrote his great epic poem, the Aeneid, Cybele was known as the "Great-Mother" of the Romans. Thus Vergil's hero, Aeneas, prayed to Cybele, calling her the

II.11.3. "*bountiful mother of the gods,*
the goddess from Mount Ida . . . "[7]
Vergil, Aeneid X. 252; 70 BCE to 19 BCE.

and he entreated her to

> II.11.4. *"be now a leader for me in battle,*
> *may you bring near an omen,*
> *according to your rites,*
> *and assist the Phrygians, oh goddess,*
> *with favorable step."*[8]
> Ibid, X. 254–255.

Not everyone appreciated her kindness, however. Other Romans were disturbed by her castrated priests or *galli*[9] with their extravagant clothing and jewelry and their weapons which showed

> II.11.5. *"signs of violent fury."*[10]
> Lucretius, de Rerum Natura II.621; *ca.* 94 BCE to *ca.* 55 BCE.

The Roman poet Catullus wrote of Cybele's priest, *Attis*, who

> II.11.6. *"loosed the weight of his loins*
> *with sharp flint . . . "*[11]
> Catullus, Carmina LXIII.5; *ca.* 84 BCE to *ca.* 54 BCE.

in frenzied homage to the goddess. With newly delicate fingers, Attis lifted up the tympanum, Cybele's sacred drum, and, shaking it, s(he) called to the other initiates to accompany her/him to the sacred groves of the goddess, on Mount Ida, where they might rejoice in the worship of the goddess. The galli (Catullus gives the word a feminine form, *gallae*) rushed up to Mount Ida, and reveled there until they reached exhaustion. Then they all fell asleep, and they slept until the new day dawned, when

> II.11.7. *"Sleep, fleeing,*
> *abruptly left the roused Attis . . . "*[12]
> Ibid, LXIII.42.

who, in the light of day, clearly remembered the irrevocable mutilation. With grief and rage (s)he cried,

> II.11.8. *"I am a woman!*
> *I was a youth, an ephebe, a boy,*
> *I was the flower of the gym,*
> *I was the ornament of the wrestling school . . .*
> *shall I now be a maid-in-waiting for the goddess,*
> *and a maid-servant for Cybele?*
> *Shall I be a Maenad, a part of myself,*
> *a sterile man?"*[13]
> Ibid, LXIII.63–69.

The answer, of course, was "yes." So Attis fled to the wild woods and there lived out her/his life as a "maid-servant" to the goddess.

Perhaps to a man like Catullus, the worst fate of all would be to lose one's virility and to become, in essence, a *woman*, losing not only his male parts, but his male privilege as well.

In spite of—or perhaps because of—the barbaric spiciness of her cult, Cybele remained quite popular among the Romans. Nor was she confused with other goddesses of foreign origin. She was sometimes synchretized to other goddesses,[14] but she was always iconographically distinct, recognizable by her *lion*. She either rides a lion or is flanked by them:

> II.11.9. *"Why does the fierce species of lion*
> *proffer their unaccustomed manes*
> *to the curved yokes*
> *for [Cybele]?"*[15]
> Ovid, Fasti IV.215–216; 43 BCE to 17? CE.

Cybele was thus an Anatolian "Mistress of Animals," mistress of the lion,[16] and also "Great-Mother."

Another foreign goddess who was quite popular in the Classical world, and who eventually took on the characteristics of many goddesses, was the Egyptian goddess, Isis. In his novel, the Metamorphoses, sometimes called The Golden Ass, the cosmopolitan poet, philosopher, and rhetorician, Apuleius, addresses Isis as follows:

> II.11.10. "*Oh, queen of heaven,*
> *whether you be the nurturing Ceres . . .*
> *or . . . the celestial Venus . . .*
> *or . . . the sister of Phoebus [Diana]*
> *or . . . Proserpine with triple face . . .*
> *by whatever name or rite or shape*
> *it is lawful to call upon you . . .* "[17]
> Apuleius, Metamorphoses XI.2; born *ca.* 123 CE.

Her Roman character was rather different from the one which she was given in Egypt: she was often depicted iconographically as a Roman matron,[18] and Apuleius gave her a unique and rather amalgamated image:

> II.11.11. "*First of all,*
> *a richness and abundance of hair flowed down*
> *and delicately dispersed and spread out*
> *about her divine neck;*
> *a garland, with varied flowers of many sorts,*
> *lightly lay on the crown of her head;*
> *in the middle of her forehead*
> *a plain circle, like a mirror—*
> *or rather, an image of the moon—*
> *shone forth with a white light;*
> *the right and left sides*
> [of the circle]
> *contained serpents,*
> *which rose up,* [as it were]
> *from the furrows of the earth,*
> *and above* [the circle]
> *extended ears of corn.*"[19]
> Ibid, XI.3.

Thus Isis here was given the ears of corn and serpents with which Demeter-Ceres was depicted. In Apuleius' representation, Isis also carried many of her attributes, including a brass timbrel, a sistrum, and a cup with a handle shaped like an asp.[20]

In Rome, Isis assimilated many functions that she did not have in Egypt. For example, she acquired power over vegetal fertility rather late, and then became assimilated to the Roman Ceres. However, she was dissimilar to Roman goddesses in that she was never assimilated into the Roman Olympian pantheon. Isis, like Cybele, was a "Great"-goddess, and, as Apuleius has Isis herself declare, her powers were potent indeed:

> II.11.12. "*I am . . . the mother of all things in nature,*
> *mistress of all the elements,*
> *the initial offspring of the ages,*
> *the greatest of all the divine powers . . .*
> *the uniform face of the gods and the goddesses.*"[21]
> Ibid, XI.5.

The idea of omnipotent power is appealing, especially to elements of society which might lack power; the adherents of the deity thus partake, albeit vicariously, of her forces. Yet, although she was lauded by her devotees, Isis' influence was feared by the State. The emperor Tiberius ordered the wholesale banishment of those Egyptians in

Italy who would not renounce the Isis-religion, hoping, one suspects, that by thus ridding the nation of Egyptians, the Roman adherents of the goddess would not be as "infected" or as powerful:

II.11.13. *"Four thousand freedmen,*
infected with that superstition,
who were of suitable age,
were to be shipped to the island of Sardinia . . .
the rest were to leave Italy,
unless they had renounced their impious rites
before a given date."[22]
Tacitus, Annals II.85; born *ca.* 55 CE.

Despite this attempt and others like it, Isis enjoyed popularity in Rome until the advent of Christianity, when she gracefully assimilated into the Virgin Mary. This assimilation is evident from similarities of iconography: the Madonna and child imagery which gained such popularity in the Christian world can be compared to the Isis and Horus imagery which prevailed among the Egyptians.[23]

Even goddesses who belonged to the Roman State pantheon often had characteristics indicative of "barbarian" goddesses. The Roman goddess *Diana* was identified early on with the Greek Artemis,[24] and, although Diana was generally a pacific goddess, there were cruel aspects to her worship in some cults—just as there may have been in the early worship of Artemis.[25] A striking example of this pre-Roman character was to be found at Diana-Trivia's shrine at Aricia; there she was indeed the "Mistress of Animals" who protected wild beasts:

II.11.14. *"And the day was already at hand . . .*
when . . . the Arician grove of Trivia
smokes, and with many a torch
the lake, which knows the secret of Hippolytus,
glitters;
Diana herself
crowns with flowers her veteran dogs
and wipes off her arrows,
and she lets wild animals go about in safety,
and at the virtuous hearths,
the whole land of Italy
honors the Ides of Hecate."[26]
Statius, Silvae III.55–60; *ca.* 45 CE to *ca.* 96 CE.

But the priesthood of the grove was obtained in an ancient manner. At Aricia, where the goddess was known as *Diana Nemorensis*, "Diana of the Grove," the priest of Diana was required to defend his office with his life: each successor won his office as *Rex Nemorensis*, "King of the Grove," by killing his predecessor in single combat.[27]

II.11.15. *"Hippolytus . . . went to the Aricians, in Italy;*
he became King there
and he dedicated a precinct to Artemis
[that is, to the Roman Diana]:
Here, until my time,
there were contests of single combat,
and the victor became the priest
of the goddess."[28]
Pausanias, Description of Greece II.27.4; *ca.* 150 CE.

Elsewhere we are told that

II.11.16. *"The strong of hand and fleet of foot*
rule [there],

and each perishes after his predecessor.''[29]
Ovid, Fasti III.271–272; 43 BCE to 17? CE.

That is, each is slain by his successor, just as he had slain his predecessor. Thus, just as Artemis, in the "Iphigeneia at Tauris," required human sacrifice, so Diana Nemorensis required that her priests rule only by engaging in a single-combat fight to the death. He who was defeated watered the grove with his blood. Although this bloody rite was ancient, it need not have been pre-Indo-European. We have no proof that pre-Indo-European cultures were more violent than the Indo-European. In fact, the opposite is probably true.[30]

Diana, like the Classical Greek Artemis, was a "Mistress of Animals" and virginal goddess of the hunt, but her earlier realm may have been, like that which one may assume for Artemis, the realm connected with fertility of animals and agriculture. Further, after she was identified with Artemis, she too became known as *Trivia*, the goddess of the three roads, and hence identified with the chthonian goddess Hecate. She acquired Hecate's "magical" aspects and her Netherworld connections. Diana was assimilated into the Roman pantheon as a huntress, but her fertility aspects were not forgotten. She was given a surface "gloss" of chastity, but her other "magical" aspects lay just below that surface.[31]

The Roman goddess of fruitfulness and prosperity, *Fortuna*, played a significant role in Roman thought and Roman religion. She was envisioned with a cornucopia:

II.11.17. ''*[Fortune] holds in her hand,*
that renowned horn of plenty,
not filled full of ever-blooming fruits,
but as much
as all the earth and all the seas
and rivers and mines and harbors
bear,
so much does she pour forth,
in plenty and abundance.''[32]
Plutarch, Moralia 318 A-B, on "The Fortune of the Romans;"
born *ca* 46 CE.

Fortuna had the ability to control mortal destiny:

II.11.18. ''*Oh goddess . . .*
ready to raise a body from the depths,
from its mortal station,
or to transform splendid triumphs
into funerals . . . ''[33]
Horace, Carmina XXXV.1–4; 65 BCE to 8 BCE.

All people fear Fortuna,

II.11.19. ''*lest with hurtful step*
you [Oh Fortuna] tumble down
the standing column
[of the state] . . .
and shatter the realm.''[34]
Ibid, XXXV.13–16.

Fortuna Primigenia, "first-born, primordial Fortune," could grant good fortune to whomever she wished, and she received dedicatory gifts from many people who were grateful for her boons:

II.11.20. ''. . . *To Fortuna Primigenia,*
child of Zeus,
I have given [this] gift.''[35]
Roman Inscription; *ca*. 200 BCE to *ca*. 300 CE.

Fortuna had an *oracular* shrine at Praeneste:

> II.11.21. "*To Fortuna Primigenia,*
> *on whatever day the oracle is manifest.*"[36]
> Roman Inscription; *ca.* 300 BCE.

Fortuna, then, contained all good things, and she could bestow them upon the fortunate or withdraw them from the less fortunate. She was thus responsible for the destinies of mortals. By an extension of these powers, she was a goddess capable of *predicting* what mortals' destinies would hold for them. The Roman Fortune, like the Fortunes of many other cultures, was therefore responsible for both fortune and fate.

The Roman goddess *Juno* corresponded to the Greek Hera, sharing many characteristics with her. Hera's pre-Greek serpent-associations were shared by Juno of Lanuvium:

> II.11.22. "*Lanuvium has been guarded for a long time*
> *by an ancient serpent . . .*
> *[who] demands his yearly sustenance*
> *and hurls forth hisses*
> *from the depths of the earth.*
> *Girls who are sent down to such rites*
> *turn pale . . .*
> *hither was my Cynthia drawn*
> *by sheared ponies:*
> *[Juno] was the [pretended] reason . . .* "[37]
> Propertius, Elegies IV.88.3–14; born *ca.* 50 BCE.

The Roman philosopher and moralist, Aelian, further described this holy place:

> II.11.23. "*. . . a grove is revered in Lavinium*
> [that is, Lanuvium],
> *both large and densely wooded,*
> *and nearby Hera of Argolis has a shrine.*
> *In the grove there is a vast and great den,*
> *and it is the resting-place of a serpent.*
> *And on allotted days*
> *sacred maidens enter the grove*
> *bearing a barley-cake in their hands . . .*
> *and if they are virgins,*
> *the serpent accepts the food as pure . . .*
> *if not, it remains untasted . . .*
> *and she who has disgraced her virginity*
> *is chastized with punishments*
> *according to the law.*"[38]
> Aelian, On Animals XI.16; *ca.* 170 CE to *ca.* 235 CE.

Sometimes young girls were chastized for "wrongdoing," and sometimes, having done nothing that would be worthy of punishment, they nonetheless received physical castigation—and, brainwashed by their society, they accepted this abuse. According to the poet, Ovid, in one ritual of Juno Lucina, in a sacred grove under the Esquiline Mount,

> II.11.24. "*There was an augur . . .*
> *He sacrificed a he-goat,*
> *and at his command*
> *the young girls offered their backs*
> *to be struck with thongs*
> *cut from hide.*"[39]
> Ovid, Fasti II.443–446; *ca.* 43 BCE to 17? CE.

The young women believed that by this means they would achieve an easy conception and delivery.

Juno was worshipped, as was Diana, in the woodland grove of Aricia:

> II.11.25. *"The inhabitants of neighboring towns [to Rome]*
> *perform for me the same service [of worship] . . .*
> *woodland Aricia, and the Laurentine people,*
> *and my own Lanuvium . . .*
> *Tibur and the sacred walls of the Praenestine goddess:*
> [in the calendars of these towns]
> *you read of the month of Juno."*[40]
> Ibid, VI.58–63.

Thus Juno, too, was involved with the grove which demanded a bloody successorship of its priests.

As was Hera, Juno was both sister and wife of the chief of the gods:

> II.11.26. *"It is something to have wed Jupiter*
> *and also to be the sister of Jupiter."*[41]
> Ibid, VI.27.

Juno was often greatly sublimated to her husband. In Vergil's epic poem, the Aeneid, Jupiter is called "the omnipotent king of Olympus,"[42] while Juno is called, simply, "wife."[43] Further, Juno, as Hera, exhausts much of her time in fruitless frustration over her husband's infidelities. Most of the tales told of Juno's impotent rage are retellings of Greek Hera-myths.[44] However, Juno seems to have fulfilled autonomous functions in cult. In many inscriptions, she is called Juno "Savior, Mother, Queen:"

> II.11.27. *"To Juno S.M.R."*[45]
> Roman Inscription; *ca*. 200 BCE to *ca*. 300 CE.

> II.11.28. *"To Juno Savior, Mother, Queen."*[46]
> Roman Inscription; *ca*. 200 BCE to *ca*. 300 CE.

As Mother, Juno was a mother-goddess and patron of mothers. On March first of each year, Roman matrons celebrated the *Matronalia,* in honor of Juno Lucina.[47] In Rome and throughout Italy, gifts were given to the goddess, in hope for and in gratitude for safe childbirths, as evidenced by inscriptions such as the following, from Norba in Latium:

> II.11.29. *"A gift for Juno Lucina*
> *on behalf of Gaius Rutilius,*
> *son of Publius."*[48]
> Roman Inscription; *ca*. 300 BCE.

Most likely, this man was a new father. It was common for the child's father to make the offering to the goddess, and to be named in the inscription instead of his wife or child.

Juno was invoked by mothers about to give birth:

> II.11.30. *"You, [Juno] Lucina . . .*
> *you pay heed to the vow*
> *of a woman in labor."*[49]
> Ovid, Fasti III.256; 43 BCE to 17? CE.

She assisted at childbirth, and she was invoked for fecundity. Thus Juno was aptly invoked as "Mother."

The Roman Juno *Regina,* "queen," received a golden sceptre on the Capitoline hill:

> II.11.31. *"Why," says Juno,*
> *am I therefore called queen,*
> *and most important of the goddesses?*
> *why is there given a golden sceptre*
> *to my right hand?"*[50]
> Ibid, VI.37–38.

Here, Juno was the essence of religious and political unity, along with the other two deities of the Capitoline Triad, Jupiter and Minerva. Sacrifice was offered to the triad by magistrates when they assumed office, and by victorious generals. In the Capitoline triad, Juno appears to be a queen of the gods in her own right, and not merely the consort of Jupiter.

Juno *Seispes*, or *Sospita*, "savior" or "unblemished," was worshipped throughout Italy:

> II.11.32. *"At the beginning of the month*
> *[the worship of] Juno Savior,*
> *the neighbor of the Phrygian Mother Goddess,*
> *is said to have been augmented*
> *with new temples."*[51]
> Ibid, II.55–56.

To this Juno Savior the dictator of Lanuvium sacrificed, as did also the highest officials of other Italic states, including Rome:

> II.11.33. *"Juno Sospita,*
> *to whom all of the consuls*
> *must make [sacrifice] . . . "*[52]
> Cicero, Pro Murena 41.90; 106 BCE to 43 BCE.

Juno thus was not only the wife of the Roman sovereign god, and therefore a ruler by proximity; she received sacrifice in her own right. Perhaps Juno was a weak goddess in Roman mythology and epic; Vergil's simple categorization of her as "wife" is certainly not an indication of power in *his* Roman pantheon. But perhaps Vergil's female pantheon was an idealization of what the Roman State *thought* its female figures should be like. By characterizing the queen of the gods as an "angry wife," Vergil was indicating to the Roman matron that she too should bow to the wishes of her husband. It would seem, at any rate, that in actual rite, Juno held much more power than she did in mythology or epic, particularly in that of Vergil.[53]

Minerva was an Italic deity who became part of the state triad, *Jupiter, Juno, Minerva*. At first, she was probably a goddess of artisans and craftspeople; later on, she was a goddess of war, when she became identified with the Greek Athena. That Minerva was important as a war-goddess is evident from her participation in the Trojan War. Her "gift" to the Trojan people was a horse,[54] even more a "machine of war" than the typical Indo-European horse, since this horse was to be filled with Greek soldiers, men who would jump out at the proper time and ravage the Trojans.

There is no doubt that Minerva was a patroness of war among the Romans, but that was not her only function:

> II.11.34. *"You yourself see that fierce wars are waged*
> *by Minerva's hands.*
> *Does she [therefore] have less leisure*
> *for the native arts?"*[55]
> Ovid, Fasti III.5–6; 43 BCE to 17? CE.

The poet Ovid goes on to declare that, after Pallas' (Minerva's) example, one should take some time to put aside the lance.[56]

Minerva, like Athena, was associated with snakes: she sent serpents as emissaries to kill the priest Laocoon, whose prophecies were warning the Trojans against her beloved Greeks and the "Trojan horse." After dispatching the priest, and his two young sons,

> II.11.35. *". . . the two serpents,*
> *slithering away,*
> *fled to the lofty sanctuaries,*

and sought the citadel
of fierce Tritonia [Minerva],
and they hid
under the feet of the goddess,
and under the circle of her shield.''[57]
Vergil, Aeneid II.225–227; 70 BCE to 19 BCE.

The snakes, in this case "ambassadors of destruction," belonged to and were sent by the "fierce" Minerva.

The oldest attestations of the goddess seem to be Etruscan; in Etruscan inscriptions she was called *Menrva, Menerva*, or *Menarva*.[58] Thus, she was originally an Italic goddess who, early on, became associated with the Greek goddess, Athena, and who then reflected the functions of her Greek sister.

The Roman goddess of love, *Venus*, the final—but not least important—goddess whom we shall discuss in this chapter, has an Indo-European name: *Venus* is related to the Sanskrit term for "loveliness," *vanas*, the Old Icelandic word for "friend," *vinr*, feminine *vina*, and the Hittite verb *wenzi*, "s(h)e has sexual intercourse." However, the name was probably given to a goddess who was worshipped in Italy before the advent of the Indo-Europeans, since there are cognate *terms* in other Indo-European languages, but no cognate *goddesses*.

Venus inherited the mythology of the Greek Aphrodite, but she was somewhat specialized among the Romans. She became a patron goddess for all sorts of people. Among the particularly chaste, she was *Venus Verticordia*, a goddess who governed the minds of chaste women.

II.11.36. ''. . . *so that the mind[s]*
of virgins and of women
might be more readily converted
from pleasure to modesty.''[59]
Valerius Maximus, Dictorum Factorumque Memorabilium VIII.15.12;
First Century CE.

As *Venus Genetrix*, she was mother of the Roman people and goddess of love—chaste or not-so-chaste. She created all of the gods, and she gave laws to heaven, earth, and sea.[60] Further,

II.11.37. ''. . . *she was the founder*
of the [human] race.''[61]
Ovid, Fasti IV.93–95; 43 BCE to 17? CE.

and she was hailed as the

II.11.38. ''. . . *first origin*
of all the elements . . .
the nurturing Venus.''[62]
Apuleius, Metamorphoses IV.30; born *ca.* 123 CE.

Perhaps because of her potency, she was often addressed as queen:

II.11.39. *''Oh, queen Venus!''*[63]
Propertius, Elegies IV.5.65; born *ca.* 50 CE.

and

II.11.40. *''Oh Venus,*
queen of Cnidus and Paphos.''[64]
Horace, Carmina I.xxx.1; 65 BCE to 8 BCE.

In fact, Venus was addressed as queen *despite the fact* that she was not married to King Jupiter. She was, therefore, a queen in her own right, and not just a consort. She must have wielded considerable power in the Roman pantheon, power which was an augmentation of her normal powers as a goddess who controlled the life force, as she controlled the act of procreation.

Venus and her son Cupid figured prominently in a tale which recalls the serpent, a creature which has manifested itself throughout several of the mythologies discussed in this book.

There was once a young woman, whose name was *Psyche*.[65] Psyche was possessed of exceptional beauty. In fact, she was so lovely that people paid homage to her as they would to a goddess. Unfortunately, they were so busy honoring the young mortal woman that they forgot to visit the temples of Venus. The goddess' statues were left ungarlanded, and her

> II.11.41. *"altars were destitute,*
> *made filthy with cold ashes,"*[66]
> Apuleius, Metamorphoses IV.29; born *ca*. 123 CE.

since, for a long time, no sacrifices had been burnt for her.

Venus was not pleased with this neglect, and she vowed to have revenge upon the young maiden:

> II.11.42. *"Now I'll make her regret*
> *her illegal beauty."*[67]
> Ibid, IV.30.

The goddess, seeking revenge, asked her son, Cupid, to use his arrows against the girl. Meanwhile, many people worshipped Psyche, but none dared to ask for her hand in marriage. All of the marriageable young men were so much in awe of her that none even dreamed of marrying her. Psyche thus remained unmarried far too long to please her father, so he went to consult Apollo's oracle, to find out what was wrong with his daughter. The oracle replied that

> II.11.43. *"a savage and wild and serpiform mischief,*
> *which, flying over the aether on its wings,*
> *exhausts one and all . . . "*[68]
> Ibid, IV.33.

would be the king's son-in-law. Psyche was to be dressed as a corpse and placed on a mountain to be wed by a terrifying serpent.[69]

Psyche was placed upon the mountain-top, and, when the mourners had left, a wind bore her to a lovely valley. She fell asleep there, and, when she awoke, refreshed, she made her way to a nearby palace. The palace was filled with exquisite treasures, and a voice told her to enjoy all of the riches, for they were hers. Invisible servants catered to her every need, and an invisible bridegroom spent enchanting nighttime hours with her.

Now, at this same time, Psyche's sisters were wondering what had happened to her, and they decided to search for her. Psyche's husband, however, aware of the approach of his sisters-in law and concerned for his own future with his wife, warned Psyche not to respond to her siblings. Psyche entreated her husband to allow her to see her sisters, and finally he consented, telling her that she must not reveal his identity to them.

The sisters visited with Psyche, and, seeing the splendor in which she lived, became jealous. They visited her two more times, and they told her that her husband was in reality an enormous serpent who would devour her. They suggested that she sneak a glance at her husband's face while he slept, and they also suggested that she cut off his serpentine head.

Psyche, heeding the words of her sisters, that night looked upon the face of her husband, Cupid; she marvelled at his beauty, his golden hair and gossamer wings. Near the bed lay Cupid's bow, arrow, and quivers. Psyche touched the tip of an arrow and pricked her finger. Because of Cupid's arrow, she was now hopelessly in love with the god. She had not the heart to attack him, so his head went unscathed. But she forgot the lamp in her hand, and dropped oil onto his shoulder. Cupid, scalded by the oil, awoke with a start, and flew away.

A sea-gull brought Venus the news that her son had fallen in love with a woman named Psyche. Venus was incensed that Psyche, of all people, should be the object of her son's love. She resolved that the girl would be sorry she had ever met Cupid.

Psyche wandered over the earth in search of a haven from the wrath of Venus, and in search of her husband as well. She finally allowed herself to be taken to Venus, where she was given difficult tasks to perform and was subjected to tortures. Worst of all, Venus would not allow Cupid and Psyche to see one another, even though both of them were at Venus' palace.

For her final task, Psyche was made to go to the Underworld, where she fell into a Stygian sleep. Cupid, recovered from his burn, hastened to rescue her, and then flew to Father Jupiter, to ask for his help. Jupiter decided that it would be a good idea to curb the young love god, and he decreed that the impetuous youth should be bound

> II.11.44. *''with the fetters of marriage.''*[70]
> Ibid, VI.23.

Psyche and Cupid should be reunited for life:

> II.11.45. *''Let him hold her, let him possess her;*
> *in Psyche's embraces*
> *let him fully take his own enjoyment*
> *forever.''*[71]
> Ibid.

Jupiter further decreed that Psyche should be made immortal. The two were married, and they lived together, at last, in happiness.

Cupid, as we see, was possessed of a periodic serpentine form, but he did *not* adopt this form at night, when he slept with Psyche. At night, he was the winged love god. The wings and serpentine form of the "Goddess of Regeneration" were thus extended to her son (that is, the Neolithic son and consort).

The female relationships in this story reflect an estrangement similar to that fostered in many patriarchal societies: according to Classical Greek and Roman mythopoets, mother-in-law is to be pitted against daughter-in-law, and sister is in competition with sister. The warrior-concept of "divide and conquer" pertains to the domestic sphere and to the battlefield.[72]

In the Roman pantheon, in summation, Cybele and Isis were borrowed directly from the Near East. Cybele, and the Roman Diana were "Mistresses of Animals." Isis, and the Roman Venus, Juno and Minerva were associated with serpents. The Roman Fortuna played a large role in the allocation of fortune and goods to the Roman people. In this, she was similar to the goddesses of fortune in many of her sister Indo-European pantheons.

All of the goddesses whom we have discussed in the last eight chapters, from *Laima* to *Fortuna*, from *Anāhitā* to *Athena*, have significance in themselves. Their individual functions reflect the places of female deities in the societies in which they were worshipped. Further, most of them were descended from the goddesses of Neolithic Europe and the Near East, as manifested in both their iconographies and their mythologies. Many of the goddesses had power over life and death, and were thus connected to the "Great-Mother" goddesses and to the bird and snake goddesses, the "Goddesses of Regeneration;" in fact, even virgin goddesses were invoked as "Mother." Huntress-goddesses such as Artemis-Diana and Skaði were "Mistresses of Animals." The mythology of Europe and related cultures changed throughout the millennia, reflecting assimilations of new peoples and new ideologies, but the goddesses indeed reflect their sources. These goddesses manifest the *resurfacings* of Neolithic European, pre-Indo-European religious beliefs in the nature and functions of the feminine.

In preceding chapters, we have focused upon individual functions of goddesses, and upon their inheritances from Neolithic Europe. In the following pages we will synthesize some of these functions, to observe the functional patterns. We will focus upon some of the more salient functions of the ideal Indo-European female figure, goddess or heroine, and we will attempt to discover the underlying service which she is expected to render to her societies.

Part Three

Energy

In the preceding pages, we have discussed goddesses from many different geographical regions, enumerating the qualities and the functions of each. The goddesses, although diverse, show recurrent patterns, with regard to their powers and functions which they fulfill in their societies.

These diverse goddesses are powerful, but the scope of their powers varies. Power may be of two sorts: power *over*, which is the power exercised by one who dominates; and power *within*, autonomy, connectedness to the life-force, which is the power of those engaged in a sharing society. This power *within* belongs to those who connect themselves to the life force and who, as nurturers, augment that life-force. The paradox of energy is that the more energy one gives to life, the more one is filled with that energy.

There are few Indo-European goddesses who have the power of domination, power *over*, but domination is part of a patriarchal world-view, not of an equalitarian world-view. In the sense of power *within*, there is variation in the amount of power retained by individual female figures in Indo-European societies. In this sense of autonomy and the ability to be "at cause" instead of "at effect," the most powerful goddesses would be the Indic Devī and the Celtic Medb. Their power is different from that of powerful goddesses within a male hierarchy, such as the Classical Greek Athena. For Athena has lost her female connectedness. Although she is important in the Greek pantheon, it is as one who serves the philosophy of the patriarchy. If she is autonomous, it is with concomitant loss of her sexuality. Patriarchal societies have taken over the powers of many divine women, just as they attempt to absorb the powers of mortal women. Thus, all of the goddesses are powerful, but the patriarchy has taken bits and pieces of many of them.

In the first part of this section, we will examine three important functions of the goddesses who were worshipped by the ancient Indo-Europeans: those of bestowing sovereignty, bestowing warrior-energy, and nurturance. The goddesses, as well as mortal women, were valued according to the quality and quantity of energy which they bestowed upon the male members of these societies. In particular the energy of female figures, and in general the energy of the nurturing classes, was thus viewed by the male mythopoets, and probably by the rulers of Indo-European societies, as a product to be commandeered by the men in charge. Nonetheless, the nurturing of a society is powerful in itself, again in the sense of power as connectedness, for it connects the nurturer to the life-force of that society, thus augmenting the life-forces of the nurturers themselves.

In the final chapter, we will examine the thesis that men's purpose for woman in these male-centered Indo-European societies was to give energy on one of these functional levels; the quality of that energy differed according to which stage of life she depicted: virgin, matron, or old woman.

CHAPTER 12

Functions of the female in male-centered society

SOVEREIGNTY

One of the more important functions of goddesses in ancient Indo-European societies was, surprisingly enough, control over kingship; goddesses were *sovereignty*-figures who determined which man should rule the kingdom. Thus, although a goddess or heroine was not the "king," only *she* had the power to bestow sovereignty over a land. In Indo-European cultures, these sovereignty-figures were *enablers*, women who gave access to the throne. A man with the proper heroic qualities would marry a foreign princess, live with her at her home, and inherit her father's kingdom. He could not become ruler of the kingdom without marrying the daughter of the king.[1]

With time, the notion of *sovereignty* often became personified as a goddess. The goddess, further, symbolically became the throne upon which she sat. The name of the Egyptian goddess *Isis*, we may recall, means "the throne." In some cultures, the throne-goddess became the judgment seat upon which the male ruler sat.

Thus, men in these male-centered cultures held the rule, but they very often had to marry the princess to gain this rule. Examples of the role of the princess abound in ancient literature. Indic princesses chose a mate in a ritual called the *svayamvara* or "self-choice." In this rite, available men would take part in various contests, to demonstrate their prowess, and each tried to prove that he was the best man. The Indic princess Draupadī, a heroine in the Mahābhārata, chose a mate by this means, and the man then inherited her father's lands.

Another heroine in the Mahābhārata, *Mādhavī*,[2] was also an intermediary of sovereignty. Mādhavī was given in marriage to three kings in succession; these kings engendered in her three sons, so that their reigns might be perpetuated. But she differed from the true "Sovereignty:" she was given to men who were already kings, and she thus did not bestow kingship *per se*. The energies of this heroine will be more thoroughly investigated in the next chapter.

Further, in India, the female figure who personified the right to rule was the goddess *Shrī Lakshmī*. Indic kings were said to have been married to her; she was the personification of "kingly fortune"[3] as well as the more common fortune, and if she abandoned a ruler, he was destined to lose his realm.

Iranian sovereignty was attained by means of the *khvarenah*, the "glory;"[4] the possessor of this glory was imbued with a special power, and he often gained the kingship. The *khvarenah* was frequently given to a male by a female intermediary:

> The mother of the hero, *Kai-Apiveh*, was *Farhank*, daughter of him who is exalted on the heavenly path. It is said that the Khvarenah of King Feredun settled on the root of a reed in the wide-formed ocean. Eventually, the glory passed to Farhank, and then to her son, whom she gave as an adoptive child to the first Kavi. The kavis became the Kayanid dynasty of kings, and they were ever accompanied by the Khvarenah given them by Farhank.

Although Farhank did endow a line of kings with sovereignty, she did so, again, as an intermediary, befitting a heroine in a post-Zoroastrian society.[5]

In early Greek tales, the rule of the land was commonly passed through a female intermediary. In Sophocles' play, Oedipus the King, Oedipus was made to marry his mother Jocasta, the Queen of Thebes.

> King Laius of Thebes was warned that if he fathered a son, that son would kill him. A son *was* born, however, and Laius exposed him, running a spike through his feet to be sure that he would stay put and succumb to the elements.
>
> A shepherd of Polybus, King of Corinth, found the baby and Polybus adopted him. The

child was called *Oedipus*, the "swollen-foot." When he was older, Oedipus went to Delphi to ask the oracle who his parents were. He was told only that he would kill his father and marry his mother. Fearing that he was meant to kill Polybus, he thus left Corinth and wandered to Thebes, killing *his real father* Laius in a chance encounter on the road.

Oedipus went on to the city, Thebes, which he found plagued by a monstrous Sphinx. He solved the riddle which the Sphinx posed, and he won Queen Jocasta, along with the kingship of Thebes. Oedipus became King of Thebes, and not simply consort of the queen:

> III.12.1. "*Creon: 'And you rule the land with her, cojointly?'*
> *Oedipus: 'She obtains from me all that she desires.'*"[6]
> Sophocles, "Oedipus the King" 579–580;
> *ca*. 496 BCE to *ca*. 406 BCE.

After some happy time spent as husband of Jocasta and king of Thebes, Oedipus found out the truth of his origins. He left his incestuous marriage, and, at the same time, gave up the kingship, for he was king of Thebes only through his marriage to the queen. The kingdom then reverted to his mother's brother, Creon, who had shared the rulership with them.

Another Greek sovereignty-figure, *Penelope*, was tenaciously wooed by suitors, the local nobles who wanted her hand. These suitors also wanted the rule of Ithaca, the island over which her absent husband Odysseus was lord.

Penelope, a heroine in Homer's Odyssey, waited faithfully for *twenty years*, for her husband Odysseus to return from the Trojan War, although she was hard-pressed to marry one of her many suitors. She pretended that she could not marry until she finished weaving a shroud for her father-in-law, Laertes.[7] But each night Penelope unraveled the work which she had accomplished during the day, and she thus extended her time of respite. Each night for three years she unraveled the shroud, until one of her maids betrayed her and revealed her subterfuge. She then had to finish the shroud; after that, she would be required to pick one of the suitors.

It was agreed that a contest would be held, and that whoever could bend Odysseus' bow would be the victor, the new husband of Penelope, and the new ruler of Ithaca. The contest, fortuitously, took place just as Odysseus—in disguise—returned home. Of course, he was victorious in the contest, and he avenged himself upon those who had so rashly believed that they could take over his rule.

In Ithaca, as we see, Penelope was a *potential* sovereignty-figure.[8] Her suitors were pragmatic; it was not Penelope, well into middle-age, whom they were anxious to possess, but her lands. The husband of Penelope would become ruler of Ithaca. Although Penelope and Odysseus had a son, Telemachus, the boy did not automatically take over his father's realm. The land did not pass from father to son but *through* a female figure. Perhaps, if Odysseus and Penelope had given birth to a daughter, the rule could have passed to *her* husband. However, no such daughter existed, and the kingship could only pass to the man who would marry Penelope.

Penelope's suitors were attempting to gain her *husband*'s kingdom. Because Odysseus was already her husband, the suitors were doomed to fail in their attempts.

If Penelope was the Greek idealization of the "perfect wife," the monogamous woman (although for half of her life, unaccompanied by her husband, she remained autonomous), her sister-in-law Helen represented the dangers (in the view of her culture) of a woman who does not remain monogamous.

Helen was the daughter of Zeus and Leda. Her father had assumed the shape of a swan, and he had seduced her mother. In due time, Helen was born—from an egg.

So from the beginning Helen had rather special status, since most mortals, even in myth, issued live from their mothers' wombs. Her special association to birds was not her chief claim to fame, however. She also was the most beautiful woman in the world. It is not surprising that there were many suitors for her hand, when she reached marriageable age.

But it was Menelaus, brother of Agamemnon, who overcame all of her other suitors, including Odysseus,

> III.12.2. *"because Menelaus gave the greatest gifts."*[9]
> Hesoid, Catalogues of Women 68.99–100; *ca.* 750? BCE.

Menelaus won not only the fair Helen, but her father's kingdom, Sparta, as well. However, his happiness was not destined to be long-lived, because there were risks involved in a marriage to the most beautiful woman in the world—not all of them her fault. In fact, she was used as a pawn by the gods, in a beauty contest.[10]

When the hero Peleus and the goddess Thetis were married, at their wedding-feast Eris, or "Strife," threw down a golden apple, inscribed "for the fairest." Just as young women often vie to catch a bride's wedding bouquet, so three goddesses: Hera, Athena, and Aphrodite, all claimed this apple. All three claimed to be the most beautiful of the goddesses. Their disagreement led to a celestial beauty contest; Paris, the most handsome mortal man in the world, was chosen judge of the beauty contest.

Each of the goddesses attempted to increase her chances of winning by doing some careful politicking. Each, in Indo-European tripartite manner, offered Paris a gift if he would cast his vote for her. Hera promised him greatness, Athena offered him success in war, and Aphrodite promised him that he would wed the most beautiful woman in the world. The latter gift appeared to Paris to be a sexual dream come true, even if Helen, his potential bride, was married.

After Aphrodite was judged by Paris to be the most beautiful of the goddesses, she helped Paris to win the lovely Helen from her husband. Paris abused Menelaus' hospitality, and the Trojan tragedy was set in motion. Helen's second husband did not gain a kingdom from her as had Menelaus. In fact, he lost his own kingdom because of her, along with the lives of Trojans and Greeks.[11]

Among the Celts, it was the earth who was "Sovereignty." She may have been symbolized by the cup-mark as early as the Neolithic;[12] this cup became, in Irish mythology, the cup of "Sovereignty" bequeathed by the goddess Flaith, who in turn became the personification of sovereignty.

There are many stories of Flaith in Irish mythology. In one tale, Conn, a famous king of Tara, was traveling with his druids and his poets. They lost their way in a mist,[13] and then came to a dwelling. There they came upon a "phantom," Lug, the god who was known as a chief of the ancient magical folk, the Túatha Dé Danann.[14]

With the phantom was a girl, and

> III.12.3. *". . . the girl was . . .*
> *the Sovereignty of Erin . . . "*[15]
> "Baile in Scail" 8.220; *ca.* 1050 CE to *ca.* 1150 CE.

She was seated on a crystal chair. A silver vat, a vessel of gold, and a golden cup lay before her. Sovereignty served Conn with mead, and she asked to whom the cup of red ale[16] should be given. She then gave the cup to Conn and to several other future kings, as Lug announced their names and reigns.[17]

The cup thus signified the bestowal *of* sovereignty *by* the goddess Sovereignty. In the story of Conn, Flaith was a lovely young woman. But she, like many other goddesses, especially in the Celtic sphere, could change her form, and her epoch of life, at will.

In another tale of Sovereignty, Flaith was neither young nor lovely. In this story, a hero, Niall of the Nine Hostages,[18] son of Eochaid Mugmedon, went hunting with his five stepbrothers. Each of the brothers went to search for drinking water and found a well guarded by an ugly old woman:

> III.12.4. *["There was] an old woman,*
> *a seeress,*
> *[seated] on the edge*
> *[of the well].*
> *She had a mouth*
> *in which there was room for a hound.*

She had a tooth-fence around her head.
She was an ugly horror of Ireland."[19]
"Echtra mac Echdach Mugmedóin" 35 (LL 4580–4583);
ca. 1100 CE.

The old woman promised water to each of the young men, in return for a kiss, but each of Niall's step-brothers, in turn, rejected her. One brother, Brian, gave her a hasty kiss, but only Niall truly embraced her, whereupon she changed into a lovely maiden and addressed Niall as king, saying,

III.12.5. "*The drink for which you came . . .*
there will be glory to drink,
from a mighty goblet.[20]
It will be mead;
it will be honey;
it will be powerful ale."[21]
LL 4668–4671; *ca.* 1100 CE.

The woman, of course, was Flaith. She bestowed sovereignty upon Niall, and Niall became high-king of Ireland. Niall's bestowal of a kiss upon a woman neither young nor lovely was probably considered to be extremely heroic by the male mythopoets. He had thus, in their view, earned the kingship with hard labor.

The most famous queen among the Celts was also an intermediary of kingship. Her name was *Medb*.[22] Although *two* Medbs appear in the texts, Medb of Cruachan and Medb Lethderg, both of them have the same function, and they are probably regional variants of the same female figure.

Medb was closely linked with Flaith. Lexically, *Medb* refers to something intoxicating, or to intoxication.[23] *Flaith*, in its primary sense, means "lordship, sovereignty, rule."[24] In modern Irish, Flaith also means "ale."[25] A ritual involving intoxication, therefore, may have been connected with the bestowal of sovereignty.

There is further evidence for the juxtaposition of the two meanings:

III.12.6. "*[He] will not be a king over Ireland*
if the ale of Cuala does not come to him."[26]
"Scéla Cano Meic Gartnáin" 452–453; *ca.* 850 CE to *ca.* 1100 CE.

and, in the Book of Leinster, Medb Lethderg is called

III.12.7. "*. . . the daughter of Conan of Cuala.*"[27]
LL 6416; *ca.* 1100 CE.

It is thus Queen Medb who is the "ale," the "intoxication" of Cuala, and she is responsible for the sovereignty of Ireland.

Folk tales linking Medb with bestowal of the kingship are numerous. In the "Cath Boinde Andso," Medb Cruachan's husbands assumed the kingship of Connacht through marriage to her and with her approval:

III.12.8. "*. . . with the consent of Medb,*"[28]
"Cath Boinde Andso" 182 (Book of Lecan 351b–353a);
ca. 1400 CE.

Eochaid Dala became king, and Ailill succeeded him.[29] Note that, when Medb was married to Eochaid Dala,

III.12.9. "*At that time,*
Ailill, son of Mata,
son of Sraibgind of the Erna,
came to Cruachan,
and Ailill was at that time
a young child."[30]
Ibid.

Medb was, therefore, much older than Ailill. The rewards derived from marriage to Medb must have been quite significant, to warrant Ailill's interest, since, again, in the male mind it was the nubile young woman who was of greatest sexual interest. In fact, Eochaid challenged Ailill to fight

> III.12.10. *"for the kingdom and for his wife."*[31]
> Ibid.

One could not gain the former without taking the latter.

Along with Medb Lethderg, too, came the sovereignty of Ireland:

> III.12.11. *"Great indeed was the power and the ability*
> *of that Medb*
> *over the men of Ireland,*
> *for she would not admit*
> *a king in Tara*
> *if she herself were not a wife for him."*[32]
> LL p. 380a; *ca.* 1100 CE.

Further, before Cormac, grandson of Conn, took the kingship of Ireland, he lived in Kells because Medb Lethderg would not let him live in Tara, the capital of North Leinster, after the death of his father, King Art. Medb thus retained the power of kingship for herself:

> III.12.12. *"Medb Lethderg of Leinster*
> *was with [King] Art,*
> *and after Art's death,*
> *she bore the kingship."*[33]
> "Esnada Tige Buchet" (LL 35383–35384); *ca.* 1100 CE.

Medb, therefore, was not only an epic queen but also the epic representation of Sovereignty. She took to herself not only the power of *enabling*, which has been considered, in male-centered societies, to belong to the sphere of women. Hers was the power of autonomy over herself and rule over others. Medb was sovereign in two different paradigms of society. Medb of Cruachan ruled equally with Ailill, in a partnership or sharing of power, and Medb Lethderg ruled in partnership with Art, and alone, after Art's death. In the latter case she followed the dominator paradigm of ruling *over*.[34]

Germanic "Sovereignty"-figures were pivotal to the throne, similar to the Irish Medb.

When Hermigisil, king of the Saxon Varini, was on his deathbed, he ordered his son Radigis to marry his stepmother, the queen. Only thus could he establish his claim to the throne:

> III.12.13. *"Let my son Radigis be married*
> *to his stepmother*
> *henceforth,*
> *just as the law of our forefathers*
> *decrees."*[35]
> Procopius, History of the Wars VIII.20.20; *ca.* 500 CE.

As late as the period of the Norman Conquest of England, Canute the Dane behaved similarly to the Saxon kings; after he overthrew Ethelred, he sent for the queen, a woman well along in years, who was living in Normandy. He did not consider the throne truly his until he had married her.[36]

In the Germanic epic, the Nibelungenlied, Queen Brynhild fulfilled the role of "Sovereignty."[37]

Brynhild was faced with many suitors, and she kept them at bay by challenging each of them to a contest of physical skills. She was their opponent, and she caused those who lost to her to pay dearly: the loser of the contest must also lose his head. Brynhild possessed great power and strength, and so she was consistently victorious in the contests:

III.12.14. "*There was a queen who lived beyond the sea,*
and no one had ever seen her like.
The maid was an incredible beauty,
and her strength was great . . .
she held shooting matches
with hefty heroes.
She threw a stone far away from her,
and then she would spring after it.
Each one who hoped to possess her
must win three games
from the high-born lady.
If he lost one game,
he also lost his head . . .
Then spoke the Lord of the Rhine,
'I will go down to the sea,
to this Brynhild,
whatever might happen to me.'"[38]
Nibelungenlied VI.2–6; *ca.* 1200 CE.

Great was the reward of sovereignty, therefore, but great was the price for those who attempted to gain it—or her—and failed. Only by such arduous contests could the superiority of the aspirant be proved.

The Scandinavian goddess, Gefjon, also served as "Sovereignty." She procured a kingdom for the god, Oðin; she mated with a giant, bearing sons who helped her to gain sufficient land to constitute Oðin's kingdom.[39]

Baltic folklore has handed down similar tales of female intermediaries in the bestowing of sovereignty.

In a Lithuanian folktale, a king forced the hero, one of his personal guards, to find a certain maiden, and to bring her back to him. The hero accomplished the task, and he was then required by the girl and the king to undertake many other feats. He successfully achieved all that was asked of him.

The king asked of the hero one feat too many, however. The last feat boomeranged, and the king was boiled to death in a vat of hot milk.[40]

And

III.12.15. "*Then the [hero], the smallest brother,*
married the beautiful girl,
and he became king . . .
When he died he left the kingdom to his children."[41]
"One Hundred and One Brothers
And One Hundred and One Stallions;" Nineteenth Century CE.

In this case we see that a transition occurred; sovereignty, after this time, no longer passed through the daughter of the king, but was handed down from father to son.

In another Lithuanian folk-tale, a king had a very pretty, but spoiled, daughter. From all over the world came young kings and princes wishing to marry her, but the princess could not make up her mind which one to choose for a husband.

Her father was perturbed, because he had to feed all of the suitors: Lithuanian suitors were as expensive to feed as the Greek suitors who depleted Penelope's stores.

Finally, the princess decided to hold a contest: the man who could speak a sackful of words would be her husband. All of the kings and dukes began to speak into their sacks, but, no matter how long they talked, their sacks remained empty. Then a young boy, keeper of the king's rabbits, began to talk, and talk, and talk. The king, unable to endure the prattling any longer, said:

> III.12.16. *''You've talked enough, silly one!*
> *Your sack is full of words!''*
> "A Sackful of Words;" Nineteenth Century CE.

So, the youth married the beautiful princess, and, when the king died, the boy succeeded him.[42]

We thus see that female "Sovereignty"-figures, in those male-centered cultures which we have been investigating, did not themselves rule. They bestowed sovereignty: a kingship, a land, or a throne, upon *men*. "Sovereignty"-figures cannot, therefore, be equated with matriarchal female rulers, although some female figures, such as the Irish Medb, did indeed share sovereignty in a pre-Indo-European manner. The female personification of sovereignty in Indo-European cultures is most likely an outgrowth of the indigenous Neolithic European matri- patrilineal descent system, and a matrifocal living pattern. The land passed to the king's *son-in-law*. Further, when the indigenous Europeans, who had owned the land, met the patrilineal Indo-European invaders, the new invaders took the land, through marriage or through force, and became the new rulers.

Sovereignty may be conceived of as a type of *energy*, which, along with martial and nurturing energies, was the gift which female figures, goddesses and heroines, bestowed upon male members of male-centered societies. Similar to the energy of the Indo Shaktī, this was an activating, vitalizing energy which enfused the Indic-European males. It is my thesis that, in patriarchal cultures, energy was regarded as the property of the male. Woman was useful, in this male-centered view, in proportion to the quantity of energy which she bestowed upon the males of her culture. With this load of energy, the males of these societies were then enabled to carry on the functions of society, as rulers or, as we shall see, as warriors.

WAR

In the function of sovereignty, an Indo-European female figure, a goddess or heroine, was usually an intermediary. The realm *passed through* her; she gave the rule to a male, and he in turn would serve as the true ruler.

The role of the Indo-European female figure in war was similar. Women who fulfilled the "warrior" function in a "male" sense, that is, in a violent, raging sense, similar to the Egyptian Hathor, the Accadian Ishtar (the Sumerian Inanna was less celebrated as a warrior than Ishtar) or the Ugaritic Anat, were few. The Amazons, so bellicose in their mythology, were represented in all myths as foreign women, never women who functioned within the Indo-European sphere.[43]

In Greece, there were isolated tales of women bearing arms out of a particular necessity. The women of Melos helped their men in time of need, but as adjuncts: each Melian woman carried a sword in the fold of her dress, and when a signal was given, each *gave her weapon to a man*; then

> III.12.17. *''the men, grabbing their swords,*
> *attacked the barbarians.''*[44]
> Plutarch, Moralia 246 F; before 50 CE to after 120 CE.

Thus, these "women warriors" bestowed power upon the warrior, just as "sovereignty"-figures bestowed power upon male rulers.

In a situation more typical of the ancient Indo-European world, the women of the Iliad occupied themselves at home while their men were out fighting:

III.12.18. *[Hector to Andromache]: "But go to your house,*
and busy yourself with your own tasks,
the loom and the distaff,
and tell your handmaids
to set about their work;
war, on the other hand,
shall be exercised by all men,
but especially by me,
among those who live in Ilium."[45]
Homer, Iliad VI.490–493; *ca.* 800? BCE.

Athena, the Greek goddess of wisdom, war, and handicrafts, was indeed a warrior-goddess, but she was in general a strategic warrior, as was her Roman counterpart, *Minerva*. Whereas her male counterpart *Ares-Mars* raged:

III.12.19. *". . . for Ares rages*
promiscuously . . . "[46]
Homer, Odyssey XI.537; *ca.* 800? BCE.

and was quite destructive:

III.12.20. *". . . annihilating Ares . . . "*[47]
Ibid, VIII.309.

on the other hand, Athena's task was to *give courage* to warriors:

III.12.21. *"So spoke Pallas Athene,*
and she breathed into
[Laertes, the father of Odysseus]
great strength."[48]
Ibid, XXIV.520.

Athena acted as general and aide rather than as a soldier. She gave advice even to wily Odysseus:

III.12.22. *". . . if fifty troops of men,*
endowed with speech,
should stand about us,
striving to slay us in battle,
well then, you should drive out
their cattle and large sheep."[49]
Ibid, XX.49–51.

Other Greek goddesses also served as inspiration and helpmeet in battle, though none played as great a role as Athena. *Artemis Agrotera* was invoked by the Spartans:

III.12.23. *". . . and when [the armies]*
were less than a stadium apart,
the Lacedaemonians sacrificed a she-goat
to [Artemis] Agrotera,
as they are accustomed,
and they marched against their enemy . . . "[50]
Xenophon, Hellenica IV.2.20; *ca.* 428/7 BCE to *ca.* 354 BCE.

Artemis of Messenia was given a martial statue:

III.12.24. *"The statue of Artemis,*
which was of bronze,
and the arms . . . "[51]
Pausanias, Description of Greece IV.13.1; *ca.* 150 CE.

As we discussed in Chapter Ten, the Spartans made a practice of martializing their goddesses.

Nerio, or Neriene, was one Roman goddess who was not borrowed from the Greeks. She was a Roman warrior-goddess who was borrowed from Rome's Italic neighbors, the Sabines:

> III.12.25. ''. . . *Nerio or Nerienes . . . is a Sabine word,*
> *and it indicates strength and fortitude . . .*
> *Nerio therefore [is] the strength and power*
> *of Mars,*
> *and a certain majesty*
> *which is shown to belong to Mars.*''[52]
> Aulus Gellius, Attic Nights XIII.xxiii.7–10;
> *ca.* 130 CE to *ca.* 180 CE.

As a warrior goddess, Nerio was often equated with Minerva:

> III.12.26. ''*Mars was conquered by Minerva*
> *[in a contest]*
> *and . . . Minerva was then called Nerio.*''[53]
> Porphyrion, Commentum in Horatium Flaccum, Epistles II.2.209;
> Early Third Century CE.

This warrior-goddess was viewed by some, appropriately enough, as the wife of the warrior-god, Mars:

> III.12:27. ''*Mars, coming from abroad,*
> *greets his wife, Nerio . . .* ''[54]
> Plautus, "Truculentus" 515; fl. *ca.* 200 BCE.

Nerio thus was "strength"[55] personified into a feminine deity, as were many abstract conceptions. Despite this personification, Nerio represented, not the act of fighting, but one who inspires the power to fight.

The situation was similar among the Irish, where the role of a warrior-goddess was *generally* to exhort men to battle, or to teach them how to fight. Thus *Scathach* taught Cu Chulainn skill of arms; the hero was directed to hold her at sword-point until she granted him three wishes:

> III.12.28. ''*Namely, instruction [in skill at arms]*
> *without neglect . . .*
> *and that she should tell him*
> *what would befall him,*
> *for she was a prophetess.*''[56]
> "Tochmarc Emire" 70; *ca.* 900 CE to *ca.* 1300 CE.

Further, Bodball the druidess and the gray one of Luachar, two female warriors, reared the hero, Finn Mac Cumaill.[57] Both of the great "warrior-goddesses," *Badb* and *Morrigan*, roused men to battle.[58]

In contrast to the role which Irish goddesses played in mythology, the role which Irish mortal women played in history, at least as reported by the Romans, was a substantive one. According to Diodorus Siculus,

> III.12.29. ''*The women of the Gauls*
> *not only resemble the men in size,*
> *but they are equal to them*
> *in prowess as well.*''[59]
> Diodorus Siculus, Bibliothecae V.32.2; fl. *ca.* 50 BCE.

Ammianus Marcellinus described the wife of the typical Gallic warrior as

> III.12.30. ''. . . *much braver than he,*
> *and bright-eyed . . .*

she puffs up her neck
and gnashes her teeth,
and, [with] her heavy, rough, snow-white arms,
she proceeds to cast punches
mingled with kicks.''[60]
Ammianus Marcellinus, History XV.12.1;
ca. 330 CE. to *ca.* 395 CE.

The Roman historian Tacitus wrote of the British Queen *Boudicca*, who led her nation in war. According to Tacitus, the British made no sexual distinction among their rulers.[61] Boudicca led her people in a military uprising against the Romans.[62]

Although it is thus most often foreigners, such as the Romans, who describe Celtic female warriors, there *is* one significant woman who was described by the Celts themselves: Queen Medb. As we discussed earlier,[63] Medb was not only general of her army: she was one of the best fighters.

Indo-Iranian goddesses generally fulfilled their martial functions more indirectly. However, the powerful, transfunctional Indic goddess, *Devī*,[64] was represented as a straightforward and rather bloodthirsty warrior-goddess. She was described as "red-toothed" from devouring her enemies:

III.12.31. *''After I shall consume*
the mighty and great Asuras . .
my teeth shall become reddened
[like] the uppermost blossoms
of the pomegranate tree.

After that the gods in heaven
and mortals on earth,
extolling [me],
shall forever speak of [me as]
the red-toothed.''[65]
Devī māhātmyam XI.44–45; *ca.* 550 CE.

This blood-red color is typical of warriors in mythology and folklore, and it is a characteristic of many female-figures who fulfill the warrior-function. We may also think of Macha *Mongrúad*, "red-maned" Macha.[66]

Remember that Devī was a Tantric goddess, and that she was probably an outgrowth of the indigenous pre-Indo-European religion; she thus did not conform to the "mental warrior" pattern portrayed by the typical Indo-European warrior-goddess. The Iranian *Anāhitā* more closely followed the Indo-European pattern. She supplied warriors, but she was not a warrior herself:

III.12.32. *''Now, then, Oh Arədvī Sūra Anāhitā. . .*
I request two heroes,
namely, a two-legged hero
and a four-legged one;
there a two-legged hero who,
at his departure to battles,
is quick,
and brings forth good for the chariots . . . ''[67]
Avesta, Yasht V.131; Fifth to First Centuries BCE.

Anāhitā, again, a bestower or procuress of warrior-prowess, probably was representative of omnipotent goddesses brought into the Indo-European religious structure.

The warrior-goddesses of the Germanic sphere were the *Valkyries*.[68] These maidens were servants of the warrior-god Oðin, and they transported those men who died courageously in battle to Valhalla:

> III.12.33. *"Gautatýr [Oðin] sent*
> *Gondul and Skogul* [two Valkyries]
> *to choose from among the kings,*
> *who, of the race of Yngvi,*
> *should go with Oðin,*
> *and stay in Valhalla."*[69]
> Hákonarmál 32.1; *ca.* 1000 CE.

Although the Valkyries *per se* did not participate in battles, but rather rallied the troops, specific warrior-maids, such as *Brynhild,*[70] fought as warriors in epic battles. Brynhild

> III.12.34. *". . . ordered and received for the battle,*
> *a good garment,*
> *a red-gold suit of armor,*
> *and a good shield."*[71]
> Nibelungenlied VII.428; *ca.* 1200 CE.

That her armor was of *red*-gold is of significance; it is yet another red symbol of a warrior-figure.

The color red also figures in the name of another warrior-maiden:

> III.12.35. *". . . the maiden Rusila,*
> *with the vow of a soldier*
> *striving after military life,*
> *overpowered in war*
> *and seized a virile glory*
> *from an effeminate enemy."*[72]
> Saxo Grammaticus, Gesta Danorum XXXVI[b]; born *ca.* 1150 CE.

The name Rusila probably is borrowed from Latin *russus*: "red." The color red is thus symbolic of the military function in the Germanic sphere and in other Indo-European spheres which we have already discussed.

The generalized Valkyries, then, as early shield maidens who were not strongly characterized, delighted in battle, but from a safe distance. Only when they became more sharply delineated heroines, such as Brynhild, did they gain intimate association with the battlefield, and status as Amazonian heroines.

Germanic mortal women remained close to their husbands and sons, when the latter performed in battle. The warriors

> III.12.36. *". . . bring their wounds*
> *to their mothers, their wives,*
> *nor are those women afraid*
> *to count or to examine the wounds;*
> *they bring food and encouragement*
> *to the warriors."*[73]
> Tacitus, Germania 7.4; born *ca.* 56 CE.

Although these women were not participants in martial endeavors, their husbands

> III.12.37. *". . . did not spurn their counsel*
> *nor disregard their answers."*[74]
> Ibid, 8.2–3.

Germanic women thus followed the Indo-European ethic of mentally and emotionally encouraging male warriors, and thus bestowing energy upon them.

Thus the female warrior-function was fulfilled in two ways by goddesses and heroines. In Egyptian, Mesopotamian, and Ugaritic myth, the female deities play out the role of raging violence, while the majority of Indo-European female warrior-figures played the role of *giving energy and encouragement to the male warriors*. In both cases, a martial mythology reflects a society's preoccupation with war. The Indo-Europeans, no less interested in war than their circum-Mediterranean and Mesopotamian neighbors, had a strong martial ethic, but their female figures were seen more as strategists and endowers of martial energy. This role of exhortation and encouragement in war is quite similar to the nurturing function, and, in fact, Indo-European female figures in all spheres were nurturers.

NURTURANCE

Nurturance applies to many spheres; all those who provide for society, as farmers, as craftspeople, as mothers, as those who assist childbirth, are nurturers. This role of sustaining the life of one's society was and is quite powerful; it underscores the fact that the nurturers in patriarchal societies have great powers, whether or not the patriarchy recognizes them. This power, of course, is not the patriarchal power *over*, but a *connectedness to the life force and a facilitation of the life force*.

Almost all of the Indo-European goddesses have as one of their functions, that of nurturing society. In Greece and Rome, first of all, even virgin goddesses such as *Artemis-Diana* and *Athena-Minerva* were connected with childbirth. It is obvious that *Aphrodite-Venus* was a goddess of fertility, and *Demeter-Ceres* was a nurturer of the soil. *Hera-Juno* was the enabling wife. The Roman *Fortuna* bestowed abundance and fortune.

Among the Balts, the earth-goddess *Lauma* was a nurturer of the soil. The Iranian "Great"-goddess, *Anāhita*, brought fertility to woman and man, and she gave energy to warriors. The Indic *Shakti* and her epiphanies represented pure, activating energy, conferring activating energy upon the passive male. The transfunctional Rigvedic goddess *Sarasvatī* bestowed abundance upon her people.

Celtic fertility goddesses also personified the nurturing function. Thus we may class *Queen Medb, Macha* (especially the third Macha), and also the Welsh King Math's virgin.

Most goddesses in the patriarchal societies which we have been exploring fall into this "nurturing" third-function slot.

In the next chapter we will discuss the fact that the primary function of the Indo-European goddess and heroine was to distribute energy to society—especially to male society. She did this in the form of a virgin, a "storehouse" of energy, or as a matron, through transmission of sexual energies. As a young maiden, and a matron in the prime of life, then, she fulfilled her allotted role: that of nurturing society in some way, whether it be through giving fertility to animate creatures or by bestowing abundance upon the earth; bestowing martial energy upon warriors; or giving sovereignty to would-be rulers. It was only as an old crone that a woman in these societies was not regarded as a nurturer, and that only in specific circumstances. In the next chapter I shall discuss energy with regard to the three life stages of woman.

CHAPTER 13

Woman's three life-phases and the distribution of energy

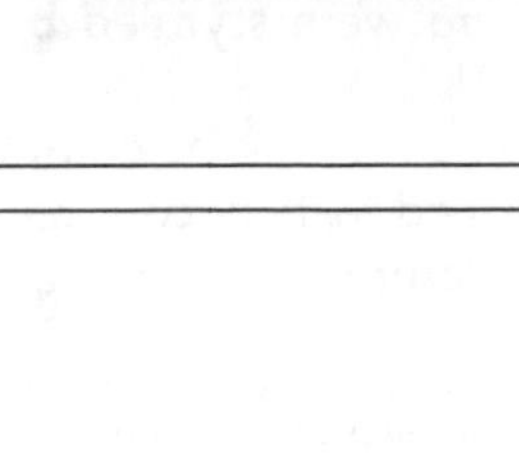

Energy is a life-force which both motivates and characterizes all people. Goddesses and heroines, in the Indo-European societies which we have been discussing, fulfilled roles, not only according to the functions which we described in the preceding chapter, but also according to the manner in which they expended energy, whether willfully or constructively. If indeed the function of these female figures was to distribute energy, then we should expect all goddesses who gave energy to others to be viewed by their societies as beneficent, and all those who, on the contrary, did *not* distribute energy, to be viewed as maleficent. A goddess, according to the Indo-European ethic, distributed or dissipated energy differently, depending upon which life phase she represented.

With few exceptions,[1] a goddess or heroine was portrayed in one of three life-epochs. In the first, she was a virgin, and her powers were in the process of being stored. In the second epoch, she released her stored powers, she was fertile, and she provided energy to males; her most common role in this epoch was that of matron. In the final epoch, that of old age, a female figure was viewed in one of two ways. She could be a nurturing grandmother, and "wise old woman;" often, however, instead of being venerated for her wealth of knowledge, she was made an object of fear or derision. The counterpoint to the wise old woman was the fearsome witch. The latter was considered a dissipator of energy, and as such she was feared.

Energy in itself is neither good nor evil: such qualities lie within the uses to which that energy is put. According to the patriarchal construct, it was the duty of the Indo-European female figure to apply her energy in a beneficent manner.

In the mythologies of the Greek and the Irish cultures, there are examples of the potency of combined female energy. Among the Irish, when the young hero Cú Chulainn was a child, he was about to turn his vast energies against his own countrymen. His uncle, King Conchobor, devised a plan to tame him:

> III.13.1. " . . . *to send a company of women out toward the boy,*
> *that is, three times fifty women,*
> *that is, ten women and seven times twenty,*
> *utterly naked,*
> *all at the same time,*
> *and the leader of the women before them,*
> *Scandlach,*
> *to expose their nakedness and their boldness to him.*
> *The whole company of women*
> *came out,*
> *and they all exposed their nakedness*
> *and their boldness to him.*
> *The boy lowered his gaze away from them*
> *and laid his face*
> *against the chariot,*
> *so that he might not see the nakedness*
> *nor the boldness of the women.*"[2]
> Táin Bó Cuailnge 1186–1192 (LL 67b);
> *ca.* 400 BCE to *ca.* 100 CE; Recorded 1st to 8th Centuries CE.

The energies of the hero were stymied by the even greater combined energies of the naked women.

The story of Cú Chulainn may be compared to that of the Greek hero, Bellerophon. The Greek hero performed feats of courage to aid the Lycians, but the latter treated him unjustly. Therefore, Bellerophon, in anger,

> III.13.2. " . . . *waded into the sea*
> *and prayed to Poseidon that,*

in revenge for this [injustice]
the land might become barren and useless.
And then, having made this prayer,
he left,
and a wave surged and inundated the land;
it was a terrible sight,
when the sea,
following him,
rose on high,
and completely concealed the plain.
Then, when the men begged Bellerophon to hold it back,
and could not persuade him,
the women, lifting up their undergarments,
came to meet him;
and when he,
out of shame,
went back again [towards the sea],
the wave too,
it is said,
withdrew along with him.''[3]
Plutarch, Moralia 248 A–B; born *ca.* 46 CE.

A man may thus comfortably face one naked woman at a time, at least when he is in control of the situation; but a crowd of uncontrolled naked women constitutes a plethora of concentrated sexuality, and the ancient hero could not stand up to so much energy.[4]

VIRGINITY

Energy, which was seen by the Indo-Europeans as unused potential, was stored by a woman while she was a virgin. Feminine virginity was an asset in ancient Indo-European mythology,[5] and often in human life as well. In other ancient cultures, women in their virgin state were often autonomous.[6] But virginity has another, also significant, function within a male-centered society: it is the state which renders a woman a "storehouse" of untapped energy, energy which she will, in her next stage, impart to man.

There are numerous illustrations throughout mythology which demonstrate that a virgin was indeed considered a repository of energy. In Rome it was the *virgo intacta,*[7] the "physically untouched unmarried girl," who stored untapped energy, although any *virgo* may be considered to be guarding her energies before she chooses a husband.

The term "virgin" did not always refer to a physical state, one which implied chastity, although the pragmatic Romans would have held strictly to its literal application.[8] In cultures other than the Roman, the term may well have been a figurative one which pertained to age, not necessarily chronologically, but qualitatively. A virgin was in the youth of her powers, in the process of storing them, and, as such, her "batteries" were "fully charged." Indeed, virgins not only stored untapped energy for men, but they were also able to transmit their powers to them, in a non-sexual manner, without diminishing those powers. Therefore, a virgin, at least on the celestial level, could be perpetually young.

Thus Aphrodite was

III.13.3. '' . . . *like an unwedded maiden*
in height and form . . . ''[9]
Homeric Hymn V.81–82; 8th to 6th Centuries BCE.

Although she was a goddess of love, she could make the Trojan Anchises believe that she was

III.13.4. ''*unwedded . . . and inexperienced in love.*''[10]
Ibid, 133.

and she could, at will, assume

> III.13.5. *"a virgin's face and appearance."*[11]
> Vergil, Aeneid I.315; 70 BCE to 19 BCE.

Aphrodite and Anchises then mated, and their union resulted in the Trojan hero, Aeneas.

Artemis was a virgin goddess, probably so characterized because she was originally a very powerful pre-Greek goddess, not merely because she stored her energies for the men and women of her society; she was a virgin by virtue of being independent, and her chastity was secondary.

Despite her virginity, the Arcadian Artemis was connected with the fertility of both man and animal, while in Chaironeia, Thespiai, Tanagra, Orchomenos, and perhaps Koronea, she was identified with *Eileithuia*, goddess of childbirth.[12]

Further, in a number of her older cults, Artemis was associated with a nature-god:

> III.13.6. *"The Eleusinians have a sanctuary of Triptolemus,*
> *of Artemis of the vestibule,*
> *and of Poseidon Father."*[13]
> Pausanias, Description of Greece I.38.6; *ca.* 150 CE.

She was connected with Father Zeus as well:

> III.13.7. *"There is a temple of Zeus,*
> *surnamed "Savior" . . .*
> *Zeus is sitting on a throne,*
> *and beside him stand Megalopolis* [on the right]
> *and a statue of Artemis Savior on the left."*[14]
> Ibid, VIII.30.10.

Although the virginity of timeless Artemis may have been figurative, at least in her earlier cults, in Classical Greece her priestesses were expected to be virgins:

> III.13.8. "[There is] *a sanctuary of Artemis,*
> *surnamed Triclaria . . .*
> *a virgin held the priesthood of the goddess*
> *until she was ready to be sent*
> *to a husband."*[15]
> Ibid, VII.19.1.

A goddess who was both "pure" and autonomous, the virgin *Athena*, was, as we have discussed, a very potent pre-Greek goddess. She was assimilated to the Indo-European Greek culture so thoroughly that she was born not of woman but of man, although, as we discussed above, Zeus' pregnancy was secondary. It was *Metis*, "wisdom," who first became pregnant with Athena. Athena emerged, with the arms that signified her warrior function, from her father's head.[16] To the androgenetic Zeus, one might compare the Iranian omnipotent god, Ahura Mazdāh, who bore the goddess Spenta Ārmaiti.[17] Further, the Indic goddess Sarasvatī was called "daughter of the lightning,"[18] a relationship bearing close resemblance to that between Athena and the thunder-god, Zeus. Androgenetic births may take place in a subtle manner. The Greek Aphrodite grew out of the foam formed from the severed genitals of Uranos, when he was castrated by his son Kronos.[19] Thus she, too, according to the male mythopoets, was not born of woman.

All of these goddesses were thus assimilated to their Indo-European cultures, and subordinated to the male deities of their respective Indo-European pantheons. Although Sarasvatī and Aphrodite were allowed sexuality, Athena and Ārmaiti sublimated their sexual natures. Athena was rendered autonomous in her celibacy, while the Iranian goddess, on the contrary, was perceived as no more than an aspect of the all-powerful Zoroastrian god.

The Greek goddess of the hearth, *Hestia*, was similar to other hearth-goddesses: as the personification of the pure core of the home, the hearth, she was required to be a virgin:

> III.13.9. *''Nor yet are Aphrodite's works*
> *for the venerable virgin, Hestia . . .*
> *she swore a mighty oath . . .*
> *that she would be a virgin all of her days . . . ''*[20]
> Homeric Hymn V.21–28; 8th to 6th Centuries BCE.

There were similar deities in many cultures, goddesses who guarded perpetual fires and who were virgins.[21] But, whereas such goddesses in other cultures were served by virgins, there were no "Vestals" in Greece. The sacred fire could even be maintained by an elderly married woman, as long as she no longer cohabited with her husband. Such was the case with the Pythia at Delphi.[22]

The Roman equivalent of Hestia, *Vesta*, was a virgin. She was the third daughter of Ops and Saturn:

> III.13.10. *''The others married . . .*
> *of the three one resisted,*
> *refusing to endure a husband . . .*
> *Do not perceive Vesta*
> *as anything but the living flame,*
> *and you see*
> *that no bodies are born of flame.*
> *Therefore, she is justly a virgin*
> *who neither sends forth*
> *nor takes seeds,*
> *and she loves companions*
> [the Vestal Virgins]
> *in her virginity.''*[23]
> Ovid, Fasti VI.287–294; 43 BCE to 17? CE.

Chastity was required of Vesta's attendants, the *Vestal Virgins*; these priestesses of the hearth cult were required to remain literal virgins. A violation of this rule resulted in live inhumation:

> III.13.11. '' . . . *nor will it be said*
> *that under [the emperor's] leadership*
> *any priestess violated her sacred fillets,*
> *and none shall be buried alive in the ground.*
> *It is thus that an unchaste [Vestal] perishes,*
> *because that [earth] which she violated,*
> *in that [earth] she is interred;*
> *and indeed Earth and Vesta are the same deity.''*[24]
> Ibid, VI.457–460.

This was a harsh form of capital punishment, indeed.

However, it was possible for a maiden to circumvent this punishment. *Rhea Silvia* was daughter of Numitor, the king of Alba Longa, and she was a Vestal Virgin:

> III.13.12. *''[Amulius] appointed her*
> *priestess of Vesta,*
> *so that she would live forever unmarried*
> *and a virgin.''*[25]
> Plutarch, Vitae Parallelae, "Romulus" III.2–3;
> born *ca*. 46 CE.

Despite her sacred appointment, Rhea Silvia became pregnant. She swore, however, that the god Mars was the father of her child. The tale she told was a convincing one:

One morning Silvia went down to the water to wash the holy accoutrement of her office. She set down her earthenware pitcher, and, tired from the walk, she sat down on the ground. She relaxed and opened up her blouse, so that the breeze might cool her. It was so peaceful in that shady spot that she fell asleep.

Now, who should be happening along at that time but the god Mars. He spied the sleeping maiden and was overcome by momentary love. He lay with her as she slept, and, when she awakened,

> III.13.13. "*She lay heavy with child:*
> *in fact, the founder of the city of Rome*
> *was already within her womb.*"[26]
> Ovid, Fasti III.24–25; 43 BCE to 17? CE.

Silvia arose, feeling heavy and languid; imagine her surprise when she discovered the twin source of that heaviness! Soon she gave birth to Romulus and Remus. Although

> III.13.14. "*they say that the figurines of Vesta*
> *covered their eyes with their virgin hands . . .* "[27]
> Ibid, III.45–46.

and

> III.13.15. "*the hearth of the goddess [Vesta]*
> *surely trembled*
> *when her servant gave birth . . .* "[28]
> Ibid, III.47.

yet it was accepted that Mars was the father of the twin heroes, and Rhea Silvia went unpunished. In fact, she was a heroine to both family and country. Upon attaining manhood, Romulus drove his uncle Amulius from the Alban throne,[29] which the latter had usurped from Silvia's father, Numitor. Thus Silvia, through Romulus, restored royal status to her father.

It would appear that cohabitation with a divine spirit did not, in the minds of the Romans, deplete a virgin's energy. On the contrary, since this might well have been regarded as a mark of divine favor, she thus posed no threat to the community of citizens. So Rhea Silvia deposited her energies in her son, Romulus, who used them to aid his deposed grandfather.

To the pragmatic Romans, lost virginity was irrevocable, at least irrevocable for their historical virgins. But even the Romans could conceive of parthenogenesis in their "mythology." One might question why it was necessary that the Vestals remain virgins. The issue was vital, perhaps, for only through virginity could their sacred energy have been saved for their office. Further, if a woman was neither virgin nor married, she became a threat to the patriarchal, patrilinear establishment, because she became autonomous. Any woman who took control of her own sexuality, in Rome as in other male-centered societies, was both condemned and feared by those societies.

It is significant that any maiden, no matter what social class she belonged to, was eligible to become a Vestal Virgin. Nor need she even be young. In 19 CE the Roman emperor Tiberius

> III.13.16. "*proposed the selection of a virgin*
> *in place of Occia,*
> *who had presided over the Vestal rites*
> *with the greatest purity*
> *for fifty-seven years.*"[30]
> Tacitus, Annals II.86; born *ca.* 55 CE.

The sacred power was present in all Roman women.

The Celts had a parallel to the Roman cult of the Vestal Virgins, although the cult was a relatively late one, following the Christianization of Ireland. The pagan Irish triple goddess *Brigid*, the daughter of the Dagda, was patroness of poets, goddess of healing, and smith-goddess. She had a son, Ruadan. When she was assimilated into Celtic Christianity, she was canonized, and she became Brigid, the virgin nun.[31] She and her attendant nuns guarded a perpetual flame:

> III.13.17. *''At the time of Brigid*
> *twenty nuns here served a master*
> *as would a soldier,*
> *she herself being the twentieth . . .*
> *when indeed every night through every succession*
> *they cared for the fire . . .*
> *on the twentieth night the last nun . . .*
> *said: 'Brigid, I have cared for your fire . . .*
> *and thus, the fire having been left . . .*
> *it was found again,*
> *unextinguished.''*[32]
> Geraldus Cambrensis, "De Igne A Brigida Sua Nocte Servato;"
> 1146? CE to 1220? CE.

Brigid was significant in the sphere of water as well as of fire; her name was given to several rivers, including the Brighid in Ireland, the Braint in Wales, and the Brent in England. Perhaps the element of water, ever-flowing, just as the element of fire, perpetually burning, is related to the notion of perpetual energy. And it would seem that virgin women were well-endowed with the stores of energy necessary to guarantee the perpetuity of the two.

St. Bride's Day—that is, St. Brigid's Day—is still celebrated, and hymns such as the following are sung to her:

> III.13.18. *''Early on Bride's morn*
> *The serpent shall come from the hole;*
> *I will not molest the serpent,*
> *nor will the serpent molest me.''*
>
> *''This is the Day of Bride.*
> *The queen will come from the mound;*
> *I will not touch the queen,*
> *nor will the queen touch me.''*[33]
> Hymn to Bride; Twentieth Century CE.

Brigid is thus associated with the female serpent, called the "queen." This female serpent is beneficent; it is not feared because it does not molest the devotee. Brigid's roots, as we can see, extend back to the Neolithic European snake goddess.

Similarities to the Roman and Celtic fire-rituals may be found in the religious rites of the Balts. A perpetual flame, sacred to the thundergod, Perkunas,[34] was tended:

> III.13.19. *''For Perkunas they used to maintain*
> *a perpetual sacred fire,*
> *in the woods,*
> *imitating Roman Vestals.''*[35]
> S. Rostowski; Eighteenth Century CE.

This flame was guarded by priests and priestesses called *Vaidelotai* or *Vaidelutes*.[36] It was probably symbolic not of female, but of male, energy. However, unmarried female Vaidelutes did serve Potrimpus, a god of rivers and springs, or his *snake-epiphany*, with a non-perpetual fire and with milk."[37] The juxtaposition of fire, waters, and snakes provides a striking parallel to the Celtic fire-cult.

Another example of the importance of virginity to the Balts may be found in the following Lithuanian folk-tale:

> When the Grand Duke of Lithuania was building the citadel of Vilnius, he asked the priests what should be offered in sacrifice to the gods, to obtain their protection over the citadel. They first decided that a mother should offer her first-born son under the corner-stone. But the gods apparently refused this sacrifice, and the priests then decided that

> III.13.20. ''*A young, beautiful, and innocent maiden*
> *must give up her life under the same stone.*''[38]
> Rev. Juozas Tumas Vaižgantas; Twentieth Century CE.

Fortuitously, the gods determined upon a lesser sacrifice. But the human sacrifice might have been completed in an earlier, more "pagan" era, and one might still compare the image of a virgin buried under a cornerstone, to ensure strength for a citadel, with that of erring Vestal Virgins buried alive for their carnal sins. The more recent tale may carry the germ of an older truth. Perhaps both concepts, although diverse, stem from the notion that a buried virgin would impart her energy, and therefore her fertility, to the land. Hence, it may be possible that the concept of an erring Vestal "virgin," punished by live inhumation, was subsequent to the notion that a true virgin might be buried not as punishment, but as a religious necessity and an honor. Thus, the live burial of erring Roman Vestals would have originated as a fertility rite.

That Classical virgins were involved in agricultural fertility rites is illustrated in the Roman ceremony of the *October Equus*, wherein the Vestal Virgins burned the blood from the tail of a sacrificed horse, to fumigate the sheep and shepherds at the Parilia-festival, and thus to purify them. The rite was intended to procure a good crop.

Even as virginity was intended to purify in agricultural rites, so it was necessary for women with special powers to be particularly "pure." Apollo's Sibyl was a virgin:

> III.13.21. ''*The Sibyl . . . the virgin said,*
> *'It is the time to ask your fate:*
> *the god, look, the god!'*''[39]
> Vergil, Aeneid VI.44–46; 70 BCE to 19 BCE.

and the Trojan seeress, *Cassandra*, was also a virgin:

> III.13.22. ''*And the son of Atreus . . .*
> *caused to perish*
> *the prophetess, [Cassandra], the virgin.*''[40]
> Pindar, Pythia XI.31–33; 518 BCE to 438 BCE.

The characteristics of virginity imbued Greek and Roman thought, so much so that one Roman author compared his heroine, *Psyche*, to:

> III.13.23. ''*Another Venus,*
> *possessed of the flower of virginity.*''[41]
> Apuleius, Metamorphoses IV.28; born *ca*. 123 CE.

Thus, a goddess of love was a wonderful figure, but when the ultimate quality of virginity was added to her attributes, she became the epitome of desirable femininity.

Among the Gaulish Celts, virginity held special powers, although it did not represent the all-pervasive virtue which it became in Rome. Pomponius Mela, in the first century CE, wrote a geographical survey of the inhabited world, in Latin, and in this survey he described the island of Sena, in the British Sea. A Gaulish god was worshipped there,

> III.13.24. *"whose priestesses [are] sanctified*
> *with perpetual virginity;*
> *their number is said to be nine.*
> *They call them Gallizenae;*
> *they think that they are furnished*
> *with extraordinary powers:*
> *to stir up seas and winds by their enchantments,*
> *and to change into whatever animals they wish;*
> *to cure whichever among them are incurable,*
> *to know and to predict the future . . . "*[42]
> Pomponius Mela, Chorographia III.6.48; 1st Century CE.

These priestesses, whether they existed in fact or in fancy, perpetuated the powers of earlier goddesses. Their abilities to arouse seas and winds remind one of the early magical races of Celts, described in Irish mythological texts.[43] Their virginity represented, not powers stored to await the need of man, but the autonomous energies which the priestesses themselves controlled. Their number, nine, is a multiple of the number three, considered a magic number in much mythology.

A very different function of virginity is illustrated in the Welsh Mabinogi, wherein *King Math* was required to keep his feet *in a virgin's lap* during the intervals between wars. One maiden who thus served Math, Goewin, daughter of Pebin, was raped by Math's nephew, Gilfaethwy. She immediately became "defused," as it were, and it became necessary for Math to seek another virgin to be his source of energy.[44] This demonstrates quite vividly how a man was able to "recharge his batteries." Since only a virgin was a "storehouse" of potential energy, a man needed to draw upon her power—in this case through a chaste sort of osmosis—to accumulate his own store of energy.

> The same theme is found in later Irish folklore. In the tale, "Thirteenth Son of the King of Erin," a hero, Sean Ruadh, wished to save a princess from a terrible monster, the Urfeist. The hero asked the princess if he might rest his head on her lap, until the time came to fight the monster. The boy fell asleep until it was time for his battle. Then, energized through his proximity to the princess, the hero vanquished the beast.[45]

Battlefield-virgins were also found in the Germanic sphere. We have already discussed the virgin *Valkyries*,[46] maidens who decided the fate of battles and who were depicted wearing battle garb. Although only a few later Valkyries actually participated in war, they did provide *encouragement* to warriors. These virgins, as we recall, also served food and mead at the table of the gods, and perhaps it was no accident that they not only aided warriors, but gave food and sustenance to both goddesses and gods. Energy and sustenance are quite closely related, and it is not difficult to correlate virgin energy with power of all sorts, in particular the power of nurturance.

Earlier, we discussed the Scandinavian giantess, *Gefjon*.[47] She procured a kingdom for Oðin, king of the gods, by means of her sons. Nonetheless, she is called by Snorri:

> III.13.25. *"A virgin,*
> *and those who die*
> *while virgins*
> *serve her."*[48]
> Snorri, Prose Edda, "Gylfaginning" 36; *ca.* 1200 CE.

The significance of Gefjon's sometime virginity was that she acted *as a virgin* toward Oðin, giving him a kingdom without mating with him. That is, the energy which Gefjon gave to Oðin was sovereignty.

Virgins also held an important place in the Indic realm. One heroine from the Indic epic, the Mahābhārata, was the maiden *Mādhavī*. The young woman was restored to a virgin state:

In the myth, Yayāti gave his daughter, the lovely virgin Mādhavī, to a young brahman, so that she might aid the youth in fulfilling a rather strange demand made of him by his guru: he must obtain eight hundred horses, each the color of the moon, and each distinguished by a black ear.

The brahman, therefore, gave Mādhavī in "temporary marriage" to three kings in succession; she bore a son to each, recovering her virginity upon the conclusion of each marriage:

> III.13.26. *"A brahman granted to me*
> *an important matter in intercourse;*
> *by means of this knowing one,*
> *thus [I am] passing for reborn."*[49]
> Mahābhārata V.114.13; *ca.* 300 BCE to *ca.* 300 CE.

Mādhavī was:

> III.13.27. " . . . *a virgin once again.*"[50]
> Ibid, V.114.21.

The brahman received two hundred horses from each king as purchase price for the maiden; unfortunately, he still lacked two hundred, and no more such horses existed. Then, the guru accepted Mādhavī in temporary marriage, in place of the last two hundred horses, and she bore a son to him as well.

Subsequently, the maiden was returned to her father, and he held a *svayamvara*, a "self-choice," for her. The *svayamvara* was an Indic ceremony wherein a young woman chose a husband from among a number of suitors who presented themselves to her. But Mādhavī chose *vana*, the forest, and an ascetic life. She thus chose perpetual virginity.

Yayāti, having fulfilled a virtuous life, died, and ascended to heaven. But one day he became guilty of overweening pride, for he said to himself that there was no one, man or god, who was as virtuous as he; and he fell from heaven back to earth. As he fell, he prayed that he might land in the midst of good men. And, indeed, he landed on that very spot where the four sons of Mādhavī were performing sacrificial rites.

Each of the four youths was very virtuous, and each surrendered a portion of his virtue to Yayāti. Even as he was refusing to accept their gifts, Mādhavī came out of her hermitage and added to the portions offered by her sons, one half of the vast virtue which she had accumulated. Yayāti accepted their gift at last, and, sustained, he was enabled to ascend to heaven once more. And his grandsons, because of their great virtue, were permitted to ascend to heaven with him.

Mādhavī was able to save her father by means of virtues apparently linked with her virginity, and through her sons, just as the Roman Rhea Silvia saved her father Numitor through *her* son, Romulus. Mādhavī gave life from her body in the form of four sons, extensions of herself and of her own virtue, and these sons gave of themselves to Yayāti. Although she had given part of her virtue to her sons, that virtue was perpetually replenished within her, "on tap" when Yayāti had great need for it. Therefore, when not only her sons, but Mādhavī herself, bestowed their virtue upon Yayāti, in effect he received a double gift.

Mādhavī possessed perpetual virginity and perpetual virtue. Not all virtue, however, need be perpetual, as one witnesses in Yayāti's lapse into *hybris*. This seems to indicate that virginity perpetuated virtue. If virginity denotes abundance, and if abundance is a life force, then perpetual virtue—perpetual virginity—spills over into the notion of perpetual energy.

As long as a woman remained a virgin, she was able to store up energy. In the act of intercourse, this energy was released and given to a man, sometimes in the concrete form of a child, and sometimes in the abstract form of revitalization. When Mādhavī's virginity was restored, she became revitalized and thus able to revitalize, to transmit energy to another, and again to another, whether it be her temporary husbands or her father. In effect, this revitalization indicated that her "batteries were recharged;" she was replete with energy.

It is significant that Mādhavī was once again a virgin when she restored her father to heaven, for she could, morally, give to Yayāti only a gift of the mind, and not of the body. Thus, she remained a virgin because her virginity served a function.

This same privilege of renewable virginity was enjoyed by other Indic heroines. Kuntī, the mother of the first three Pāṇḍavas in the same epic, the Mahābhārata, and Satyavatī, their great-grandmother, were also renewed virgins. And Draupadī, the common wife of the Pāṇḍavas, became a virgin again each time she left one husband and went to another.

Satyavatī was the grandmother of the Pāṇḍavas and the Kauravas, the rivals in the great war of the Bhāratas, the *Mahābhārata*. She bore Vyāsa, the author of the poem, to the seer, Parāsara. Although she thus bore a son, she yet *remained a virgin*. She then married an old king; she bore to him two sons, both of whom died without leaving heirs.

The younger son had left two widows, and Satyavatī invoked her son Vyāsa, who was an ascete, to impregnate the two widows, according to the law. The widows bore sons, Dhṛta-rāshṭra, a blind man, ancestor of the Kauravas, and Pāṇḍu, "the white one," step-father of the Pāṇḍavas. (All of the Pāṇḍavas had immortal natural fathers.)

The Pāṇḍavas, upon the death of their father, were brought to their uncle, Dhṛta-rāshṭra, who cared for them well. However, a rivalry grew between his sons, the Kauravas, and the Pāṇḍavas, and this rivalry developed into a violent hatred on the part of the Kauravas. Dhṛta-rāshṭra sent his nephews away, to live in retirement, to keep the peace with his sons. Nonetheless, one of his sons, Duryodhana, still plotted to kill his cousins, by setting fire to their house. The five brothers were thought to have perished in the fire, but they escaped to the forest.

Now, at this time, a neighboring king, Draupada, declared a svayamvara for his daughter,

> III.13.28. " . . . *Draupadī, the slender-waisted,*
> *who has a faultless body,*
> *whose hair has a scent*
> *equal to the blue lotus . . .* "[51]
> Ibid, I.175.10.

and many noble suitors came to woo her. The eager suitors

> III.13.29. " . . . *watched her walking about*
> *and they competed amongst themselves,*
> *biting their lips,*
> *contorting them*
> *[until they were] copper-red.*"[52]
> Ibid, I.178.11.

The Pāṇḍava brothers went to the svayamvara, and they were victorious in all of the contests. One of them, Arjuna, won the maiden Draupadī, and the brothers conducted her to their home. They told their mother, Kuntī, that they had acquired something wonderful. The boys were outside the house and she was within. Without looking, she said,

> III.13.30. "*Now, let everyone share it!*"[53]
> Ibid, I.182.2.

And they did.

Draupadī therefore became the joint wife of all five brothers. It was arranged that she should dwell for two days in the house of each of the brothers in succession:

> III.13.31. "*And then the learned sage*
> *related this marvellous happening,*
> *[one] exceeding that*
> *apportioned to humankind;*
> *that in fact the noble,*
> *slender-waisted woman*
> *with the advent of each day,*

became a virgin again.''[54]
Ibid, I.190.14.

Thus the renewable features of virginity were elastic, conforming to the exigencies of the roles which the society dictated, evincing that woman's energy must be renewed for man. This elasticity, of course, was not necessarily beneficial to the women experiencing it.

"Recovered virginity" was a phenomenon experienced by women of other ancient cultures. The Greek *Hera* restored her virginity by bathing yearly in a river:

III.13.32. *''In Nauplia [there is]*
a spring called the Canathus.
The Argives say that in this place
Hera bathes each year,
and becomes a virgin [again].''[55]
Pausanias, Description of Greece II.38.2–3; *ca.* 150 CE.

One may recall the bathing of images of the Germanic goddess, Nerthus, and that of the Romanized Cybele. Water was considered a purifying agent which, through its energies, renewed the powers of those who bathed in it. Revitalized by the energies of the waters, a goddess could be strengthened; further, if it was desirable, she could be "re-purified" in a masculist sense, that is, caused to become a virgin once again.

Hera had three surnames which reflect her three life-stages. According to Pausanias, she was reared by Temenos, who established three sanctuaries for her and gave her three corresponding epithets:

III.13.33. *'' . . . when she was still a virgin*
[he called her] 'Child,'[56]
when she was married to Zeus,
he called her 'The Completed One,'[57]
when for some reason she quarreled with Zeus
and returned to Stymphalos,
Temenos named her 'Widow.' ''[58]
Ibid, VIII.22.2.

As "Child," she was a virgin, as yet unwed, or *unwed again*. As the "Completed One," or the "Perfect One," she was full-grown, and in an "appropriate" state of matrimony. As "Widow," she was not a woman whose husband had died, but an abstinent woman; this period may be related to that of the mensis, the *katamenia*. According to Aristotle, this latter period occurred at the time of the waning moon.[59] Thus, Hera's three stages of life may be related to new moon ("Child"), full moon (the "Completed One"), and waning moon ("widow").

Although her periods of abstinence were cyclic, Hera was always to be a model of purity. We are told that Zeus made Hera his

III.13.34. *''respectable and modest-appearing wife . . . ''*[60]
Homeric Hymn V.44; 8th to 6th Centuries BCE.

and even Hera's clothing is called "pure."[61] Hera was thus the "perfect" wife of Zeus, a woman who, at regular intervals, renewed her virginity and her energies to benefit her husband and her society.

Hera's Roman counterpart, *Juno,* was viewed in two life-stages, those of virgin and of matron. Apuleius wrote that Juno was worshipped in Carthage as a maid who was carried through the sky by a lion,[62] the animal which often accompanies Near Eastern goddesses. In this case Juno was probably an assimilation of a local goddess, perhaps

Ashtarte. Her "virginity" was indicative of her youth and of her autonomous powers in the Near East.

Both the Indic Sarasvatī and the Iranian Arədvī Sūrā Anāhitā were self-regulating "virgins," and both were filled with energy. These two goddesses, whether of a river or of a "watery province,"[63] seem not only to have given, but to have *denoted* perpetual forces within themselves. The waters flow for all eternity and thus represent boundless, infinite energy. And water is, in fact, a *literal* source of energy.[64]

From their unlimited resources, Anāhitā and Sarasvatī gave sustenance to men:

> III.13.35. "*For him Sarasvatī pours forth*
> *milk, ghee, honey, and water.*"[65]
> Rigveda IX.67.32; *ca.* 1200 BCE.

Anāhitā was

> III.13.36. "*. . . increasing the herd . . .*
> *increasing mankind,*"[66]
> Avesta, Yasht V.1; 5th to 1st Centuries BCE.

and to this end she

> III.13.37. "*makes perfect the semen*
> *of all men*
> *and makes perfect the uteri*
> *of all women*
> *for birth . . .* "[67]
> Ibid, V.2.

Life energy, therefore, was perpetuated through semen and the uterus, both a gift of the goddess. Anāhitā was energy personified, giving to men and to women the furtherance of life; she was literally invoked as a "storehouse" of energy:

> III.13.38. "*May I bring to the storehouse at will,*
> *all good life, copiously,*
> *and may I win a growing realm.*"[68]
> Ibid, V.130.

Although Anāhitā bestowed fertility upon mortals, she was not an active participant in the act leading to propagation.[69] Under the influence of the Iranian prophet Zarathustra, the Indo-European pantheon was altered, so that it might conform to the doctrine celebrating Ahura Mazdāh, the great spirit, as the supreme deity. Other deities were but "aspects" of this god,[70] and those gods who could not be integrated into the Zarathustrian pantheon were transformed into demons or simply deleted from the pantheon.

The Zarathustrian goddess Ārmaiti, "right thought," was imbued with the purity which one would expect of a goddess representing the mind of the supreme god. This virgin represented a pure wisdom, giving advice about the role of the spirit whenever there was hesitation;[71] she also ruled the land and its fruits.[72]

The river-goddess Anāhitā was more richly personified than her Zoroastrian sister. She was given feminine characteristics by the Avestan mythopoets, but she did not assume the fertility characteristics of an Aphrodite or even of her Indic sister, Sarasvatī. For, whereas Sarasvatī was described as a maiden only once, and in a context which precludes the translation "virgin:"

> III.13.39. "*May the daughter of lightning,*
> *the maiden,*
> *possessed of wonderful vitality,*

Sarasvatī,
the wife of a hero,
bring [us] wisdom . . . ''[73]
Rigveda VI.49.7; *ca.* 1200 BCE.

Anāhitā, on the other hand, was indeed called a maiden:

III.13.40. '' . . . *Arədvī Sūrā Anāhitā,*
who always is perceived
in the body of a beautiful maiden . . . ''[74]
Avesta, Yasht V.120; 5th to 1st Centuries BCE.

but she was a maiden who did not marry. In fact mythologists have often compared her to the Greek virgin, *Artemis*.[75]

Finally, *Anāhitā*, literally, means "faultless."[76] The notions of "purity" and "immaculateness" are often morally and philosophically connected with virginity. Those women who store up vital forces for men are thus endowed with a quality of purity which assumes a mystical connotation bordering on holiness; the accumulation and "storehousing" of energy was, according to the Indo-Europeans, vital to the maintenance of humanity.

Since many powerful goddesses were envisioned as virgins, because of their independence of consorts, by a natural progression such a goddess was believed to conceive without the intervention of a male, man or god. This belief in *parthenogenesis* was aided by the fact that in prehistory the biological role of the father was not completely understood. The belief in parthenogenesis that was incorporated into Indo-European Greek myth reflects that the powerful position held by the feminine persisted through even androcentric Greek thought.

The Greek Hera conceived Hephaestus without the intervention of her husband, Zeus:

III.13.41. ''*But Hera bore famous Hephaestus*
without mingling in love [with Zeus],
for she quarreled violently with her husband.''[77]
Hesiod, Theogony 927–928; *ca.* 750? BCE.

She also bore the monster Typhaon:

III.13.42. ''*Typhaon . . . once upon a time*
Hera, being angry with Zeus the father,
bore him,
when the son of Cronos
bore glorious Athena
from within the top of his head.''[78]
Homeric Hymn III.306–309; 8th to 6th Centuries BCE.

Hera said:

III.13.43. ''*All right, now I will work it out*
that there will be born to me,
a son,
who will be excellent among the immortal gods,
and [I will do this]
disgracing neither your sacred marriage-bed
—nor mine.
Nor will I go to your bed.''[79]
Ibid, III.326–329.

Recall that Zeus had given *androgenetic* birth to Athena, although we may just as easily think of Metis as Athena's *parthenogenetic* mother;[80] Hera perhaps felt that her husband's liaisons were aggravating enough, but taking over the realm of childbirth was more than she could stand. Hera thus joined in competition with Zeus, in the realm of solo birth-giving.

Although the earliest Greek literature tells us that Hera conceived Ares with Zeus,[81] the Roman Ovid, on the other hand, describes Juno (Greek Hera) as the parthenogenetic mother of Mars, Ares' Roman equivalent:

> III.13.44. *"The divine Juno grieved*
> *that Jupiter had not pursued her services,*
> *as Minerva was born without a mother . . . "*[82]
> Ovid, Fasti V.231–232; 43 BCE to 17? CE.

The goddess Flora touched Juno with a flower

> III.13.45. *"and she conceived*
> *as it touched her lap . . .*
> *Mars was begotten."*[83]
> Ibid, V.256–258.

In pre-Greek religious imagery, the bee motif was quite prevalent.[84] Bees were idealized because they are able to conceive by parthenogenesis.[85] In the historical period, the poet Pindar called the priestess of Delphi the "Delphic bee,"[86] and the priestesses of Demeter and other goddesses were also called *Melissae*, "bees."[87]

It is apparent that, as it applied to the descendants of a "Great"-goddess, the term *virginity* signified *autonomy*. Parthenogenesis was but one example of her independence.[88]

Virginity was thus a "storehouse" of energy to the patriarchal, patrilineal Indo-European peoples. Perhaps virginity was also revered because the virgin had not yet *taken the strength of* (rather than given strength to) the male.

The two opposites are constantly interwoven throughout the tapestry of ancient Indo-European myth and legend. The "good wife," for example the *Third Macha*, brings wealth of all sorts to a marriage. But in the married state she may be overseen and controlled by her husband. However, a woman who was not under the control of a husband should, and must, remain a virgin. In early Rome, thus, the only females who were not under the guardianship of their fathers, or their husbands, were the Vestal Virgins. Their loss of virginity, as we have discussed, was speedily rewarded by capital punishment. To allow the degenerate female to live was to undermine the fabric of Roman morality. Therefore, if one was neither virgin nor married, one was a threat to the patriarchal establishment.

And so the virgin, the maiden who stored her powers and held them in abeyance for the men of her society, was a woman who was cherished and revered.

MATRIMONY

In pre-Indo-European Europe and the Near East, energy was derived from both male and female. In the *hieros gamos*, the "sacred marriage" ritual, the goddess: Cybele, Inanna-Ishtar, Aphrodite, mated with her consort: Attis, Dumuzi, Tammuz, Adonis, and then, whether by accident or through the purpose of the goddess, the consort lost his life.[89] His vital forces joined those of the universe, revitalizing it, so that the society and all of its fruits might be replenished.

In later Indo-European societies, matrons expended energy, transmitting it to their consorts. They gave energy to their husbands in two ways. First, women bore children to their husbands; from a male perspective, this continued the paternal blood line. To bear a child is to use one's powers to create another life, thus ensuring the perpetuation of life forces. The second means of energy transfer is the act of intercourse. Copulation involves the transmission of energy. Although the transmission should, from a physical point of view, be mutual, the Indo-European patriarchs viewed it as energy given *by* a woman *to* a man.

That the Greek goddess of fertility, *Aphrodite*, was born of the foam of the sea, is therefore not surprising. Aphrodite and her Roman counterpart, *Venus*, were worshipped as goddesses of love. And as the eternal flow of waters, from which Aphrodite arose, was a constant source of energy, so was such energy symbolic of the goddess; symbolically, this goddess thus transmitted the forces of life to mortals. Water was indicative of energy, whether that energy be mobile, as with Aphrodite-Venus, or stored, as with Anāhitā, Sarasvatī, and Brigid.

Hera, in her married state, was "perfect" or "fulfilled," as we discussed above. Complying to the role of matron goddess, Hera, Juno, the Germanic Frigg and the Indic Shakti were usually petrified in that phase of life wherein wedded woman transmits energy to a consort.

Female energy was worshipped as such in post-Rigvedic India, by adherents of the Tantric religion.[90] In one text,

> III.13.46. *"The husband,*
> *having joined in intercourse*
> *with his wife,*
> *being an embryo [again],*
> *is born at this time.*
> *This conception [is] the characteristic of a wife,*
> *that he is born again in her."*[91]
> Manu Smṛtiḥ IX.8; 5th Century BCE.

Indeed, as we have seen, the Sanskrit term *shakti*, "power, energy, ability," came to mean the active power of a deity, a goddess-consort and queen.[92] Shaktī was to the god Shiva where Hera and Juno were to Zeus and Jupiter. But the power of the queen-consort was revered in Tantrist India, while it was sublimated in Classical Greece and Rome. Shakti was power.

There were many goddesses who existed in this transmission stage, some of whom, even if married, were not attached to one man. In this case, they willfully chose to disperse their energies. Examples abound in the Celtic sphere: *Queen Medb* was married, several times, but she was not wont to reserve her sexuality for her husband. The warrior-goddess *Morrigan* served the martial function in much the same manner as did the Germanic Valkyries, but whereas the latter were virgins, Morrigan transmitted warrior-energies through sexual intercourse.

> In the Battle of Moytura, Morrigan helped the "People of the goddess Danu," the Túatha Dé Danann, to defeat their enemy, the Fomorians. Just before this great battle, and near the magical time of Samain, the Celtic Halloween, the Dagda, the great chieftain god of Danu's people, met Morrigan in Glen Etin, near the river Unius. There the two had union.
>
> Afterward, Morrigan prophesied to the Dagda, telling him where the Fomorians would land, and that he should summon the warriors of Erin to meet her at the Ford of Unius. She would then go to destroy the king of the Fomorians. She later gave two handsful of the enemy's blood to the Dagda's hosts, which were waiting at the Ford of Unius.
>
> Morrigan came to the battlefield and heartened the People of the Goddess, so that they fought the battle fiercely, routing the Fomorians. After the battle was over, Morrigan proclaimed that battle and its victory throughout Ireland.

The many-faceted Morrigan was warrior-goddess and seeress. She both took and gave blood, the stream of life. As did the Valkyries, she exhorted men on the field of battle, without engaging in battle herself. And she bestowed prowess in battle through the transmission of her sexual powers.

There were thus two means of transmitting energy. In both there were matrons, or women in the ripeness of their sexual lives: in the first, a woman reserved her energies for her husband or lover. In the second stage a woman was more independent, and she bestowed her powers upon those men whom she wished to aid, never completely depleting her own forces.

When a woman does deplete her own forces, her energies may be misused. When a goddess or mortal woman totally gives over her powers to another, foregoing the self-regulation of those powers, she runs the risk of having her powers abused. This is particularly true if she has not been wise, or fortunate, in her choice of a mate. Thus the Greek "barbarian" princess, *Medea,* who aided the hero Jason in his quest for the *golden fleece,* made tragic use of her powers for her lover, and was subsequently deserted by him.

In the story of Jason and the Argonauts,[93] Jason undertook the task of recovering the golden fleece for King Pelias, his maleficent uncle who had usurped the throne of Iolcus, in Thessaly.

After many adventures, Jason and his crew reached Colchis and found the golden fleece. Aeetes, king of Colchis, agreed to give Jason the fleece if he would first perform some almost impossible tasks. Medea, daughter of the king, helped Jason by means of her magic art, for she had fallen in love with him. He completed the tasks, and he and his Argonauts returned to Iolcus with the golden fleece, and with Medea in tow.

Escape from Colchis was not a simple matter, and in that task too Medea helped Jason. While they were in flight, Medea murdered her young brother Absyrtus, cut him into pieces, and scattered the fragments, so that her father would have to stop to gather them up, and would thus be hindered in his pursuit.

Finally, the group arrived at Iolcus. There, Medea murdered Jason's uncle Pelias, because of the wrongs which the latter had perpetrated upon Jason's family: she had restored his half-brother Aeson to youth by boiling him in a cauldron with magic herbs. Then she suggested to Pelias' daughters that they do the same with their father. However, this time the restorative herbs were left out, and Pelias was not rejuvenated, but simply boiled. His son, understandably angry, drove Jason and Medea out of Iolcus.

From there the two travelled about, and they finally took refuge at Corinth.[94] Jason, tired of his exciting life with Medea, decided to marry the daughter of Creon, king of Corinth: he resolved to desert Medea, being unencumbered by feelings of gratitude for the evils she had perpetrated for him, or even loyalty to her as mother of his children. Of course, he may also have been interested in Creon's kingdom, as well as his daughter.

If Jason thought that Medea would give her blessing to his happy new life, he was naïve indeed. Medea raged, causing Jason's future father-in-law some consternation. Creon decided that it was in his best interests to banish Medea and her children.

Medea appeared to accept this further humiliation stoically, and she merely asked for a day's respite. The relieved Creon granted her this wish, and she used her time carefully. She arranged the deaths of Jason's bride-to-be and of Creon. Then she killed her own children, out of resentment for Jason and fear that her children would die in exile, and she escaped to Athens.

Medea's story is an example of energy misused. It is also a story which illustrates shifts of power: Medea, the barbarian princess, killed her brother to effect Jason's escape from Colchis. The Colchian society was a barbarian one, and it was probably matrilineal or patri-matrilineal. Recall that in such societies the closest male-female tie is often that of brother and sister. Thus Medea's fratricide represented a cutting off of her matrilineal ties. She truly gave up all of her old life for the man she loved. Once again myth gives heroic sanction to the shift to patriarchy and patrilineality.

Consorts of heroines such as Medea often depleted the women of their energies. Another depleted heroine was the Carthaginian queen, *Dido.* Her life may be viewed in the three phases of virgin or celibate, matron or professed matron, and, if not old woman, at least "used up" woman.

Dido had been married once, to a man named Sychaeus, and after he died, for a long time she felt love for no other man. Indeed, she repeatedly rejected requests from many suitors.[95] She remained celibate for many years. When the hero *Aeneas* first saw her, she appeared

III.13.47. " . . . *as Diana,*
[when] she causes her dancers to dance . . .
thus was Dido."[96]
Vergil, Aeneid 498–503; 70 BCE to 19 BCE.

Dido, having stored up her virgin energies, was thus compared to the virgin goddess Diana-Artemis.

Having acted upon advice from her husband Sychaeus, Dido had gained wealth.[97] When she fell in love with Aeneas, she shared her wealth with him, thereby helping him to regain his strength, for Aeneas' ship, fleeing from burning Troy, had found port at Dido's city when the hero and all of his men were suffering from greatly depleted energies.

Therefore, when Dido was in her second phase, when she was no longer professed virgin but instead professed matron, then she imparted to Aeneas not only abstract "stored energies," but actual material wealth.

Dido was fated to pass quickly from her second to her last stage. She had not long enjoyed her "marriage" to Aeneas when the hero was enjoined by the gods to set sail once more for Italy and the new society which he was destined to found. Aeneas stood firm against Dido's entreaties to remain with her, and he sailed away from Carthage in the night.

When she saw Aeneas' ships, moving away from the harbor, Dido aged overnight. She changed into a Medea-figure, but an ineffectual one. Aware that her fate could only be the angry attacks of rejected suitors, who would not fail to take advantage of Dido's abandoned state, the heroine decided to take fate into her own hands. Hurling imprecations at Aeneas and his tribe, she committed suicide.

Perhaps all that saved Dido from acts of malevolent retribution, worthy of a Medea, was a miscalculation in time. Indeed, she reproached herself for failing to wreak vengeance upon her estranged lover before he sailed. But Vergil saved his readers from an ignominious ending, and was content with the dramatic impact of having Dido turn the forces of her wrath against herself. She brought, not blood upon Aeneas' head, but only tears to his eyes, when, later in the Aeneid, as a shade in the Underworld, she refused to answer or to look upon him.[98]

Dido thus saw her energies abused when her lover abandoned her to fulfill his destiny. Her energies spent in vain, Dido died and became a shade,[99] a shadow of a woman.

Another heroine-goddess whose energies were misused was the Irish third *Macha*, wife of the farmer, Cruin.[100] Recall that her husband boasted of her running abilities to King Conchobor, who then forced her to race his horses, even though she was pregnant. Upon winning the race, Macha's labor culminated. She died as she gave birth to twins. This Macha was possessed of great powers, and she was quite willing to transmit them to her husband. But Cruin, by a tragic decision worthy of a Sophocles, misused her great gift, and not only did she die because of his misuse, but he lost the gifts of plenty which she had brought to him. Further the warriors in the "Cattle-Raid of Cooley" were rendered incapacitated by her dying curse.

There are many tragedies of misused powers throughout the mythologies of ancient cultures. Through the story of the Trojan War runs a thread of energy misspent.

When the Greek hero Peleus and the Nereid Thetis were married, at their wedding-feast the goddess Eris, "strife," threw down to the guests a golden apple,[101] inscribed "for the fairest."

Hera and Athena and Aphrodite all claimed this apple: that is, all claimed to be the most beautiful. Paris, the most handsome mortal man in the world, was asked to judge which of the goddesses was most worthy of the apple.

The goddesses, not content to let the verdict of this beauty contest lie upon anything as tenuous as their beauty, decided to take political action. Each of the three offered to give Paris wonderful gifts if he would cast his vote for her. Hera promised him greatness, Athena offered him success in war, and Aphrodite offered him the loveliest woman in the world for his wife.

Paris chose Aphrodite's gift. One might speculate about the significance of this sexual choice, as opposed to the choice of fame or martial prowess. Perhaps the energies which are transmitted through the sexual act are primary; if a man is thus fulfilled, he then has the energies to pursue greatness. His prowess is increased proportionately to the beauty of his woman. If she is very beautiful, he is suffused with energy.

> After she was judged by Paris to be the most beautiful of the goddesses, Aphrodite helped Paris to win the lovely Helen from her husband, Menelaus. Paris abused the hospitality of the cuckolded Menelaus, and therefore he abused love. The forces of love having been misdirected, love became a destructive force, leading to war between Menelaus, with the confederated Greeks as his allies, and Paris, with those Trojans who had the ill-fortune to be associated with him.[102]

In fact, the tragedy of the fall of Troy might have been averted, had the Trojans given ear to the prophecies of Cassandra. Before the birth of Paris, Cassandra had announced that the unborn child of her parents, Priam and Hecuba, would grow up to be the ruin of his country.[103] But, since the virgin Cassandra had resisted the love of the powerful deity, Apollo, the god negated the gift of prophecy which he had given to her. (This, we must understand, is a creation of the patriarchy; it was the snakes who had originally conferred the gift of prophecy upon Cassandra, not the late-comer, Apollo.[104]) Cassandra bore the stigma of madness, and therefore her prophecies went unheeded. So her great forces were suppressed, spent in vain, and the Trojan tragedy took place.

OLD AGE AND WITCHES, YOUNG AND OLD

In a balanced, equalitarian society, one might expect that the old woman, full of wisdom and experience, would be highly valued. In patriarchal Indo-European societies in which women had little status, however, the old woman, the crone, was least respected. When a woman had "run down her batteries," and thus no longer had enough energy to give to others, she then became the antithesis of the young virgin who stored energy, or of the matron who transmitted it. Although some old women dispensed both herbs and wise advice, and thus benefitted humanity, for the most part, ancient mythology depicted the old woman as evil crone. Whether virgin or matron, she was depicted as a barren creature who was said to use the energies of others to supplement her own wasted forces. Whereas the young virgin represents potential energy, the aged virgin represents the sterility, the barrenness of a woman who has never borne children, and who will never change her barren state. She will, therefore, never bear sons for the patriarchy.

Some goddesses could represent both the matron and the aged states, as did Hera when she was *widow*.[105] Another Greek matron- or mother-goddess, Demeter, was also depicted in an aged state when she was sorrowing for her stolen daughter, Persephone.[106] Demeter was

> III.13.48. " . . . *like an old woman,*
> *born long ago,*
> *who is excluded from childbearing*
> *and the gifts of garland-loving Aphrodite* . . . "[107]
> Homeric Hymn II.101–102; 8th to 6th Centuries BCE.

Bereft of her daughter, barren in her solitude, Demeter caused all of the earth to become barren as well.[108]

Although Demeter created havoc among gods and mortals, she was not metamorphosed into a bogey-woman, but gods and men treated her with respect and awe. She was, after all, a mother, and, primarily, a goddess of vegetal *fertility*, and she caused the earth to blossom again. She *controlled* her own, and the world's, fertility. She used her barrenness as a weapon. But because there was a possibility that she would renew fertility, the gods and men, in spite of their fear, showed her respect. Not all goddesses received such respect. Those who were frozen in their aged state, who even potentially would not energize the men of their society, were often depicted as frightful hags, women who were to be avoided at all cost. One such woman was the Germanic goddess, *Rán*. This goddess was an old, withered crone, wife of the sea-king, Aegir. She used to drag her net under the ocean, following ships, and waiting for those sailors who might chance to fall overboard:

III.13.49. *"But Sigrún, from above,*
[was] bold in battle,
so that he saved them,
and their ships as well;
he powerfully wrested
out of Rán's hand,
the king's sea-steed [ship],
at Gnipa Grove."[109]
Helgakviða Hundingsbana I.30; *ca.* 550 CE to *ca.* 1000 CE.

Since age had caused her energies to run down, Rán needed the life force of the sailors to revitalize herself.

The Greek goddess *Hecate* was powerful in the heavens, on earth, and in the underworld.[110] She was a goddess of herbal magic; Classical "witches," such as Medea, were her followers. The Greek poet Theocritus sang

III.13.50. " . . . *to Hecate of the Underworld,*
in whose wake young pups tremble,
as she traverses the tombs
and black blood
of the dead.
Hail, hard-striking Hecate!
Attend me in my goal,
making potions that are no less potent
than those of Circe
or Medea,
or golden-haired Perimede."[111]
Theocritus, Idyll II.12–16; *ca.* 310 BCE to *ca.* 250 BCE.

The witch, although in a sense a mortal follower of the chthonic goddess, was also herself a transmutation of the more ancient goddess. Whereas the powers over both life and death were natural to the prehistoric goddess, her powers over death were feared by many of the assimilating historical male-centered cultures. Her vast powers were detrited into negative magic that a clever hero, or anyone who knew the proper apotropaic chant, might hope to avoid. The witch was generally a woman,[112] and always a person with connections to the Underworld. She could be old or young, ugly or beautiful.

One of the most beautiful Classical-age witches was the "lovely-haired"[113] *Circe*, a "terrible goddess,"[114] around whose house were

III.13.51. " . . . *mountain wolves and lions,*
whom [Circe] herself had enchanted,
when she gave them harmful drugs."[115]
Homer, Odyssey X.212–213; *ca.* 800? BCE.

Circe, a descendant of the ancient "Mistress of Animals," sang with "lovely voice,"[116] and was a most alluring sorceress, as the hero Odysseus discovered.

The hero Odysseus found himself in her domain, and he found his companions bewitched by the lovely goddess. She would give the men a potion to drink,[117] and then, striking them with her wand, she would turn them into animals and pen them into pig-sties.

But, as Odysseus was on his way to rescue his metamorphosed friends, hurrying forth somewhat rashly, the god Hermes, in disguise, met him and gave him a potent herb, which would render the hero impervious to Circe's magic potion. Further, the god told Odysseus that, just as Circe was about to strike him with her wand, he must draw his sword threateningly. He must then make her swear an oath, that she would not plot any new misdeeds against him. Then, he could enjoy her couch in safety.

All came to pass as the god had foretold. Circe, out of love for Odysseus' masculine strength, even freed his comrades. Odysseus, with a little help from the god, had saved the day for his friends and for himself. And the beautiful witch was not boiled in oil or even baked in her own oven, but simply found herself alone again.

It would appear that a witch such as Circe could not be punished by the gods for her "transgressions," for she herself was a goddess, a "Mistress of Animals," and it was thus her function to have magical relations with animals, even if they had once been human.

Other Classical-age goddesses were closely linked with animals of various sorts; many were maiden-animal hybrids. All were female and all were terrifying creatures. The Greek Scylla was a terrifying female monster who was endowed with twelve feet and six heads.[118] As did the Germanic Rán, Scylla seized and devoured sailors, but she was not an underwater-creature:

> III.13.52. "*Up to her middle*
> *she lies hidden in a hollow cavern,*
> *but she holds her head out*
> *beyond the terrible gulf,*
> *and she fishes there . . .*
> *no sailors yet may profess*
> *that they have fled close by her,*
> *unharmed, in their ship.*"[119]
> Ibid, XII.93–99.

Further,

> III.13.53. "*A cavern confines Scylla*
> *in blind recesses,*
> *from which she thrusts forward her mouths*
> *and draws ships into her rocks.*
> *Above, she is of human shape:*
> *as far as her waist a virgin*
> *with a beautiful bosom;*
> *below she is a sea-monster*
> *with a huge body,*
> *with dolphins' tails*
> *connected to a belly of wolves.*"[120]
> Vergil, Aeneid III.424–428; 70 BCE to 19 BCE.

Many monster-goddesses, including Scylla and the Irish Morrigan, inhabited the caves. The cave was the womb of the Mother and was thus the Goddess herself.

Another female monster was the nursery bogey *Lamia,*[121] who had unwashed genitals.[122] She stole children from their own beds and devoured them.[123]

Some female monsters had their origins in the Neolithic bird and snake goddesses. The Greek *Gorgons* retained the ancient European snake-symbols, but their "snaky hair" became a terrifying attribute. These women were monsters whose eyes turned anyone who met their gaze to stone. *Medusa* was the most famous of the Gorgons, and the only mortal among them. The hero Perseus cut off her head, and the winged horse Pegasus sprang forth from the wound.[124] The *snaky-haired* goddess was thus destroyed, and from her body came the *winged* horse.

The *Furies* or *Erinyes* were snaky virgin goddesses who brought punishment for those who deserved it, especially those who committed murder of kin.[125] Vergil describes one of the Furies, *Tisiphone*:

> III.13.54. "*At once avenging Tisiphone,*
> *equipped with a whip,*
> *leaping on the guilty,*
> *harasses them,*
> *and, her left hand brandishing her fierce snakes,*

she calls on her raging band of sisters.''[126]
Ibid, VI.570–572.

Another Fury, *Allecto*, set people on fire. She was

III.13.55. ''*infected with Gorgon's venom.*''[127]
Ibid, VII.341.

and her

III.13.56. '' . . . *heart [loves] sad wars,*
rages, plots, and noxious crimes . . .
she changes herself into so many forms,
such fierce shapes,
so many black serpents
sprout up.''[128]
Ibid, VII.324–329.

All of the Furies had viper-like hair. They not only brandished snakes; they assimilated the snake into their *persona*.

Other female monsters were, like the Furies and Gorgons, associated with snakes. The *Dirae* were dread creatures, endowed with "snaky coils" and clothed with "windy wings:" they were descended from both the snake goddess *and* the bird-goddess:

III.13.57. ''*They say that there are twin plagues,*
named the Dirae,
whom timeless Night bore with Tartarean Megaera
in one and the same birth;
they fastened the coils of a snake
around both of them
and added windy wings.''[129]
Ibid, XII.845–848.

The *Harpies* also embodied characteristics of the bird-goddess. They were Greco-Roman female demons who brought doubt and destroyed hope, and they darted out from blind shadows.[130] Like many other female monsters, they were both human and beast:

III.13.58. ''*These birds have the faces of young women,*
the filthiest refuse [comes] from their belly,
they have clawed hands,
and their faces are always pale with hunger.''[131]
Ibid, III.216–218.

The *Sirens* were bird-woman hybrids, similar to the Harpies in form. They lived on rocky islands, and with their songs they enticed passing sailors to their destruction. Odysseus was warned:

III.13.59. ''*Whoever approaches the Sirens*
in ignorance,
and hears their song,
he never returns home . . .
but the Sirens enchant him
with their clear-toned song,
as they sit in a meadow,
and about them is a large pile of bones
of rotting men . . .
but you, row past them,
and put honey-sweet wax,
which you have softened,
in your companions' ears . . . ''[132]
Homer, Odyssey XII.41–48; *ca.* 800? BCE.

These Greco-Roman monsters had several characteristics in common. First, many of them, such as the Sirens, the Harpies, and Scylla, were half lovely young woman and half animal. Generally, in this case, they had *beautiful breasts*. Secondly, young, heroic males often conquered them, usually with the help and wisdom of a god, as Hermes aiding Odysseus with Circe, or a goddess, as Circe aiding Odysseus with Scylla. In conquering these "monsters," the warriors were symbolically overcoming *very powerful* goddesses of the pre-Indo-European societies; conquering these goddesses was both a reality and a metaphor for conquering the goddess-centered people. Finally, these female figures often had the attributes of birds or snakes. Although they continued the personification of Neolithic European bird and snake goddesses, they were reduced to dire monsters rather than powerful goddesses who ruled life and death. All of these female monsters were perhaps projections of Classical men's fears—and of their desires. Under Greek and Roman sway, the potency of these once-potent goddesses was held in check.

The Indic *Nirṛti* was a goddess of destruction and death. She was associated with the house of the neglected woman, and to her care fell the old spinster, the barren woman. She followed closely upon old age:

> III.13.60. *''Thus may Nirṛti*
> *devour my old age.''*[133]
> Rigveda V.41.17; *ca.* 1200 BCE.

and, like the underworld-goddess, Hecate, she also represented the state which followed old age, that of death."[134] She was to be avoided, as a goddess who brought destruction:

> III.13.61. *''Let not Nirṛti,*
> *distributing ill,*
> *have power over us.''*[135]
> Ibid, X.36.2.

The Celtic *Badb* fulfilled a similar function. She was a crow-goddess[136] who brought death. The bird-goddess *Morrigan* too could bring death on the battlefield, as well as victory.

Baltic witches, *raganas*, were often depicted as old, evil women, although they could at times be beautiful and young—as was the Greek Circe. In a Lithuanian folk-tale,[137] a king's mother hated her daughter-in-law, and, as her two grandchildren were born, she substituted a cat for each of them. She was called, in the tale, "the old witch"[138] and "the old worn-out woman."[139]

A *ragana* was

> III.13.62. *''A flying witch,*
> *who changes herself into a cat . . .*
> *and rides through the air on a ram.''*[140]
> Mannhardt: 628; Twentieth Century CE.

We see that the ragana, according to the Balts, *was* a cat; other folk-beliefs have deemed the cat her companion. Perhaps the tiny feline inherited the job of the earlier lions, consorts of the "Mistress of Animals."

The Slavic witch, the *Vyed'ma*, was similar to the Baltic ragana. Her name means the "knowing woman,"[141] and she was originally an old woman, wise in herbal magic. But, by the time the Slavic folk-tales were written down, the Vyed'ma had become a female fiend.[142] She was a "winged old woman" who "spread her wings, flying in the air . . ."[143]

The Vyed'ma could be born of mortal parents. *Baba*[144] *Yaga*, another Slavic witch, was of more supernatural descent.[145] She was an old woman who often lived in the woods, similar to the witch who tried to eat Hansel and Gretel. Her hut stood "on fowls' legs,"[146] and she devoured any mortals who strayed too close to her.[147] She rode in a mortar, propelled by a pestle, and she swept away her traces with a broom.[148]

In most historical cultures, goddesses who took the energies of others for themselves were regarded as evil witches. In some cultures, however, the more ancient goddess was visible among other, more assimilated deities. She remained the goddess who both gave life and brought death.

Among the Celts, as among the Germans who worshipped Nerthus, a virgin-goddess augmented her fecundating powers through the sacrifice of men who wooed her: she absorbed their energy.

> At the time of Samain, a maiden was wooed at Bri Ele by the men of Ireland, and for each man who wooed her, one of his people was slain, no-one knowing who did the deed. Each invoking community had to sacrifice one man each year, to secure the "good will" of the goddess.[149]

Bri Ele was another name for Cruachan, the royal center of Connacht, where Queen Medb had ruled. So this maiden perpetuated the great powers of the Irish "queen," who, in turn, had perpetuated the powers and prerogatives of the more ancient goddesses.

Thus there were goddesses who aided men but who remained autonomous and powerful. They continued the traditions of prehistoric goddesses, somehow escaping the assimilation into Indo-European male-centered society, and concomitant loss of powers, which most of their sister-goddesses underwent. Many autonomous goddesses were transmuted to witches by the Greeks, Romans, and other Indo-Europeans, and they were often removed to far-away islands or stuck underwater, perhaps thus lurking just at the periphery of men's consciousness. Although some male-centered cultures refused to venerate them, they could not eradicate them. Further, other cultures did continue to worship both the life-giving and the death-giving aspect of the goddess.

Even today the goddess Devī, in all of her manifestations, is a very important force in Indic religion.[150] More commonly, however, the goddess in her death aspect was viewed not as goddess, but as "witch;" her meaning, "wise woman," was forgotten and she was regarded as a sterile woman to be feared because she would not give her energy to men. In fact, even when "the wise woman" has been herbswoman and healer—one who lived in harmony with her physical and social environment, a nurturer—even then, she has been despised and persecuted by the leaders of male-centered cultures. After the advent of Christianity, throughout the centuries of the Middle Ages, such healers were hunted down and persecuted. The excuse was given that the female witch consorted with the devil, that the devil had given her the knowledge of healing, and that she was, therefore, an embodiment of evil herself. The real reason, of course, was that these healers posed a threat to the power which the rising class of medical doctors wielded over the populace. The "witches" represented the power of autonomy, which threatened those who believed in power *over*.[151]

Throughout history, there have been, in the folktales and myths of many cultures, various sorts of witches, young and old, described by male mythopoets as evil and not so evil. But they all possessed one characteristic in common: they were autonomous; they possessed powers which were not controlled by men. They were thus, in one way, *a projection of men's fears*, fears of energies which they did not control. Whereas virgins and matrons have been tied to the patriarchal culture, and have given energy in some form to man, the witch, whether old, depleted woman or simply woman who has reserved her powers for herself, has not been possessed by the patriarchy. Patriarchal men have always feared powerful women.

Any autonomous woman is a candidate for the "fear-inspiring goddess." Whether maiden or crone, the autonomous woman is feared as one who can emasculate men verbally as surely as Circe transformed unlucky men into lions and wolves with a tap of her wand. The rigid patriarch seems to fear that autonomous women will transform men into mice.

Increasing numbers of women are recognizing their power and their autonomy, but men's fear of this power is a projection of their own world-view. Women do not use their power to dominate or to subordinate, as is typical of a dominator society. Rather, women use their power to increase the well-being of their environment. Men who fear women's strength fear a matriarchy, the inverse of a patriarchal society, and they do not wish to be subordinates in such a society. But there is no evidence that a matriarchal dominant-subordinate society has ever existed. What may indeed have existed is *partnership*[152] societies in which women and men held equally valuable roles.

We have re-examined the goddesses through several millennia, and we have seen a radical change in how the divine feminine has been viewed, first by the goddess-centered societies of the Neolithic, then by the assimilated societies made up of male-centered Indo-Europeans and the more equalitarian folk whom they conquered; and finally by modern societies, many of which worship no personification of the feminine at all. There is a lack of balance in much of modern religion, an imbalance in the character of the divine. This imbalance reflects upon the wellness, in all of its aspects, of our world.

CHAPTER 14

Conclusion: Bestowal of energy and reciprocity the challenges of the future

Throughout the past few millennia there have been great advances in technology which have raised standards of living in many areas of the world. At the same time, we have reduced our standard of life: our quality of air, purity of rivers and oceans, wellness of the land; and we have increased world hunger, extinction of whole species of animals, depletion of natural resources. Improved technology is not leading to greater peace and harmony among nations, between individuals, even within the self. The patriarchal world is out of balance. The worship of the male energy has led to rape of our natural resources and poisoning of our environment. What is missing, particularly in Western culture, is respect for an energy which makes things whole, an energy which honors life.

The goddesses provide a clue to how we must restructure our world if it is to survive, a clue both to our past and to our future. The fact that there were powerful goddesses disproves the claim that woman has "always" been powerless and secondary, and that this "second rank" is thus a natural phenomenon. This frees us to move into a balancing.

The goddesses are multiple but the goddess-energy is a unity, and just as all people are part of a divine essence which is at once unified and diverse, just as there is both unity and duality in the forces of life and death. The goddess of life and death, the "Goddess of the Life Continuum" who endured from at least the sixth millennium BCE, from Neolithic iconography through the mythologies of most Indo-European societies, had as her iconographic representations the bird and the snake. These figures span all of the spacial possibilities: the bird flies to the sky, while the snake is a chthonic creature of earth and underworld. They span the temporal possibilities as well: birds such as the dove represent life, while birds such as the crow represent death, in particular death on the battlefield; the snake was linked to rebirth, for it sloughed its skin and acquired a new one, in continual cycles. Thus, the composite of bird and snake matched the continuum of birth, death and rebirth which the "Goddess of the Life Continuum," the "Goddess of Regeneration" encompassed. Contained within the sphere of rebirth was the mystic: the snake as seeress, embodiment of wisdom; the wisdom which is not just autocratic Mistress of the world, but compassionate guide.

This feminine wisdom, lauded throughout the myths of the Indo-Europeans, despite their women's lack of stature in their societies, must be the thread which leads us out of the labyrinth of destruction in which this world finds itself enmeshed. The feminine energy, the energy which nurtures one's children, one's environment, and *oneself*, must attain the stature of the masculine; the two must be in balance with one another so that the world itself will be in balance, physically, emotionally, and spiritually. Only in harmony with true wisdom and spirituality can intellectuality lead to growth for humanity, and only if the feminine spirit is honored can spirit be in harmony. Many philosophies teach us that it is the inner realms which are important, that the physical world is delusion. But if that is so, then it is moral to neglect our physical universe. The disaster attendant upon that conclusion is obvious. We must attend to not only the inner realms, but the outer as well, for if we do not care about our physical universe, we will perish. Just as the outer world sustains us, so we must all, women and men, nurture it. We need, therefore, a balance among all levels: physical, spiritual, intellectual, emotional.

The ancient "Great"-goddesses bestowed life and brought death. Since the goddesses and gods whom we worship reflect our own world-view, worship of ancient goddesses reflected the balance of respecting both life and death. Today, those who construct ever more potent death machines have become more involved with death than with life. We need not only to re-evaluate our respect for life; we need to promote a better quality of life for all of humanity. We must use our powers for growth and autonomy rather than as power *over*.

I believe that we are in the process of returning to that necessary balance, and to the wisdom that all things are interconnected. Although many in the world are indeed promoting technology without ethics and religion without the compassion and love of true spirituality; although many still feed on violence and negativity; nevertheless there are increasing numbers of people who are rejecting these systems, who are using their energies to promote world peace and to raise the quality of the environment. In awakening their own nurturing energies, more and more people are taking individual responsibility for the welfare of our planet and for all of its inhabitants. The divine energy which we worship in goddesses and gods is in all of us, and we have the ability to use that energy to begin our healing.

End Notes
Abbreviations
Selected Bibliography
Glossary

ENDNOTES

INTRODUCTION

1. Rāmāyaṇa 1.45.
2. Harivaṁśa II App.1.41.525.
3. Hesiod, Theogony 190–197:

> . . . ἀμφὶ δὲ λευκὸς
> ἀφρὸς ἀπ' ἀθανάτου χροὸς ὤρνυτο·
>   τῷ δ' ἔνι κούρη
> ἐθρέφθη· πρῶτον δὲ Κυθήροισιν ζαθέοισιν
> ἔπλητ',
>   ἔνθεν ἔπειτα περίρρυτον ἵκετο Κύπρον.
> ἐκ δ' ἔβη αἰδοίη καλὴ θεός . . .
> . . . τὴν δ' Ἀφροδίτην . . .
> κικλήσκουσι θεοί τε καὶ ἀνέρες . . .

4. Myth is either inherited or borrowed. Although both India and Greece share a common heritage, as Indo-European cultures which derived language, social structure, and much of their religion from a common ancestor, the Proto-Indo-European, the love-goddess was most likely *not* a part of that inheritance (v. Chapter One); one must therefore search for the origins of the goddesses Aphrodite and Shrī Lakshmī in cultural areas other than the Indo-European, most likely in the Near East, in Mesopotamia, since echoes of a similar myth can be found there.
5. cf. Puhvel (1987): 1–4 and 7–20, on mythological methodologies and the monogenetic approach.
6. "Primary" source is a *philological* term indicating the source itself, rather than later commentary on the source: for example, a poem by the Greek poet Sappho rather than a discussion of that poem by a modern scholar. "Primary" can be an ambiguous term, however. Since, in most patriarchal cultures, myths were most commonly written by men, giving "divine" explanations for contemporary political practice, the myths themselves become political discussions. Thus, the true primary sources, from the perspective of ancient women, have reached us in hugely atrophied form. We study patriarchal myth, therefore, to determine what happened to the role of the female, divine and mortal, after the advent of the patriarchs. v. Daly (1978): 27 on male-authored texts as secondary sources.

PART ONE: CHAPTER ONE

1. *BCE*, "before the common era," is used in place of BC, "before Christ," to divide time in a manner inclusive of both Christians and non-Christians. Likewise, *CE*, "common era," is used instead of AD, *anno domini*, "in the year of the Lord."
2. Gimbutas (1982): 4–8; (1977): 281; and written communication.
3. Ibid: 8.
4. Furthermore, this ritual pottery was most likely made only by women. v. Gimbutas (1982): 7,9.
5. cf. Goldenburg (1979): 96 ff, on *thealogy*.
6. According to Gimbutas, personal communication, male figures compose only two to three percent of figurines found in European excavations of Neolithic date. Further, at least forty percent of the figurines are bird-woman and snake-woman hybrids (Gimbutas, 1982: 13). v. below.
7. The faces are masked: v. Gimbutas (1974): 57–66.
8. v. Powell (1966): 14 ff; v. Kurtz (1975): 111.
9. v. Chapter Two, below.
10. Ovid, Fasti III.21; 45:

> *Mars videt hanc visamque cupit*
>   *potiturque cupita . . .*
> *Silvia fit mater.*

    Cf. Chapter Thirteen, below, on the miraculous conceptions of the Roman Vestal Virgin Rhea Silvia and others.
11. Apollodorus, Atheniensis Bibliothecae I.iii.5:

Ἥρα δὲ χωρὶς εὐνῆς ἐγέννησεν Ἥφαιστον·

v. Chapter Twelve, below.

12. Gimbutas (1974): 74.
13. Literally, "truly, I stand as one." Devī-māhātmyam X.8:

. . . ekaiva tiṣṭām . . .

v. Chapter Seven, below.

14. v. Gimbutas (1974): 152 et passim.
15. v. Chapter Two, below.
16. v. Gimbutas (1974): 112 ff.
17. v. Gimbutas (1982): 13.
18. v. Marshack (1972). Note the schematized figures of birds in figures 70b and 72b, a fragment from La Vache, an Upper Palaeolithic site in France; the engraving of a wide-eyed bird in figure 76, from the cave site of Paglicci, an Upper Palaeolithic site in southeastern Italy; the composition on bone representing a snake, a duck, and a smaller bird in figure 77, also from Paglicci; and the long baton of reindeer antler depicting salmon, two seals, and serpents in figure 61, from Montgaudier, an Upper Palaeolithic site in France.
19. v., for example, Gimbutas' (1987) excavation report for the Neolithic Greek site in Thessaly, Achilleion: plates 10a, 13; figures 29, 31. Finds are in the Larissa Museum. The snake-figurines from Achilleion were excavated from shrines.
20. v. Vasić (1936): Vol. III, figures 384, 448, 467.
21. v. endnote 19, above.
22. v. Theochares (1973): Plate 75; cf. Gimbutas (1974): 94–95; pl 54, 65.
23. Ibid, Plate 56, a clay figurine of a woman holding a child (kourotrophos), National Archaeological Museum, No. NM 5937. The figure dates to the Late Neolithic.
24. The uraeus was probably a stylization of the sacred asp. It appeared on the headdress or crown of Egyptian rulers, gods, and goddesses.
25. The spelling *Uatchit* is sometimes found, but *Uatchet* will be used throughout this book for consistency. V. Budge (1904; 1969), Vol. I:24.
26. v. Lewis and Short (1962): 256.
27. v. Budge (1904; 1969) Vol. I:442. Cf. Lanzone (1974–75), plates 58–60.
28. v. Budge (1910; 1983): 33. Budge (1920; 1978) Vol. II: CXViii.
29.  Budge (1920; 1978), Vol. I: 401.
30. cf. the Sumerian cylinder seal depicted in Campbell (1974): 295, dating to 2500 BCE. On it are represented a Sumerian goddess and god with snakes and a sacred tree. v. the Tiamat-Marduk myth below.
31. Syrian seated goddess with snakes. Ivory from Ras Shamra, Syria, dating to ca. 2000 BCE. The Louvre, No. AO 19397. cf. Amiet (1980), No. 16.
32. Gimbutas (1974): 74–75.
33. Ibid: 75; Nilsson (1950): 80–82.
34. Two chryselephantine figures from Knossos may be found in the Heraklion Museum, Crete, Nos. 63 and 65. cf. Kurtz (1975): 209; Alexiou (1973): Plate 12.
35. Taylour (1970): 278. The snakes discovered in this building may or may not have been worshipped by themselves. They were found along with several idols, the majority of which were female.
36. Campbell (1974): 287. The figure of Hygieia dates to 400 BCE.
37. v. Apollodorus, Atheniensis Bibliothecae I.iv.1.
38. v. Anticlides, in Scholiast on Homer's Iliad, viii.44.
39. Apollodorus, Atheniensis Bibliothecae, I.ix.11:

. . . παραστάντες
αὐτῷ κοιμωμένῳ τῶν ὤμων ἐξ ἑκατέρου
τὰς ἀκοὰς
ταῖς γλώσσαις ἐξεκάθαιρον.
ὁ δὲ ἀναστὰς καὶ
γενόμενος περιδεὴς
τῶν ὑπερπετομένων ὀρνέων
τὰς φωνὰς συνίει,
καὶ παρ' ἐκείνων μανθάνων
προύλεγε τοῖς ἀνθρώποις τὰ μέλλοντα.

40. For discussion of *Tantra* and *shakti*, v. Chapter Seven, below.
41. v. Monier-Williams (1899; 1964): 380.
42. v. Avalon (1978): 675 ff.
43. Several figurines of this Indic goddess are extant. A bronze statue of *Manasā* from Bihar, dating to *circa* 900 CE, may be seen at the Los Angeles County Museum of Art, No. M.83.1.2. A canopy of cobra hoods rises above her head.
44. Los Angeles County Museum of Art, No. M.82.42.1. The schist figurine was found in Rajasthan; three arms hold a horn, a lance, and a water-pot. Cf. the depiction of *Hygieia* described above.
45. v. Chapter Five, below.
46. v. Mannhardt (1936).
47. "Aukso Žiedas," "The Gold Ring," a Lithuanian folk-tale in Užburta Karalystė (1957), 160ff:

    —Nebijok, žmogau! Tu mane
    išgelbėjai nuo mirties . . .
    gyvatę, o tu ją išpirkai.

48. v. Ralston (1872): 115.
49. v. Chapter Five, below, for a discussion of the Lithuanian folk-tale, "Eglė, the Queen of Serpents."
50. "Psalms" 74.14:

    . . . ritsats'tā rā'she liv'yātān . . .

    Cf. "Job" 26.13: Yahweh created the "fleeing serpent,"

    nāchāsh bāriāch.

51. Ibid: 74.13:

    . . . shibar'tā rā'she taninim al-hamāyim

52. "Isaiah" 27.1:

    . . . yiph'qid adonai
    b'char'bu haqāshāh
    v'hag'dulāh v'hachazāqāh
    al liv'yātan
    nāchāsh bāriach
    v'al liv'yātān
    nāchāsh 'aqalāton
    v'hārag et-hatanin bayam.

    The serpents are used in a metaphorical sense here, to indicate enemies of Israel.
53. Campbell (1974): 294.
54. The Ugaritic text is KTU 1.5 (=UT 67). For the name of *Mot*, cf. Ugaritic *mwt*, "to die."
55. KTU 1.5 vi.
56. Ibid 1.6.i (=UT 49).
57. Ibid 1.6.ii.
58. Ibid 1.6.iii.
59. Ibid 1.6.v.
60. Ibid 1.2.iv (=UT 68).
61. v. Cassuto (1951): 133.
62. or "I destroyed the great god, Nahar." KTU 1.3.iii (=UT 'nt III.35–36) 38–39:

    lmḫšt . mdd
    il ym . lklt nhr . il rbm.

63. v. Chapter Two, below.
64. A full description of the battle is not found in extant Egyptian literature. It is alluded to in the "Hymn to Osiris" 22 (inscribed on the stele of Ahenmose, dating to *ca.* 1500 BCE), where Horus, son of Osiris, is described as the "avenger of his father." The hieroglyphic text may be found in Budge (1904; 1969) II.173. A more detailed description is given in Plutarch, Moralia 356 C–D, "On Isis and Osiris" XIII.
65. v. the Egyptian Book of the Dead, passim.
66. "Hymn to Osiris" 13–17. Text may be found in Budge (1904; 1969) II: 168–170.
67. Enuma Elish: IV.71:

    . . . Ti-amat ul u-ta-ri ki-šad-sa

    " . . . and Tiamat did not turn back her neck."

cf. IV.90: *šur-šiš* "roots, limbs"

68. Marduk was also known as *Bel*: Enuma Elish IV.33. Ugaritic *b'l* indicates "owner of the house, lord." v. Gordon (1955): 247.
69. Enuma Elish: IV.101:

is-suk mulmul-la
ich-te-pi ka-ras-sa

''He loosed an arrow;
it split open (lit. ''broke'') her stomach.''

According to Langdon (1923): 141, *is-suk* appears for *nasaku*, "throw."

70. Ibid: IV.102:

u-šal-liṭ lib-ba

'' . . . and it plundered her inner parts.''

71. Ibid IV.103:

ik-mi-ši-ma nap-ša-taš u-bal-li

"He captured her and extinguished her soul."

72. Homeric Hymn to Pythian Apollo 351 ff. For the iconography of Typhon, v. the detail from a red-figured vase depicted in Larousse (1959, 1968): 91.
73. Ibid: 300 ff.
74. Apollodorus, Atheniensis Bibliothecae I.iv.1–2.
75. cf. Plutarch, Moralia, "Quaestiones Graecae" 12:

οἱ μὲν γὰρ φυγεῖν
ἐπὶ τῷ φόνῳ φασὶ
χρῄζοντα καθαρσίων . . .

''Some indeed say that [Apollo] fled
because he wished for a cleansing
for the murder [which he had committed].''

76. Apollodorus, Atheniensis Bibliothecae II.v.2. For the iconography, v. the votive relief from Lerna, in the Peloponnese Argolis, now in the National Archaeological Museum, Crete (No. N.M. 3617).
77. Apollodorus, Atheniensis Bibliothecae III,iv.1. v. Campbell (1974): figure 315, a Laconian cup now in the Louvre, Paris, No. N 3157. Note that several birds and snakes appear here; bird and snake iconography, with the two often shown in concert, as on this cup, continued to proliferate in Classical cultures long after the original mythological significance of the bird and snake were forgotten.
78. v. the metope from Selinus, depicted in Larousse (1959; 1968): 184. v. Chapter Thirteen, below, for a discussion of the goddess-turned-witch, Medusa.
79. Apollodorus, Atheniensis Bibliothecae II.iv.2. For the iconography, see the plate from Rhodes, British Museum No. GR 1860.4–4.2, dated *ca.* 600 BCE. v. also the winged Gorgon's head (No. GR 1888.6-1.127), and the terracotta jar decorated by a Gorgon's head surmounted by wings (No. 1862.7-12.2), both in the British Museum.
80. cf. CIA I.2.1578:

Ἡδίστιον Διὶ Μιλιχίῳ

"Most pleasing to the God Meilichios."

Further,

in parte inferiore lapidis
imago serpentis sculpta fuit.

''On the lower part of the stone
a likeness of a serpent was carved.''

cf. CIA 2.1579–1583.
v. Campbell (1964): 18, figure 8, a votive tablet, dating to the fourth century BCE. From The Piraeus, Greece.

81. The epithet Meilichios means "the gracious one." v. Liddell and Scott (1856): 1093.
82. cf. Farnell (1896): I.65.

83. v. Chapter Three, below.
84. Ibid.
85. Ibid.
86. v., for example, Raphael's depiction (1504–1506 CE) in Campbell (1974): 343. Cf. Gustav Moreau's painting in Allen (1979): 118.
87. v. the portrait of Saint Michael from Valencia (1400–1425 CE) shown at the New York Metropolitan Museum (Hibbard (1980): No. 353).
88. v. the portrayal in the Shahnamah, the Persian "Book of Kings," in Allen (1979): 123.
89. Vasić (1936): Vol. II, figure 95; Vol. III, figures 448, 460, 466, 467.
90. Vasić (1936): Vol. III, figures 384, 467, 539.
91. v. endnote 19, above.
92. These are calibrated carbon 14-tree ring dates. The excavator, Marija Gimbutas, has indicated that 98 percent of the figurines excavated at Achilleion were female figures.
93. v. Gimbutas (1987) plates 6, 7.
94. Ibid: plate 8.
95. Ibid: figures 19,4; 19,6; 21,1; 24,1.
96. v. Theochares (1973) figure 204, a Neolithic clay "mask"-shaped head from Dikili Tas. Philippi Museum 64; Plate XVIII, a figure with "mask"-like head on a painted pot. Late Neolithic (*ca.* 3500–2800 BCE). cf. Tsounta, excavation report on the Neolithic Acropolis of Dimini (1908), plate 27, No. 5.
97. Ibid 145.
98. Ibid 377; cf. figure 262, Heraklion Archaeological Museum; No. 2716. cf. Tsounta (1908), plate 37, No. 12; plate 38, No. 3, both from Dimini.
99. v. Wagner y Wagner (1934): 121 *et passim*.
100. cf. the ivory plaques, depicting winged female figures with palm trees: *ca.* 900 BCE, Syria; Louvre, Nos. 11468 and 11469.
101. v. the cylinder seal, dating to *ca.* 2300 BCE, representing the joint appearance of the Great Gods on the morning of the New Year; a winged goddess, often identified as the planet Venus—that is, Inanna-Ishtar—is depicted among the deities. Louvre, No. AO 11569. cf. Amiet (1980) 21 (772). Another cylinder seal, portrayed in Wolkstein and Kramer (1983): 92, depicts the winged Inanna with weapons issuing from her shoulders.
102. Gimbutas (1974): 146.
103. cf. Plutarch, Parallel Lives, "Life of Theseus" 21:

> *ἐκ δὲ τῆς Κρήτης ἀποπλέων εἰς Δῆλον κατέσχε . . .*
> *. . . ἐχόρευσε μετὰ τῶν ἠϊθέων χορείαν*
> *ἣν ἔτι νῦν ἐπιτελεῖν Δηλίους λέγουσι,*
> *μίμημα τῶν ἐν τῷ Λαβυρίνθῳ*
> *περιόδων καὶ διεξόδων,*
> *ἔν τινι ῥυθμῷ παραλλάξεις*
> *καὶ ἀνελίξεις ἔχοντι γιγνομένην.*
> *καλεῖται δὲ τὸ γένος τοῦτο τῆς*
> *χορείας ὑπὸ Δηλίων γέρανος . . .*
>
> *''Sailing home from Crete,*
> *[Theseus] came to Delos and . . .*
> *he danced with his youths a dance*
> *which they say is even now performed*
> *by the Delians,*
> *an imitation of the circuits and passages*
> *in the Labyrinth,*
> *consisting of alternating*
> *motions and evolutions*
> *in a certain rhythm.*
> *This kind of dance is called*
> *by the Delians the Crane . . . ''*

To the Greek *geranos*, "crane," cf. Lithuanian *garnys*, "stork."

104. Los Angeles County Museum Nos. M.51.1.9; M.51.1.10; M.51.1.11; M.51.1.12. Similar figurines are found at the British Museum: Nos. GR 1864.2-20.32; GR 1864.2-20.33; GR 1871.5-15.3. These figures date to *ca.* 1300 BCE. cf. the Late Neolithic clay schematic figures from Knossos, described above.
105. v. Chapter Two, below.

106. v. Chapters Six and Eight, below.

PART ONE: CHAPTER TWO

1. v. Kramer (1963a): 3.
2. Ibid: 29.
3. v. Chapter Three, below.
4. v. Delitzsch (1914): *nin*, 204; *lil*, 171. *lil* can also mean "ghost" or "demon." cf. the Sumerian flying demons, the *lili*; the Hebrew goddess *Lilith* probably has her source in the Sumerian spirit. v. below on Inanna and the Lili-demon.
5. v. ANET (1955): 575.
6. v. Jacobsen (1976): 131; v. Delitzsch (1914): *hursag*, 211; *nin*, 204.
7. v. Jacobsen (1976): 10.
8. v. below, on the Descent of Inanna to the Underworld.
9. v. Kramer, (1963a): 157.
10. v. Jacobsen (1976): 84.
11. v. Kramer (1963a): 124.
12. Kramer (1963a): 197–198.
13. ANET 103–104.
14. Ibid 507–512.
15. v. Chapter Ten, below.
16. This belongs to the Accadian version of the myth. v. ANET (1969): 108.
17. v. Perera (1981) for a Jungian analysis of the "Descent of Inanna," and the death and rebirth of the goddess.
18. v. ANET (1969) 53–57.
19. v. Kramer, (1963b): 492–493; 515–516.
20. Ibid 515, line 10:

    . . . -zu mu-maš-àm
    nin$_9$-zu mu-maš-àm.

21. Ibid, lines 14–15:

    kù-^{d}ereš-ki-gal-la-ke$_4$
    zà-sal-zu dùg-ga-àm.

22. Ibid: 511, lines 227–228; 232–233:

    ama-gan-a nam-dumu-ne-ne-šè
    ^{d}ereš-ki-gal-la-ke$_4$ . . .
    síg-ni garaš^{sar}-gim
    sag-gá-na mu-un-tuku-tuku
    ù-u$_8$ a-šà-mu dug$_4$-ga-ni.

23. cf. Delitzsch (1914): 83.
24. v. Chapter Ten, below.
25. v. Chapter Seven, and Chapter Thirteen, below.
26. v. Chapter Ten, and Chapter Thirteen, below.
27. Exaltation of Inanna, ed. Hallo (1968) line 12:

    sag-kal an-ki-a
    ^{d}inanna . . .

28. Ibid, line 112:

    an-úr an-pa
    nin-gal-bi-me-en.

29. v. Kramer (1979): 73; 85–86.
30. Hallo, ed. (1968) lines 9–11:

    ušumgal-gim kur-ra
    uš$_x$ ba-e-sì
    ^{d}iškur-gim ki-sig$_x$-gi$_4$-za
    ^{d}ezinu la-ba-ši-gál
    a-ma-ru kur-bi-ta
    e$_{11}$-dè.

31. Ibid, line 43:

hur-sag ki-za ba-e-dù-sù-dè
^{d}ezinu nì-gig-bi.

32. v. Wolkstein and Kramer (1983): 52.
33. Hallo, ed. (1968) line 14:

nin-ur-ra u_5-a.

34. Gadd (1924) 67, No. VII.14 (inscription of Utu-hegal, king of Erech):

. . . ug-me^{2} . . .

35. v. Wolkstein and Kramer (1983): 92.
36. Hallo, ed. (1968) lines 26–27:

igi-mè-ta
nì ma-ra-ta-si-ig
nin-mu á-ní-za
KA.KA *ì-durud$_x$-e.*

cf. the Canaanite myth in ANET: 519, wherein *Ishtar* became a *ḫapupiš*-bird and flew off to the storm-god.

37. Ibid, lines 125; 127–130; 132:

ki-bala-gul-gul-lu-za
hé-zu-ám . . .
ur-gim adda$_x$-kú-za
hé-zu-ám;
igi-huš-a-za
hé-zu-ám;
igi-huš-bi-íl-íl(i)-za
hé-zu-ám;
igi-gùn-gùn-na-za
hé-zu-ám . . .
ù-ma gub-gub-bu-za
hé-zu-ám.

38. Gadd (1924) 77, No. IX.7–8 (Gudea, Statue C):

u(d) ^{d}inanna-ge igi-nam-ti-ka-ni
mu-ši-bar-ra-a . . .

39. v. Part Two, below.
40. v. Kramer (1963b): 503, line 57:

ama-^{d}inanna ^{d}inanna-dingir-an-na
túg-zu túg-zu.

41. Hallo, ed. (1968) lines 55, 57:

mí-bé dam-a-ni-ta
ša$_6$-ga na-an-da-ab-bé . . .
nì-kù-šà-ga-na
nam-mu-da-an-búr-re.

42. v. Jacobsen (1976): 24.
43. Ibid. v. Chapter Six, below, on the Iranian storehouse-goddess.
44. Ibid: 39. cf. Kramer (1963a): 260.
45. v. Wolkstein and Kramer (1983): ii, a fragment of a relief vessel, dating to *ca.* 2400 BCE. Stalks grow from the shoulders of the goddess. cf. Ibid 3, a cylinder seal dating to *ca.* 2350–2150 BCE; two seated female figures face a date palm.
46. The rosettes became a popular religious symbol in the subsequent millennia; the Thraco-Phrygian god Sabazius was depicted with rosettes (v. Godwin (1981): 160, No. 130), and rosettes accompanied the symbolism of the Christian cross (v. Godwin: 92, No. 56).
47. v. Wolkstein and Kramer (1983): 27: a cylinder seal dating to *ca.* 3000 BCE; a city shrine is surrounded by the rosettes, face, and gateposts of Inanna.
48. v. Delitzsch (1914): 151.
49. v. Kramer, (1963b): 505, lines 5; 8–9; 16–21; 26–30:

. . . ga-ša-an-an-na me-[*e*] *. . .*
mu-ud-na-mu . . .
am-^{d}dumu-zi . . .

^{d}*inanna-ke*$_4$ . . .
SAL-la-ni sir-ra . . .
SAL-la . . .
si-gim . . .
ma-an-na . . .
u$_4$*-sar-gibil-gim* . . .

ki-sikil-mèn a-ba-a ur$_x$*-ru-a-bi*
SAL-la-mu . . .
ga-ša-an-mèn gu$_4$ *a-ba-a bí-íb-gub-bé*
in-nin$_9$ *lugal-e ḫa-ra-an-ur*$_x$*-ru*
^{d}*dumu-zi lugal-e ḫa-ra-ur*$_x$*-ru.*

50. Ibid: 508, line 21:

igi-mà làl-bi-im
šà-mà ḫi-(is)^{sar}*-bi-im.*

51. v. above.
52. For example, v. the myth of "Inanna and Bilulu," in Jacobsen and Kramer (1953): 172–187.
53. v. below.
54. v. Apollodorus, Atheniensis Bibliothecae, III.xiv.4.
55. Hallo, ed. (1968) lines 1; 5–6:

nin-me-šár-ra . . .
me-imin-bé
šu sá-du$_{11}$*-ga*
nin-mu me-gal-gal-la
sag-kešda-bi za-e-me-en.

56. v. Wolkstein and Kramer (1983): 16–18.
57. v. Kramer (1979): 86.
58. Ibid: 89–90.
59. Hallo, ed. (1968) line 62:

gal-zu igi-gál
nin-kur-kur-ra.

60. Ibid 153:

nin-mu hi-li gú-è
^{d}*inanna zà-mí.*

61. v. Parts Two–Three, below, for ancient goddesses who embodied wisdom.
62. v. Hallo (1968): 8.
63. Kramer (1979): 27.
64. v. Kramer (1963a): 78. v. the Lipit-Ishtar Law Code, dating to *ca*. 1700 BCE, translated by Kramer (1963a): 336–340.
65. Lau (1906; 1966) 18 [No. 95, obverse]:

93 GEME.DA *10* . . . *ta*
42 GEME *30 ta* . . .
6 GEME.DA SHU.GI *20 ta*
38 DUMU *20 ta.*

66. Ibid 33 [No. 69, obverse]:

7 KAL *50 ta* . . .
33 KAL *60 ta.*

67. v. Budge (1904; 1969) I: 222, describing the illustrated version of the fifth hour of the "Book of that which is in the Underworld."
68. v. Chapter One, above.
69. v. Gardiner (1927; 1964): 1.
70. v. Budge (1904; 1969) I: 40–41; for example, *ṭu-t*, "a bird;" *ṭuat*, "bird-death," an ancient name for the land of the dead (Budge [1920; 1978] II: 871–872); *ṭua*, "to adore, to honor, to praise" (Ibid: 871).
71. Ibid (1904; 1969) I: 439; v. illustration facing page 438.
72. Ibid. cf. the goddess *Isis*, mother of *Horus*; Horus' nurse was Isis' sister, *Nephthys*. A similar relationship is found in the Indic Rigveda, where the sisters *Uṣas* and *Rātrī* are described as

mother and nurse of the sun-god, and the Roman *Matralia*-festival shows the same triad. v. Chapter Three, below.

73. v. Lanzone (1881–1884; 1974) I, plate 58, figure 4.
74. Ibid, figure 3.
75. v. Budge (1904; 1969) I: illustrations facing pages 514, 516, and 517.
76. Ibid: 515.
77. For Anat, v. below, this chapter; for Athena, v. Chapter Ten.
78. v. Budge (1904; 1969) II: illustration, page 277; cf. Lanzone (1881–1884; 1974) I, plate 43, figure 1: Anat holds a lance and a shield.
79. v. below.
80. v. Budge (1904; 1969) II: illustration, page 279; cf. Lanzone (1881–1884; 1974) I, plate 47.
81. Egyptian *ṭefṭef* indicates "to spit, to exude moisture." v. Budge (1920; 1978) II: 877.
82. v. Budge (1904; 1969) II: illustration facing page 89.
83. Ibid I: illustration facing page 418.
84. v. Lanzone (1881–1884; 1974) I, plate 108, figure 2.
85. v. Budge (1904; 1969) I: 418. A double Maāt, also winged, is depicted in Lanzone (1881–1884; 1974) I, plate 109, figure 1.
86. Ibid I: 113.
87. Her name is composed of the signs for three vases, outstretched heaven, water, and female deity.
88. v. Budge (1904; 1969) II: illustration facing page 102; cf. Lanzone (1881–1884; 1974) I, plate 150, figure 4.
89. v. Lanzone (1881–1884; 1974) I, plate 150, figures 1–2.
90. Ibid I: 287–288.
91. v. Chapter One, above.
92. v. Budge (1904; 1969) II: illustrations facing pages 95 and 99.
93. Ibid I: illustrations facing pages 369 and 423.
94. Ibid II: 104.
95. Ibid II: 94; 98. This myth is later than the one which represents *Nut* and *Nu* as consorts.
96. Budge (1904; 1969) I: 428.
97. Ibid I, illustration facing page 427.
98. Ibid I, illustration facing page 434.
99. Ibid I, illustration facing page 435.
100. v. Chapter Ten, below.
101. Text is in Gardiner (1931), from Papyrus Chester Beatty I, *verso* C, page 3 (plate XXIV) (The text dates to the New Kingdom, 1550–1080 BCE):

Nubit s-šua-à
ḥem set s-qai-à
nebt pet àri-à àut
en Ḥet-Ḥert ḥeknu-à
en ḥenut
smà-à en-s
setchem set speru-à
utch set en-à henut.

102. v. Chapter Ten, below.
103. v. Budge (1904; 1969) I: 435.
104. Ibid I: 210.
105. Inscription of Petosiris from the Tomb of Petosiris in the necropolis of Hermopolis. v. Lefebvre (1924) II. 56:

khus-à . . .
per-n Ḥet-Ḥer
neh Res-t.

The sycamore tree was also sacred to the goddess Nut. v. the Book of the Dead lix, Papyrus of Ani.

106. Ibid; v. Budge (1895; 1967) 171 (Book of the Dead lxxxii.7):

qeq-à . . .
kher semam àmi
Ḥet-ḥert, ḥent-à.

107. v. above.
108. v. Lichtheim (1976) II: 200, "The Doomed Prince;" for the text, v. Gardiner (1932):1–9: from Papyrus Harris 500, *verso*.
109. cf. the birth of the Indic goddess *Devī*. v. Chapter Seven, below.
110. The sacred feminine often is found in sets of seven; cf. the Indic *Saptamatrika*, the "Seven Mothers." A *Saptamatrika* plaque is in the Los Angeles County Museum of Art, No. M.80.157.
111. v. Lichtheim (1976) II: 207, "The Two Brothers." For the text, v. Gardiner (1932): 9–29: from the d'Orbiney Papyrus.
112. v. Budge (1904; 1969) I: illustration facing page 434.
113. Ibid I: 437.
114. Ibid I 392:

Ḥet-Ḥert
iu ȧn eref netert ten,
smam-nes reth . . .

115. Ibid I 393:

ȧu sekhem-nȧ
em reth
ȧu netchem ḥer ȧb-ȧ.

116. Ibid I: 393–398.
117. v. Chapter Ten, below.
118. v. Budge (1904; 1969) I: illustration facing page 450; Lanzone (1881–1884; 1974) I, plate 175, figure 2; plate 177, figure 3.
119. Ibid I: 103.
120. Ibid I: 30; 78; 92.
121. Ibid I: 93.
122. Ibid I: 459:

ȧ mut ur
ȧn sefekh mesu-s.

Sefekh literally means "to loosen, to unbind;" v. Budge (1920; 1978) II: 665. The text is late, dating to *ca*. 550 BCE.

123. v. Brugsch (1968) IV: 637, Naophore Statue, Vatican, No. 1370, d.8:

Net ur mut
mes Rā . . .

124. v. Budge (1904; 1969) I: 451; (1920; 1978) II: 399.
125. Ibid I: 462.
126. v. Budge (1920; 1978) II: 399.
127. The text may be found in Budge (1904; 1969) I 386:

ȧst ur
ḥent neteru.

128. v. Budge (1904; 1969) II: illustration facing page 202.
129. Ibid.
130. v. Lanzone (1884–1885; 1974) II, plate 292.
131. Ibid: illustration facing page 206; cf. Lanzone (1884–1885; 1974) II, plate 292.
132. v. Budge (1895; 1967) 229 (Book of the Dead, Chapter CLI.I.1):

i-ȧ un-ȧ em sa-k.

133. v. Budge (1904; 1969) II: 169, from the Hymn to Osiris, *ca*. 1500 BCE, 14–15:

Ȧst . . .
khepert nef em ṭenḥui
ȧrit hennu menȧt sen-s.

134. v. Lichtheim (1976) II: 217; the text, from Papyrus Chester Beatty I, is in Gardiner (1931).
135. *Demotic* indicates Egyptian cursive writing and language. Demotic literature dates from the seventh century BCE, and it reflects Hellenic influence.
136. v. Lichtheim (1980) III: 149. The text is from Papyrus British Museum 604 *verso*.

137. v. Budge (1904; 1969) II 169, Hymn to Osiris 14–15:

Ȧst . . .
reret ta pen em ḥai
ȧn khen-nes ȧn qemtu-s su . . .

138. Ibid 169–170, Hymn to Osiris 16:

setheset nenu en urṭ-ȧb
khenpet mu-f
ȧrit ȧuāu . . .

139. v. Part Two, below.
140. v. Budge (1895; 1967) 144 (Book of the Dead, Chapter CXXXIV, plate XXII.11–12):

mes en su mut-f Ȧuset,
renen en su Nebt-ḥet,
mȧ ȧrit en sen en Ḥeru . . .

141. Ibid 32 (Chapter XVII, plate VII.33–35); 229–231 (Chapter CLI.I.1, II.1).
142. Ibid 227 (Chapter CLVI.I):

. . . ḥekau en Ȧst . . .
utchat ser pen . . .

143. cf. the Ugaritic god El, below.
144. The text is in Budge (1904; 1969) I 374:

ȧaut netri
ennu-nef re-f
pegas en su
sekher ḥer set.
sek-nes Ȧst em ṭet-set
ḥenā ta unnet ḥer-set
qeṭ-nes-set em tcheṭfeti shepsi . . .

145. Ibid 375:

. . . khet ānkhet . . .

146. Literally "place of mouth."
147. Budge (1904; 1969) I 380:

ȧst re-set
em nefu en ānkh
thes-set ḥer ṭer ment . . .

148. v. above in this chapter and v. Chapter Six, below, on the Mesopotamian goddess Ninhursag.
149. v. Budge (1904; 1969) I 382:

ȧ tcheṭ-nȧ ren-k
ȧtef neter
ānkh sa
ṭemu-tu ḥer ren-f.

150. Ibid 384:

ȧn ren-k ȧpu
em na tcheṭu-k-nȧ
ȧ tcheṭ-k set nȧ
peri ta metu.

151. Plutarch, Isis and Osiris IX (354 C).
152. v. Budge (1904; 1969) II: 217.
153. cf. Apuleius, Metamorphoses, *passim*.
154. v. Moss and Cappannari (1982): 65; and v. Begg (1985): 153–264 for a gazetteer of the areas in which Black Virgins have been found.
155. Apuleius, in the Metamorphoses IX.2; IX.5, describes Isis as an amalgam of deities. cf. Solmsen (1979): 24.
156. v. Lichtheim (1973) I: 87, Stela of the butler Merer of Edfu, Cracow National Museum.
157. Ibid I: 90, Stela of the soldier Qedes from Gebelein, Berlin 24032.

158. Ibid I 19: the Autobiography of Weni, Cairo Museum 1435; Ibid 100, 107: the Instruction to King Merikare, Papyrus Leningrad 1116A; Papyrus Moscow 4658; Papyrus Carlsberg 6.
159. v. Pomeroy (1975) passim.
160. v. Lichtheim (1973) I 227; 231, from the Story of Sinuhe, Berlin 3022, 10499.
161. Ibid (1976) II 25–29, Obelisk inscriptions of Queen Hatshepsut in the Temple of Karnak.
162. Ibid II 12–14, from the Autobiography of Ahmose, son of Abana, Tomb at El-Kab.
163. Ibid II 149, from the Instruction of Amenemope, 1290–1280 BCE, British Museum 10474.
164. From the Legend of King Keret, composed *ca.* 1350 BCE: KTU 1.14.iii.39–42 (=UT Krt 143–146):

tn . ly . mṯt . ḥry
n'mt . špḥ . bkrk
dk . n'm . 'nt . n'mh
km . tsm . 'ṯṯrt . tsmh.

165. cf. Patai (1967): illustration within pp. 82–83.
166. v. Chapter One, endnote 31.
167. v. Chapter One, above.
168. v. above.
169. v. Chapter One, above.
170. v. ANET: 249–250.
171. cf. Deuteronomy 16:21, forbidding the planting of a tree as an *Asherah* beside the altar of Jehovah (Yahweh), the Hebrew God. It would be unnecessary, of course, to forbid what was not practiced. Inscriptions discovered in the last few years bear out the biblical testimony. The *Khirbet el-Qôm* inscription (v. Naveh (1979): 27–30) and the inscription from *Kuntillet 'Ajrud* (v. Meshel [1978]) both invoke blessings by the Hebrew God *and by his Asherah*. But v. Zevit (1984): 39–47, who argues that pronominal suffixes are not attested as affixes to personal names in biblical Hebrew, and that the inscription should be read *Yahweh and Asherata*. For a synopsis of Asherah in Near Eastern myth and iconography, v. Maier (1986).
172. The appellation *Elohenu*, "our God," is found prominently in Hebrew prayers, including the *Shema*. As a common noun, the word means "a mighty one, a hero." Cf. Gesenius (1846): 45.
173. cf. Pope (1955): 36.
174. KTU 1.4.iv.49 (=UT 51):

aṯrt . wbnh . ilt . wṣbrt.

175. KTU 1.4.i.21–22 (=UT 51.i.22–23):

mgn . rbt . aṯrt ym
mǵẓ . qnyt . ilm.

176. cf. Maier (1986): 36.
177. KTU 1.4.vi.45–47 (=UT 51):

. . . ṣḥ
šb'm . bn. aṯrt
špq . ilm . . .

178. v. Oldenburg (1969): 28.
179. v. ANET: 519.
180. v. above.
181. KTU 1.15.ii.26–28 (UT 128):

ynq . ḥlb . a[ṯ]rt
mṣṣ . ṯd . btlt ['nt]
mšnq

To *btlt*, a "young girl" cf. Hebrew *b'tulah*. v. Gordon's notes on *btlt* (1955) 249: in the ancient Near Eastern languages, there *was* no term that, by itself, indicated *virgo intacta*.
182. KTU 1.10.ii–iii (=UT 76).
183. v. Chapter One, above.
184. Ibid; v. KTU 1.5.vi (=UT 67).
185. v. Chapter One, above.
186. KTU 1.3.iii.41–42 (=UT 'nt iii.38–39):

mḫšt . bṯn . 'qltn
šlyṭ . d. šb't . rašm.

187. v. Apollodorus, Atheniensis Bibliothecae I.vi. 1–2. As the giant Enceladus was fleeing from

battle, Athena threw the whole island of Sicily upon him. The similarity of the two names, *Anat* and *Athena* (Linear B *A-ta-na*), and functions, may be due to intercourse between the Greeks and their Near Eastern neighbors. The Greeks equated the two goddesses: a Greek-Phoenician bilingual inscription, found on Cyprus, reads in Phoenician "To Anat . . . " and is translated into Greek as "To Athena . . . " cf. Oldenburg (1969): 86.

188. KTU 1.3.ii.5–14; 24–26 (=UT 'nt ii):

'nt . . .
. . . b'mq . tḫtṣb . bn
qrytm tmḫṣ . lim . ḫp . y[m]
tṣmt . adm . ṣat . špš
tḥth . kkdrt . ri[š]
'lh . kirbym kp . . .
. . . 'tkt
rišt . lbmth . šnst . [ ]
kpt . bḥbšh . brkm . tǵl[l]
bdm . . .
tḫtṣb . wtḥdy . 'nt
tǵdd . kbdh . bṣḥq . ymlu
lbh . bšmḫt . . .

For the translations of *'tkt* and *šnst* v. Cassuto (1951; 1971): 87.

189. KTU 1.3.v.19–25 (=UT 'nt v.27–33):

wt'n . btlt . 'n[t . . .
. . . a[l tš]mḫ
al . tšmḫ . . .
al . aḫdhm . . .
qdqdk . ašhlk . šbtk [. dmm]
šbt . dqnk . mm'm . . .

190. KTU 1.3.v.27–29 (=UT 'nt v.35–37):

. . . yd'[tk] bt . kan[št] . . .
. . . mh . tarš[n]
lbtlt . 'nt.

For the translation of *kanšt,* v. Cassuto (1951; 1971): 149–150.

191. v. ANET: 149 ff; for the text, v. KTU 1.17–1.19 (=UT Aqht). The legend of Aqhat dates to *ca.* 1350 BCE.

192. KTU 1.10.ii.10–11 (=UT 76):

tšu knp btlt . 'n[t]
tšu . knp . wtr . b'p.

PART ONE: CHAPTER THREE

1. For variant hypotheses regarding the Proto-Indo-European homeland, v. Gimbutas (1985); Mallory (1989): 143–185; Gamkrelidze and Ivanov (1985 a, b, c); D'iakonov (1985); Bosch-Gimpera (1980). The major problem posed by the Pontic-Caspian theory is that it is difficult to prove a link between that area and Central and Northern Europe.
2. Gimbutas (1977): 281–308. Equipment such as cheek pieces made of antler, dating to *circa* 4500 BCE, were found in the Volga and Dnieper steppes. Further, large numbers of horse-bones were found in the lower Dnieper. Horse-sacrifice is also attested in south Russia, dating to the fourth millennium BCE: horse-skulls were interred in separate graves in the district of Kherson and in the region of Odessa.
3. Ibid. *circa* 3400 BCE, Proto-Indo-European warriors first used wheeled vehicles in Europe.
4. v. Mallory (1989): 186–221 for a summary of present information on Proto-Indo-European archaeology.
5. Gimbutas (1977): 277–278; (1982): 18–19.
6. Daggers, battle-axes, and arrowheads proliferated in chieftains' tombs. v. Gimbutas (1977): 284.
7. *Suttee* burial is evidenced in a tomb from the cemetery at Ponte San Pietro, Tuscany, dating to the early part of the second millennium BCE. There were two skeletons in this "Tomb of the Widow." The skeleton of a middle-aged man surrounded by pottery and several weapons, including copper axes and daggers, lay to the right of the doorway. To the left of the doorway,

and against the wall, lay the skeleton of a young adult female, accompanied only by a jar and a necklace. The skull of the young woman showed signs of injury. Cf. Trump (1965): 82–84.

8. Gimbutas (1977): 285; 304–305.
9. Indic mythology reflected the practice of *suttee*, and described its "origins." In the Bhagavata Purāṇa IV, *Satī*, a wife of the god *Śiva*, killed herself by suppressing her breath, because her father Dakṣa had insulted her husband. (Cf. Kalidasa, Kumara Sambhavam I.21.) She was considered the perfect sort of wife.
10. Gimbutas (1977): 284.
11. For the view that we have insufficient evidence to posit a Proto-Indo-European "warrior"-society, v. Mallory (1989): 111. Mallory does concede sufficient Proto-Indo-European terminology to indicate a military of some sort (125).
12. v. Dumézil (1958): 11 et passim. For a review of Dumézil's work through 1971, v. Littleton (1973).
13. Deborah Dickmann Boedeker (1974), *passim*, has attempted to identify the Greek love-goddess *Aphrodite* with the dawn-goddess *Eos*. Boedeker presents good evidence that both dawn and sun-maiden mythology accrued to Aphrodite, although she conflates the dawn and sun-maiden functions. If Aphrodite *were* Indo-European, she would as likely be a sun-maiden as a dawn goddess, particularly since she may be identified with the epic love-figure, Helen, who, as I demonstrate below, was very likely a sun-maiden. Although Boedeker has assembled excellent evidence that Aphrodite embodies Indo-European Dawn-mythology, nonetheless, I believe that the dawn and solar functions are superpositions upon a pre-Indo-European goddess of regeneration. Her powers, as progenitress of deities and mortals, are great, while the powers of the Indo-European dawn goddess and sun-maiden are limited to the naturalistic.

    Paul Friedrich (1978) compared Aphrodite to the Vedic dawn-goddess Ushas, as did Boedeker. However, Friedrich recognized that Aphrodite was composed of a synthesis of characteristics from Indo-European, Phoenician, Sumerian-Accadian, Egyptian, Minoan, and the Old European mother-goddess/bird-goddess. (I disagree, however, with his assumption that Aphrodite's solarity links her to a "masculine principle" [page 80], just as I cannot agree that Athena's intellect is "masculine" [page 90]). I would describe the Neolithic European stratum as that of the "Goddess of Regeneration," of birth, life, and death, who was represented as both bird and snake. See below, Chapter Ten.
14. Antipater, Palatine Anthology V.3:

    γηράσκεις τιθωνέ.
    τί γὰρ σὴν εὐνέτιν Ἠῶ
    οὕτως ὀρθριδίην
    ἤλασας ἐκ λεχέων;

15. Propertius, Elegies II.18 A 7f:

    ''[Aurora] . . .
    invitum et terris praestitit officium.''

16. Ovid, Amores I.13:

    seniore marito . . . flavia . . .

17. Ovid, Fasti IV.713–714, called her:

    Memnonis lutea mater,

    "Memnon's saffron-yellow mother."

18. Ibid: VI.473–568:

    Iam, Phryx, a nupta quereris, Tithone, relinqui,
    et vigil Eois Lucifer exit aquis:
    ite, bonae matres (vestrum Matralia festum)
    flavaque Thebanae reddite liba deae . . .
    . . . Matutae sacra parenti
    sceptriferas Servi templa dedisse manus.
    . . . famulas a limine templi
    arceat . . . libaque tosta petat . . .

non . . . hanc pro stirpe sua pia mater adoret:
ipsa parum felix visa fuisse parens
alterius prolem melius mandabitis illi . . .

19. Plutarch, Parallel Lives, "Life of Camillus," V.2:

καὶ γὰρ ϑεράπαιναν είς τὸν σηκὸν
ἐισάγουσαι ῥαπίζουσιν,
εἶτ' ἐξελαύνουσι καὶ τὰ τῶν ἀδελφῶν
τέκνα πρὸ τῶν ἰδίων ἐναγκαλίζονται . . .

20. Rigveda IV.30, 8, 10:

striyam yad durhanāyuvam vadhir
duhitaram divaḥ . . .

apoṣā anasaḥ sarat sampiṣṭāt
aha bibhyusī ni yat sīm śiśnathat vṛṣa.

21. Ibid: I.96.5:

naktoṣasā varṇamāmemyāne
dhāpayete śiśumekam samīcī
dyāvākṣāmā rukmo antarvi bhāti
devā agnim dhārayandraviṇodām.

22. v. Robbins (1978): Appendix: Agni very possibly functioned as both sun and moon in this hymn.
23. Rigveda I.48.14, 16; III.61.7:

mahi; mahī

24. Ibid: III.61.1:

pracetāḥ

25. Ibid:

vājena vājini

26. Ibid:

viśvavāre.

27. Ibid I.113.19:

mātā devānām.

28. From a Lithuanian folk-song "O Vakar Vakarati," in Korsakas (1954) 50:

Išėjau pas aušrinę.
Aušrinė atsiliepė:
—aš anksti ryt saulelei
turiu prakurti ugnelę.''

29. Ibid: 51, from "Miela Saulyte, Dievo Dukryte":

—Miela saulyte, dievo dukryte,
Kas rytais, vakarėliais,
Prakūrė tau ugnelę,
Tau klojo patalėlį?

—Aušrinė, Vakarinė:
Aušrinė ugni prakāre
Vakarinė patalą klojo . . .

30. Jonval (1929): No. 364 (B34001):

Saules meita gulētāja
ar to rīta Auseklīti.

31. Ibid: No. 424 (B34022):

Trīs rītiņi neredzēja
Auseklīša uzlecam:
Saules meita ieslēguse
ozolina kambarī.

32. Ibid: No. 418 (B33831):

> *Kur tas rīta Ausekliņš?*
> *Kā neredz uzlecot?*
> *—Ausekliņš Vāczemē*
> *samta svārkus šūdināja.*

33. The Russian goddess of the dawn, *Zarya*, did not bear a name cognate to the goddesses in this section. She will be discussed in Chapter Six, below.
34. v. Matys Stryjkowski, in Mannhardt (1936) 356:

> *Ausca dea est radiorum solis,*
> *vel occumbentis,*
> *vel supra horizontem ascendentis.*

35. v. (Robbins) Dexter (1984): 137–144.
36. Rigveda IV.43.6, to the Ashvins, the divine twin horsemen:

> *patī bhavathaḥ sūryāyāḥ*

Sūryā was the sun-maiden, while *Sūryă* was her father, the sun. The long *"a"* in *Sūryā* indicates feminine gender.

37. Ibid: X.85.9:

> *somo vadhūyur abhavat,*
> *aśvinā āstam,*
> *ubha varā sūryām yat patye śansantīm*
> *manasā savitā adadāt.*

38. cf. the Old Slavic *Perun*; v. Chapter Six, below.
39. Uzburta Karalystė (1957) 193:

> *[Perkūnas] tarė griausmingu balsu:*
> *—Tegul bus taip:*
> *Saulė dieną saugos*
> *savo dukterį Zemę,*
> *o Mėnuo—naktį.*

40. Old Lithuanian folksong translated by Adrian Paterson (1939): 82, (No. XLI).
41. Latvian folksong. Text is from Mannhardt (1936) 623:

> *"Kur palikke Deewa sirgi?*
> *Deewa Dehls jahdija.*
> *Kur asijahje Deewa Dehli?*
> *Saules Meitas raudsitees . . . "*

Cf. Jonval No. 105 (B33867):

> *"Dieva dēli brīkšķināja*
> *kumeliņus ganīdami."*

> "The sons of God make cracking noises
> while protecting the horses."

42. An anonymous Latvian folk-song from the 19th–20th centuries, in Hatto (1965): 702, No. 15 (Jonval No. 405):

> *sudrabiņa gaiļi djied*
> *zeltupītes maliņa.*
> *Tia piecēla Dieva dēlus,*
> *Saules meitas preciniekus.*

43. An anonymous Latvian folk-song in Hatto (1965): 701, No. 11 (Jonval No. 362).

> *Mēness nēma Saules Meitu*
> *Lūdza mani vedībās . . .*
> *nu varēju droshi jat*
> *Dieva Delu pulciņa.*

44. Euripides, Trojan Women 893–894:

> πίμπρησι δ' οἶκους.

45. Proto-Indo-European **su̯el*. Cf. the root-word for sun, **sAu̯el, *sAu̯ol*.
46. v. Gregoire (1953): 452–464, for a discussion of Helen and the Dioskouroi, reflecting on their origins in the primal egg.
47. Homeric Hymn XXXIII.3 described Kastor as *ἱππόδαμον*, "tamer of horses." One may have been a horseman and the other a cattleman. v. Ward (1968).
48. Euripides, Helen 1495–1507:

> *μόλοιτέ ποθ' ἵππιον ἅρμα*
> *δι' αἰθέρος ἱέμενοι . . .*
> *σωτῆρες τᾶς Ἑλένας . . .*
> *δύσκλειαν δ' ἀπὸ συγγόνου*
> *βάλετε βάρβάρων λεχέων . . .*

The Dioskouroi were asked to protect Helen on her sea-journey home from Troy.
49. Hesiod, Catalogues of Women 68.13–15:

> *καί νύ κε δὴ Κάστορ*
> *τε καὶ ὁ κρατερὸς Πολυδεύκης*
> *γαμβρὸν ποιήσαντο κατὰ κράτος.*
> *ἀλλ' Ἀγαμέμνων*
> *γαμβρὸς ἐὼν ἐμνᾶτο κασιγνήτῳ*
> *Μενελάῳ*

50. v. (Robbins) Dexter (1984): 139–142.
51. cf. Godwin (1981): figures 128, 131, 136.
52. The name *Semele* may have been borrowed by the Greeks from Phrygio-Thracian.
53. cf. Hesiod, Theogony, 940–942.
54. Ovid, Metamorphoses III.261–263:

> *. . . dum linguam ad iurgia solvit,*
> *"profeci quid enim totiens*
> *per iurgia?" dixit,*
> *"ipsa petenda mihi est . . . "*

55. A similar "testing" of the divine lover occurs in the Cupid and Psyche story. cf. the notes to Chapter Five, and cf. Chapter Ten, below.
56. v. Ovid, Metamorphoses 3.259 ff; Apollodorus, Atheniensis Bibliothecae III.iv.3. cf. Athena, born from her father's head, and the Iranian Spənta Ārmaiti, born of her father Ahura Mazdah, discussed in Part Two, below. Thus, in male-god-centered religion, the male has expropriated the female act of giving birth.
57. Hesiod, Theogony 942:

> *νῦν δ' ἀμφότεροι*
> *θεοί εἰσιν.*

58. Cf. Latvian *zeme*, "earth," Turkina (1964): 379; Latvian *māte*, "mother," Turkina: 158.
59. Cf. Lithuanian *žemė*, "earth," Pēteraitis (1960): 560.
60. Gimbutas (1984) 48:

> *tyra ir teisinga*

61. Ibid:

> *Žemyna, žiedkelėle*
> *žydėk rugiais,*
> *miežiais ir visais javais.*

62. Alexandrow (1919): 266.
63. Ibid: 626.
64. Ibid: 188.
65. cf. Hubbs (1982): 123–144, on modern worship of Mother Earth in Russian culture.
66. v. Ralston (1872): 248.
67. Gimbutas (1967): 754.
68. Ibid: Orel District, Central Russia, 1870.
69. Sanskrit *vṛtratara*.
70. Rigveda I.32.1–9. Since the text is quite long, I have omitted it here. It is found in Müller (1877) I: 23–24.
71. Ibid: V.29.4; V.32.1.
72. Ibid: X.120.6:

. . . śavasā sapta dānūnpra sākṣate
pratimānāni bhūri.

73. Avesta Yašt V.73:

āaṯ hīm jaiδyən:
avaṯ āyaptəm dazdi.nō
vaŋuhi səviste
ardvī sūre anāhite,
yaṯ bavāma aiwi.vanyā̊
dānavō tūrą . . .

74. Lebor Gabála Érenn, VII.366.K:

is i in Danand sin
mathair na ndee.

75. Ibid VII.310 R[1]:

dorat . . . alt fri halt
⁊ feith fri feith
dia laim dair,
⁊ icaid
fri teora nomaidhi . . .

76. Ibid VIII.414:

con ro chansat
a ndruideseom ⁊ a filid
airchetla dóib,
conacatar-ni bátir
fóit móna ⁊ sléibi.

77. Ibid VIII.415:

. . . focherdsat na druidhi
gáetha druidhechta na ndegaidh,
co tochradh in murgriain n-íchtrach
for úachtar in mara.

78. Ibid VIII.435:

for demna ⁊ fomhmhoire (sic)
.i. for Túathaib Dé Danann.

79. Book of Taliesin XXXVI.10:

dylaw adaw
doethaw don.

80. Book of Taliesin XVI.26:

Rym gelwir kyfrwys
yn llys don.

81. The name *Belus* may be related to that for the Near Eastern god, *Baal*. v. Chapter Two, above.
82. Apollodorus, Atheniensis Bibliothecae II.i.4.

αὑτῃ Ποσειδῶν τὰς ἐν Λέρνῃ
πηγὰς ἐμήνυσεν.

83. Strabo, Geographus VIII.6.8:

φρεάτων . . . ἃ ταῖς Δαναίσιν
ἀνάπτουσιν ὡς ἐκείνων ἐξευρουσῶν.

" . . . wells . . . which they ascribe to the Danaïds,
believing that they discovered them."

84. Apollodorus, Atheniensis Bibliothecae II.i.5:

αἱ δε κοιμωμένους τοῦς
νυμφίους ἀπέκτειναν

Cf. Ovid, Heroides XIV.

85. Horace, Odes III.11.23–28:

. . . inane lymphae dolum
fundo pereuntis imo . . .

". . . and their cask,
empty of water
which passes away
through the bottom."

86. However, the Greeks did certainly regard husband-killing as a monstrous crime; cf. Aeschylus' "Eumenides," lines 584-591; 627ff; 704ff, where Orestes' matricide of Clytemnestra is regarded as less worthy of punishment than Clytemnestra's murder of her husband, King Agamemnon.
87. v. Apollodorus, Atheniensis Bibliothecae II.ii.2.
88. According to Apollodorus, Atheniensis Bibliothecae II.iv.1, the chamber was underground. The Roman poet Horace, on the other hand, wrote (in Odes III.16.1 ff.) that Danaë was incarcerated in a bronze tower.
89. Apollodorus, Atheniensis Bibliothecae II.iv.1:

τὴν ϑυγατέρα μετὰ τοῦ παιδὸς
έις λάρνακα βαλὼν
'έρριψεν έις ϑάλασσαν.

90. Ovid, Metamorphoses IV.734:

ter quater exegit repetita
per ilia ferrum.

Cf. Apollodorus, Atheniensis Bibliothecae II.iv.3.

91. Ovid, Metamorphoses IV.670–739. Cf. Apollodorus, Atheniensis Bibliothecae II.iv.3.
92. Cf. the "Fall of the Sacred Serpent" in Chapter One, above.
93. Fraenkel (1965): I.111:

. . . an Kalno nemunelis,
po Kalnu dunojelis.

"On the mountain is (the river) Nemunas;
at the foot of the mountain is the (little river)
Dunõjus."

94. Ibid:

par didžias marias,
par Dunojeḷi.

" . . . over the great sea,
over the deep stream."

95. Mülenbachs (1923–25): 518.
96. Rigveda I.136.3:

. . . dānunaspatī mitrastayorvaruṇo.

97. v. Oldenburg (1969): 154 ff. for a reconsideration of the original Semitic homeland and migrations.
98. Patai (1967) writes cogently of goddess-worship among the Hebrews in the first millennium BCE.
99. v. Gesenius (1949) 661.
100. Hebrew Old Testament, "Genesis" 3.
101. v. the writings of Naomi Goldenberg, Mary Daly, Judith Ochshorn, and others writing in the Judeo-Christian feminist spiritualist tradition.
102. Kramer (1963a): 147 ff. On the relationships of Hebrew and Mesopotamian female figures, v. Teubal (1984): *passim*.
103. cf. the Egyptian goddess Isis, who caused the sun-god Rā to be bitten by a deadly *serpent*: only the goddess could cure him. v. Chapter Two, above.
104. Delitzsch (1914): 156–157.
105. Gesenius (1846; 1949): 263–264.
106. v. Gimbutas (1974): 216 ff. for Neolithic iconography.

107. v. Chapter One, above.
108. v. Campbell (1974): figure 241, an Egyptian figure dating to *circa* 1400 BCE; Ibid: figure 240, a figure from the Indus Valley, dating to *circa* 2000 BCE; Alexiou (1973): figures 37, 38, and 39: gold rings from Mycenae, Vaphio, and Phaistos. Figures of Indic *Yakskis*, or tree-spirits, are at the Los Angeles County Art Museum (Nos. M.85.2.1 and M.80.62). Syrian ivory plaques, dating to *circa* 800 BCE, depict female cherubs with palm trees (Louvre: Nos. 11468, 11469).
109. cf. Craven (1976?): 175, a painting dating to *circa* 1565 CE: a tree blossoms at the touch of a lovely woman; in this case, it is the fertility of the woman which brings out the fruitfulness of the tree. Compare this to the Indic Saundaryalaharī, plate 37 c,d, accompanying stanza 85: in a grove, the "Great"-goddess *Devī* is kicking the *aśoka* tree, thereby stimulating it to blossom. In Asia Minor, the Ephesian "Artemis" is represented with a plethora of "breasts;" there has long been controversy regarding the possibility that these breasts are, in reality, fruit. v. Chapter Ten, below. cf. the Hebrew "Song of Songs," VII. 8, wherein the Beloved is compared to a towering palm tree, and the breasts of the Beloved are like its clusters.

PART TWO: INTRODUCTION

1. Gimbutas (1977): 281, 289, 291, 292.
2. For example, the Tiszapolgar group in east Hungary; in many cases, male graves showed Proto-Europid skeletons, while female graves showed (local) Mediterranean skeletal types (Ibid: 294).
3. Ibid: 290; Gimbutas cites the dislocation of the southeast-European Karanovo, Vinča, Butmir, and Lengyel populations.
4. Ibid: *passim*.
5. For a discussion of Proto-Indo-European goddesses, v. Chapter Three, above.

PART TWO: CHAPTER FOUR

1. v. Chapter Three, above.
2. v. Chapter One, above.
3. v. Chapter Thirteen, below, on Vestals and the sacred fire.
4. Basanavičius (1902): 194:

   jos katrą vieną žmogų
   tuoj' užgimusi palaimindayusēs . . .

   cf. Paul Einhorn, from the Historica Lettica (17th century) in Mannhardt (1936): 620.
5. Ibid:

   o tos laimēs kasdien' mainydavusiosēs:
   viena dien' turtinga, kitą dien'
   —vidutinē, kitą dien'
   su visu nieko ne turēdavusi
   . . . dabar sakoma:
   ''teip laimē lēmē'' arba:
   ''katram vienam no Dievo yra
   laimē duota, bet ne visi tegal' atrasti.

6. cf. the Germanic Valkyries, below; they too were clothed in the plumage of birds, and they too fell into the power of whomever seized their feathers. cf. also the bird-maidens celebrated in classical ballet, as in Peter Tschaikovsky's "The Swan Lake."
7. v. Zobarskas (1958): 193–196.
8. v. Balys (1936): 36, No. 404. This tale is one variant of a folk-tale also found in other European areas.
9. Biezais (1955) 120, No. 16415:

   '' . . . laba laime . . . ''

10. Ibid 123, No. 9208,1:

    Kur, Laimiņa, tu sēdēji,
    Kad es dzimu māmiņai?
    Vai sēdēji laimes krēslā,
    Vai asaru lāmiņā?

11. Ibid 124, No. 1216,1:

Laimiņ' man mūžu lēm',
Trīs krēslē sēdēdam'.
Sēd', Laimiņ', vien' krēslē,
Lem man vienu labu mūžu.

12. Ibid 129, No. 27684:

Dievam dieniņ' i aizgāja,
Ar Laimiņu runājot,
Kam būs mirt,
Kam dzīvot
Šai baltā saulītē.

13. v. Gimbutas (1984) 44:

naktinės bātybės . . .
labiau žemiškos negu kitos dievės.

14. Turkina (1964): 143.
15. Gimbutas (1984) 44:

žemes moterys

16. Pēteraitis (1960): 205.
17. v. Korsakas (1954) 340:

laumė ragana

"Laumė the witch . . . "

cf. the Baltic *raganas* in Chapter Thirteen, below.

18. Gimbutas (1984) 44:

Laumių kasos ilgos . . .
geltoni plaukai.
Krūtys labai didelės . . .

19. Basanavičius (1902): 195.
20. Ibid:

senovēje laumēs labai tankei rodydavos
irgi ant lieptų skalbdavo,
o jei joms kas, pro sali eidams,
ką pasakydavo, arba jas pasveikindavo,
tai jos labai linksmai dēkavodavo.

21. Translated by Irina Zheleznova, undated.
22. cf. the Slavic folk-tale, "Marya Morevna" in Ralston (1872): 85 ff. (Afanas'ev (1865–69) viii, No. 8.) Here the part of Lauma is played by the Baba Yaga. v. Chapter Thirteen, below.
23. The tale brings to mind the Greek myth of Pegasus, the flying horse which was born from the neck of the witch-goddess Medusa as she was being beheaded by the young hero, Perseus. cf. Chapter Thirteen, below.
24. Balys (1936): 246 No. 3695. Cf. Basanavičius (1902): 195.
25. Balys (1936): 246 No. 3694.
26. Ibid: No. 3693.
27. Gimbutas (1984): 47.
28. Ibid 46:

Pasirodo . . .
žmogiškame pavidale,
bet su vištos kojomis.

29. Homer, Odyssey X. Cf. Chapter Thirteen, below.
30. v. Chapter Thirteen, below, on the crone-witch aspect of the goddess.
31. v. Chapter Twelve, above.
32. cf. the Slavic folk-tale, "The Water Snake," discussed below.
33. Korsakas (1965) III: 296:

—Duok,—sako,
—Eglute, zodį,
jog tekėsi už manęs,
tai pats gražumu išlisiu.

34. cf. the "Cupid and Psyche" story in Chapter Eleven, below. The envious and mendacious sisters of Psyche told her that her mysterious husband, whose face she was forbidden to look upon, was a terrible serpent. In reality, it was quite the contrary: Psyche's husband was the handsome god of love.
35. Korsakas (1965) III: 297:

    —Gerai,—sako,
    —atsilankyti leisiu,
    bet pirma suverpk
    šitą šilkų kuodelį . . .

    One is reminded of the Greek personification of the perfect wife, the faithful *Penelope*, wife of Odysseus. To keep at bay the suitors who wished to marry her and, thus, to take the place of Odysseus, whom they presumed to be dead, she asked that the suitors grant her respite: she would not have to make a choice among them until she had finished weaving a shroud for her father-in-law, Laertes. She wove by day and unraveled her work by night. v. Chapter Ten and Chapter Twelve, below.
36. Ibid 298:

    Žilvine Žilvinėli!

    Jei tu gyvas, pieno puta,
    jei negyvas, kraujo puta!

37. On the secret name, which represents the essence of the powers of the person who owns it, v. Part One, Chapter Two, above; the Egyptian goddess Isis forced the sun-god Rā to reveal his secret name to her, and she thereby came into possession of his powers.
38. v. Chapter One, above.
39. v. Chapter Three, above.
40. Juška III (1882; 1954) 423, No. 1252, 14–17:

    Saulė motušė
    Saulė motušė
    kraitelį krovė;

    Mėnuo tėvužis
    Mėnuo tėvužis
    dalelę skyrė.

    Žvaigždė sesutė
    Žvaigždė sesutė
    suole sėdėjo;

    sietyns brolelis
    sietyns brolelis
    lauku lydėjo.

PART TWO: CHAPTER FIVE

1. Herodotus, Histories IV, 105:

    . . . ἔτεος ἑκάστου ἅπαξ
    τῶν Νευρῶν ἕκαστος λύκος γίνεται
    ἡμέρας ὀλίγας
    καὶ αὖτις ὀπίσω ἐς τὠυτὸ κατίσταται.
    ἐμὲ μέν νυν ταῦτα λέγοντες οὐ πείθουσι . . .

    On the ancient identity of the Neuri, v. Trubačev (1985): 238–240. The author believes that the Neuri were originally *Celts* rather than *Slavs*; he connects *Neuroi* with the Celtic Gaulish tribal name, *Nervii*. Further, he connects the periodic transformation of the Neuroi into wolves with the Celtic tribal name *Volcae*, perhaps "wolves," and he asserts that the Herodotean passage is concerned with an ethnic memory of kinship ties, rather than with superstitions about lycanthropy. Another archaeological view regards the Neuri as Balts. v. Gimbutas (1963): 22; 97–101.
2. Gimbutas (1967): 755.
3. Ibid: 756.
4. Ibid: 755.

5. Ibid: 755–756. cf. the *Baltic Laumas*, who were also responsible for the hail.
6. Ralston (1872): 181–182.
7. cf. the Germanic swan-maidens in Chapter Nine, below, and v. Chapter One, above, on Neolithic bird-goddesses.
8. v. Ralston (1872): 179.
9. Ibid: 104–105. cf. Russian *lad*, "harmony, concord:" Akhmanova (1971): 264.
10. Ibid: 213.
11. v. Chapter Four, above.
12. The tale is found in Ralston (1872): 116 (Erlenvein, No. 2). From the Tula Government. The cuckoo, by the way, was respected by the Slavs. Cuckoos were believed to be the god Zywic, the "Lord of Life," in bird-form. v. Ralston (1872): 214 and Grimm, Deutsche Mythologie: 565–566, quoting the Old Polish Chronicle of Prokosz.
13. Her name means "birth-giver." Through the nineteenth century, Slavic peasants believed that birth-fairies appeared at the bedside of a newborn baby and determined its destiny. (Compare also the Germanic *Norns*, Chapter Nine, below). v. Gimbutas (1967): 755; 758.
14. v. Afanas'ev (1865–1869) III.403 ff.
15. Ibid: 409; 411.
16. Ibid: 410.
17. Ibid: 411.
18. Ibid:

    dobra ti Sreča!

19. Ibid:

    zla ti Sreča.

20. v. Chapter Eleven, below.
21. v. Chapter Seven, below, on the Indic goddesses of fortune and misfortune.
22. Akhmanova (1971): 295.
23. Afanas'ev (1865–1869) II.101.
24. Ibid:

    . . . stariya, malen'kiya sushchestva
    zhenskago pola,
    kotoriya sidyat na pechi,
    pryadut po nocham pryazhu . . .

25. Ibid 101; 103.
26. Ibid 101.
27. Ibid 103.
28. cf. Akhmanova (1971): 586.
29. Afanas'ev (1865–1869) II.365:

    kostlyavoi skelet . . .

30. Ibid I.566–567:

    Na krutoi gore vysokoi
    kipyat kotly kipuchie,
    vo tex kotlax kipuchiix
    gorit ognem negasimyim
    vsyak zhivot podnebesnoi;
    vokrug kotlov kipuchiix
    stoyat startsy starye;
    poyut startsy starye
    pro zhivot, pro smert',
    pro ves' rod chelovech . . .
    Sulyat startsy starye
    vsemu miru zhivoty dolgie,
    kak na tu-li zluyu Smert'
    kladut startsy starye
    proklyat'itse velikoe!

31. v. Ralston (1872): 87 ff.
32. Ibid: 85.
33. Ibid.
34. Svarogits, "Svarog's son," was sometimes called *ogon'*, "fire;" v. Ralston (1872): 85. He cites the

Slovo nyekoego khristolyubtsa, a thirteenth-century writing, which states that the Slavic people "pray to Ogon', whom they call Svarozhich." cf. Sanskrit *agni*, Latin *ignis*, "fire."

35. To Veles/Volos, compare the Lithuanian god, *Velinas*. v. Ralston (1872): 252.
36. Ralston (1872): 251.
37. v. Chapter Three, above.
38. Akhmanova (1971): 199.
39. Ibid.
40. v. Ralston (1872): 349.
41. Afanas'ev (1865–1869) I. 273.
42. Ibid 273–274:

vyn' ty, Devitsa,
otecheskii mech'-kladenets,
dostan' pantsyr' dedovskii,
shlem bogatyrskii,
otopri konya vorona;
vyidi ty . . .
vo chistom pole
stoit rat' moguchaya . . .
Zakroi ty, devitsa,
menya svoeyu phatoi
ot sily vrazh'ei . . .

43. Lebesgue (1920): 38. Translated from the French.
44. Sobolevskii (1895–1902) IV:366–367, No. 468:

"Ty nochui, nochui, lyubeznyi,
Nochui nochku u menya!"—
—"Rad by, dushechka, ostat'sya,
U menya volya ne svoya . . .
Ya esche bol'she boyusya,
Boyus'—do svetu prosplyu!"—
—"Ty ne bois', ne bois', lyubeznyi:
Vo vsyu nochky ne usnu,
Do zoryushki razbuzhu,
Do zoryushki do utryanoi,
Ya daleko provozhu!"

45. Ibid IV: 373, No.475:

" . . . Razbudi, milaya,
po utru ranen'ko,
do beliya zoryushki,
chtob ne razsvetalo!"

46. Hatto (1965): 675 (No. 426), Anonymous folksong, Ukranian, nineteenth century; translated by the author with Benee Dean:

"Oi misyatsyu, misyachen'ku,
Zaidi za komoru,
Nekhai z'svoiim milisen'kim
Troshki pogovoru.

Oi misyatsyu, misyachen'ku,
Sviti, ne khovaisya—
Khot' poidesh', mii milen'kii,
Khutko povertaisya!"

47. Alexandrow (1923): 286.
48. Ibid: 595.
49. Transl. Ralston (1872) 188.
50. Ibid.
51. Hatto (1965): 668 (No. 411), Anonymous, Russian, nineteenth century (Original: fifteenth century):

chudo:

na nebe solntse - v tereme solntse;

na nebe mesyats - v tereme mesyats;
na nebe zvezdy - v tereme zvezdy;
na nebe zarya - v tereme zarya,

i vsya krasota podnebesnaya . . .

52. Afanas'ev I (1865–1869): 730.
53. Ibid 730–731:

lyubit oxotit'sya
v svetliya lunniya nochi;
s oruzhiem v rukax
mchitsya ona
na borzom kone po lesam,
soprovozhdaemaya lovchimi psami,
i gonit ubegayushchago zverya.

54. Ibid 731.
55. Ibid.

PART TWO: CHAPTER SIX

1. Artaxerxes II (Mnemon), Susa A (405–359 BCE):

. . . vasnā AM
Anahata utā Miϑra . . .
AM Anahata utā Miϑra
mām pātuv . . .

2. Avesta, Yasht (Yašt) V.86–87:

tuvąm naraciṱ yōi taxma
jaiδʿyą̊nte āsu.aspiδəm
x^{v}arnaŋhasca uparatātō.
ϑwąm āϑravąnō . . .
maʿstīm jaiδyą̊nte spānəmca . . .

ϑwąm kaininō . . .
xšaʿϑra huāpā̊ jaiδyą̊nte
tax(ə)məmca nmānō.paitīm.
ϑwąm carāitiš zizanāitiš
jaiδʿyą̊nte huzāmiδəm.

3. Ibid: V.78:

upatacaṱ
ardvī sūra anāhita . . .
armaēstā̊ anyā̊ āpō kṛnaoṱ
fraša anyā̊ fratācayaṱ,
huškəm pərətum raēcayaṱ
tarō vaŋhvīm vītaŋhvaitīm.

4. Khvarənah (*X^{v}arənah*) was perhaps similar to the Homeric Greek χάρις. In Homer, Odyssey 11.12, for example, χάρις connotes the *aura* which the goddess *Athena* conferred upon Telemachos, the son of Odysseus and Penelope, to increase the charisma of the youth when he appeared before the Greek Assembly. The Indic attribute, *tejas*, may have a similar meaning. This is a Sanskrit term often given to the light surrounding a deity, for example, the energy-filled light emanating from the gods when they created the "Great"-goddess, Devī: v. Devī māhātmyam II.10 ff.
5. Avesta, Yašt V.89:

. . .mana raya x^{v}arənaŋha . . .

6. *Zoroaster*, or *Zarathustra*, in his group of hymns known collectively as the *Gathas (Gāϑās)* or Gatha Avesta, divided into chapters called *Yasnas*, posited an ethical dualism between *Asha*, "Truth," and *Drug*, "Falsehood." This dualism was actually promoted by one Iranian sect, but popularized throughout Iran under the Sassanian dynasty, when the Zend-Avesta was recorded.
7. v. Avesta, Yasna 33.11.

8. Avesta, Yasna 44.7:

ahurā
kə bərəχδąm tāšt
xšaϑrā mąt̰
ārmaitīm:
azəm tāiš ϑωā
fraxšnī avāmī
mazdā . . .
vispanąm dātārəm.

Further, cf. Yasna 45.4:

. . . at̰ hoi dugədā
hušyaoϑanā ārmaitiš . . .

"[Ahura Mazdāh's] daughter
is Armaiti of good deeds."

cf. the Greek goddess Athena, whom we will discuss below; she was said to have been born of Zeus alone. (Hesiod, Theogony: 924)

9. Ibid: Yasna 31.12:

ānuš.haxš ārmaitiš
mainyū pərəsaitē
yaϑrā maēϑā.

10. Ibid: Yasna 33.13:

frō spəntā ārmaitē
ašā daēnå fradaxšayā.

11. Ibid:

ašiča ārmaitī . . .

But cf. also *Ashi Vaŋguhi* (Aši Vaŋuhi), "Good Ashi;" in Yasna seventeen, she too is invoked as a goddess of *wisdom* (XVII.1–2 *et passim*) and *wealth* and *happiness* (XVII.6 ff). She is thus a goddess of *good fortune*. In this hymn, Spēnta Ārmaiti is described as her *mother* (XVII.16).

12. Ibid: Yasna 43.1:

. . . tat̰ mōi då ārmaitē
rāyō ašīš . . .

13. Ibid: Yasna 47.3:

at̰ hōi vāstrāi
rāmā.då ārmaitīm.

14. Ibid: Yasna 28.3:

xšaϑrəmča
aγžō.nvamnəm
varədaitī ārmaitiš . . .

15. Ibid: Yasna 33.12:

. . . ahurā
ārmaitī
təvīsīm dasvā . . .

cf. Avesta, Yašt 1.27 ff. and cf. Dumézil (1947): 60.

16. Bundahišn XV.1–2.

PART TWO: CHAPTER SEVEN

1. However, the Indians and Iranians may have left their Steppe homeland in two different migrations. v. Polomé (1983): 1–2.
2. v. Mackay (1948): 53.
3. v. Campbell (1974), figure 240; cf. the Sumerian cylinder-seal from Tello, illustrated in Wolkstein and Kramer (1983): 40, depicting horned deities facing a sacred tree. Trees were worshipped throughout ancient Europe and the Near East. cf. also Mackay (1948), plate XVI,8, and Vermeule (1964), figure 44. cf. Chapter Three, above, on the sacred tree.

4. The Rigveda dates to *ca*. 1200 BCE.
5. Rigveda I.41.1–4; I.191.9; II.27.1; VII.41.2; X.72.4,8; X.132.6.
6. Ibid X.72.4:

aditerdakṣo ajāyata
dakṣādvaditiḥ pari.

cf. Sanskrit *dakṣ*, "to be able, to be strong."

7. Ibid I.89.10:

aditidyauraditirantarikṣamaditirmātā
sa pitā sa putraḥ;
viśve devā aditiḥ panca janā
aditirjātamaditirjanitvam.

To Aditi's plurality of roles, compare the later Christian Trinity.

8. Ibid II.40.6:

. . . devyaditir anarvā . . .

9. Ibid X.70.7:

. . . priyā dhāmāny
aditer upasthe . . .

10. Ibid I.185.3:

aneho dātramaditer
anarvam huve
svarvadavadham
namasvat.

11. Ibid I.162.22:

anāgāstvam no
aditiḥ kṛṇotu . . .

12. Ibid I.94.16; I.95.11; I.96.9 *et alia*:

tanno mitro varuṇo
māmahantāmaditiḥ
sindhuḥ pṛthivī uta dyauḥ

13. Ibid VII.104.9:

yo pākaśansam
viharanta [=viharante] evair
ye vā bhadram
dūṣayanti svadhābhiḥ
ahaye vā tānpradadātu soma
ā vā dadhātu
nirṛterupasthe.

14. Atharvaveda VI.63.1:

yatte devī nirṛtirābabandha
dāma grīvāsvavimokyam yat.
tatte vi ṣyāmyāyuṣe varcase
balāyādomadamannamaddhi prasūtaḥ

15. v. Chapter Three, above.
16. Atharvaveda VII.64:

idam yatkṛṣṇaḥ
śakunirabhiniṣpatannapīpatat;
āpo mā tasmāt-

sarvasmādduritātpāntvamhasaḥ

idam yatkṛṣṇaḥ
śakuniravāmṛkṣannirṛte
te mukhena;
agnirmā tasmādenaso gārhapatyaḥ
pra muñcatu.

17. There is a striking similarity between Nirṛti and the Celtic goddess *Badb,* who also appeared as a black bird. v. Chapter Eight, below.
18. On *Devī* see below.
19. The Purāṇas (2nd to 16th centuries CE; dates per O'Flaherty [1975] 16–18) are verse-writings which celebrate the powers and acts of gods and goddesses.
20. Rigveda I.3.12:

. . . maho arṇaḥ sarasvatī . . .

21. Ibid IX.67.32:

. . . tasmai sarasvatī
duhe kṣīram
sarpirmadhūdakam.

22. Ibid X.30.12:

. . . sarasvatī tad
gṛṇate
vayo dhāt.

23. Ibid II.41.16:

ambitame.

24. Ibid II.41.17:

. . . sarasvati . . .
prajām devi
dididḍhi naḥ

25. Ibid X.184.1–2:

Viṣṇur yonīm kalpayatu . . .
garbham dhehi sarasvati . . .

26. Ibid I.164.49:

. . . yo ratnadhā vasuvidyaḥ
sudatraḥ sarasvati . . .

cf. X.17.9:

Sarasvatīm yām pitaro havante . . .
rāyasposam yajamāneṣu dhehi.

"Sarasvatī,
whom the fathers call upon . . .
give increase of wealth
to those who make sacrifice."

27. Ibid VII.96.3:

. . . bhadramidbhadrā
kṛṇavat sarasvaty . . .

28. Ibid VI.61.7:

vṛtraghnī

cf. II.30.8:

. . . Sarasvati . . .
dhṛṣatī
jeṣi śatrūn.

"O Sarasvatī . . .
courageous,
you conquer our enemies."

29. Ibid VI.61.3:

Sarasvati devanido ni barhaya.

30. Ibid VI.49.7:

vīrapatnī

31. Ibid VI.61.4:

. . . pra no devī
Sarasvatī
vājebhir vājinīvatī
dhīnāmavitry avatu.

32. Ibid I.3.12:

. . . Sarasvatī . . .
dhiyo viśva
vi rājati . . .

33. Ibid II.3.8:

. . . sarasvatī
sādhayantī dhiyam . . .

34. Monier-Williams, (1899): 1182; Saundarylaharī: 98.
35. Lalita, (1978) 107:

om aing
Sarasvatyai namaḥ

36. Sarasvatī is regarded today as both individual personification of wisdom and as one aspect of an omnipotent and more removed deity.
37. Rigveda VII.42.3:

yajñiyamaramatim.

38. cf. Rigveda VII.36.8:

mahīmaramatim.

39. Ibid V.43.6:

mahīmaramatim . . . gnām
devīm namasā ratahavyām . . .
bṛhatīmṛtajñām . . .

40. Ibid X.92.5:

pra . . . yanti sindhavastiro
mahīmaramatim dadhanvire.

41. cf. Reichelt (1967): 428. Old Iranian *arəm*, Sanskrit *arám*, "right, correct" +*matay*, from the verbal root *man*, "to think." Aramati, Ārmaiti thus mean "right thought."
42. Grassman, (1976): 1187.
43. Monier-Williams, (1899): 892.
44. Ibid.
45. Ibid.
46. Mahābhārata I.92.3; I.189.39; I.203.16 *et passim*.
47. Śatapatha Brāhmaṇa XI.4.3.3.
48. v. Chapter Eleven, below.
49. v. Hesiod, Works and Days 60 ff. According to Hesiod, Pandora was endowed by all of the Olympian deities, but was the *dispenser* of all *evils*.
50. Hesiod, Theogony 190 ff. v. Chapter Ten, below, and the Introduction, above.
51. Rāmāyaṇa I.45. Mahābhārata I.16.34. Pañcarātra III.
There are other stories of her birth: cf. Śatapatha Brāhmaṇa III.1.
52. v. Monier-Williams (1899): 25.
53. Rāmāyaṇa I.45.
54. Mahābhārata I.92.26–27. Saundaryalaharī 98.
55. Meditation of Mahālakṣmī, preceding Devī māhātmyam I.
56. cf. Sappho, Fragment 198 [Scholia on Theocritus xiii.1–2c, in Page, (1955) 105]:

Ἔρωτα . . .
Ἀφροδίτης καὶ Οὐρανοῦ

"Eros, son of
Aphrodite and Ouranos."

Eros was, early on, given widely differing genealogies; even Sappho gave him two different sets of parents. Later, Eros, and particularly his Roman counterpart, Cupid, became more widely accepted as son of Aphrodite/Venus. v. Ovid, Metamorphoses I.463; IX.482; Apuleius, Metamorphoses, IV.30–31 *et passim*; Horace, Carmina I.19.1. Note that Eros had both a physical and a *cosmic* significance; in the latter, he was one of the three primeval beings, along with Chaos and Earth, which were created before all else. Cf. Hesiod, Theogony 120.

57. Harivaṁśa II. App. I.41.525: 541:

dharmāllakṣmyudbhavaḥ kāmaḥ

58. Devī māhātmyam IV.11:

gaurī tvameva
śaśimaulikṛtapratiṣṭā.

cf. V.11.

59. Ibid IV.11:

śrī kaiṭabhāri-
hṛdayaikakṛtādhivāsā.

60. Ibid I.85–87:

devi . . .
prabodham ca
jagatsvāmī . . .

61. Harivaṁśa 99.2:

rukmiṇyām . . . lakṣmī . . .

"Rukmini [who was] Lakṣmī"

cf. Homer, Odyssey XVII.36–37; XIX.53–54, wherein the heroine Penelope is compared to the goddess Aphrodite:

. . . Πηνελόπεια
. . . ἰκέλη . . . χρυσέῃ Ἀφροδίτῃ

" . . . Penelope,
resembling . . . golden Aphrodite"

62. Ibid I.88.34; I.98.3 *et passim*.

63. Saundaryalaharī I:

śiva śaktyā yukto
yadi bhavati śaktaḥ prabhavitum.
na cedevam devo na khalu
kuśalaḥ spanditum api.

64. Female counterparts existed early on: recall the Egyptian double-deities such as *Nu* and *Nut* and other pairs in their company, including *Kekui* and *Kekuit*, *Ḥeḥu* and *Ḥeḥut*. (v. Chapter Two, above.) The Indic form of the female counterpart, the *śaktis*, became a predominant religious form *ca*. 500 CE.

65. v. Monier-Williams: 443.

66. Mahābhārata V.3972; Harivaṁśa 1340 ff.

67. Devī māhātmyam II.17 *et passim*. Devī's multiplicity of eyes was sometimes great indeed. Cf. Pañcarātra IX, where she calls herself the "hundred-eyed."

68. Devī māhātmyam II.10–11.

69. Ibid: II.12:

. . . atīva . . .
jvalantamiva parvatam . . .
jvālāvyāptadigantaram.

70. Ibid II.13:

. . . ekastham tadabhūnnārī
vyāptalokatrayam tviṣā.

71. Ibid II.20–32.
72. Ibid X.5:

. . . dvitīyā
kā mamāparā . . .

73. Ibid:

. . . maṭyeva viśantyo
madvibhūtayaḥ

74. Ibid X.6:

tasyā devyāstanau
jagmur . . .

Similarly, the goddesses are assimilated to *Lakṣmī* as Devī: cf. the Pañcarātra IX.

75. Monier-Williams: 217; Mahābhārata I.207.18 *et passim;* Saundaryalaharī 71; App. 2.
76. Monier-Williams: 609; Devī māhātmyam V.84. Here, Devī is said to have sprung from Pārvatī's physical sheath. On Pārvatī as *Gaurī*, the "white goddess," the "shining, brilliant goddess," v. Devī māhātmyam IV.11, 41; V.10. As Gaurī, she is still a fierce warrior-maiden, rather than the more pacific personification customary for Pārvatī. Cf. also Saundaryalaharī 81.
77. cf. Devī māhātmyam XI.23. On Sarasvatī, see above.
78. Monier-Williams: 277; Devī māhātmyam VII.6 *et passim*. Kālī issued from the forehead of Devī, armed, just as did Athena from the brow of her father, Zeus.
79. Devī māhātmyam VII.7. She was given the epithet *Durgā* because she slew the demon or *Asura, Durgā,* "the unattainable, the one who is difficult of access." (Pañcarātra IX.)
80. Monier-Williams: 487; Devī māhātmyam IV.11 *et passim*. Saundaryalaharī 89.
81. Monier-Williams: 383; Devī māhātmyam II–III *passim*.
82. Monier-Williams: 743; Devī māhātmyam IV *passim*.
83. Devī māhātmyam XI.54:

bhrāmarīti ca mām
lokāstadā
stoṣyanti sarvataḥ

This name was also given to her *Yoginīs* or attendants; cf. Monier-Williams 770. Compare the epithet given to the attendants of the greek goddess Demeter: *melissa*, "bee-(goddess)." v. on Demeter, Chapter Ten, below.

84. Monier-Williams: 83; Devī māhātmyam II.52 *et passim*.
85. Monier-Williams: 171; Devī māhātmyam II.51 *et passim*.
86. Devī māhātmyam XII.40:

bhavakāle nṛṇām saiva
lakṣmīrvṛddhipradāgṛhe.
saivābhāve
tathālakṣmīrvanāśāyopajāyate.

cf. Devī māhātmyam V.11.

87. Harivaṁśa Appendix 1.8.19–20:

prakīrṇakési mṛtyuśca
tathā mānsaudanapriya
lakṣmīralakṣmi . . .

88. Devī māhātmyam I.64:

nityaiva sā
jaganmūrtistayā . . .

89. Ibid II.38:

kirīṭollikhitāmbarām.

90. Ibid IV.9:

vidyā . . . paramā

91. Ibid IV.11:

medhāsi devi
viditākhilaśastrasāra . . .

92. Ibid III.42:

mahāsīnā devyā
śiraścchittvā
nipātitaḥ

93. Ibid II.9–33.
94. Ibid: Meditations preceding Chapters One and Two; with regard to the noose, thunderbolt, and trident, cf. the Germanic Oðin, the Greco-Roman Zeus/Jupiter, and the Greco-Roman Poseidon/Neptune, with their respective attributes. Most often, a god was provided with one particular attribute. However, this was not always the case with regard to female deities. Devī, who was a *multifunctional goddess*, was endowed with multiple *attributes*.
95. Ibid I.75:

tvayaitaddhāryate
viśvam
tvayaitat ṛjyate
jagat.

96. Ibid IV.5.
97. Ibid XI.13. Here Devī is addressed as *Brahmāṇī*, another name for the goddess Sarasvatī:

haṅsayukta
vimānasthe brahmāṅī

The swan was the vehicle of Brahmā, Brahmāṇī's consort. The concept of the goddesses Devī, Sarasvatī, and Brahmāṇī riding on the swan (*haṇsa* is also a name for *goose* in Sanskrit) evokes that of the Greek goddess, *Aphrodite*, who was also depicted riding a swan (v. Chapter Ten, below), and, further, that of the later patroness of nursery-rhymes, *Mother Goose*. One might also recall the swan-maidens of Germanic and Balto-Slavic folk-tales. (v. Chapters Four, Five, and Nine.)

98. Ibid XI.14:

triśūlacandrāhidhare.

99. On the Indic "snake"-energy, v. Part One, Chapter One, above.
100. v. the magnesian schist figurine from Orissa, dating to the eleventh century CE, at the Los Angeles County Museum of Art, No. M.77.82.
101. Devī māhātmyam XII.41:

stutā sampūjitā
puṣpairdhūpagandhādibhistathā
dadāti vittam putranśca matim
dharme gatim śubhām.

102. Manu Smṛti IX.3:

pitā rakṣati kaumāre
bhartā rakṣati yauvane
rakṣanti sthavire putrā
na ratrī svātantryamarhati.

103. v. Preston (1982) 215: her festival is today "one of the most important festivals of the state of Bengal and its principal city, Calcutta."

PART TWO: CHAPTER EIGHT

1. v. Larousse (1965): 345. In one figure, the antlered Cernunnos holds a purse from which grain and coins flow.
2. For the iconography, v. Larousse (1965): 346.
3. v. Chapter Three, above.
4. v. below and cf. Chapter Three, above, on the tripartite theory of the French mythologist Georges Dumézil.
5. There is dispute regarding the meaning of her name. It may mean "great queen," from O.Ir. *mōr*, "great," and *ri*, *rig*, "king," *rigain*, "queen," or it may mean the "queen of nightmares," from *mŏr*, "nightmare." Morrigan became a feared goddess,

in Mórrígan úathmar

''the horrid Morrigan.''

(Metrical Dindshenchas "Odras" 55.) The text for the Metrical Dindshenchas may be found in Gwynn (1924).

6. Metrical Dindshenchas "Odras" 56:

a húaim chrúachan cubaid.

On a subliminal level, the cave may have represented the womb. cf. the Greco-Roman Hecate and Scylla, who also inhabited caves.

7. Táin Bó Cuailnge 1992–1993:

Táinic ieramh in Morrígan ann sin
i rriocht samhaisci finne óderge . . .

The text for the Táin is taken from O'Rahilly (1967).

8. Ibid 1997–1998:

Táinic dano in Morríghan ann sin
i rriocht escuinge slemne . . .

9. Ibid 2001:

Táinic ieramh in Morrígan
i riocht saidhi gairbi glasrúaidhi.

10. Windisch II.2 (1887): 239 believes that *Regamna* is a corruption of *Mórrigna*. The tale, therefore, would originally have been called the "Cattle-Raid of the Cow of Morrigan."
11. Táin Bó Regamna 5:

. . . hen-si dub forsin craib ina ḟarrad.

For the text, v. Windisch (1887).

12. Táin Bó Cuailnge 1094 (Ó Fiannachta text, 1966) = LL 9500:

. . . Lóch
co lleith Bodba . . .

13. Dineen (1927): 68.
14. Táin Bó Cuailnge 2808:

. áth fors ṅgéra in Badb.

15. Ibid 3431:

Baidbi béldergi.

16. v. Chapter Twelve, below.
17. v. also below.
18. Táin Bó Cuailnge 205 ff:

''a Ḟeidelm banḟáid,
cia ḟacci ar slúag?''

19. Ibid 207 ff:

''Atchíu forderg ḟorro,
atchíu rúad.''

20. Compert Cú Chulainn, "The Birth of Cú Chulainn" 4:

. . . hi rict enlaithe . . .

Text for this version may be found in Windisch (1880) I: 143 ff.

21. Metrical Dindshenchas "Ard Macha" 10:

Macha ben nemid

To O.Ir. *nemed*, "sacred," cf. Skt. *namas*, "a bow, a gesture of reverence," thus, "to pay homage;" Lat. *nemus*, "grove (often a sacred place)."

22. Metrical Dindshenchas "Ard Macha" 81 ff. v. below on the "pangs" of the Ulstermen.
23. *comḟlathius*, "co-sovereigns." Do Ḟlathiusaib Hérend 20 a–b (LL 2514–2559).
24. LL 2530.
25. Metrical Dindshenchas "Ard Macha" 13 ff.
26. Ibid: 12.
27. LL 14547 ff:

co mbert emun .i. mac ⁊ ingen.

''She bore twins, that is, a son and a daughter.''

The plain, *Emain Macha*, is named for the twins, O.Ir. *emon*. Cf. Metrical Dindshenchas "Ard Macha" 73–80 and LL 14573–14574.

28. The mare was believed to have been *Liath Macha*, the Grey of Macha. cf. Gricourt (1954): 82–83.
29. Metrical Dindshenchas "Ard Macha" 93 ff:

andsin robomarb in ben
don galur garb roglinned . . .

''Then the woman died
of that difficult illness,
it was certain.''

30. LL 14574 ff.
31. cf. Dumézil (1954): 17.
32. cf. also the Welsh goddess Rhiannon, below. Several other goddesses were given equine shape or function: the Greek *Demeter Erinys* changed into a mare when she was pursued by Poseidon as stallion, and was raped by him. She gave birth to hippomorphous offspring. The Indic *Saraṇyū* assumed the shape of a mare to escape from *her* pursuer, Vivasvat, and she, just as Demeter, was caught and raped. She subsequently gave birth to the twin horse-deities, the *Ashvins* (Aśvins).
33. Her name is related to the Indo-European word for honey, and it perhaps refers to intoxication from drinking mead. According to Puhvel (1970): 167, her name is part of a compound indicating a horse-ritual involving drunkenness, and she is thus connected with the Indo-European ritual known in India as the *Aśvamedha*, and in Rome as the *October Equus*. There was a Celtic equivalent to this horse-ritual. Geraldus Cambrensis described it in his Topographia Hibernica: 168, wherein he who was to become king mated with a white mare, which was then sacrificed. After some rituals which Cambrensis finds quite barbaric, the king's

''sovereignty and dominion are established.''

(*regnum illius et dominium est confirmatum.*)

The horse represented sovereignty and bestowed it upon the man who mated with it; and the male attained the kingship. Perhaps Medb, as personification of sovereignty, was the anthropomorphic equivalent—albeit unsacrificed—of the white mare.

34. Táin Bó Cuailnge 27–28:

Dáig is mé ra chunnig
in coibchi n-ingnaid
nára chunnig ben ríam
remom ar fer d' ḟeraib Hérend,
.i. cen neóit, cen ét, cen omon.

35. Ibid 36–37:

Dámbad étaid in fer 'cá mbeind,
níbad chomdas béus,
dáig níraba-sa ríam
can fer ar scáth araile ocum.

36. v. Chapter Thirteen, below, on virginity and chastity among Indo-European women.
37. v. (Robbins) Dexter (1985): 57–74, on the relationship between virginity and autonomy among Indo-European female figures.
38. v. Thurneysen *et al.* (1936b) 104: an heiress was called a *banchomarba*. Further, (page 133) (H.3.18,221a 3):

ranna[it] ingena fri macu
dlighthecha séta saindilsi
athar ilchoraigh.

''Daughters divide with sons
lawful chattel
[which is] the private property
of a father of many pledges.''

(that is, the father has many business dealings.)

If there was no male heir, a daughter could inherit all of her father's or mother's estate, including property (pages 134–136).

39. v. Chapter Ten, and Chapter Thirteen, below.
40. Thurneysen *et al*. (1936b) 82 (Cāin Lānamna 5):

bē cuitc[h]ernsa

41. Ibid 81:

fer for bantinc[h]ur co fognam

42. Metrical Dindshenchas "Ath Luain" 17:

. . . co mbrig brotha . . .

43. Táin Bó Cuailnge 16:

. . . ferr im chath ⁊ comrac ⁊ comlund . . .

44. Ibid 15–16:

. . . ferr im rath ⁊ tidnacul . . .

45. v. further, Chapter Twelve, on the goddesses as personifications of sovereignty.
46. On the naming of the Mabinogi, v. Ford (1977): 1; Evans (1907) xxvi.
47. Mabinogi, "Pwyll Pendeuic Dyuet" 614–615:

"Y rof i a Duw . . .
oed escor nym pryder
im pei gwir hynny."

The text may be found in Thomson (1957).

48. *Epona* is derived from PIE **ekwo-*, which gave Gaulish *epo*, Lat. *equus*, Skt. *aśva*; the Greek ἵππος is a borrowed word.
49. v. Chapter Thirteen, below.
50. v. Chapter Ten, below.

PART TWO: CHAPTER NINE

1. Tacitus, Germania 20:

eadem iuventa, similis proceritas;
pares validaeque miscentur . . .
sororum filiis idem apud avunculum
qui apud patrem honor.
quidam sanctiorem artioremque
hunc nexum sanguinis arbitrantur.

2. v. Mallory (1989): 124.
3. Tacitus, Germania 19:

paucissima
in tam numerosa gente
adulteria,
quorum poena praesens
et maritis permissa . . .

4. For depiction of goddesses with torques v. the early Iron Age Gundestrup Cauldron, which is found in the National Museum at Copenhagen. v. also Glob (1969), illustrations 47 and 48: front and back views of a Bronze-Age female figure from the Danish peat bog at Viksø.
5. cf. Glob (1969): illustrations Nos. 1, 2, 4, 5, 25, 35, 51, 52, 53.
6. Ibid: 116.
7. The masculine equivalent of *Nerthus*, described in the Scandinavian Edda, was the god

Njǫrðr. Both are derived from Proto-Germanic * ner þuz. v. Polomé (1954) and (1987): 460. Polomé is skeptical, however, about the possibility of a Viking-Age "masculinization" of the deity along with a "masculinization" of agriculture.

8. Tacitus, Germania 40:

(. . . in commune Nerthum,
id est Terram matrem, colunt . . .)

mox vehiculum et vestis et,
si credere velis,
numen ipsum
secreto lacu abluitur.
servi ministrant,
quos statim idem lacus haurit.

9. v. The Predynastic Egyptian figurines dating to *ca.* 3500 BCE (British Museum Nos. 32139, 32141), and Sumerian figures dating to 2000–1500 BCE (British Museum, Near Eastern Care 13).
10. Endnote Four, above.
11. cf. Polomé (1954): 184 ff; 199–200. The name of the goddess may be related to the Greek ἀνήρ, Skt. *nára*, "man, virile force," the Indo-European translation of what the life force really meant. cf. also Turville-Petre (1964): 171.
12. Snorri, "Gylfaginning" 34:

. . . vald yfir IX heimum,
at hon skipti ǫllum vistum
með þeim er til hennar varu sendir,
enn þat eru sóttdauðir menn
ok ellidauðir.

Text for this and the following reading are from the Jónsson edition (1875).

13. Ibid:

Hon er blá hálf,
enn hálf með hǫrundarlit.
Því er hon auðkend,
ok heldr gnúpleit
ok grimmlig.

14. Saxo Grammaticus, Gesta Danorum VI.12.
15. *Urth* means "fate," that is, the "past," in Old Norse. It is the past tense of *verða*, "to come to pass." cf. Taylor (1927; 1957): 392.
16. *Verðandi* means the "being" in Old Norse, thence "present," from *verða*. v. Vigfusson (1874): 695.
17. *Skuld* indicates "future" in Old Norse, from *skula*, "shall, must." v. Vigfusson (1874): 560. Note that the names of all three Norns were late inventions: attempts to explain, through the naming process, the functions of the goddesses.
18. Poetic Edda, "Vǫluspá" 20:

þaðan koma meyiar
margs vitandi
þriar . . .
Urð héto eina,
aðra Verðandi . . .
Skuld ina þriðio;
þær lǫg lǫgðo,
þær líf kuro
alda bornom,
ørlǫg seggia.

Text for the Poetic Edda may be found in Kuhn (1968).

19. Tacitus, Germania 8:

inesse quin etiam
sanctum aliquid et providum putant,
nec aut consilia earum aspernantur

aut responsa neglegunt.

20. Caesar, de Bello Gallico 1.50:

. . . apud Germanos
ea consuetudo esset,
ut matres familiae eorum
sortibus et vaticinationibus declararent,
utrum proelium committi ex usu esset,
necne . . .

21. Strabo, Geography VII.2,3:

. . . ἱέρειαι πολιότριχες,
λευχείμονες . . .
αἰχμαλώτοις διὰ τοῦ στρατοπέδου
συνήντων ξιφήρεις . . .
ἐλαιμοτόμει ἕκαστον . . .
ἐκ δὲ τοῦ προχεομένου αἵματος
εἰς τὸν κρατῆρα
μαντείαν τινὰ ἐποιοῦντο . . .

22. Snorri, "Bragarœður" 2:

Enn Skąði,
dóttir Þjassa jǫtuns,
tók hjalm ok brynju
ok ǫll hervópn,
ok ferr til Ásgarðs,
at hefna fǫður síns.
enn Æsir buðu henni
sætt ok yfirbœtr;
ok hit fyrsta,
at hon skal kjósa sér
mann af Ásum,
ok kjósa af fótum,
ok sjá ekki fleira af.
Þa sá hon eins manns fœtr
forkunnar fagra,
ok mælti:
"Þenna kýs ek,
fátt mun ljótt
á Baldri.
Enn þat var Njǫrðr
or Nóatúnum.

23. cf. the Indic *svayamvara*, the "self-choice," where a noble Indian woman was allowed to choose a husband from among a number of suitors. The phenomenon was also similar to the races and other games which were held in Greece for a noble woman's hand. v. Chapter Twelve, below.
24. Njörð was the Scandinavian male counterpart of Nerthus, who was worshipped in Germany.
25. Snorri, "Gylfaginning" 23 (the numbering of the chapters of the "Gylfaginning," in this selection and in following selections, is taken from the Faulkes (1982) edition):

. . . ferr hon mjǫk á skiðum
ok með boga,
ok skýtr dýr.

26. Ibid 24.
27. Ibid. cf. also the Poetic Edda, "Grímnismál" 14.
28. Snorri, "Gylfaginning" 24.
29. v. Part One, Chapter One, above, on the "Mistress of Animals" and her lions.
30. Snorri, "Gylfaginning" 24.
31. Ibid 35.
32. Poetic Edda, "Lokasenna" 30:

" . . . Freyia! . . .
ása oc álfa
er hér inni ero,
hverr hefir þinn hór verið."

33. Ibid 32:

" . . . Freyia!
þú ert fordæða
oc meini blandin miǫc,
síztik at brœðr þinom
stóðo blíð regin . . .

34. Snorri, "Gylfaginning" 42.
35. "Sǫrla Þattr" I.
36. In Poetic Edda, " Þrymskviða" 3, Thor (Þor) asks Freyja to lend him her *fiaðrhams*, her "feather garment."
37. Snorri, "Gylfaginning" 1:

en plógrinn gekk
svá hart ok djúpt,
at upp leysti landit;
ok drógu øxninir þat land
út á hafit,
ok vestr,
ok námu staðar
í sundi nøkkvoru.
Þar setti Gefjun landit,
ok gaf nafn,
ok kallaði Selund.

38. Ibid 35:

. . . Gefjun,
hon er mær,
ok henni þjóna þær
er meyjar andask.

39. Poetic Edda, "For Skírnis" 6:

"Í Gymis gǫrðom
ec sá ganga
mér tíða mey;
armar lýsto
enn af þaðan
alt lopt oc lǫgr."

40. Snorri, "Gylfaginning" 37:

. . . er hon tók upp hǫndum,
ok lauk hurð fyrir sér,
þá lýsti af hǫndum hennar
bæði í lopt
ok á lǫg,
ok allir heimar birtust
af henni.

41. This was Oðin's ring; it had the power to renew itself.
42. Poetic Edda, "For Skírnis" 42:

"lǫng er nótt
langar ro tvær,
hve um þreyiak þriár?"

43. v. Chapter Three, above.
44. The Old Icelandic *Valkyrja* is composed of two linguistic elements: *valr*, "the dead in the place of battle" (cf. OEng *wœl*, "the fallen," OS, OHG *wal*, "battlefield," Toch A *wäl*, "to die," *wlalune*, "death", Lith *vẽles*, "dead spirit," OIr *fuil*, from *u̯oli*, "blood") and *kyrja*, from *kjosa*, "to choose, to select." cf. De Vries (1962): 642. Thus the Valkyries were goddesses who chose those who were to die on the battlefield.
45. v. above.
46. Snorri, "Gylfaginning" 36.

47. Ibid. The names of some of the most ancient Valkyries are found in the Poetic Edda, "Grímnismál" 36.
48. cf. the tales of Slavic *Vilas*, and of *Vassilissa the Wise*, in Chapter Five, above.
49. cf. Chapter Eight, above, where *Dechtire*, the mother of the Irish hero Cú Chulainn, appeared as one of a flock of birds. Again, when avian attributes are assimilated to a heroine, she is rendered magical; this is the epic and folkloristic survival of the mythological bird-goddess.
50. Vǫlsunga Saga 21:

. . . sá at þat var kona.
Hon var í brynju,
ok var svá fǫst
sem hon væri holdgróin.

Text for the Vǫlsunga Saga is found in Finch (1965).
51. Ibid:

vænleik ok vitru

52. Ibid 22:

"Aldri finnsk þér vitrari kona
í verǫldu,
ok kenn enn fleiri spekiráð."

53. Ibid:

. . . þess sver ek
at þik skal ek eiga,
ok þú ert
við mitt œði.

54. Old Saxon *frigu*, "love." cf. Vigfusson (1874): 174. cf. Old High German *Fri(j)a*. The Germanic day-name, *Freitag*, "Frigg's day," Old Saxon *Frigedæg* (cf. Modern English *Friday*) is paralleled in the Romance languages by names for the Roman goddess of love, Venus (cf. French *Vendredi*, Spanish *Viernis*, from Latin *Veneris dies*, "Venus' day"), rather than for the matron-goddess Hera/Juno.
55. Poetic Edda, "Lokasenna" 26:

" . . . Frigg! . . .
oc hefir æ vergiǫrn verið,
er þá Véa oc Vilia
léztu þér,
Viðris qvæn,
báða í baðm um tekit."

56. v. Vigfusson (1874): 706.
57. Ibid: 687.
58. Poetic Edda, "Grímnismál" 7. cf. Old Norse *segia*, "to say;" v. Vigfusson (1874): 518.
59. Poetic Edda, "Lokasenna" 29.

" . . . ørlǫg Frigg
hugg ec at
ǫll viti,
þótt hon siálfgi segi."

60. v. Chapter Thirteen, below, on the relationship between *virginity* and *prophecy*.

PART TWO: CHAPTER TEN

1. PY 172=Tn 316, a Mycenaean tablet from Pylos:

"*di-we* GOLD BOWL *1* MAN *1*
e-ra GOLD BOWL *1* WOMAN *1*

Other deities are mentioned in this hymn, including Poseidon (*po-si-da-i-jo*), Hermes (*e-ma-a*$_2$), and possibly a dove-goddess (*pe-re-*82*, perhaps for Πέλεια). v. Ventris and Chadwick (1973): 286–289.

2. Homer's precise dates are not known; in fact, some Classicists believe that there may have been *two* Homers, and some believe that he (or she) did not exist. For further reading, v. Davison in Wace and Stubbings (1962): 234–266.
3. v. Chapter One, above, on the origins of Apollo's patronage of Delphi.
4. v. Chapter Thirteen, below.
5. Greek goddesses of Proto-Indo-European origin have already been discussed in Chapter Three, above.
6. v. Pomeroy (1975) *passim*.
7. Homer, Odyssey VI.92:

στεῖβον δ' ἐν βόθροισι . . .

8. Ibid VI.139–141:

οἴη δ' Ἀλκινόου θυγάτηρ μένε·
τῇ γὰρ Ἀθήνη θάρσος
ἐνὶ φρεσὶ θῆκε
καὶ ἐκ δέος εἵλετο γυίων.
στῆ δ' ἄντα σχομένη . . .

9. Ibid VI.199:

πόσε φεύγετε φῶτα ἰδοῦσαι;

10. Ibid VI.235:

τῷ κατέχευε χάριν
κεφαλῇ τε καὶ ὤμοις . . .

11. Ibid VI.237:

θηεῖτο δὲ κούρη.

12. Ibid VI.303–315:

ἀλλ' ὁπότ' ἄν σε
δόμοι κεκύθωσι καὶ αὐλή,
ὦκα μάλα μεγάροιο διελθέμεν,
ὄφρ' ἂν ἵκηαι μητέρ' ἐμήν·
ἡ δ' ἧ σται ἐπ' ἐσχάρῃ
ἐν πυρὸς αὐγῇ,
ἠλάκατα στρωφῶσ' ἁλιπόρφυρα . . .
ἔνθα δὲ πατρὸς ἐμοῖο θρόνος . . .
τὸν παραμειψάμενος
μητρὸς περὶ γούνασι χεῖρας
βάλλειν ἡμετέρης . . .
εἴ κ έν τοι κείνη γε
φίλα φρονέῃσ' ἐνὶ θυμῷ,
ἐλπωρή τοι ἔπειτα
φίλους τ' ἰδέειν
καὶ ἱκέσθαι οἶκον ἐϋκτίμενον
καὶ σὴν ἐς πατρίδα γαῖαν.

13. Ibid VII.49–50.
14. Ibid VII.13:

εἴσω δόρπον ἐκόσμει.

Another Greek custom, mentioned by Homer in passing, is pertinent here: an upper-class Greek woman often wore a *κρήδεμνον*, a veil or mantilla which was drawn across the face to protect a woman from the gaze of strangers. In Homer's Iliad 22.470, Aphrodite gave a κρήδεμνον to the Trojan princess, Andromache. Further, in Odyssey 1.334, Odysseus' faithful wife, *Penelope*, leaving her chamber accompanied by two female attendants, descended the stairs to the main floor of her palace, where her suitors were waiting. Downstairs, she stood by the doorpost,

ἄντα παρειάων σχομένη
λιπαρὰ κρήδεμνα

"holding before her cheeks
her shining veil(s)."

The veil was used, in both Greek and in earlier Near Eastern cultures, as a badge of the "respectable woman." cf. Lerner (1986): 134–140.

15. v. Chapter Twelve, on goddesses who confer sovereignty. The Phaeacian society may have followed the equalitarian "partnership" model rather than the male-centered "dominator" model. v. Eisler (1987) XVII ff; 20; *et passim*.
16. v. Glossary below; cf. Chapter Eight, above, on Irish inheritance patterns.
17. Homer, Odyssey VII.73:

ου' μὲν γάρ τι νόου
γε καὶ αὐτὴ δεύεται ἐσθλοῦ·

18. Ibid VII.66–68:

τὴν δ' Ἀλκίνοος ποιήσατ' ἄκοιτιν,
καί μιν ἔτισ',
ὡς οὔ τις ἐπὶ χθονὶ
τίεται ἄλλη,
ὅσσαι νῦν γε γυναῖκες
ὑπ' ἀνδράσιν οἶκον ἔχουσιν.

19. Aeschylus, "Eumenides" 605:

οὐκ ἦν ὅμαιμος
φωτὸς ὃν κατέκτανεν.

20. Ibid 658–659:

οὐκ ἔστι μήτηρ
ἡ κεκλημένου τέκνου
τοκεύς, τροφὸς δὲ
κύματος νεοσπόρου.

21. v. below.
22. Aeschylus, "Eumenides" 734–741:

ἐμὸν τόδ' ἔργον,
λοισθίαν κρῖναι δίκην·
ψῆφον δ' Ὀρέστῃ τήνδ'
ἐγὼ προσθήσομαι.
μήτηρ γὰρ οὔτις ἐστὶν
ἥ μ' ἐγείνατο,
τὸ δ' ἄρσεν αἰνῶ πάντα,
πλὴν γάμου τυχεῖν,
ἅπαντι θυμῷ,
κάρτα δ' εἰμὶ τοῦ πατρός·
οὕτω γυναικὸς οὐ προτιμήσω μόρον
ἄνδρα κτανούσης
δωμάτων ἐπίσκοπον.
νικᾷ δ' Ὀρέστης,
κἂν ἰσόψηφος κριθῇ.

23. Homer, Odyssey VIII.308:

. . . Διὸς θυγάτηρ Ἀφροδίτη . . .

24. Cythera lies off the Laconian coast of the southeastern Peloponnese; Cyprus is a large island located south of Cythera.
25. Hesiod, Theogony 190–197:

. . . ἀμφὶ δὲ λευκὸς
ἀφρὸς ἀπ' ἀθανάτου χροὸς ὤρνυτο·

τῷ δ' ἔνι κούρῃ
ἐθρέφθη· πρῶτον δὲ Κυθήροισιν ζαθέοισιν
ἔπλητ',
ἔνθεν ἔπειτα περίρρυτον ἵκετο Κύπρον.
ἐκ δ' ἔβη αἰδοίη καλὴ θεός . . .
. . . τὴν δ' Ἀφροδίτην . . .
κικλήσκουσι θεοί τε καὶ ἀνέρες . . .

cf. Chapter Seven, above, on the goddess Shrī Lakshmī and v. also the Introduction, above.

26. Pausanias, Description of Greece I.14.7:

. . . ἱερόν ἐστιν Ἀφροδίτης Οὐρανίας . . .
πρώτοις δὲ ἀνθρώπων Ἀσσυρίοις
κατέστη σέβεσθαι τὴν Οὐρανίαν,
μετὰ δὲ Ἀσσυρίους
Κυπρίων Παφίοις
καὶ Φοινίκων τοῖς Ἀσκάλωνα ἔχουσιν
ἐν τῇ Παλαιστίνῃ,
παρὰ δὲ Φοινίκων Κυθήριοι
μαθόντες σέβουσιν·

27. Herodotus, The History I.105:

. . . τῆς οὐρανίης Ἀφροδίτης
τὸ ἱρόν . . .
πάντων ἀρχαιότατον ἱρῶν
ὅσα ταύτης τῆς θεοῦ·

28. The "popular-" or "folk-" etymology for Aphrodite is that the first part of her name is derived from Greek ἀφρός, "foam;" according to Hesiod, Theogony 195–198:

. . . τὴν δ' Ἀφροδίτην . . .
κικλήσκουσι θεοί τε καὶ ἀνέρες,
οὕνεκ' ἐν ἀφρῷ
θρέφθη·

"Gods and men have called her Aphrodite,
because she grew in the foam."

Most modern etymologists have agreed that this is *not* a valid etymology for the "foam-born" goddess. For discussion of etymological attempts on her name, v. Robbins (1978): 47 ff. On modern attempts to decipher her origins, v. Endnote 13, Chapter Three.

29. Clay drinking cup from Rhodes, Attic, *ca.* 460 BCE. British Museum No. D 2. For other female figurines associated with geese, cf. Chapter Seven, Endnote 97.
30. Terracotta figurine from Tarentum, *ca.* 380 BCE. British Museum No. 1308.
31. The orginal was crafted by Diodalses of Bithynia, *ca.* 250 BCE. v. the marble Roman copy, dating to the first century CE, in the British Museum, No. 1963.10-29.1. and v. the Roman copy in the J. Paul Getty Museum, No. 55.AA.10, dating from the first to the second centuries CE. The latter depicts Eros along with Aphrodite, and it has a more prominent snake coiled around Aphrodite's left arm. Beneath Aphrodite is a fragmentary goose. Thus she is depicted with snake and bird.
32. Pindar, poetic Fragment 122:

Πολύξεναι νεάνιδες,
ἀμφίπολοι
Πειθοῦς ἐν ἀφνειῷ Κορίνθῳ . . .
. . . ματέρ' ἐρώτων
οὐρανίαν πτάμεναι
νόημα ποτ' τὰν Ἀφροδίταν . . .

33. Pausanias, Description of Greece II.34.11.
34. Ibid I.1.3.
35. Homer, Odyssey IV.14:

Ἑρμιόνην,
ἣ εἶδος ἔχε χρυσέης Ἀφροδίτης.

36. Homeric Hymn V.70–74:

σαίνοντες πολιοί τε λύκοι
χαροποί τε λέοντες,
ἄρκτοι παρδαλιές τε θοαὶ
προκάδων ἀκόρητοι
. . . ἡ δ' ὁρόωσα μετὰ φρεσὶ
τέρπετο θυμὸν
καὶ τοῖς ἐν στήθεσσι βάλ' ἵμερον·
οἱ δ' ἅμα πάντες
σύνδυο κοιμήσαντο
κατὰ σκιόεντας ἐναύλους.

cf. Homeric Hymn XIV.1–4, to the "Mother of all the Gods and Men," who

Μητέρα μοι πάντων τε θεόν
πάντων τ' ἀνθρώπων . . .
ᾗ κροτάλων τυπάνων τ' ἰαχὴ
σύν τε βρόμος αὐλῶν
εὔαδεν ἠδὲ λύκων κλαγγὴ
χαροπῶν τε λεόντων . . .

"delighted in the sound
of rattles and drums
together with the hum of flutes
and the roar of wolves
and of bright-eyed lions . . . "

37. Homer, Iliad V.311–313:

καί νύ κεν ἔνθ' ἀπόλοιτο
ἄναξ ἀνδρῶν Αἰνείας
εἰ μὴ ἄρ' ὀξὺ νόησε
Διὸς θυγάτηρ Ἀφροδίτη,
μήτηρ, ἥ μιν ὑπ' Ἀγχίσῃ
τέκε βουκολέοντι·

38. Pausanias, Description of Greece III.17.5–6 on Laconia:

ὄπισθεν δὲ τῆς Χαλκιοίκου
ναός ἐστιν Ἀφροδίτης Ἀρείας·
τὰ δὲ ξόανα ἀρχαῖα
εἴπερ τι ἄλλο ἐν Ἕλλησιν.

cf. Lactantius, Divinarum Institutionum I.20:

. . . aedem Veneri armatae
simulacrumque posuerunt.

"They dedicated a temple
to the armed Venus
and a statue."

39. This may also have been the case with Athena, the protective goddess of the city of Mycenae, or her martial ability may have led to her function as protective goddess.
40. Homer, Odyssey VIII.292:

"Δεῦρο, φίλη,
λέκτρονδε τραπείομεν . . . "

41. Ibid 326:

ἄσβεστος δ' ἄρ' ἐνῶρτο γέλως
μακάρεσσι θεοῖσι . . .

42. cf. also Ovid, Metamorphoses IV.171–189.
43. Linear B Text PY ES 650, a Mycenaean text from Pylos:

ai-ki-wa-ro a-ti-mi-to do-e-ro.

cf. PY Un 219:

a-ti-mi-te.

44. The "many-breasted" Artemis has been a favorite of sculptors for at least the past two millennia. She is represented even today in figurines made by the modern Ephesians. For an illustration of a "Classical" Ephesian Artemis, v. Roscher I (1884–1886): 588. There has been

disagreement over the significance of the many "breasts:" some see them as fruit of the date palm. cf. Chapter Three, Endnote 109, on the Hebraic metaphor of the date palm.

45. cf. Pausanias, Description of Greece III.12.8 and III.22.8, describing her temples in Laconia.
46. v. Chapter One, above, on the "Mistress of Animals."
47. Xenophon, Hellenica IV.2,20:

οὐκέτι δὲ στάδιον ἀπεχόντων,
σφαγιασάμενοι οἱ Λακεδαιμόνιοι
τῇ Ἀγροτέρᾳ
ὥσπερ νομίζεται,
τὴν χίμαιραν,
ἡγοῦντο ἐπὶ τοὺς ἐναντίους . . .

48. Homer, Odyssey XX.71:

Ἄρτεμις ἁγνή . . .

49. Homer, Iliad XXI.470–471:

πότνια θερῶν,
Ἄρτεμις ἀγροτέρη . . .

50. Aristophanes, "Lysistrata" 645:

. . . κᾆτ' ἔχουσα τὸν κροκωτὸν
ἄρκτος ἦ Βραυρωνίοις.

51. A linguistic connection between Ἄρτεμις and ἄρκτος has been posited, but it is disputed.
52. "Hesiod," Astronomia 3:

ἑλέσθαι δὲ μετὰ Ἀρτέμιδος
τὴν περὶ τὰς θήρας ἀγωγὴν
ἐν τοῖς ὄρεσι ποιεῖσθαι.

53. Ovid, Metamorphoses II.464–485, declares that it was Juno (Hera), angry with her husband's infidelity, who changed Callisto into a bear. Diana (Artemis) only banished the pregnant girl from her company.
54. "Hesiod," Astronomia 3.
55. cf. Ovid, Metamorphoses II.505–507.
56. Pausanias, Description of Greece I.29.2:

. . . περίβολός ἐστιν Ἀρτέμιδος
καὶ ξόανα Ἀρίστης καὶ Καλλίστης·
ὡς μὲν ἐγὼ
δοκῶ . . . τῆς Ἀρτέμιδός
εἰσιν ἐπικλήσεις αὗται . . .

57. Homeric Hymn XXVII.1–2, 10:

Αρτεμιν . . .
. . . ἐλαφηβόλον, ἰοχέαιραν . . .
. . . θερῶν ὀλέκουσα γενέθλην . . .

58. Ibid 15:

Μουσῶν καὶ Χαρίτων
καλὸν χορὸν ἀρτυνέουσα.
ἔνθα κατακρεμάσασα,
παλίντονα τόξα καὶ ἰοὺς
ἡγεῖται χαρίεντα περὶ χροὶ
κόσμον ἔχουσα,
ἐξάρχουσα χορούς·

59. v. the dancing group from Palaikastro, Crete, in Alexiou (1973), plate 22.
60. v. Pausanias, Description of Greece III.23.10:

. . . Ἀρτέμιδος ἱερόν ἐστιν
ἐν τῇ Ἐπιδαυρίων Λιμνάτιδος.

" . . . there is a shrine

of Artemis Limnatis
in the land of the Epidaurians.''

Ibid III.2.6:

. . . ἐν Ἀρτέμιδος ἱερῷ·
τὸ δὲ ἱερὸν τοῦτο
ἐν μεθορίῳ τῆς τε Λακωνικῆς
καὶ τῆς Μεσσηνίας ἐπεποίητο
ἐν χωρίῳ καλουμένῳ Λίμναις·

'' . . . in a shrine of Artemis;
This shrine was built
on the border
of Laconia and Messenia,
in a region called Limnae.''

v. also Strabo, Geography 8.362.

61. v. Nilsson (1941): 150. Some of these cymbals were inscribed. One inscription reads:

In parte interiore
cymboli aenei . . .
'Λιμνατις'.

''In the interior
of a bronze cymbal,
'Limnatis'.''

v. Roehl (1882), No. 20.

62. Timotheus, Fragment 1, in Bergk (1882) III 620:

εἰς Ἄρτεμιν . . .
Μαινάδα, Θυιάδα, Φοιβάδα, Λυσσάδα.

Mainas (acc. -ada) indicated a "maenad, a mad woman;" a *Thuias* was a "possessed woman;" a *Phoibas* was a "priestess of Phoebus (Apollo), an inspired woman;" and a *Lussas* was a "raging, mad woman."

63. Pausanias, Description of Greece VIII.37.4 on Arcadia:

. . . Ἄρτεμις . . .
ἕστηκεν ἀμπεχομένη δέρμα ἐλάφου
καὶ ἐπὶ τῶν ὤμων φαρέτραν ἔχουσα,
ἐν δὲ ταῖς χερσὶ
τῇ μὲν λαμπάδα ἔχει,
τῇ δὲ δράκοντας δύο.

Pausanias refers here to a work by Damophon. cf. Pauly-Wissowa (1894) III: 1439.

64. v. Alexiou (1973), plate 12; v. Kurtz (1975) 209.
65. v. Chapters One and Two, above.
66. v. below.
67. Euripides, "Iphigeneia at Aulis" 1590–1595:

κἀν τῷ δε Κάλχας
πῶςδοκεῖς χαίρων ἔφη·
ὦ τοῦδ' Ἀχαιῶν κοίρανοι
κοινοῦ στρατοῦ,
†ὁρᾶτε τήνδε θυσίαν,
ἣν ἡ θεὸς†
προύθηκε βωμίαν,
ἔλαφον ὀρειδρόμον;
ταύτην μάλιστα
τῆς κόρης ἀσπάζεται,
ὡς μὴ μιάνῃ βωμὸν
εὐγενεῖ φόνῳ.

cf. the Hebrew Old Testament, Genesis 22: 1–18, wherein a ram was substituted in burnt offering for Abraham's son, Isaac. Such stories may indicate the mitigation of a deity who had once demanded human sacrifice.

68. Euripides, "Iphigeneia in Taurus" 34–41:

ναοῖσι δ' ἐν τοῖσδ'
ἱερίαν τίθεσί με·
ὅθεν νόμοισι τοῖσιν ἥδεται θεὰ
Ἄρτεμις ἑορτῆς—
τοὔνομ' ἧς καλὸν μόνον,
τὰ δ' ἄλλα σιγῶ,
τὴν θεὸν φοβουμένη—
θύω γάρ,
ὄντος τοῦ νόμου
καὶ πρὶν πόλει,
ὃς ἂν κατέλθῃ
τήνδε γῆν Ἕλλην ἀνήρ.
κατάρχομαι μέν,
σφάγια δ' ἄλλοισιν μέλει
ἄρρητ' ἔσωθεν τῶνδ' ἀνακτόρων θεᾶς.

69. Homer, Odyssey XX.61–63:

"Ἄρτεμι, πότνα θεά,
θύγατερ Διός,
αἴθε μοι ἤδη
ἰὸν ἐνὶ στήθεσσι βαλοῦσ'
ἐκ θυμὸν ἕλοιο
αὐτίκα νῦν . . . "

70. v. (Robbins) Dexter (1985): 57–74 and v. Chapter Thirteen, below.
71. Plato, Theaetetus 149 B:

. . . τὴν Ἄρτεμιν,
. . . ἄλοχος οὖσα
τὴν λοχείαν εἴληχε.

72. Hesiod, Theogony 924:

Αὐτὸς δ' ἐκ κεφαλῆς
γλαυκώπιδα Τριτογένειαν . . .

The exact meaning of the cult-name Tritogeneia, "born of Trito," is unknown, although Trito appears to have some connection with water—perhaps the Libyan river Trito. The difficulty is that Athena was not worshipped as a water-deity. v. Farnell (1896): I.266–270.

73. Homer, Odyssey III.371–372:

. . . ἀπέβη γλαυκῶπις Ἀθήνη
φήνῃ εἰδομένη·

74. Ibid I.319–320:

. . . ἀπέβη γλαυκῶπις Ἀθήνη,
ὄρνις δ' ὣς ἀνόπαια διέπτατο·

75. For coins depicting Athena and the owl, v. those on display at the British Museum, Department of Coins and Medals.
76. The figure, a copy of Pheidias' chryselephantine Athena Parthenos, dates to *ca.* 400 BCE and is in the National Archaeological Museum, Greece, No. N.M. 129.
77. Apollodorus, Atheniensis Bibliothecae II.iv.3. For the mythology of Medusa, v. Chapter Thirteen, below.
78. The figure, dating to *ca.* 520 BCE, is in the Acropolis Museum in Athens, Greece (No. 631).
79. cf. the bronze water-jug, dating from *ca.* 350 to *ca.* 325 BCE, under the handle of which Athena is depicted slaying the giant. J. Paul Getty Museum No. 73.AC.15.
80. v. Chapter Two, above.
81. In a variant of this myth, Poseidon gave the *horse*, a symbol *par excellence* of the Indo-Europeans, to the Athenians. v. Vergil, Georgics I.12–14.
82. Augustinus, De Civitate Dei 18.9:

. . . quia una plus inventa est feminarum,
Minerva vicit.

"Because one more woman was found,
Minerva [that is, Athena] *prevailed."*

83. Apollodorus, Atheniensis Bibliothecae III.xiv.1:

> *Ἀθηνᾶ μὲν οὖν ἀφ' ἑαυτῆς*
> *τὴν πόλιν ἐκάλεσεν Ἀθήνας,*
> *Ποσειδῶν δὲ θυμῷ ὀργισθεὶς*
> *τὸ Θριάσιον πεδίον ἐπέκλυσε*
> *καὶ τὴν Ἀττικὴν*
> *ὕφαλον ἐποίησε.*

cf. Hyginus, Fabula 164.3:

> *. . . itaque Minerva ex suo nomine*
> *Athenas condidit . . .*
>
> "*And so Minerva* [Athena]
> *founded* [the city] *Athens*
> *after her name.*"

cf. also Herodotus, The History VIII.55 and Ovid, Metamorphoses VI. 72–82; in the latter, Minerva depicts the contest between herself and Poseidon/Neptune on a tapestry which she was weaving in a contest between herself and the mortal weaver, Arachne. Minerva was victor in the second contest as well.

84. Augustinus, De Civitate Dei 18.9:

> *ut nulla ulterius ferrent suffragia,*
> *ut nullus nascentium*
> *maternum nomen acciperet,*
> *ut ne quis eas Athenaeas vocaret.*

St. Augustine gives Marcus Varro (116 BCE to 27 BCE) as his source for this information.

85. cf. *Aphrodite Areia* and the Laconian *Artemis Agrotera*, whom we discussed earlier in this chapter. The pre-Athena may have been the house-goddess of the Mycenaean king. She would have taken over the war-like cult because the Mycenaean princes were involved in war and needed her protection. Later, when the kingship was abolished, Athena would have become the goddess and protectress of the democratic city. v. Nilsson (1950): 496, 501. On the other hand, we cannot be certain that her function as *patroness* preceded her function as *warrior*. v. above.
86. v. the discussion of the "tripartite theory" in Chapter Three, above.
87. cf. the following Panathenaic sacrificial dedication:

> *τῆι Ἀθηνᾶι τῆι Ὑγιείαι . . .*
> *τῆι Ἀθηνᾶι τῆι Πολιάδι*
> *καὶ τῆι Ἀθηνᾶι τῆι Νίκηι.*
>
> "*To Athena Hygieia (health),*
> *to Athena Polias (of the city),*
> *and to Athena Nike (victory).*"

The text is from Roehl (1882): IG 2–3[1], 334.9; 21–22 (Editio Minor).

88. Pausanias, Description of Greece V.3.2 on Elis:

> *τῶν δὲ Ἠλείων αἱ γυναῖκες,*
> *ἅτε τῶν ἐν ἡλικίᾳ*
> *σφίσιν ἠρημωμένης τῆς χώρας,*
> *εὔξασθαι τῇ Ἀθηνᾷ*
> *λέγονται κυῆσαι παραυτίκα,*
> *ἐπειδὰν μιχθῶσι τοῖς ἀνδράσι·*
> *καὶ ἥ τε εὐχή σφισιν ἐτελέσθη*
> *καὶ Ἀθηνᾶς ἱερὸν ἐπίκλησιν*
> *Μητρὸς ἱδρύσαντο.*

89. v. Chapter Twelve, below.
90. Homer, Iliad V.778:

> *Αἱ δὲ βάτην τρήρωσι*
> *πελειάσιν ἴθμαθ' ὁμοῖαι . . .*

91. Gimbutas (1974): 149–150.
92. Homer, Iliad I.551:

τὸν δ' ἠμείβετ' ἔπειτα
βοῶπις πότνια Ἥρη·

cf. Iliad XIV.263 *et passim*; Homeric Hymn III.332 *et passim*.

93. Kerenyi (1975): 127 connects her bovine characteristic with the moon-cult. cf. Plutarch, Moralia 282 C:

. . . τὴν Ἥραν ἐν ὕλῃ
τὴν σελήνην.
διὸ καὶ 'Ιουνῶνεμ
ἐπονομάζουσι τὴν Ἥραν,
τὸ νέον ἢ τὸ νεώτερον ἐμφαίνοντος
τοῦ ὀνόματος ἀπὸ τῆς σελήνης·

'' . . . the moon is Hera
in material form.
For this reason,
[the Romans] call Hera
by the name ''Juno,''
''the new'' or ''younger,''
apparently named for the moon.''

v. Chapter Thirteen, below, on sexual abstinence by both Hera and Juno. Hera's relationship with the moon may be linked to the time of the menses.

94. Pausanias, Description of Greece V.17.1, on Elis:

τῆς Ἥρας δέ ἐστιν
ἐν τῷ ναῷ Διός,
τὸ δὲ Ἥρας ἄγαλμα
καθήμενόν ἐστιν
ἐπὶ θρόνῳ·
παρέστηκε δὲ γένειά τε ἔχων
καὶ ἐπικείμενος κυνῆν
ἐπὶ τῇ κεφαλῇ,
ἔργα δέ ἐστιν ἁπλᾶ.

95. Alcaeus, poem GI.6–7 (Text is in Page, 1955: 161):

cὲ δ' Αἰολήιαν [κ]υδαλίμαν θέον
πάντων γενέθλαν . . .

96. Scholia on Homer, Iliad I.609 (on Zeus and Hera):

ἀδέλφη μόνη
ἀνδρὸς ἔτυχε τοιούτου.

''This is the only sister
[who] obtained such a husband.''

97. Scholia on Theocritus XV.64:

ἐπιβουλεύειν τῇ Ἥρᾳ μιγῆναι,
ὅτε αὐτὴν ἴδοι χωρισθεῖσαν
ἀπὸ τῶν ἄλλων θεῶν.
βουλόμενος δὲ ἀφανὴς γενέσθαι
καὶ μὴ ὀφθῆναι ὑπ' αὐτῆς
τὴν ὄψιν μεταβάλλει εἰς κόκκυγα
καὶ καθέζεται εἰς ὄρος . . .
τὴν δὲ Ἥραν πορευομένην μόνην
ἀφικέσθαι πρὸς τὸ ὄρος
καὶ καθέζεσθαι εἰς αὐτό,
ὅπου νῦν ἐστιν ἱερὸν Ἥρας τελείας.
τὸν δὲ κόκκυγα ἰδόντα
καταπετασθῆναι καὶ καθεσθῆναι
ἐπὶ τὰ γόνατα αὐτῆς
πεφρικότα καὶ ῥιγῶντα
ὑπὸ τοῦ χειμῶνος.
τὴν δὲ Ἥραν ἰδοῦσαν αὐτὸν
οἰκτεῖραι καὶ περιβαλεῖν

τῇ ἀμπεχόνῃ.
τὸν δὲ Δία εὐθέως
μεταβαλεῖν τὴν ὄψιν
καὶ ἐπιλαβέσθαι τῆς Ἥρας.
τῆς δὲ τὴν μίξιν παραιτουμένης
διὰ τὴν μητέρα,
αὐτὸν ὑποσχέσθαι
γυναῖκα αὐτὴν ποιήσασθαι.
καὶ παρ' Ἀργείοις δέ,
οἳ μέγιστα τῶν Ἑλλήνων
τιμῶσι τὴν θεόν,
τὸ [δὲ] ἄγαλμα τῆς Ἥρας
ἐν τῷ ναῷ καθήμενον
ἐν [τῷ] θρόνῳ
τῇ χειρὶ ἔχει σκῆπτρον,
καὶ ἐπ' αὐτῷ τῷ σκήπτρῳ
κόκκυξ.

cf. Diodorus Siculus, Bibliothecae V.72; Pausanias, Description of Greece II.36.2 and II.17.4.

98. Scholia on Homer, Iliad I.609:

τὸν δὲ Δία καὶ Ἥραν
ἐπὶ ἐνιαυτοὺς τριακοσίους . . .

99. Ibid XIX.407:

αὐδήεντα δ' ἔθηκε
θεὰ λευκώλενος Ἥρη·

100. Homeric Hymn III.345–346, to Pythian Apollo:

. . . ἐς θῶκον πολυδαίδαλον . . .
αὐτῷ ἐφεζομένη
πυκινὰς φραζέσκετο βουλάς·

101. v. Chapter Three, above, on the three Proto-Indo-European functions.
102. v. Chapter Twelve, below.
103. Hesiod, Theogony 211:

Νὺξ δ' ἔτεκεν
στυγερόν τε Μόρον . . .

104. Ibid 904:

. . . ᾗς πλείστην τιμὴν
πόρε μητίετα Ζεὺς . . .

105. Plutarch, Moralia 398 C–D:

. . . οὐδ' ἀποθανοῦσα λήξει μαντικῆς,
ἀλλ' αὐτὴ μὲν
ἐν τῇ σελήνῃ περίεισι
τὸ καλούμενον φαινόμενον γενομένη
πρόσωπον . . .

106. Libanius, Orations XII.60:

ὥσπερ οὖν οὐ τῆς Πυθίας
ἡγούμεθα τοὺς χρησμούς,
ἀλλὰ τοῦ πέμποντος
ἐπὶ τὸ στόμα τὰ λόγια . . .

107. v. Chapter One, above.
108. Ibid.
109. Hesiod, Theogony 360.
110. Ibid 126–136.
111. Homeric Hymn II, to Demeter: 420.
112. Alcman, poetic Fragment 62 (Bergk numeration):

Εὐνομίας [τε] καὶ Πειθοῦς ἀδελφὰ
καὶ Προμαθείας θυγάτηρ . . .

113. v. Mikalson (1983): 61.
114. Ibid: 60.
115. Archilochus, poetic Fragment 16 (Bergk):

> *Πάντα τύχη καὶ μοῖρα,*
> *Περίκλεες,*
> *ἀνδρὶ δίδωσιν.*

116. Hesiod, <u>Theogony</u> 423–427:

> *οὐδέ τί μιν Κρονίδης ἐβιήσατο*
> *οὐδέ τ' ἀπηύρα,*
> *ὅσσ' ἔλαχεν Τιτῆσι*
> *μετὰ προτέροισι θεοῖσιν,*
> *ἀλλ' ἔχει . . .*
> *καὶ γέρας ἐν γαίῃ*
> *τε καὶ οὐρανῷ*
> *ἠδὲ θαλάσσῃ·*

Some scholars consider the passage in Hesiod to be an interpolation. cf. Farnell (1896) II: 504. Hecate might have been a goddess whose cult was newly imported into Boeotia.
117. v. above on Athena, and v. Glossary, below.
118. Hesiod, <u>Theogony</u> 434:

> *ἔν τε δίκῃ*
> *βασιλεῦσι παρ' αἰδοίοισι*
> *καθίζει . . .*

119. Ibid 430:

> *ἔν τ' ἀγορῇ λαοῖσι μεταπρέπει,*
> *ὅν κ' ἐθέλῃσιν·*

120. Ibid 431–433:

> *ἠδ' ὁπότ' ἐς πόλεμον*
> *φθεισήνορα θωρήσσωνται*
> *ἀνέρες,*
> *ἔνθα θεὰ παραγίγνεται,*
> *οἷς κ' ἐθέλῃσι*
> *νίκην προφρονέως ὀπάσαι*
> *καὶ κῦδος ὀρέξαι.*

121. v. Chapters Eight and Nine, above.
122. Hesiod, <u>Theogony</u> 450:

> *. . . κουροτρόφον . . .*

123. Ibid 444–447:

> *. . . ληίδ' ἀέξειν·*
> *. . . θυμῷ γ' ἐθέλουσα,*
> *ἐξ ὀλίγων βριάει*
> *καὶ ἐκ πολλῶν μείονα θῆκεν.*

Note all of the times that Hesiod uses the verb ἐθέλειν, "to wish, to will," with regard to the goddess, Hecate. She was obviously an autonomous goddess, one who could do what she wished, to whom she wished.
124. v. Chapter Thirteen, below.
125. Vergil, <u>Aeneid</u> IV.609:

> *nocturnisque Hecate*
> *triviis ululata*
> *per urbes.*

126. Ovid, <u>Fasti</u> I.141–142:

> *ora vides Hecates*
> *in tres vertentia partes,*
> *servet ut in ternas*
> *compita secta vias . . .*

127. <u>Homeric Hymn</u> II, to Demeter: 24–25. Hecate lived in a cave; caves were believed by many to

be the entrance to the Netherworld. cf. Endnote Six, Chapter Eight, above, on the Celtic goddess Morrigan. Morrigan also inhabited a cave.

128. Ibid, 438–440:

. . . Ἑκάτη . . .
πολλὰ δ' ἀρ' ἀμφαγάπησε
κόρην Δημήτερος ἁγνήν·
ἐκ τοῦ οἱ πρόπολος
καὶ ὀπάων ἔπλετ' ἄνασσα.

129. Apollonius Rhodius, Argonautica III.1211–1215:

Βριμὼ . . . Ἑκάτην . . .
. . . πέριξ δέ μιν ἐστεφάνωντο
σμερδαλέοι δρυίνοισι
μετὰ πτόρθοισι δράκοντες·

130. *Kore* indicates the "girl," the "maiden," the "daughter."
131. Homeric Hymn II, to Demeter: 83–84:

. . . οὔ τοι ἀεικὴς
γαμβρὸς ἐν ἀθανάτοις
Πολυσημάντωρ Ἀιδωνεύς . . .

132. v. Chapter Two, above.
133. Both priests and priestesses officiated in these rites; among the latter were those called *Melissae*, bees. According to Porphyrion, de Antro Nympharum 18,

Καὶ τὰς Δήμητρος ἱερείας
ὡς τῆς χθονίας θεᾶς μύστιδας
μελίσσας,
οἱ παλαιοὶ ἐκάλουν . . .

" . . . and
the priestesses of Demeter,
as also the female initiates of the chthonian goddess,
the ancients used to call
Melissae . . . "

cf. Servius, Commentaria in Vergili Aeneid I. 430, wherein the Roman goddess *Ceres*, whom the Romans considered to be the equivalent of Demeter, taught the secrets of her rites to an old woman named *Melissa*:

Apud Isthmum anus quaedam nomine Melissa fuit:
Hanc Ceres sacrorum suorum cum secreta docuisset . . .

"Among the Isthmians there was an old woman,
Melissa by name:
Her Ceres taught her sacraments,
along with hidden things . . . "

One is reminded of the scene on several gold signet-rings which date from *ca.* 1500–1400 BCE: female figures are portrayed, each apparently with head and hands of an insect. These women, perhaps a goddess with her priestesses, may be Melissae. Thus, we see that the Greek goddess Demeter has received the heritage of ancient Minoan goddesses. v. the gold ring from Phaestos, Heraklion Archaeological Museum, Crete, No. 424. cf. Higgins (1967): figures 239–240.

134. Homeric Hymn II, to Demeter: 393–394:

τέκνον, μή ῥά τι μοι σ[ύ γε
πάσσαο νέρθεν ἐοῦσα]
βρώμης;

135. v. Chapter Two, above.
136. Homeric Hymn II, to Demeter: 445–448. But cf. Ovid, Metamorphoses V.564–567: Persephone

spends half of the year with her mother, and half with her husband. (Further, according to Metamorphoses V.534–538, Persephone *herself* plucked seven pomegranate seeds and ate them, thus consigning *herself*, in her childlike innocence, to the Underworld.) In Fasti IV. 614, however, Ovid declares that Persephone dwells with her mother for *nine* months out of every year. cf. the Sumerian myth of Dumuzi and Geshtinanna, in Chapter Two, above.

137. According to Ovid, Fasti IV.550–560, the Eleusinian child whom Demeter nursed was Triptolemus, and the goddess foretold that the boy would be

. . . primus arabit
et seret et culta praemia tollet humo.

" . . . the first who will plough
and sow and reap the harvest
from the cultivated earth."

138. Pausanias, Description of Greece VIII.25.4, on Arcadia:

καλοῦσι δὲ Ἐρινὺν
οἱ Θελπούσιοι τὴν θεόν . . .

"The Thelpusians call the goddess Erinys."

139. v. Chapter Thirteen, below.
140. v. Rohde (1925) I. 270. But cf. Farnell (1909) V 437–439; Farnell believes that the Erinyes were personified curses, or "the curse-force externalized."
141. Pausanias, Description of Greece VIII.25.6, on Arcadia:

τὸ μὲν δὴ παραυτίκα
τὴν Δήμητρα ἐπὶ τῷ συμβάντι
ἔχειν ὀργίλως,
χρόνῳ δὲ ὕστερον
τοῦ τε θυμοῦ παύσασθαι . . .

142. cf. Pausanias, Description of Greece VIII.5.8, on Arcadia:

ἐπὶ δὲ Σίμου τοῦ Φιάλου
βασιλεύοντος
ἠφανίσθη Φιγαλεῦσιν ὑπὸ πυρὸς
τῆς Μελαίνης Δήμητρος
τὸ ἀρχαῖον ξόανον·

"When Simus, the son of Phialus, was king,
the people of Phigalia lost by fire
the ancient wooden image
of Black Demeter."

143. This iconography is shown in the terracotta figurine of Demeter with sheaves of corn, poppies, and snakes, which is displayed in the Terme Museum, Rome. cf. Larousse (1959; 1968): 148.
144. v. Chapter Two, above.
145. Pindar, "Olympia" II.68 f.
146. Pindar, poetic Fragment 133.
147. Homer, Odyssey X.527–529:

ἔνθ' ὄιν ἀρνειὸν ῥέζειν
    θῆλυν τε μέλαιναν
εἰς Ἔρεβος στρέψας,
    αὐτὸς δ' ἀπονόσφι τραπέσθαι
ἱέμενος ποταμοῖο ῥοάων·

148. Ibid X.533–534:

. . . ἐπεύξασθαι δὲ θεοῖσιν,
ἰφθίμῳ τ' Ἀίδῃ
    καὶ ἐπαινῇ Περσεφονείῃ·

149. v. also Chapter Thirteen, below, on renewable virginity.

PART TWO: CHAPTER ELEVEN

1. Ovid, Fasti IV. 255–256:

   . . . ut Roma potens opibus
   iam saecula quinque
   vidit . . .

   "When Rome, mighty in power,
   had already seen five centuries . . . "

   By Roman reckoning, the year was 549.
2. Ibid IV. 264–265.
3. Ibid IV.337–345:

   . . . in Tiberim qua lubricus
   influit Almo . . .
   illic purpurea canus
   cum veste sacerdos
   Almonis dominam sacraque
   lavit aquis . . .
   ipsa sedens plaustro
   porta est invecta Capena . . .

4. v. Chapter Nine, above.
5. v. Chapter Thirteen, below.
6. Livy, Ab Urbe Condita XXIX.xiv.14:

   in aedem Victoriae
   quae est in Palatio,
   pertulere deam pridie idus Apriles . . .
   Populus frequens dona deae
   in Palatium tulit,
   lectisterniumque et ludi fuere,
   Megalesia appellata.

7. Vergil, Aeneid X.252:

   alma parens Idaea deum . . .

8. Ibid X.254–255:

   tu mihi nunc pugnae princeps
   tu rite propinques
   augurium Phrygibusque adsis
   pede, diva, secundo.

9. For the iconography of a "gallus," v. Godwin (1981), figure v; a relief from the Appian Way, *ca.* 150 CE.
10. Lucretius, de Rerum Natura II.621:

    . . . violenti signa furoris . . .

11. Catullus, Carmina LXIII.5:

    devolsit ili
    acuto sibi pondera silice . . .

12. Ibid LXIII.42:

    ibi Somnus excitam Attin
    fugiens citus abiit . . .

13. Ibid LXIII.63–69:

> *ego mulier,*
> *ego adolescens, ego ephebus, ego puer,*
> *ego gymnasi fui flos,*
> *ego eram decus olei . . .*
> *ego nunc deum ministra*
> *et Cybeles famula ferar?*
> *ego Maenas, ego mei pars,*
> *ego vir sterilis ero?*

14. cf. Apuleius on Isis, below.
15. Ovid, Fasti IV. 215–216:

> *cur huic*
> *genus acre leonum*
> *praebent insolitas*
> *ad iuga curva iubas?*

16. v. Louvre figure MA 2604, a marble Cybele with a small lion in her lap. The figure dates from the fourth to the third centuries BCE. cf. Godwin (1981) figure 76: Cybele riding a lion.
17. Apuleius, Metamorphoses XI.2:

> *Regina caeli,*
> *sive tu Ceres alma . . .*
> *seu tu caelestis Venus . . .*
> *seu Phoebi soror . . .*
> *seu . . . Proserpina triformi facie . . .*
> *quoque nomine, quoque ritu,*
> *quaque facie,*
> *te fas est invocare . . .*

18. v. the bronze figure of Isis with her son Horus, Louvre, Room 248, 7th–4th centuries BCE. cf. the silver statuette of Isis Fortuna from Macon, 1st–3rd centuries CE. British Museum, No. 1824.4–26.5.
19. Apuleius, Metamorphoses XI.3:

> *Iam primum*
> *crines uberrimi prolixique*
> *et sensim intorti*
> *per divina colla*
> *passive dispersi molliter defluebant.*
> *Corona multiformis variis floribus*
> *sublimem destrinxerat verticem,*
> *cuius media quidem super frontem*
> *plana rotunditas in modum speculi*
> *vel immo argumentum lunae*
> *candidum lumen emicabat,*
> *dextra laevaque sulcis*
> *insurgentium viperarum cohibita,*
> *spicis etiam Cerialibus desuper porrectis.*

20. Ibid XI.4.
21. Ibid XI.5:

> *adsum . . . rerum naturae parens,*
> *elementorum omnium domina,*
> *saeculorum progenies initialis,*
> *summa numinum . . .*
> *deorum dearum facies uniformis . . .*

22. Tacitus, Annals II.85:

> *. . . quattuor milia libertini generis*
> *ea superstitione infecta,*
> *quis idonea aetas,*
> *in insulam Sardiniam veherentur . . .*
> *ceteri cederent Italia,*
> *nisi certam ante diem*
> *profanos ritus exuissent.*

However, this "superstition" may also have referred to the Jewish religion, rather than to the Egyptian.

23. v. above on the Roman Isis; further, v. Larousse (1965): 47, a bronze statuette of Isis suckling Horus; fourth to second centuries BCE. v. also Budge (1904; 1969) II, plate 35. Regarding traits shared by Isis and the Virgin Mary, v. Begg (1985): 13 ff.
24. In the "Chryses," a play by Pacuvius (220 BCE to *ca.* 132 BCE) which may use some material from Euripides' "Iphigeneia in Tauris," the goddess Artemis is known as Diana.
25. v. Chapter Ten, above.
26. Statius, Silvae III.55–60:

   Iamque dies aderat,
   . . . cum . . .
   fumat Aricinum Triviae nemus
   et face multa
   conscius Hippolyti splendet lacus;
   ipsa coronat
   emeritos Diana canes
   et spicula terget
   et tutas sinit ire feras,
   omnisque pudicis
   Itala terra focis
   Hecateidas excolit idus.

27. cf. also Frazer (1935): 1–3.
28. Pausanias, Description of Greece II.27.4, on Corinth:

   Ἱππόλυτον . . .
   ἐς Ἰταλίαν ἔρχεται
   παρὰ τοὺς Ἀρικιεῖς,
   καὶ ἐβασίλευσέ τε αὐτόθι
   καὶ ἀνῆκε τῇ Ἀρτέμιδι τέμενος,
   ἔνθα ἄχρι ἐμοῦ
   μονομαχίας ἆθλα ᾗν
   καὶ ἱερᾶσθαι τῇ θεῷ
   τὸν νικῶντα·

29. Ovid, Fasti III.271–272:

   regna tenent fortes
   manibus pedibusque fugaces,
   et perit exemplo postmodo
   quisque suo.

30. v. Eisler (1987): *passim*.
31. Diana's name may be derived from the Latin term for "divinity," **divios*; cf. Latin *dius*, "divine." If so, there are two Eastern European terms that would be cognate with *Diana*: Rumanian *zīna*, "fairy," and Albanian *zane*, "mountain-fairy." Both fairies and witches work magic, and both are no doubt descendants of earlier goddesses, rendered less potent than the more august goddesses through the attrition of time and the workings of male-god-centered cultures.
32. Plutarch, Moralia 318 A–B, on "The Fortune of the Romans:"

   τὸ δ' ὑμνούμενον ἐκεῖνο
   τοῦ πλούτου κέρας
   ἔχει διὰ χειρός,
   οὐκ ὀπώρας ἀεὶ θαλλούσης μεστόν,
   ἀλλ' ὅσα φέρει πᾶσα γῆ
   πᾶσα δὲ θάλαττα
   καὶ ποταμοὶ καὶ μέταλλα
   καὶ λιμένες,
   ἄφθονα καὶ ῥύδην ἐπιχεαμένη.

33. Horace, Carmina XXXV.1–4:

   O Diva . . .
   praesens vel imo tollere de gradu

mortale corpus vel superbos
vertere funeribus triumphos . . .

34. Ibid XXXV.13–16:

iniurioso ne pede proruas
stantem columnam . . .
concitet imperiumque frangat.

35. <u>C.I.L.</u> XIV (1887) 2863:

. . . Fortuna Diovo Fili . . .
Primogenia
donom dedi.

cf. similar inscriptions in this volume, Nos. 2849–2888.

36. Ibid I^1 page 339, municipal and private inscriptions:

. . . Fortunae prim[i]g(eniae),
utro eorum die oraclum patet . . .

37. Propertius, <u>Elegies</u> IV.8.3–14:

Lanuvium annosi vetus est
tutela draconis . . .
. . . cum pabula poscit
annua
et ex ima sibila
torquet humo.
talia demissae pallent
ad sacra puellae . . .
huc mea detonsis avecta est
Cynthia mannis:
causa fuit Juno . . .

38. Aelian, <u>On Animals</u> XI.16:

οὐκοῦν ἐν τῷ Λαουινίῳ
ἄλσος τιμᾶται
μέγα καὶ δασύ,
καὶ ἔχει πλησίον νεὼν
Ἥρας Ἀργολίδος.
ἐν δὲ τῷ ἄλσει
φωλεός ἐστι μέγας καὶ βαθύς,
καὶ ἔστι κοίτη δράκοντος.
παρθένοι τε ἱεραὶ
νενομισμέναις ἡμέραις
παρίασιν ἐς τὸ ἄλσος
ἐν τοῖν χεροῖν
φέρουσαι μάζαν . . .
καὶ ἐὰν μὲν παρθένοι ὦσι,
προσίεται τὰς τροφὰς [ἅτε] ἁγνὰς
ὁ δράκων . . .
εἰ δὲ μή,
ἄπαστοι μένουσι . . .
καὶ ἥ γε τὴν παρθενίαν αἰσχύνασα
ταῖς ἐκ τοῦ νόμου
κολάζεται τιμωρίαις.

39. Ovid, <u>Fasti</u> II.443–446:

augur erat . . .
ille caprum mactat,
iussae sua terga puellae

pellibus exsectis percutienda dabant.

40. Ibid VI.58–63:

. . . suburbani dant mihi munus idem . . .
nemoralis Aricia . . .
et populus Laurens
Lanuviumque meum . . .
Tibur
et Praenestinae moenia
sacra deae:
Iunonale leges tempus.

41. Ibid VI.27:

est aliquid nupsisse Iovi,
Iovis esse sororem . . .

42. Vergil, Aeneid XII.791:

. . . rex omnipotentis Olympi . . .

43. Ibid XII.793:

. . . coniunx . . .

44. cf. Ovid, Fasti II.177 ff, where Juno changed Callisto into a bear; and Fasti VI.487 ff, where Juno caused Ino's husband to go insane and subsequently murder his son.
45. C.I.L. XIV.2091:

. . . Iunoni S.M.R . . .

46. Ibid XIV.2090:

. . . Iunone Seispitei
Matri Reginae . . .

47. Ovid, Fasti III.245 ff; cf. Horace, Carmina III.4.59.
48. C.I.L. I^2, No. 359, bronze tablet from Norba:

Iunone Locina dono
pro C. Rutilio P.f.

cf. Ibid Nos. 360 and 362.
49. Ovid, Fasti III.256:

tu voto parturientis ades.

50. Ibid VI.37–38:

"Cur igitur Regina vocor,
princepsque dearum?
Aurea cur dextrae sceptra
dedere meae?"

51. Ibid II.55–56:

Principio mensis
Phrygiae contermina Matri
Sospita delubris dicitur
aucta novis.

52. Cicero, Pro Murena 41.90:

Iunonis sospitae,
cui omnes consules
facere necesse est . . .

53. The Etruscans borrowed Juno, calling her *uni*. In the bilingual Punic-Etruscan dedication found in the harbor town of Pyrgi, in Etruria, she was identified with the "Great"-goddess, Ashtarte, v. Pfiffig (1965).
54. Vergil, Aeneid II.150 ff.
55. Ovid, Fasti III.5–6:

ipse vides manibus peragi
fera bella Minervae:
num minus ingenuis artibus
illa vacat?

56. Ibid III.7–8.
57. Vergil, Aeneid II.225–227:

at gemini lapsu delubra
ad summa dracones
effugiunt saevaeque petunt
Tritonidis arcem,
sub pedibusque deae
clipeique sub orbe teguntur.

According to Herodotus IV.180, Athena (by Vergil's extension, Minerva) was the daughter of Poseidon and the Tritonian Lake, in Libya. She was therefore called the Tritonian goddess. v. also Endnotes, Chapter Ten, above.

58. v. Hofmann II 1938): 90–91; the Etruscan triad *Tinia, Uni, Menerva* reached Rome in the sixth century BCE.
59. Valerius Maximus VIII.15.12:

quo facilius virginum mulierumque mens
a libidine ad pudicitiam
converteretur . . .

60. Ovid, Fasti IV.93–95.
61. Ibid I.40:

Haec generis princeps . . .

62. Apuleius, Metamorphoses IV.30:

. . . elementorum origo initialis . . .
orbis totius
alma Venus.

63. Propertius, Elegies IV.5.65:

. . . Venus O Regina . . .

64. Horace, Carmina I.xxx.1:

O Venus,
regina Cnidi Paphique . . .

65. *Psyche* means "spirit, soul, mind" in Greek, so the love-affair between Psyche and Cupid was one between "spirit" and "love."
66. Apuleius, Metamorphoses IV.29:

arae viduae
frigido cinere foedatae.

67. Ibid IV.30:

iam faxo huius etiam
ipsius inlicitae formisitatis paeniteat.

68. Ibid IV.33:

saevum atque ferum vipereumque malum,
quod pinnis volitans super aethera cuncta fatigat . . .

69. Note that Psyche, who was dressed as a corpse, had her mortal clothing removed. She was thus discovered by Cupid, who took her to his palace. Similarly, the Baltic Eglė took off her clothes and went swimming. When she returned to her clothes, the serpent was sitting upon them. Both young girls, when divested of their mortal clothing, aroused the interest of the young god in serpent-disguise. v. Chapter One, above, for the story of Eglė and the serpent.
70. Apuleius, Metamorphoses VI.23:

nuptalibus pedicis

71. Ibid:

> *''teneat, possideat,*
> *amplexus Psychen semper suis amoribus perfruatur.''*

72. In Aeschylus' play, the "Agamemnon," the Trojan Cassandra and the Greek Clytaemnestra are pitted against one another in similar manner, when, on the contrary, they should have united against the cruelty and dominance of Agamemnon.

PART THREE: CHAPTER TWELVE

1. If he did not marry the king's daughter, he must marry the ruler's wife or wives. In the Ancient Near East, a victor would often acquire the harem of the former king, and he would thus legitimize his takeover of the throne. v. Lerner (1986): 70; 256, footnote 41.
2. Her name, which has reference to a flower rich in honey, or to an intoxicating drink made from honey, is probably related to that of the Irish *Medb*. v. below.
3. *rāja-lakṣmī*. v. Monier-Williams 874.
4. v. Chapter Six, above.
5. In many ancient cultures, among them the ancient Hebrews, daughters received an inheritance in the form of a dowry. Thus, property *per se* passed from man to man, but it passed *through* women. v. Lerner (1986): 107–109, discussing the Hebrew Covenant Code (Exodus 21: 2–11).
6. Sophocles, "Oedipus the King" 579–580:

> ΚΡ: *ἄρχεις δ' ἐκείνῃ*
> *ταὐτὰ γῆς ἴσον νέμων;*
> ΟΙΔ: *ἃν ᾖ θέλουσα*
> *πάντ' ἐμοῦ κομίζεται.*

7. Elizabeth Barber, in an unpublished paper, gives the metaphor of Laertes as "dowager king," consigned to spend his time tending the vineyard after the death of the queen.
8. Hera too *could have been* a sovereignty figure. When the monstrous Typhoeus wanted to take over the kingdom of Zeus, he intended to take over Hera as well. Thus Typhoeus would have legitimized his hold on the throne. v. Nonnos, Dionysiaca II.314–333.
9. Hesiod, Catalogues of Women 68.99–100:

> . . . *Μενέλαος πλεῖστα πορών.*

10. Proclus, Chrestomathy in Homer, Opera, ed. Munro (1912–1919): 102–103.
11. v. Chapter Thirteen, below.
12. v. Glob (1970): 167; figures 53, 58, 59.
13. The mist probably represents separation of this world from the other world.
14. v. Chapter Six, above.
15. Baile in Scail 8 (Thurneysen, ed. (1936a) 220:

> . . . *ba sii ind ingen* . . .
> *flaith Herenn.*

16. This is called *dergflaith.*
17. Baile in Scail, *passim.*
18. Niall was high-king of Ireland 379–405 CE.
19. "Echtra mac Echdach Mugmedóin" 35 (LL 4580–4583 [p.34 a]):

> *Eces senmna fora brú.*
>
> *bel aicce i tallfad cú*
> *clethchur fiacal imma cend.*
> *grannu anathu Her*[end].

20. v. Quin (1976) II: 124.
21. LL 4668–4671 [p.34 b]:

> *In lind ara tánac cend* . . .
> *bid buaid do dig a dind chuirn,*
> *bid mid bid mil bid morch*[uirm].

22. v. Chapter Eight, above.
23. Quin (1976) III: 78.
24. Ibid II.160. cf. Welsh *gwlad,* "land."
25. Ibid II.161; cf. Dineen (1927): 462.
26. Scéla Cano Meic Gartnáin 452–453, ed. Binchy (1963).

niba rí aran Érind
mani toro coirm Chualand.

27. LL 6416 [p. 44 b]:

Medb Lethderg
ingen Chonáin Chualand . . .

28. "Cath Boinde Andso," ed. O'Neill (1905) 182. [Book of Lecan 351 b–353 a]:

do deoin Meadba . . .

29. Ibid. Further, on Medb and Ailill, v. Chapter Eight, above.
30. Ibid:

Is an aimsir sin
tainic Ailill, mac Mata
mic Sraibgind, do Ernaib,
co Cruachain, ⁊
ba leanb óc Ailill
in tan sin . . .

31. Ibid:

na rigi ⁊ a mna.

32. O'Máille (1927): 137 [LL p. 380 a]:

Roba mor tra nert
⁊ cumachta Meidhbhe insin
for firu Erenn
air isi na leigedh
ri a Temair gan a beth
fein aigi na mnái . . .

33. "Esnada Tige Buchet," "The Songs of Buchet's House," LL 35383–35384 [p. 270 b]:

i fail Airt ro boí
in Medb Lethderg do Laignib.
⁊ arrobertside in rige
iar n-ecaib Airt.

34. Procopius, History of the Wars VIII.20.20:

'Ράδιγις δὲ ὁ παῖς
ξυνοικιζέσθω τῇ μητρυιᾷ
τὸ λοιπὸν τῇ αὑτοῦ,
καθάπερ ὁ πάτριος
ἡυῖν ἐφίησι νόμος.

35. v. Freeman (1867) I.410 ff.
36. v. Chapter Nine, above.
37. Nibelungenlied VI.2–6:

Ez was ein küneginne
gesezzen über sê,
ir geliche enheine
man wesse ninder mê
diu was unmâzen scœne,
vil michel was ir kraft.
si scôz mit snellen denegen
umbe mínne den scaft.

Den stein den warf si verre,
dar nâch si witen spranc.
swer ir mínne gerte,
der muose âne wanc
driu spil an gewinnen
der frouwen wol geborn.
gebrast im an dem einen,

er hete daz houbet sin verloren . . .

Dô sprach der vogt von Rine:
''Ich wil nider an den sê
hin ze Prünhilde,
swi ez mir ergê . . . ''

38. v. Chapter Nine, above.
39. cf. the Greek Pelias and the "barbarian" witch, Medea, in Chapter Thirteen, below.
40. "One Hundred and One Brothers and One Hundred and One Stallions," in Korsakas (1954) 321:

tada tas maželis
vedė tą paną
ir karaliavo . . .
O po mirties karalystę
paliko savo vaikams.

41. "A Sackful of Words," in Zobarskas (1958): 112–118.
42. v. Robbins (1978): 31–39.
43. Plutarch, Moralia 246F:

οἱ δὲ τὰ ξίφη λαβόντες
ἐπέθεντο τοῖς βαρβάροις . . .

44. Homer, Iliad VI. 490–493:

" . . . ἀλλ' εἰς οἶκον ἰοῦσα
τὰ σ' αὐτῆς ἔργα κόμιζε,
ἱστόν τ' ἠλακάτην τε,
καὶ ἀμφιπόλοισι κέλευε
ἔργον ἐποίχεσθαι·
πόλεμος δ' ἄνδρεσσι μελήσει
πᾶσι, μάλιστα δ' ἐμοί,
τοὶ Ἰλίῳ ἐγγεγάασιν."

45. Ibid, Odyssey XI. 537:

ἐπιμὶξ δέ τε
μαίνεται Ἄρης.

46. Ibid VIII. 309:

. . . ἀίδηλον Ἄρηα . . .

That is, Ares destroys so thoroughly that he makes one "unseen."

47. Ibid XXIV.520:

Ὣς φάτο,
καί ῥ' ἔμπνευσε μένος μέγα
Παλλὰς Ἀθήνη . . .

48. Ibid XX.49–51:

εἴ περ πεντήκοντα λόχοι
μερόπων ἀνθρώπων
νῶϊ περισταῖεν,
κτεῖναι μεμαῶτες Ἄρηϊ,
καί κεν τῶν ἐλάσαιο βόας
καὶ ἴφια μῆλα.

49. Xenophon, Hellenica IV.2.20:

οὐκέτι δὲ στάδιον ἀπεχόντων,
σφαγιασάμενοι οἱ Λακεδαιμόνιοι
τῇ Ἀγροτᾳ,
ὥσπερ νομίζεται,
τὴν χίμαιραν,
ἡγοῦντο ἐπὶ τοὺς ἐναντίους . . .

50. Pausanias, Description of Greece IV.13.1, on Messenia:

τό τε γὰρ τῆς Ἀρτέμιδος ἄγαλμα,
ὃν χαλκοῦν
καὶ αὐτὸ καὶ τὰ ὅπλα . . .

51. Aulus Gellius, Attic Nights XIII.xxiii.7–10:

. . . "Nerio" sive "Nerienes" . . .
Sabinum verbum est,
eoque significatur virtus et fortitudo . . .
"Nerio" igitur Martis vis et potentia
et maiestas quaedam
esse Martis demonstratur.

52. Porphyrion, Commentum in Horatium Flaccum, Epistles II.2,209:

. . . a Minerva Mars victus est,
et . . . Minerva Neriene est appellata.

53. Plautus, "Truculentus" 515:

Mars peregre adveniens
salutat Nerienem uxorem suam.

54. To *Nerio* compare Sanskrit *nara*, "man;" Greek ἀνήρ, "man" (both the Sanskrit and the Greek terms indicate *heroic* man); and the Germanic goddess *Nerthus*.
55. "Tochmarc Emire" in Van Hamel (1956) 70:

.i. a forcetal cen díchell . . .
⁊ epert fris nech aridmbai,
ar ba fáithsi.

56. v. the "Macgnimartha Find," the "Boyhood Deeds of Finn," 4; text in Meyer (1881–1883): 198.
57. v. Chapter Eight, above.
58. Diodorus Siculus, Bibliothecae V.32.2:

Αἱ δὲ γυναῖκες τῶν Γαλατῶν
οὐ μόνον τοῖς μεγέθεσι
παραπλήσιοι τοῖς ἀνδράσιν εἰσίν,
ἀλλὰ καὶ
ταῖς ἀλκαῖς ἐνάμιλλοι.

59. Ammianus Marcellinus, History XV.12.1:

. . . multo se fortiore
et glauca . . .
illa inflata cervice suffrendens,
ponderansque niveas ulnas et vastas,
admixtis calcibus emittere coeperit pugnos . . .

60. Tacitus, Agricola XVI.
61. Ibid; Tacitus, Annals XIV.31,35,37.
62. v. Chapter Eight, above.
63. v. Chapter Seven, above.
64. Devī māhātmyam XI. 44–45:

Bhakṣayantyāśca tānugrān . . . mahāsurān
raktā dantā bhaviṣyanti
dāḍimīkusumopamāḥ

tato mām devatāḥ svarge
martyaloke ca mānavāḥ
stuvanto vyāhariṣyanti satataṁ
raktadantikām.

65. v. Chapter Eight, above.
66. Avesta, Yašt V. 131:

āaṯ
. . . ardvī sūre anāhite
duva aurvanta yāsāmi
yimca bi-paitištānəm [aurvantəm],
yimca caϑwar-paitištānəm:
a-om bi-paitištānəm
aurvantəm, yō anhat āsuš
uzgąstō hufrao-urvaēsō
vāšå pəšanaēsŭca . . .

67. v. Chapter Nine, above.
68. Eyvind Skáldaspillir, Hákonarmál 32.1, transmitted by Snorri Sturluson in the Heimskringla:

Gǫndul ok Skǫgul
sendi Gautatýr
at kjósa of konunga,
hverr Yngva ættar,
skyldi með Oðni fara
ok í Valhǫll at vesa.

69. v. also Chapter Nine, above.
70. Nibelungenlied VII. 428:

si hiez ir gewinnen
ze strîte guot gewant,
eine brünne rôtes goldes
unt einen guoten schildes rant.

71. Saxo Grammaticus, Gesta Danorum XXXVI[b]:

. . . Rusilam virginem
militari voto
res bellicas emulatam
armis oppressit,
virilemque gloriam
ex muliebri hoste corripuit.

72. Tacitus, Germania 7.4:

. . . ad matres, ad coniuges
vulnera ferunt:
nec illae numerare aut exigere
plagas pavent,
cibosque et hortamina
pugnantibus gestant.

73. Ibid 8.2–3:

. . . nec aut consilia earum aspernantur
aut responsa neglegunt.

PART THREE: CHAPTER THIRTEEN

1. "Great"-goddesses personified the totality of energy; they embraced all goods within the life force, and, if they wished, they could cut off that force. They thus represented both the dispensation and the expropriation of energy: they brought both life and death. Because a "Great"-goddess was so powerful, she not only bestowed energy upon men; she also retained power for herself.
2. Táin Bó Cuailnge 1186–1192 (LL page 67b):

. . . in bantrocht da lécud
immach do ṡaigid in meic
.i. trí coícait ban
.i. deich mnáa ⁊ secht fichit díscir
derglomnocht i n-óenfecht uili
⁊ a mbantóesech rempo, Scandlach,
do thócbáil a nnochta ⁊ a nnáre dó.
Táncatar immach in banmaccrad uile
⁊ túargbatar a nnochta
⁊ a nnáre uile dó.
Foilgid in mac a gnúis forru
⁊ dobretha a dreich frisin carpat
arná acced nochta nó náre na mban.

3. Plutarch, Moralia 248 A–B:

. . . εἰς τὴν θάλατταν ἐμβὰς
εὔξατο κατ' αὐτοῦ τῷ Ποσειδῶνι
τὴν χώραν ἄκαρπον γενέσθαι

καὶ ἀνόνητον.
εἶθ' ὁ μὲν ἀπῄει κατευξάμενος,
κῦμα δὲ διαρθὲν
ἐπέκλυζε τὴν γῆν·
καὶ θέαμα δεινὸν ἦν,
ἑπομένες μετεώρου τῆς θαλάττης
καὶ ἀποκρυπτούσης τὸ πεδίον.
ἐπεὶ δέ,
τῶν ἀνδρῶν δεομένων
τὸν Βελλεροφόντην ἐπισχεῖν,
οὐδὲν ἔπειθον,
αἱ γυναῖκες ἀνασυράμεναι
τοὺς χιτωνίσκους
ἀπήντησαν αὐτῷ·
πάλιν οὖν ὑπ' αἰσχύνης
ἀναχωροῦντος ὀπίσω
καὶ τὸ κῦμα λέγεται συνυποχωρῆσαι.

4. However, in another tale, the "Mesca Ulad," the "Intoxication of the Ulstermen" (lines 1040–1043), the hero was stymied when the female satirist, *Riches*, took off her clothes before him. He hid his face, so that he might not see her nakedness. The Celtic hero needed to be *in control* of his own sexuality.
5. v. Pandian (1982) 181: in South Indian Tamil society, chaste women were believed to possess a sacred power.
6. v. (Robbins) Dexter (1985): 57–74.
7. cf. Vergil, Aeneid I.345: Dido had been *intacta* as a maiden. It is significant, with regard to the "maiden"-state, that Lat. *vidua*, "widow" and *virgo* came to be used interchangeably. v. Juvenal, Satires IV.4, where *vidua* means "unwedded." *Vidua*, indeed, is cognate with Greek ἠίθεος, "bachelor."
8. v. Chapter Eleven, above, on the sacred snakes and the virgins of Lanuvium.
9. Homeric Hymn V.81–82 [to Aphrodite]:

. . . Ἀφροδίτη
παρθένῳ ἀδμήτῃ
μέγεθος καὶ εἶδος ὁμοίη . . .

10. Ibid 133:

ἀδμήτην . . .
καὶ ἀπειρήτην φιλότητος . . .

ἀδμήτην comes from ἀ + δαμάω, literally "not tamed, unsubdued." Thus, to marry a woman, among the Greeks, was to *subdue* her, to *bring her under the yoke.*

11. Vergil, Aeneid I.315:

virginis os habitumque gerens . . .

12. v. Roscher (1884–1886) I: 559, 571.
13. Pausanias, Description of Greece I.38.6, on Attica:

Ἐλευσινίοις δὲ ἔστι μὲν
Τριπτολέμου ναός,
ἔστι δὲ Προπυλαίας Ἀρτέμιδος
καὶ Ποσειδῶνος Πατρός . . .

14. Ibid VIII.30.10, on Arcadia:

ἔστιν . . .
ἱερὸν Σωτῆρος ἐπίκλησιν Διός·
. . . καθεζομένῳ δὲ τῷ Διὶ ἐν θρόνῳ
παρεστήκασι τῇ μὲν ἡ Μεγάλη πόλις,
ἐν ἀριστερᾷ δὲ
Ἀρτέμιδος Σωτείρας ἄγαλμα.

15. Ibid VII.19.1, on Achaia:

. . . ναὸς Ἀρτέμιδος
Τρικλαρίας ἐπίκλησιν . . .
ἱερωσύνην δὲ εἶχε
τῆς θεοῦ παρθένος,

ἐς ὅ ἀποστέλλεσθαι
παρὰ ἄνδρα ἔμελλε.

16. v. Chapter Ten, above.
17. v. Chapter Six, above.
18. Rigveda VI.49.7:

. . . *pāvīravī* . . .

19. v. Chapter Ten, above. This androgenetic birth is evidence, not of Indo-European assimilation, but of patriarchal Near-Eastern assimilation. This birth is parallel to that of the Hittite-Hurrian river Aranzah/Tigris/Ishtar, the Phoenician Ashtarte, and perhaps the Babylonian River, sister of Son of Sea, in the Near-Eastern Kingship in Heaven myths.
20. Homeric Hymn V.21–28, to Aphrodite:

οὐδὲ μὲν αἰδοίῃ κούρῃ
ἅδε ἔργ' Ἀφροδίτης,
Ἱστίῃ . . .
ὤμοσε δὲ μέγαν ὅρκον . . .
παρθένος ἔσσεσθαι
πάντ' ἤματα . . .

21. Vestals have attended a sacred fire in many cultures throughout the world. v. Frazer II (1935): 243–246.
22. v. Farnell V (1896): 352.
23. Ovid, Fasti VI.287–294:

utraque nupserunt . . .
de tribus impatiens
restitit una viri . . .
nec tu aliud Vestam quam vivam
intellege flammam,
nataque de flamma corpora nulla vides.
Iure igitur virgo est,
quae semina nulla remittit
nec capit
et comites virginitatis amat.

24. Ibid VI.457–460:

''nullaque dicitur vittas temerasse sacerdos
hoc duce nec viva defodietur humo.
Sic incesta perit,
quia quam violavit, in illam
conditur,
et Tellus Vestaque numen idem.''

25. Plutarch, Vitae Parallelae "Romulus" III.2–3:

. . . ἱέρειαν τῆς Ἑστίας
ἀπέδειξεν
ἄγαμον καὶ παρθένον
ἀεὶ βιωσομένην.

26. Ovid, Fasti III.24–25:

. . . iacet ipsa gravis:
iam scilicet intra
viscera Romanae conditor urbis erat.

27. Ibid III.45–46:

. . . Vestae simulacra feruntur
virgineas oculis opposuisse manus . . .

28. Ibid III.47:

ara deae certe tremuit
pariente ministra . . .

29. v. L. Annaeus Florus, Epitome I.1.
30. Tacitus, Annals II.86:

rettulit . . . capiendam virginem
in locum Occiae,
quae septem et quinquaginta per annos
summa sanctimonia
Vestalibus sacris praesederat.

31. v. Ó Cathasaigh (1982) 86, for discussion regarding Saint Brigid as the euhemerization of the ancient goddess.
32. Geraldus Cambrensis, "De Igne A Brigida Sua Nocte Servato;" text is in Proceedings of the Royal Irish Academy Vol. 52 Sect. C, No. 4 (1948) 150:

Cum tempore Brigide xx moniales hic Domino militassent,
ipsa vicesima existente . . .
Cum vero singulis noctibus
singule per ordinem ignem custodiant,
nocte vicesima monialis ultima . . .
inquit: ''Brigida, custodi ignem tuum . . . ''
Et sic, igne relicto . . .
inextinctus reperitur.

33. Text is in Ross (1976): 129.
34. v. Chapter Four, above.
35. S. Rostowski (Eighteenth Century) in Mannhardt (1936) 435:

Perkuno ignem in sylvis sacrum,
vestales Romanas imitati,
perpetuum alebant.

36. The terms for the Lithuanian priests and priestesses may be derived from Proto-Indo-European **weid*, "to know." cf. Sanskrit *Veda*.
37. v. Mannhardt (1936): 222.
38. Rev. Juozas Tumas Vaižgantas, "The Marian," transl. by Rev. A. P. Naudžiūnas, in Beliajus (1954): 72.
39. Vergil, Aeneid VI.44–46:

Sibyllae . . .
virgo, ''poscere fata
tempus'' ait: ''deus, ecce, deus!''

40. Pindar, Pythia XI. 31–33:

Ἀτρείδας . . .
μάντιν τ' ὄλεσσε κόραν . . .

v. also Aeschylus, "Agamemnon" 1202 ff, for the story of Cassandra and Apollo.

41. Apuleius, The Golden Ass IV.28:

Venerem aliam
virginali flore praeditam . . .

cf. Chapter Eleven, above.

42. Pomponius Mela, Chorographia III.6.48:

cuius antistites perpetua virginitate sanctae
numero novem esse traduntur:
Gallizenas vocant,
putantque ingeniis singularibus praeditas
maria ac ventos concitare carminibus,
seque in quae velint animalia vertere,
sanare quae apud alios insanabilia sunt,
scire ventura et praedicare . . .

43. v. Chapter Three, above.
44. Mabinogi IV.

45. v. Curtin (1975) 105–109.
46. v. Chapter Nine, and Chapter Twelve, above.
47. Ibid.
48. Snorri, "Gylfaginning" 36:

. . . Gefjon,
hon er mœr,
ok henni þjóna
þær er meyjar andast.

49. Mahābhārata V.114.13:

Kriyatāṁ mama saṁhāro
gurvartha dvijasattama;
eṣā tāvan mama prajñā
yathā vā manyase dvija.

50. Ibid V.114.21:

Kumārī kāmato bhūtvā . . .

51. Ibid I.175.10:

. . . tasyānavadyāṅgī draupadī tanumadhyamā
nīlotpalasamo gandho yasyāḥ kośāt . . .

52. Ibid I.178.11:

vyāyacchamānā dadṛśurbhramantīṁ
saṁdaṣṭadantacchadatāmravakrāḥ.

53. Ibid I.182.2:

. . . bhuṅkṣeti sametya sarve.

54. Ibid I.190.14:

idaṁ ca tatrādbhutarūpamuttamaṁ
jagāda viprarṣiratītamānuṣam;
mahānubhāvā kila sā sumadhyamā
babhūva kanyaiva gate gate'hani.

55. Pausanias, Description of Greece II.38.2–3, on Corinth:

. . . ἐν Ναυπλίᾳ καὶ πηγὴ
Κάναθος καλουμένη·
ἐνταῦθα τὴν Ἥραν
φασὶν Ἀργεῖοι
κατὰ ἔτος λουμένην
παρθένον γίνεσθαι.

56. v. Inscriptiones Graecae XIV.665:

τᾶς θε[οῦ τᾶς] παιδός ἠμί.

"To the goddess, to the Child,
I belong."

57. v. Plutarch, Moralia 264 B:

Διὸς τελείου καὶ Ἥρας τελείας . . .

"Zeus Perfect and Hera Perfect . . . "

The Greek term τέλειος is derived from τέλος, "an end accomplished," "completion."
58. Pausanias, Description of Greece VIII.22.2, on Arcadia:

παρθένῳ μὲν ἔτι οὔσῃ Παιδί,
γημαμένην δὲ τῷ
ἐκάλεσεν αὐτὴν Τελείαν,
διενεχθεῖσαν δὲ ἐφ' ὅτῳ δὴ
ἐς τὸν Δία
καὶ ἐπανήκουσαν
ἐς τὴν Στύμφαλον
ὠνόμασεν ὁ Τήμενος Χήραν.

59. Aristotle, History of Animals VII.2 (582 a–b).
60. Homeric Hymn V.44, to Aphrodite:

. . . αἰδοίην ἄλοχον . . .
κέδν' εἰδυῖαν.

61. v. Callimachus, Aetia III, fragment 66.2–3:

. . . Ἥρης
ἁγνὸν . . . πάτος . . .

62. Apuleius, Metamorphoses VI.4.
63. According to Lommel (1954): 412–413, the original name of the Old Iranian goddess Anāhitā was **Harahvati*; cf. Avest. *Haraxvaiti*, Old Persian *hara[h]uvati*. *Harahvati is not attested as the name of a goddess, but is the name of the region, Arachosia. Perhaps the region was a watery one, thus giving rise to the river-goddesses which became Anāhitā and Sarasvatī v. Puhvel (1978): 356.
64. cf. the Irish Brigid, above.
65. Rigveda IX.67.32:

tasmai sarasvatī duhe
kṣīram sarpirmadhūdakaṁ.

66. Avesta, Yašt V.1:

. . . vaϑwō.frāδanąm ašaonīm
gaēϑō.frāδanąm . . .

67. Ibid V.2:

. . . vīspanąm aršnąm
xšudrå yaožda δāiti . . .
vīspanąm hāirišinąm zaϑāi
garəwąn yaoždaδāiti . . .

68. Ibid V.130:

. . . upa stṛmaēšu vārəma daiδe
parnaŋhvaṭ vīspąm hujyāitīm,
uruδyəntəm xšaϑrəm zazāite.

69. But v. Widengren (1965): 179. Further, in the Iranian Shahnamah, Gushtasp's *wife* was Nahid. Anāhitā thus, in the later literature, lost her virginity.
70. v. Chapter Six, above; v. Duchesne-Guillemin (1952): 15.
71. v. Chapter Six, above.
72. Ibid.
73. Rigveda VI.49.7:

pāvīravī kanyā
citrāyuḥ sarasvatī
vīrapatnī
dhiyaṁ dhāt.

74. Avesta, Yašt V. 126:

yā hištaite fravaēδəmna
Arədvī Sūrā Anāhitā
kaininō kəhrpa srīrayå . . .

75. cf. Widengren (1965): 123.
76. cf. Bartholomae (1961): 125.
77. Hesiod, Theogony 927–928:

Ἥρη δ' Ἥφαιστον κλυτὸν
οὐ φιλότητι μιγεῖσα
γείνατο,
καὶ ζαμένησε
καὶ ἤρισε
ᾧ παρακοίτῃ . . .

78. Homeric Hymn III.306–309, to Apollo:

. . . Τυφάονα . . .
ὅν ποτ' ἄρ' Ἥρη ἔτικτε
χολωσαμένη Διὶ πατρί,

ἥνικ᾽ ἄρα Κρονίδης
ἐρικυδέα γείνατ᾽ Ἀθήνην
ἐν κορυφῇ·

79. Ibid III.326–329:

καὶ νῦν μέντοι
ἐγὼ τεχνήσομαι,
ὥς κε γένηται
παῖς ἐμός,
ὅς κε θεοῖσι μεταπρέποι ἀθανάτοισιν,
οὔτε σὸν αἰσχύνασ᾽ ἱερὸν λέχος
οὔτ᾽ ἐμὸν αὐτῆς.
οὐδέ τοι εἰς εὐνὴν πωλήσομαι . . .

80. v. Chapter Ten, above. cf. Daly (1978): 13. Remember that Zeus' androgenesis is merely patriarchal propaganda; Athena's mother simply gave birth from within Zeus' body. Daly reminds us that swallowing Metis is, in fact, "male cannibalism."
81. cf. Hesiod, Theogony 921–923.
82. Ovid, Fasti V.231–232:

sancta Iovem Iuno,
nata sine matre Minerva,
officio doluit
non eguisse suo.

83. Ibid V.256–258:

. . . tacto concipit illa sinu . . .
Marsque creatus erat.

84. v. Vermeule (1964): plate XLIII f; Gimbutas (1974): 181–185, text figures 139–146.
85. cf. Auerbach (1961): 108.
86. cf. Pindar, Pythia IV.60:

. . . μελίσσας Δελφίδος . . .

87. cf. Porphyrion, De Antro Nympharum 18 and v. Endnotes, Chapter Ten.
88. Parthenogenesis came to have a spiritual meaning. Since such a form of conception was "supernatural," one that was not effected in a carnal manner, it was considered to be more evolved, more spiritual, than normal conception.
89. v. Chapter Two, above.
90. v. Chapter Seven, above.
91. Manu Smṛtiḥ IX.8:

patirbhāryāṁ saṁpraviśya
garbho bhūtveha jāyate;
jāyāyāstaddhi jāyātvaṁ yadasyāṁ
jāyate punaḥ

92. v. Chapter Seven, above.
93. v. Apollonius Rhodius, Argonautica.
94. v. Euripides, "Medea."
95. Vergil, Aeneid I.720–722; IV.15 ff.
96. Ibid I.498–503:

qualis . . . exercet Diana choros . . .
talis erat Dido . . .

In fact, Aeneas, one thinks, forgot that Dido was anything but a *virgo intacta*. cf. West (1975) 150.

This comparison was a traditional one; cf. Apollonius Rhodius, Argonautica III. 876–885, where Medea was compared to Artemis and her nymphs, and cf. Homer, Odyssey VI. 102–109, where Nausikaa was also compared to Artemis and her nymphs. But Dido was only *compared* to a virgin; she was not, of course, a *virgo intacta*.
97. Ibid I.357–364.
98. Ibid VI.450–476.
99. Vergil's land of the dead was a shady place, peopled by shades. The Stygian boatman Charon announces, in Aeneid VI.390, that

"This is the land of the shades."

umbrarum hic locus est . . .

In Aeneid VI.452, Dido wandered *per umbras*, "through the shadows."

100. v. Chapter Eight, above.
101. cf. the modern bride, throwing the wedding bouquet into the midst of her eligible young female guests.
102. v. Proclus, Chrestomathy, in Homeri Opera, ed. Munro (1912–1919) V: 102–103.
103. v. Euripides, "Andromache" 293 ff. However, according to Apollodorus, Atheniensis Bibliothecae 3.12.5, it was Hecuba who foresaw that she would bear the "firebrand" of her city.
104. Her struggle was against superimposed patriarchy. v. Wolf (1984): 264. The inner history of Christa Wolf's Cassandra is "the struggle for autonomy."
105. v. above.
106. Demeter has been identified with her daughter, Persephone, as two aspects of the same goddess; she may thus be viewed as *maiden*; she was also *mother* of Persephone; and she was *old woman* when she sorrowed for her daughter. She therefore depicts the spectrum of woman's life.
107. Homeric Hymn II.101–102, to Demeter:

γρηὶ παλαιγενέι ἐναλίγκιος,
    ἥτε τόκοιο
εἴργηται δώρων τε
    φιλοστεφάνου Ἀφροδίτης . . .

108. v. Chapter Ten, above.
109. Helgakviða Hundingsbana I.30:

Enn þeim sidlfom
*   Sigrún ofan,*
fólcdiǫrf, um barg
*   oc fari þeira;*
snøriz ramliga
*   Rán ór hendi*
giálfrdýr konungs
*   at Gnipalundi.*

The text may be found in Kuhn (1962).

110. v. Godwin (1981) 23, figure vi: a triple Hecate, a miniature bronze altar for use in sympathetic magic; from Pergamum, 200–250 CE; Berlin, Staatliche Museum.
111. Theocritus, Idyll II.12–16:

τᾷ χθονίᾳ θ' Ἑκάτᾳ,
    τὰν καὶ σκύλακες τρομέοντι
ἐρχομέναν νεκύων ἀνά τ' ἠρία
    καὶ μέλαν αἷμα.
χαῖρ' Ἑκάτα δασπλῆτι
    καὶ ἐς τέλος ἄμμιν ὀπάδει
φάρμακα ταῦτ' ἔρδοισα
    χερείονα μήτε τι Κίρκας
μήτε τι Μηδείας
    μήτε ξανθᾶς Περιμήδας.

112. Medieval and modern witches have been both women and men.
113. Homer, Odyssey X.136:

. . . εὐπλόκαμος . . .

114. Ibid:

. . . δεινὴ θεὸς . . .

115. Ibid 212–213:

. . . λύκοι ἦσαν ὀρέστεροι
    ἠδὲ λέοντες,
τοὺς αὐτὴ κατέθελξεν,
    ἐπεὶ κακὰ φάρμακ' ἔδωκεν.

116. Ibid 221:

. . . ὀπὶ καλῇ . . .

117. In Aeneid VII.19–20, Vergil too indicates that Circe charmed by means of potent herbs. However, in Eclogues VIII.70, he contends that she transformed the men by songs (*carminibus*), associating them, perhaps, with the Sirens.
118. Homer, Odyssey XII. 89–91.
119. Ibid XII.93–99:

μέσση μέν τε κατὰ σπείους
κοίλοιο δέδυκεν,
ἔξω δ' ἐξίσχει κεφαλὰς
δεινοῖο βερέϑρον,
αὐτοῦ δ' ἰχϑυάᾳ . . .
τῇ δ' οὔ πώ ποτε ναῦται
ἀκήριοι εὐχετόωνται
παρφυγέειν σὺν νηί·

120. Vergil, Aeneid III.424–428:

at Scyllam caecis cohibet spelunca latebris
ora exsertantem
et navis in saxa trahentem.
prima hominis facies
et pulchro pectore virgo
pube tenus,
postrema immani corpore pistrix,
delphinum caudas
utero commissa luporum.

121. Scholia on Aristophanes, Wasps 1035c:

. . . Λαμία ϑηρίον . . .

122. Aristophanes, "Wasps" 1035c = "Peace" 758:

. . . Λαμίας ὄρχεις ἀπλύτους . . .

123. v. Rogers (1916) II: 158, note on Wasps 1035. The Greek *Lamia* may possibly be related to the Baltic goddess who determines the fate of children, *Laima*, or to the chthonic goddess, *Lauma*. v. Chapter Four. cf. Keats' *Lamia*, who turns into a *serpent* on her wedding night.
124. v. Hesiod, Theogony 276 ff.
125. v. Chapter Ten, above.
126. Vergil, Aeneid VI.570–572:

continuo sontis ultrix accincta flagello
Tisiphone quatit insultans,
torvosque sinistra
intentans anguis vocat agmina saeva sororum.

127. Ibid VII.341:

. . . *Gorgoneis* . . . *infecta venenis* . . .

128. Ibid VII.324–329:

. . . *Allecto* . . .
. . . *cui tristia bella*
iraeque insidiaeque et crimina noxia cordi . . .
. . . *tot sese vertit in ora,*
tam saevae facies,
tot pullulat atra colubris.

129. Ibid XII.845–848:

dicuntur geminae pestes cognomine Dirae,
quas et Tartaream Nox intempesta Megaeram
uno eodemque tulit partu,
paribusque revinxit
serpentum spiris
ventosasque addidit alas.

130. Ibid III.232:

. . . *caecisque latebris* . . .

131. Ibid III.216–218:

> *virginei volucrum voltus,*
> *foedissima ventris*
> *proluvies, uncaeque manus,*
> *et pallida semper*
> *ora fame.*

132. Homer, Odyssey XII.41–48:

> ὅς τις ἀϊδρείῃ πελάσῃ
> καὶ φθόγγον ἀκούσῃ
> Σειρήνων, τῷ δ' οὔ τι . . .
> οἴκαδε νοστήσαντι . . .
> ἀλλά τε Σειρῆνες
> λιγυρῇ θέλγουσιν ἀοιδῇ
> ἥμεναι ἐν λειμῶνι,
> πολὺς δ' ἀμφ' ὀστεόφιν θὶς
> ἀνδρῶν πυθομένων . . .
> ἀλλὰ παρεξ ελάαν,
> ἐπὶ δ' οὔατ' ἀλεῖψαι ἑταίρων
> κηρὸν δεψήσας μελιηδέα . . .

133. Rigveda V.41.17:

> *atrā śivāṁ tanvo dhāsimasyā*
> *jarāṁ cinme nirṛtirjagrasīta.*

134. v. Chapter Seven, above, on Rigveda VII.104.9.
135. Rigveda X.36.2:

> *mā durvidatrā nirṛtirna īśata . . .*

136. v. Chapter Eight, above, and v. Dineen (1927) 68.
137. "Auksaplaukis ir Auksažvaigždė," in Korsakas (1965): 459–464.
138. Ibid 467:

> *ta senoji ragana.*

139. Ibid:

> *senoji bobpalaike . . .*

cf. Lith. *boba*, "old woman," and *palaikis*, "worn-out," from *laikas*, "time."
140. Mannhardt (1936): 628. My translation from the German.
141. cf. Russian *vyedat'*, "to know."
142. v. Ralston (1872) 168.
143. Curčija-Prodanović (1957) 97–98.
144. cf. Lithuanian *boba*, "old woman, wife"; cf. Pēteraitis (1960): 45.
145. Ralston (1872) 170.
146. v. Downing (1956) 177.
147. Ibid.
148. Ibid 179.
149. v. T.G.E. Powell (1958) 152.
150. v. Chapter Seven, above.
151. v. Ehrenreich and English (1973): 4–13.
152. v. Eisler (1987): *passim* on "partnership" societies and "dominator" societies.

ABBREVIATIONS AND PHRASES

acc.	accusative
AJP	American Journal of Philology
ANET	Ancient Near Eastern Texts Relating to the Old Testament
Av.	Avesta(n)
b	born
BCE	*before the common era*, used in place of BC, "before Christ"
ca.	*circa* (about; approximately)
CE	*common era*, used in place of AD, "anno domini."
CIA	Corpus Inscriptionum Atticarum
CIL	Corpus Inscriptionum Latinarum
cf.	*confer* (compare)
col.	column
d	died
D.Mah.	Devī māhātmyam
dat.	dative
e.g.	*exempli gratia* (for example)
et al.	*et alia* (and others)
(et) passim	(and) throughout (the text or passage)
f.	feminine (gender)
fig.	figure
fl.	*floruit* (flourished, did one's major work during that time)
gen.	genitive (case)
Gk.	Greek
ibid	the same (text as in the preceding footnote)
Ir.	Irish
JAOS	Journal of the American Oriental Society
JIES	Journal of Indo-European Studies
KTU	Keilscriftliche Texte aus Ugarit
lit.	literally
LL	Book of Leinster
m.	masculine (gender)
Mbh.	Mahābhārata
neut.	neuter (gender)
O.Ir.	Old Irish
PAPS	Proceedings of the American Philosophical Society
PIE	Proto-Indo-European
pl.	plate
RIA Dict.	Dictionary of the Irish Language, Royal Irish Academy
sg.	singular
UT	Ugaritic Textbook
v.	*vide* (see)
Y.	Yašt

SELECTED BIBLIOGRAPHY

Note: The majority of the Greek and Roman texts used may be found either in Oxford Classical Texts or in the Loeb Classical Library; the latter is given in Greek-English and Latin-English. For those authors not readily available in these publications I have cited texts below.

Afanas'ev, Aleksandr Nikolaevich. *Poet'cheskiia Vozzrenia Claviani na Prirodu*. Vol I-III. Paris: Mouton, 1969–70 (Moscow: Soldateikov, 1865–69).
Akhmanova, O. S., ed. *Russko-Angliiskii Slovari*. Moscow: "Soviet Encyclopaedia,"1971.
Alexandrow, A. *Polnii Russko-Angliiskii Slovar'*. New York: Maisel, 1919.
Alexiou, Stylianos; Cressida Ridley, transl. *Minoan Civilization*. Heraklion: Alexiou Sons, 1973.
Allen, Judy and Griffiths, Jeanne. *The Book of the Dragon*. New Jersey: Chartwell, 1979.
Amiet, Pierre. *Art of the Ancient Near East*. New York: Abrams, 1980.
Auerbach, Charlotte. *The Science of Genetics*. New York: Harper, 1961.
Avalon, Arthur (Sir John Woodroffe). *Shakti and Shakta*. New York: Dover, 1978.
Balys, Jonas. *Motif-Index of Lithuanian Narrative Folk-Lore*. Kaunas: Lithuanian Folk-Lore Archives, 1936.
Bartholomae, Christian. *Altiranisches Wörterbuch*. Berlin: De Gruyter, 1904, 1961.
Basanavičius, J. *Lietuviškos Pasakos*. Shenandoah, PA: Stagaro, 1902.
Begg, Ean. *The Cult of the Black Virgin*. London: Arkana, 1985.
Beliajus, Vytutes, ed. *Vakarinė Daina (The Evening Song)*. Los Angeles: Bonnie Press, 1954.
Bergk, Theodorus, ed. *Poetae Lyrici Graeci* III. Fourth Edition. Leipzig: Teubner, 1882.
Best, R. I. and Bergin, Osborn, ed. *The Book of Leinster (LL)* I-II-III. Dublin: Thom & Co., 1954.
Biezais, Haralds. *Die Hauptgöttinnen der Alte Letten*. Uppsala: Almqvist & Wiksells, 1955.
Binchy, Daniel A. *Scéla Cano Meic Gartnáin*. Dublin: Institute for Advanced Studies, 1963.
Boedeker, Deborah Dickmann. *Aphrodite's Entry into Greek Epic*. Leiden: Brill, 1974.
Bosch-Gimpera, P. *Les Indo-Européens: Problèmes archéologiques*. Paris: Payot, 1980.
Brackert, Helmut, ed. *Das Nibelungenlied*. Frankfurt am Main: Fischer, 1970.
Brugsch, Karl Heinrich. *Thesaurus Inscriptionum Aegyptiacarum* IV. Austria: Akademische Druck-u. Verlagsanstalt, 1968.
Budge, E. A. Wallis. *The Egyptian Book of the Dead*. New York: Dover, 1895, 1967.
Budge, E. A. Wallis. *The Gods of the Egyptians* I-II. New York: Dover, 1904, 1969.
Budge, E. A. Wallis. *Egyptian Language*. New York: Dover, 1910, 1983.
Budge, E. A. Wallis. *An Egyptian Hieroglyphic Dictionary* I-II. New York: Dover, 1920, 1978.
Campbell, Joseph. *The Mythic Image*. Princeton: Princeton University Press, 1974.
Cassuto, U. *The Goddess Anath*. Jerusalem: Magnes Press, 1951.
Corpus Inscriptionum Latinarum. Berlin: Reimer, 1873–1918.
Craven, Roy C. *A Concise History of Indian Art*. New York: Oxford University Press, undated, probably 1976.
Curčija-Prodanović, Nada. *Yugoslav Folk-Tales*. London: Oxford University Press, 1957.
Curtin, Jeremiah. *Myths and Folktales of Ireland*. New York: Dover, 1975.
Daly, Mary. *Gyn-Ecology: The Metaethics of Radical Feminism*. Boston: Beacon Press, 1978.
Davison, J. A. "The Homeric Question" in Wace (1962): 234–266.
Delitzsch, Friedrich. *Sumerisches Glossar*. Leipzig: Hinrichs, 1914.
(Dexter), Miriam Robbins. *Indo-European Female Figures*. Unpublished Dissertation, University of California, Los Angeles, 1978.
Dexter, Miriam Robbins. "Proto-Indo-European Sun-Maidens and Gods of the Moon." *Mankind Quarterly* XXV 1-2: 137–144, 1984.
Dexter, Miriam Robbins. "Indo-European Reflection of Virginity and Autonomy." *Mankind Quarterly* XXVI 1-2: 57–74, 1985.
D'Iakonov, I. M. "On the Original Home of the Speakers of Indo-European." *Journal of Indo-European Studies (JIES)* 13.1–2: 92–174, 1985.
Dietrich, Manfried, *et al. Die keilalphabetischen Texte aus Ugarit* (KTU). Butzon & Bercker: Kevelaer, 1976.
Dindorf, Wilhelm, ed. *Scholia Graeca in Homeri Iliadem* I. Oxford: Clarendon Press, 1875–78.
Dineen, P. S. *An Irish-English Dictionary*. Dublin: Educational Co. of Ireland, 1927.
Downing, Charles. *Russian Tales and Legends*. London: Oxford University Press, 1956.

Duchesne-Guillemin, Jacques; M. Henning, transl. *The Hymns of Zarathustra.* Boston: Beacon Press, 1952, 1963.
Dumézil, Georges. *Tarpeia.* Paris: Gallimard, 1947.
Dumézil, Georges. "Le Trio des Macha." *Revue de L'Histoire des Religions* 146:5–17, 1954.
Dumézil, Georges. *L'Ideologie Tripartie des Indo-Européens.* Brussels: Latomus, 1958.
Ehrenreich, Barbara and English, Deirdre. *Witches, Midwives, and Nurses: A History of Women Healers.* New York: The Feminist Press, 1973.
Eisler, Riane. *The Chalice and the Blade.* San Francisco: Harper and Row, 1987.
Eliade, Mircea, ed. *The Encyclopedia of Religion.* New York: Macmillan, 1987.
Evans, J. Gwenogvryn, ed. *The White Book Mabinogíon.* Pwllheli: Private Issue, 1907.
Farnell, Lewis R. *Cults of the Greek States* I-V. Oxford: Clarendon Press, 1896.
Faulkes, Anthony. *Snorri Sturluson, Edda, Prologue and Gylfaginning.* Oxford: Clarendon Press, 1982.
Finch, R. G., ed. *Vǫlsunga Saga.* London: Nelson, 1965.
Ford, Patrick. *The Mabinogi and Other Medieval Welsh Tales.* Los Angeles: University of California Press, 1977.
Fraenkel, Ernst. *Litauisches Etymologisches Wörterbuch.* Heidelberg: Carl Winter, 1965.
Frazer, Sir James George. *The Golden Bough* I-II. New York: Macmillan, 1935.
Freeman, E. A. *History of the Norman Conquest of England* I. Oxford: Clarendon Press, 1867.
Frick, Carl, ed. *Pomponius Mela, De Chorographia.* Leipzig: Teubner, 1880.
Friedrich, Paul. *The Meaning of Aphrodite.* Chicago: University of Chicago Press, 1978.
Fritzsche, O. Fridolenus, ed. *Lactantius, Opera* I. Leipzig: Tauchnitz, 1842.
Gadd, C. J. *A Sumerian Reading Book.* Oxford: Clarendon Press, 1924.
Gamkrelidze, T. V. and Ivanov, V. V. "The Ancient Near East and the Indo-European Question: Temporal and Territorial Characteristics of Proto-Indo-European based on Linguistic and Historico-Cultural Data." *JIES* 13.1–2: 3–48, 1985a.
Gamkrelidze, T. V. and Ivanov, V. V. "The Migrations of Tribes Speaking Indo-European Dialects from their Original Homeland in the Near East to their Historical Habitations in Eurasia." *JIES* 13.1–2: 49–91, 1985b.
Gamkrelidze, T. V. and Ivanov, V. V. "The Problem of the Original Homeland of the Speakers of Indo-European Languages in Response to I.M. Diakonoff's Article." *JIES* 13.1–2: 175–184, 1985c.
Gardiner, Sir Alan H. *Egyptian Grammar.* London: Oxford University Press, 1927, 1964.
Gardiner, Sir Alan H. *The Library of A. Chester Beatty: The Chester Beatty Papyri* I. London: Walker (Oxford University Press), 1931.
Gardiner, Sir Alan H. *Late Egyptian Stories.* Brussels: Bibliotheca Aegyptiaca, 1932.
Geldner, Karl F., ed. *Avesta.* Stuttgart: Kohlhammer, 1896.
Gesenius, Friedrich Heinrich Wilhelm, ed.; S.P. Tregelles, transl. *Hebrew and Chaldee Lexicon to the Old Testament Scriptures.* Grand Rapids: Eerdmans, 1846, 1949.
Gimbutas, Marija. *The Balts.* New York: Praeger, 1963.
Gimbutas, Marija. "Ancient Slavic Religion: A Synopsis" in *To Honor Roman Jacobson:* 738–759. Paris: Mouton, 1967.
Gimbutas, Marija. *The Gods and Goddesses of Old Europe 7000–3500 BC: Legends and Cult Images.* Los Angeles: University of California Press, 1974.
Gimbutas, Marija. "The First Wave of Eurasian Steppe Pastoralists into Copper Age Europe." *JIES* V.4:277–338, 1977.
Gimbutas, Marija. "Old Europe in the Fifth Millennium B.C." in Polomé (1982):1–59.
Gimbutas, Marija. "Senosios Europos Dievės ir Dievai Lietuvių Mitologijoje." *Metmenys* 48: 28–57, 1984.
Gimbutas, Marija. "Primary and Secondary Homeland of the Indo-Europeans: Comments on the Gamkrelidze-Ivanov Articles." *JIES* 13.1–2: 185–202, 1985.
Gimbutas, Marija. *Achilleion, Neolithic Site in Thessaly.* Institute of Archaeology, UCLA, Monomenta Archaeological Monograph Series, 1987.
Glob, P. V.; R. Bruce-Mitford, transl. *The Bog People.* New York: Ballantine, 1969.
Glob, P. V.; J. Bulman, transl. *The Mound People.* New York: Cornell University Press, 1970, 1974.
Godwin, Joscelyn. *Mystery Religions in the Ancient World.* London: Harper and Row, 1981.
Goldenburg, Naomi. *Changing of the Gods.* Boston: Beacon Press, 1979.
Gordon, Cyrus H. *Ugaritic Manual.* Rome: Pontifical Biblical Institute, 1955.
Gordon, Cyrus H. *Ugaritic Textbook* (UT). Rome: Pontifical Biblical Institute, 1965.
Grassmann, Hermann. *Wörterbuch zum Rigveda,* Fifth Edition. Wiesbaden: Harrassowitz, 1976.
Gregoire, Henri. "La Nativité des Dioscures dans la Mosaïque de la Johann Philippstrasse, à Trèves." *La Nouvelle Clio* V.5–6: 452–464, 1953.
Gricourt, Jean. "Epona, Rhiannon, Macha." *Ogam* VI II: 82–83, 1954.

Grimal, Pierre, ed. *Larousse World Mythology.* New Jersey: Chartwell, 1965.
Grimm, Jacob. *Deutsche Mythologie.* Göttingen: Dieterich, 1835.
Guirand, Felix, ed. *New Larousse Encyclopedia of Mythology.* New York: Hamlyn, 1959, 1968.
Gwynn, Edward, ed. *Metrical Dindshenchas.* Dublin: Hodges, Figgis & Co., 1924.
Hallo, William W. and Van Dijk, J. J. A. *Exaltation of Inanna.* New Haven: Yale University Press, 1968.
Hatto, Arthur T. *Eos: An Inquiry into the Theme of Lovers' Meetings and Partings at Dawn in Poetry.* The Hague: Mouton, 1965.
Havthal, Ferdinand, ed. *Porphyrion, Commentarii in Q. Horatium Flaccum.* Berlin: Springer, 1864–66.
Hibbard, Howard. *The Metropolitan Museum of Art.* New York: Harper and Row, 1980.
Higgins, Richard. *Minoan and Mycenaean Art.* New York: Praeger, 1967.
Hofmann, J. B. *Walde's Lateinisches Etymologisches Wörterbuch.* Heidelberg: Carl Winter, 1938.
Hubbs, Joanna. "The Worship of Mother Earth in Russian Culture" in Preston (1982): 123–144.
Jacobsen, Thorkild and Kramer, Samuel N. "The Myth of Inanna and Bilulu." *Journal of Near Eastern Studies* XII.3: 160–188, 1953.
Jacobsen, Thorkild. *The Treasures of Darkness: A History of Mesopotamian Religion.* New Haven: Yale University Press, 1976.
Jagadiswarananda, Swami, ed. *Mārkāṇḍeya Purāṇa: Devī-māhātmyam.* Madras: Sri Ramakrishna Math, 1969.
Jónsson, Finnur. *Snorri Sturlusonar, Heimskringla.* Gads: Copenhagen, 1911.
Jónsson, Þorleifr. *Edda Snorra Sturlusonar.* Kaupmannahöfn: Gyldendals Bókverzlun, 1875.
Jonval, Michel. *Latviešu Mitologiskās Dainas.* Paris: Picart, 1929.
Juška, Antanas. *Lietuviškos Dainos.* Vilnius?: Valstybinė Grožinės Literatūros Leidykla, 1954.
Kerényi, Karl; Christopher Holme, transl. *Zeus and Hera.* New Jersey: Princeton University Press, Bollingen Series LXV.5, 1975.
Kohlmann, Philip and Jahnke, Richard, eds. *Statius, Opera* I II. Leipzig: Teubner, 1876–98.
Korsakas, Kostas, ed. *Lietuvių Tautosakos Rinktinė* Vol. III, "Pasakos." Vilnius: State Publishing House, 1954.
Korsakas, Kostas, ed. *Lietuvių Tautosaka* III. Vilnius: Mintis, 1965.
Kramer, Samuel Noah. *The Sumerians.* Chicago: University of Chicago Press, 1963a.
Kramer, Samuel Noah. "Cuneiform Studies and the History of Literature: The Sumerian Sacred Marriage Texts." *PAPS* 107.6:485–516, 1963b.
Kramer, Samuel Noah.*From the Poetry of Sumer.* Berkeley: University of California Press, 1979.
Kuhn, Hans. *Edda: Die Lieder des Codex Regius Nebst Verwandten Denkmälern* I-II. Heidelberg: Carl Winter, 1962–1968.
Kurtz, Seymour. *The World Guide to Antiquities.* New York: Crown, 1975.
Lalita. *Choose Your Own Mantra.* New York: Bantam, 1978.
Langdon, S., ed. *The Babylonian Epic of Creation.* Oxford: Clarendon Press, 1923.
Lanzone, Ridolfo. *Dizionario di mitologia egizia.* Amsterdam: J. Benjamin, 1881–84; 1974–75.
Lau, Robert Julius. *Old Babylonian Temple Records.* New York: AMS Press, 1906, 1966.
Lebesque, Phileas. *Les Chants Feminins Serbes.* Paris: Sansot, 1920.
Lefebvre, Gustave. *Le Tombeau de Petosiris* II: texts. Paris: Institut Français d'Archéologie Orientale, 1924.
Lerner, Gerda. *The Creation of Patriarchy.* Oxford: Oxford University Press, 1986.
Lewis, Charlton T. and Short, Charles. *A Latin Dictionary.* Oxford: Clarendon Press, 1879, 1962.
Lichtheim, Miriam. *Ancient Egyptian Literature* I. Berkeley: University of California Press, 1973.
Lichtheim, Miriam. *Ancient Egyptian Literature* II. Berkeley: University of California Press, 1976.
Liddell, Henry G. and Scott, Robert. *A Greek-English Lexicon.* New York: Harper and Brothers, 1856.
Littleton, C. Scott. *The New Comparative Mythology,* Second Edition. Los Angeles: University of California Press, 1973.
Lommel, H. "Anahita-Sarasvati" in *Asiatica: Festschrift Friedrich Weller:* 405–413. Leipzig: Harrassowitz, 1954.
Mackay, Dorothy. *Early Indus Civilizations.* London: Cuzac, 1948.
Maier, Walter A., III. *'Ašerah: Extrabiblical Evidence.* Atlanta: Scholars Press, 1986.
Mallory, J. P. *In Search of the Indo-Europeans: Language, Archaeology and Myth.* London: Thames and Hudson, 1989.
Mannhardt, Wilhelm. *Letto-Preussische Götterlehre.* Riga: Lettisch-Literärische Gesellschaft, 1936.
Marshack, Alexander. *The Roots of Civilization: The Cognitive Beginnings of Man's First Art, Symbol, and Notation.* New York: McGraw Hill, 1972.
Meshel, Zeev. *Kuntillet 'Ajrud, A Religious Centre from the Time of the Judaean Monarchy on the Border of Sinai.* Jerusalem: The Israel Museum, Catalogue No. 175, Spartus Hall, 1978.

Meyer, Kuno, ed. "'Macgnimartha Find,' the 'Boyhood Deeds of Finn.'" *Revue Celtique* V:195–204, 1881–1883.

Mikalson, Jon D. *Athenian Popular Religion*. Chapel Hill: University of North Carolina Press, 1983.

Monier-Williams, Sir M. *Sanskrit-English Dictionary*. Oxford: Clarendon Press, 1899.

Moss, Leonard W. and Cappannari, Stephen C. "In Quest of the Black Virgin" in Preston (1982): 53–74.

Mülenbachs, Karlis, ed. J. Endzelin. *Latviesu Valodas Vardnica (Lettish-deutsches Wörterbuch)* I. Riga: Izdevusi Izgitibas Ministrija, 1923–1932.

Müller, F. Max, ed. *Rigveda Saṁhita* I-II. London: Trübner, 1877.

Munro, David B. and Allen, Thomas W., ed. *Homer: Opera*, Third Edition. Oxford: Clarendon Press, 1912–19.

Naveh, J. "Graffiti and Dedications." *Bulletin of the American Schools of Oriental Research* 235: 27–30, 1979.

Nilsson, Martin. *Geschichte der Griechischen Religion*. Munich: Beck, 1941.

Nilsson, Martin. *The Minoan-Mycenaean Religion and its Survival in Greek Religion*, Second Revised Edition. Lund: Gleerup, 1950.

Ó Cathasaigh, Donál. "The Cult of Brigid: A Study of Pagan-Christian Syncretism in Ireland" in Preston (1982): 75–94.

Ó Fiannachta, Pádraig. *Táin Bó Cuailnge*. Dublin: Dublin Institute for Advanced Studies, 1966.

O'Flaherty, Wendy Doniger. *Hindu Myths*. Middlesex, England: Penguin, 1975.

Olrik, J. and Raeder, H., ed. *Saxo Grammaticus: Saxonis Gesta Danorum* I. Haunia: Levin and Munksgaard, 1931.

O'Máille, Tomas. "Medb Chruachna." *Zeitschrift für Celtische Philologie* XVII: 129–146, 1927.

O'Meara, John, ed. *Giraldus Cambrensis, Topographia Hiberniae* in *Royal Irish Academy Proceedings* 52 C 4, Dublin: Hodges, Figgis & Co., 1949.

O'Neill, Joseph, ed. "Cath Boinde Andso." *Eriu* II[2]: 174–185,1905.

O'Rahilly, Cecile, ed. *Táin Bó Cuailnge*. Dublin: Dublin Institute for Advanced Studies, 1967.

Oldenburg, Ulf. *The Conflict Between El and Ba'al in Canaanite Religion*. Leiden: J. Brill, 1969.

Page, Denys. *Sappho and Alcaeus*. Oxford: Clarendon Press, 1955.

Pandian, Jacob. "The Goddess Kannagi: A Dominant Symbol of South Indian Tamil Society" in Preston (1982): 177–191.

Patai, Raphael. *The Hebrew Goddess*. New York: Avon, 1967.

Paterson, Adrian, transl. *Old Lithuanian Songs*. Kaunas: Pirbačis, 1939.

Perera, Sylvia Brinton. *Descent to the Goddess*. Toronto: Inner City Books, 1981.

Pēteraitis, Vilius. *Lietuviškai Angliškas Žodynas*. Chicago: Lietuviškos Knygos Klubas, 1960.

Pfiffig, A.J. *Uni-Hera-Aśtarte*. Österreichische Academie der Wissenschaften, Böhlaus, Wien, 1965.

Polomé, Edgar. "A Propos de la Déesse Nerthus." *Latomus* XIII: 167–200, 1954.

Polomé, Edgar. *The Indo-Europeans in the Fourth and Third Millennia*. Ann Arbor: Karoma, 1982.

Polomé, Edgar. "Vedic Religion and its Indo-European Background" in Sarasvati (1983): 108–116.

Polomé, Edgar. "njǫrðr" in Eliade (1987)X: 459–460.

Pomeroy, Sarah B. *Goddesses, Whores, Wives, and Slaves: Women in Classical Antiquity*. New York: Schocken, 1975.

Pope, Marvin H. *El in the Ugaritic Texts*. Leiden: J. Brill, 1955.

Powell, T. G. E. *The Celts*. New York: Praeger, 1958.

Powell, T. G. E. *Prehistoric Art*. London: Thames and Hudson, 1966.

Preston, James J. "The Goddess Chandi as an Agent of Change" in Preston (1982): 210–226.

Preston, James J., ed. *Mother Worship: Themes and Variations*. Chapel Hill: University of North Carolina Press, 1982.

Pritchard, James B., ed. *Ancient Near Eastern Texts Relating to the Old Testament (ANET)*, Second Edition. Princeton, New Jersey: Princeton University Press, 1969.

Puhvel, Jaan, ed. *Myth and Law Among the Indo-Europeans*. Los Angeles: University of California Press, 1970.

Puhvel, Jaan. *Comparative Mythology*. Baltimore: Johns Hopkins University Press, 1987.

Puhvel, Jaan. "Victimal Hierarchies in Indo-European Animal Sacrifice" *AJP* 99: 354–362.

Quin, E. G., ed. *Dictionary of the Irish Language*. Dublin: Royal Irish Academy, 1976.

Ralston, W. R. S. *The Songs of the Russian People*. London: Ellis and Green, 1872.

Reichelt, Hans. *Awestisches Elementarbuch*. Heidelberg: Carl Winter, 1967.

Roehl, Hermann, ed. *Inscriptiones Graecae Antiquissimae Praeter Atticas in Attica Repertas*. Berlin: Reimer, 1882.

Rogers, Benjamin, ed. *The Comedies of Aristophanes* Vol. II. London: Bell, 1916.

Rohde, Erwin. *Psyche: Seelencult und Unsterblichkeitsglaube der Griechen*. Mohr: Tübingen, 1925.

Roscher, W. H. *Ausführliches Lexikon der Griechischen und Römischen Mythologie* I. Leipzig: Teubner, 1884-86.

Ross, Anne. *The Folklore of the Scottish Highlands.* London: Batsford, 1976.

Roth R. and Whitney, W. D., ed. *Atharvaveda Saṁhita.* Berlin: Dümmler, 1924.

Sarasvati, Svami Satya Prakash, ed. *Dayananda Commemoration Volume.* Paropkarini Sabha, Dayanand Ashram, Ajmer, 1983.

Śāstrī, Haragovinda, ed. *Manusmṛtiḥ.* Varanasi: Chowkhamba Sanskrit Series, 1965.

Sobolevskii, A. I. *Velikorusskaya Narodnye Pesni.* Petersburg: Gosudarstva, 1895–1902.

Solmsen, Friedrich. *Isis Among the Greeks and Romans.* Cambridge: Harvard University Press, 1979.

Sukthankar, Vishnu S., ed.*The Mahābhārata.* Poona: Bhandarkar, 1940.

Taylor, A. R. *An Introduction to Old Norse.* Oxford: Clarendon Press, 1927, 1957.

Taylour, Lord William. "New Light on Mycenaean Religion." *Antiquity* XLIV: 270–279, 1970.

Teubal, Savina J. *Sarah the Priestess.* Athens, Ohio: Swallow Press, 1984.

Theochares, Demetres Rega, ed. *Neolithic Greece.* Athens: National Bank of Greece, 1973.

Thilo, George and Hagen, Hermann, eds. *Servii Grammatici qui feruntur Vergilii Carmina Commentarii* I-II. Hildesheim: Olms, 1961.

Thomson, R. L., ed. *Pwyll Pendeuic Dyuet.* Dublin: Institute for Advanced Studies, 1957.

Thurneysen, R., ed. "Baile in Scāil." *Zeitschrift für Celtischen Philologie* XX: 213–227, 1936a.

Thurneysen, R. *et al. Studies in Early Irish Law.* Dublin: Figgis, 1936b.

Trubačev, O. N. "Linguistics and Ethnogenesis of the Slavs: The Ancient Slavs as Evidenced by Etymology and Onomastics." *JIES* 13.1–2: 203–256, 1985.

Trump, David. *Central and Southern Italy Before Rome.* New York: Praeger, 1965.

Tsounta, Xristou. *Diminiou kai Sesklou.* Athens: Sakellarios, 1908.

Tsounta, Xristou. *Diminiou kai Sesklou.* Athens; Sakellarios, 1908.

Turkina, E. *Latvian-English Dictionary.* New York: Saphragraph, 1964.

Turville-Petre, E. O. G. *Myth and Religion of the North: The Religion of Ancient Scandinavia.* New York: Holt, Rinehart and Winston, 1964.

Užburta Karalystė: Lietuvių Liaudies Pasakos. Vilnius: Valstybinė Grožinis Literatūros Leidykla, 1957.

Vaidya, P. L., ed. *Harivaṁśa.* Poona: Bhandarkar, 1969–71.

Van Hamel, A. G., ed. *Compert Con Culainn and Other Stories.* Dublin: Institute for Advanced Studies, 1956.

Vasić, Miloje M. *Preistoriska Vinča* II. Beograd: Izdanie Državne Shtamparije, 1932–1936.

Ventris, Michael and Chadwick, John. *Documents in Mycenaean Greek.* London: Cambridge University Press, 1973.

Vermeule, Emily. *Greece in the Bronze Age.* Chicago: University of Chicago Press, 1964.

Vigfusson, Gudbrand. *Icelandic-English Dictionary.* Oxford: Clarendon Press, 1874.

Wace, Alan and Stubbings, Frank H. *A Companion to Homer.* New York: Macmillan, 1962.

Wagner, E. R. and Wagner, D. L. *La Civilizacion Chaco-Santiagueña* I. Buenos Aires: Compania Impresora Argentina, 1934.

Ward, Donald. *The Divine Twins: An Indo-European Myth in Germanic Tradition.* Berkeley: University of California Press, 1968.

Wendel, C., ed. *Scholia in Theocritum Vetera.* Stüttgart: Teubner, 1851, 1914.

West, E. W., transl. *The Great Bundahišn* in *Sacred Books of the East* V. Pahlevi Texts, Delhi, Motilal Banarsidass, Oxford University Press, 1880.

West, Grace. *Women in Vergil's Aeneid.* Unpublished Dissertation. University of California, Los Angeles, 1975.

Widengren, Geo. *Die Religionen Irans.* Stüttgart: Kohlhammer, 1965.

Windisch, Ernst, ed. *Irische Texte mit Wörterbuch.* Leipzig: Hirzel, 1880.

Windisch, Ernst, ed. *Irische Texte* II^2. Leipzig: Hirzel, 1887.

Wissowa, Georg, ed. *Paulys Real-Encyclopädie der Classischen Altertumswissenschaft.* Stüttgart: Metzler, 1894.

Wolf, Christa; Jan Van Heurck, transl. *Cassandra: A Novel and Four Essays.* New York: Farrar, Straus, Giroux, 1984.

Wolkstein, Diane and Kramer, Samuel Noah. *Inanna: Queen of Heaven and Earth.* New York: Harper and Row, 1983.

Zevit, Ziony. "The Khirbet-el-Qôm Inscription Mentioning a Goddess." *Basor* 255, 1984.

Zheleznova, Irina. *The Sun Princess and Her Deliverer.* Moscow: Progress Publishers, undated.

Zobarskas, Stepas. *Lithuanian Folk Tales.* New York: Rickard, 1958.

GLOSSARY

amazons: mythological female warriors who always lived just beyond the bounds of the "civilized" world.

androgenesis: When used mythologically, this term indicates birth through a father alone; the child is thus not born from its mother's womb. Zeus gave androgenetic birth to Athena.

avunculate: a type of relationship whereby responsibility for one's sons is given over to their maternal uncles. That is, a special relationship exists between maternal uncle and nephew.

cognate: As a linguistic term, *cognate* indicates sister-languages or words which are related by descent from the same ancestral language. For example, Sanskrit, Latin, Greek, and Lithuanian are cognate languages. An example of cognate words or names exists in the names of the Latin dawn-goddess *Aurora* and the Indic dawn-goddess, *Ushas.* The two cognates are descended from the Proto-Indo-European term for the dawn-goddess, **Ausosa.*

divine pantheons: groups of gods and goddesses forming a stratified society, each performing a specific function or functions. An example of a divine pantheon is that group of deities which were believed to dwell upon the Greek Mount Olympus.

equalitarian society: the Neolithic European societies were very possibly equalitarian: that is, both functions or jobs within the society and *respect* were equally divided between women and men. Equalitarian societies were probably matrilineal or matri-patrilineal rather than patrilineal, with regard to inheritance.

etymology: a word traced back to its earliest components in the earliest possible languages. For example, the Indo-European goddess of the dawn was *Eos* in Greek, *Aurora* in Latin, *Ushas* in Sanskrit.

gynecocracy: rule by a woman or women.

gynomorphic: "shaped like a human woman."

indigenous peoples: those living in a geographical area before another, often invading, tribe migrates into that area. Examples of such societies were the Dravidians in pre-patriarchal India and the pre-Greek Minoans before the arrival of the Greeks. These indigenous peoples, when they assimilate with the invaders, contribute to a new combined culture; the mythology and even the new language often reflect the influence of the earlier peoples.

karma: in Hindu and Buddhist philosophy, the total of a person's good and bad actions, which bear consequences upon her or his subsequent lives.

matriarchy: a society in which the mother or female authority-figure rules. The term means, literally, "mother-rule," rather than descent or inheritance through the female line. Although some nineteenth- and early twentieth-century anthropologists believed that a matriarchal stage preceded the (supposedly superior) patriarchal stage in world history, no evidence of any historical matriarchal society has ever been found, although several *matrilinear* societies have existed.

matrilinear or *matrilineal society:* a society in which descent and inheritance are traced through the female line. In such societies the mother's brother is often a powerful authority-figure in the family, and he is sometimes the guardian of his sister's sons. (see *avunculate*) A matrilinear society in no way presupposes a matriarchy; in attested societies which practice matrilinear descent, most authority is still held by men.

matrilocal society: a society wherein men, upon marriage, go to their wives' family homes.

pantheon: the group of goddesses and gods recognized as the major deities of a particular society. For example, the Olympic or Olympian pantheon was composed of the major Greek (or Greco-Roman) goddesses and gods.

parthenogenesis: birth through a mother with no male participation. Thus, Hera gave birth to Hephaestus without the participation of Zeus.

patriarchy: a society in which the father or male authority-figure rules. In a patriarchal society males are dominant and, generally, they serve as the rulers and politicians of that society. Although the terms *patriarchal* and *patriarchy* have often been overused, I nonetheless use them synonymously with *male-centered* and *male-centered society,* since these societies are literally "male-ruled." For the time frame of this book we are discussing both Indo-European patriarchal societies which embrace(d) male-centered religious pantheons, and patriarchal Near-Eastern societies which embraced somewhat more equalitarian pantheons. v. Lerner (1986) on ancient patriarchy in the Near East.

patrilinear or *patrilineal society:* a society in which descent and inheritance are traced through the male bloodline.

patrilocal society: a society whose women, upon marriage, go to their husbands' family homes.

proto-language: the earliest, ancestral form of a language or group of related dialects; a hypothetical form which existed before the language achieved written status. For example, the ancestor of modern English, modern German, Old English, Old Saxon, and Old High German, is "Proto-Germanic;" the ancestor of the Germanic languages, Greek, the Italic languages, Hittite, Sanskrit, and modern Irish, among many others, is "Proto-Indo-European." Words and forms in proto-languages are indicated by an asterisk, *, to indicate that they are hypothetical.

theacentric societies: goddess-centered societies.

theagony: origins of the goddess(es).

thealatry: worship of the goddess(es).

transfunctional: fulfilling several functions, such as those of nurturing, providing martial strength, and serving as a seat of sovereignty. Indo-European goddesses are often transfunctional, while Indo-European gods generally fulfill one role.

Skirnir, 104
Skuld, 100
Smert, 64
Snake-woman goddesses, 2, 6–11, 95, 186
  Baltic, 8, 54, 57–59
  Celtic, 165–166, 177
  Egyptian, 6, 8, 10, 22
  European neolithic, 5–13, 179–181
  Greek, 7–8, 10–11, 18, 113, 117, 119–123, 127–128
  Hebraic, 8, 11, 46, 48
  Indic, 7–8, 11
  Roman, 7, 135, 137–138, 140
  Slavic, 8, 63
  Sumerian, 8–11
  Ugarit, 28, 30–31, 88
Snorri Sturleson, 98–99
  "Gylfaginning," 98–100, 103–104, 167
Solntee, 66
Soma, 38–40, 77, 80, 82
Sophocles, *Oedipus the King*, 146
Sovereignity and powers of goddesses, 2, 26–27, 146–152
Spendarmat, 72
Spenta Ārmaiti, 71–72, 162
Sreča, 63
Statius, *Silvae*, 133
Strabo, *Geography*, 101
Sun-goddesses, 57, 66
Sun-maiden, 36, 59
  Baltic, 39–41, 54
  Greek, 40
  Indic, 39–41
  Nordic, 104
Sūryā, 39–40, 76
Svarog, 64
Svaroghits, 64

Tacitus, 98–99, 101, 155
  Annals, 133, 164
  Germania, 98–99, 101, 156
Táin Bó Cuailnge, 88–93, 160
Táin Bó Ragamma, 89
Tamuz, 21, 48, 173
Tara, 82
Tawoare, 28
Tefnut, 23
Telemachuss, 147
Temenos, 168
Teyrnon Twrf Liant, 93–94
Theaetetus (Plato), 118
Themis, 7
Theocritus, *Idyll*, 178
Theogony (Hesiod), 1, 112, 118, 123–125, 172
Thetis, 148, 176
Tiamat, 10–11, 23
Tiberius, Emperor, 164
Tisiphone, 179–180
Tithonus, 36–37
"Tochmarc Emire," 154
"Tranculentus" (Plautus), 154
Tuatha Dé Dānann, 43–45, 88
Tvastr, 80
Tyche, 85, 124, 128
Typhon, 10, 172
Tyr (Tiwaz), 98

Uatchet, 6
Ubaid, 16
Ulmá, 83
Umá, 5
Underworld deities:
  Egyptian, 22
  Greek, 17–18, 125–128
  Indic, 78
  Sumerian, 16–17
  Ugarit, 28–29
Uranos, 160
Urth, 100
Ushas, 36–38, 46, 76
Utatchet, 22
Utu-hegal, King, 19

Vahruna, 11
Vaižgantas, Juozas Tomas, 166
Valerius Maximus, *Dictorum Factorumque, Memorabilium*, 138
Valkyries, 104–105, 155–156, 167, 173
Varuna, 45, 76–77, 80
Vassilissa the Wise, 62–63
Ve, 105
Veles/Volos, 64–65
"Veluspa," 100
Venus, 1, 48, 103, 132, 138–140, 157, 174
Vergil, *Aeneid*, 125, 130–131, 136, 138, 162, 166, 176, 179–180
Verthandi, 100
Vesta, 163
Veyed'ma, 181
Vila, 62
Vili, 105
Virginity of goddesses, 161–173
  Baltic, 54–57
  Celtic, 165–167
  Egyptian, 25
  Greek, 25, 112, 118, 120, 161–163, 166, 169–170, 172–173
  Indic, 167–169, 170
  Iranian, 171–172
  Nordic, 167, 170
  Roman, 161, 163
Vishnu (Visnu), 78, 80–82
Vitae Parallelae (Plutarch), 163
Vladimir, Prince, 62

ABOUT THE AUTHOR

Miriam Robbins Dexter is a lecturer in the department of Classics at the University of Southern California, where she teaches courses in Latin, Greek, and Sanskrit language and literature. She received her Ph.D. from UCLA in Indo-European Studies (comparative linguistics, archaeology, and mythology). Her doctoral dissertation, *Indo-European Female Figures*, along with courses she taught at UCLA and USC in ancient goddesses and heroines, evolved into *Whence the Goddesses: A Source Book*. She is also the author of several journal articles on ancient female figures.

Miriam's interest in ancient women, both divine and mortal, coupled with a concern for contemporary women, led her to teach courses in Women's Studies at California State University, Northridge. This interest grew into an involvement in the National Women's Studies Association, as a member of its Coordinating Council, which has continued for the past five years.

The ATHENE Series

The Athene Series assumes that all those who are concerned with formulating explanations of the way the world works need to know and appreciate the significance of basic feminist principles.

The growth of feminist research has challenged almost all aspects of social organization in our culture. The Athene Series focuses on the construction of knowledge and the exclusion of women from the process—both as theorists and subjects of study—and offers innovative studies that challenge established theories and research.

On Athene—When Metis, goddess of wisdom who presided over all knowledge was pregnant with Athene, she was swallowed up by Zeus who then gave birth to Athene from his head. The original Athene is thus the parthenogenetic daughter of a strong mother and as the feminist myth goes, at the "third birth" of Athene she stops being Zeus' obedient mouthpiece and returns to her real source: the science and wisdom of womankind.

THE ATHENE SERIES

An International Collection of Feminist Books
General Editors: Gloria Bowles, Renate D. Klein, and Janice Raymond
Consulting Editor: Dale Spender

MEN'S STUDIES MODIFIED The Impact of Feminism on the Academic Disciplines
Dale Spender, editor

WOMAN'S NATURE Rationalizations of Inequality
Marian Lowe and *Ruth Hubbard*, editors

MACHINA EX DEA Feminist Perspectives on Technology
Joan Rothschild, editor

SCIENCE AND GENDER A Critique of Biology and Its Theories on Women
Ruth Bleier

WOMAN IN THE MUSLIM UNCONSCIOUS
Fatna A. Sabbah

MEN'S IDEAS/WOMEN'S REALITIES *Popular Science*, 1870-1915
Louise Michele Newman, editor

BLACK FEMINIST CRITICISM Perspectives on Black Women Writers
Barbara Christian

THE SISTER BOND A Feminist View of a Timeless Connection
Toni A.H. McNaron, editor

EDUCATING FOR PEACE A Feminist Perspective
Birgit Brock-Utne

STOPPING RAPE Successful Survival Strategies
Pauline B. Bart and *Patricia H. O'Brien*

TEACHING SCIENCE AND HEALTH FROM A FEMINIST PERSPECTIVE
A Practical Guide
Sue V. Rosser

FEMINIST APPROACHES TO SCIENCE
Ruth Bleier, editor

INSPIRING WOMEN Reimagining the Muse
Mary K. DeShazer

MADE TO ORDER The Myth of Reproductive and Genetic Progress
Patricia Spallone and *Deborah L. Steinberg,* editors

TEACHING TECHNOLOGY FROM A FEMINIST PERSPECTIVE
A Practical Guide
Joan Rothschild

FEMINISM WITHIN THE SCIENCE AND HEALTH CARE PROFESSIONS
Overcoming Resistance
Sue V. Rosser

RUSSIAN WOMEN'S STUDIES Essays on Sexism in Soviet Culture
Tatyana Mamonova

TAKING OUR TIME Feminist Perspectives on Temporality
Frieda Johles Forman, editor, with *Caoran Sowton*

RADICAL VOICES A Decade of Feminist Resistance from *Women's Studies International Forum*
Renate Klein and *Deborah L. Steinberg*, editors

THE RECURRING SILENT SPRING
H. Patricia Hynes

EXPOSING NUCLEAR PHALLACIES
Diana E.H. Russell, editor

THE WRITING OR THE SEX? or why you don't have to read women's writing to know it's no good
Dale Spender

FEMINIST PERSPECTIVES ON PEACE AND PEACE EDUCATION
Birgit Brock-Utne

WHENCE THE GODDESSES A Source Book
Miriam Robbins Dexter